The Merchant Adventurers
General Editor: Ralph Davis, Ph.D.

The Wine Trade

The Merchant Adventurers

The Wine Trade

A. D. FRANCIS
C.B.E., M.V.O., F.R.HIST.S

Adam & Charles Black
London

First published 1972
A. & C. Black Ltd.
4, 5 & 6 Soho Square London W1V 6AD
ISBN 0 7136 1308 4

Printed in Great Britain by
T. & A. Constable Ltd., Edinburgh

Contents

Maps

Acknowledgments

My grateful acknowledgments are due to the Public Records Office; the British Museum and the London Library and their staffs, who have helped me so much. I also have to thank Dr Hull of the Kent Record Office, the University Library of Coimbra and the University of Kansas for permission to use some quotations from their manuscripts, and Earl Spencer and Lord Methuen for references to their archives. The following kindly allowed me to use quotations from published works: Messrs. Hutchinson from the *Journal of Edward Barlow*, Ed. J. Lubbock; Miss F. F. Andrews from the *Torrington Diaries* published by Messrs. Eyre & Spottiswood in 1934; the Clarendon Press, Oxford, for statistics published by E. B. Schumpeter, in *English Overseas Statistics;* Messrs. Antony Gibbs & Sons from the *History of Antony and Dorothea Gibbs*.

Many other people have helped me in my researches, but my particular thanks are due to Professor Ragnhild Hatton of the University of London, Professor John Bromley of Southampton and last but not least the editor of this series, Professor Ralph Davis of Leicester University.

CHAPTER I

The Early Days of Wine in England

THE first wine to reach England was probably an amphora presented as a propitiatory gift with other trade goods to a local chief. We do not know when this event occurred. Articles of Mediterranean manufacture reached England when Avebury and Stonehenge were being built. We do not know whether they changed hands many times or how soon there were regular voyages made by traders from the Mediterranean. Vineyards were perhaps planted at Marseilles and in Spain and Portugal before 500 B.C., but wine is a bulky and perishable product, so it is unlikely that it was carried as far as England before it was well established in Spain and traders became accustomed to make the journey in a single voyage. The first definite evidence of wine in England is provided by the tombs of Belgic chieftains in the first century before Christ. The presence of a silver Roman wine cup does not necessarily prove that wine was drunk from it, but that of an amphora suggests that wine was already a feature in a chieftain's life of which it was proper that he should not be deprived beyond the grave.

Wine quickly followed the passage of the Roman legionaries and according to Diodorus Siculus was already penetrating far into France in the first century B.C. The same writer reports that the natives were crazy for wine, which played much the same part in the advance of Italian traders as fire-water and rum did in the infiltration of their European successors into Africa and into Red Indian territory many centuries later. The merchants found that with an amphora of wine they could purchase a handsome slave and, attracted by the large profits, they ascended all the rivers of Gaul and even began to carry wine by waggon overland. Narbonne was an early centre for vineyards and it is not unlikely that at this period not only wine but vineyards spread from the Mediterranean to the valley of the Garonne.

It took some time for the cultivation of the vine to extend even to the north of Italy, and the climate of central and northern France was not propitious. But attempts would be made by enterprising natives or homesick Romans to grow wines on the periphery, and in the course of a century or two some of these would succeed and hardier strains of vine would be developed. The Allobriges living in the valleys of the Rhône and of the Isère were early wine-growers, and by the fourth century A.D. the poet Ausonius was writing of the wines of the Moselle, which reminded him of the Gironde, his own birthplace. Such was the development of the production of wine in the Roman provinces that by the time of Martial and Plutarch it was being imported on some scale from France and Spain into Italy and was of a quality to win the approval of Roman connoisseurs. This competition aroused the resentment of the Italian wine-growers, who persuaded Domitian and some other emperors to restrict the expansion of vineyards in Italy and to issue decrees for the destruction of a number of vineyards in the provinces. It is interesting that already the complaint arose that the undue growth of vineyards diminished the production of corn and was a cause of famines. This complaint and laws to remedy it were often to recur throughout the centuries. Various authorities indeed have held that there is a direct relationship between the production of corn and of wine, and that when corn is cheap vineyards expand, and vice versa. This could be so in a country which was a regular importer or exporter of corn but famines were usually the result of a local failure of a crop. Prices responded very rapidly, but it was seldom that supplies of corn could be brought from elsewhere in the same season. Even in Roman times transport was uncertain and expensive, and after the fall of the Roman empire trade was largely restricted to goods which were valuable, durable and portable. The area under corn could be expanded fairly rapidly, if land was available, but not in time to make up for the failure of the harvest and by the next year the increase in production might not be necessary. The creation of a vineyard on the other hand required some years, so the relationship between the production of corn and of wine was not very flexible.

Owing to the prevalence of forests in Britain, Germany and much of France, the climate was damper than in our day and perhaps even less suitable for wine growing, but no doubt Roman colonists liked to see vines growing up their walls to remind them of home and were tempted to try to make some wine whenever a good summer ripened the grapes sufficiently. We know that quite improbable and bulky commodities such as marbles and building stones from the Greek islands were imported to Chichester as ballast, so it is likely that wine, which could be fetched from much nearer places, for instance from Auxerre down the Seine, was imported in fair quantities. The urbanized Roman centres would have supplied a steady demand, and although the British as a race drank their native mead or beer, their chieftains and other Romanized British prized wine both for its prestige and for its intoxicating properties. Throughout the centuries wine in northern countries seldom became a drink for the people on account of the expense, but remained aristocratic, ecclesiastic and bourgeois. This was natural where wine could only be grown with difficulty or not at all, but in the Middle Ages, owing to the influence of Islam, the consumption of wine became restricted in much of southern Europe.

The pleasures of wine and its aristocratic connotation would not perhaps have been enough to keep its memory alive in England after the Romans left if it had not been for its religious associations. Wine already had a religious significance in connection with the mysteries of Mythras and of Dionysus, and was a favourite theme of classical poets. Its use for the Christian Mass gave it a new importance and made it a universal necessity. Christian missionaries took wine with them wherever they preached the gospel, so St Columba is said to have carried wine from the Loire with him when he made his first journey from Brittany to Ireland. Bishops, subsequently canonized, did not think it beneath them to cultivate vineyards, and the wine of Auxerre is said to owe its first reputation to St Germanus who visited England twice in the fifth century. In modern times some writers influenced by a morbid fear of the horrors of alcoholism have tried to argue that the word 'wine' in its early Christian context really meant grape-juice or unfermented wine. This suggestion is belied by the pronouncements of the early fathers who made it clear that the use for the Communion of the fermented juice of the grape was indispensable and forbade the substitution of the juice of apples or of any other fruit. In England in the year 676 at the Council of Winchester it was laid down that no priest must celebrate the Mass with water unmixed with wine or with beer. Therefore the keeping at all seasons of a small store of wine was essential, for although only a token sip was required, Communion in both kinds was usual and was recommended to be frequent. The Venerable Bede deplored that many people only took Communion three times a year and recommended that all who felt themselves fit to receive Communion should do so often. He also said that vineyards were not uncommon in England. Indeed, religious institutions often planted vineyards. They had the money and the labour to tend them, and often land in favourable situations. A good vintage was rare, but they did not worry about quality, and were satisfied if they could produce enough for their ecclesiastical needs. When there was a surplus it could always be used both by themselves and by the many guests to whom it was their duty to give hospitality.

In this way the tradition of wine, which might have died out in England during the Dark Ages, was kept alive. Long before the Norman Conquest a substantial trade in wine with the continent was resumed, but English vineyards were still kept up. Domesday Book specifically mentioned thirty-eight vineyards in the area covered by its survey. As early as the year 629 an annual fair was held at the time of the vintage at St Denis near Paris and was attended by merchants from Rouen. By the time of Charlemagne, Rouen was a busy port and the centre of a trade in wine with England from the Ile de France, parts of Burgundy, and perhaps from the Loire. By this time Frisian traders were navigating the Rhine in flat-bottomed boats and bringing down wine from the Rhine and the Moselle. For Rhenish wine, wooden casks had been used already in Roman times. Remains of them have been found in England. But the German merchants who were established in London in the tenth century, in the reign of King Ethelred, and paid their dues in kind did so in pepper, in cloth and in vinegar, which were brought to Mainz or Cologne by the overland route. There is no mention of wine, so most of that imported probably came from Rouen. The amount was already sufficient to attract the notice of the tax-gatherer, who collected a duty of six shillings on each incoming cargo.

The Normans were more familiar with wine than the Anglo-

Saxons and their coming reinforced the consumption of wine and also its aristocratic connection. But it was not only the nobles who drank wine, for it formed a normal part of the board of all the royal household and of the dependents of men of high degree, who counted for this purpose as part of their families. The consumption of wine was further encouraged by the fact that payment in kind was very usual. The king had the right of prisage, which entitled him to a tun of wine from before the mast and a tun of wine from after the mast from each ship carrying over twenty tuns and to a tun from ships between ten and twenty tuns. The right of prisage was often parcelled out to favoured noblemen and the king could also exercise a right to purchase any incoming wines at a favourable price, if he needed them for his own use or that of his armies. The king and many Norman barons also had estates in France, from which they could bring wine, so that a good part of the wine coming in was a perquisite of the governing class and did not enter through commercial channels. Some of it was sold to merchants, but a large proportion was expended either in the form of allowances or of hospitality to dependents or guests.

The eleventh and twelfth centuries saw an expansion of vineyards in northern Europe, which perhaps spread to England. In 1125 William of Malmsbury spoke of a number of vineyards in Gloucestershire which produced wines of as good a quality as those of France. This would have been easier if many of the wines still came from the neighbourhood of Paris rather than from Bordeaux, but there is some evidence that between 1150 and 1300 climatic conditions in England were a little more favourable than they had been before or than they became later. Opponents of this theory point out that the period included a great number of cold winters and of wet and stormy summers. Its defendants suggest that in spite of much bad weather the temperature in the late summer was a little higher and the incidence of late frosts a little less and that these were the most important factors. Such an absence of damaging cold winds is borne out by the existence of vineyards in rather unexpected places in the eastern half of England. It is hard to tell whether the expansion of vineyards was caused by any temporary amelioration of the climate or only by increased prosperity and increased demand. There were a number of wet summers in the fourteenth century, which may have reversed the process, but any decline may equally have been

due to the fact that it was the hey-day of the union of England
with Aquitaine and of the Bordeaux trade. In 1179, for instance,
King Louis VII of France made a pilgrimage to Canterbury and
gave the monks of the shrine of St Thomas a benefaction of an
annual 100 muys or 66 pipes of wine from his vineyards near
Paris. But the monks complained that the wine was thin and harsh
and too sour, by the time it reached England, to be used. They
obtained permission to sell the wine for what it would fetch. The
payment was often interrupted by war but was finally renewed
in 1477 by King Louis XI. By that time his Paris vineyards had
entirely disappeared so the king ordered that the monks should
have wine from Gascony, and this was duly delivered to them free
of French duties.

There have been runs of good and bad years but wine-growing
in England has never been more than marginal. In spite of this
there have always been a few vineyards, as there are at the present
day. Some wine could indeed always be grown here, if there were
sufficient inducement. The climate in favoured parts of the
country is very little worse for the purpose than that of the Rhineland for instance. At Eastbourne there is actually a little more sun
in the early months of the summer and only a little less in the
ripening season. The principal difference is that the sun is a little
less hot in the late summer months and the average temperature
is a little lower and the nights colder. As regards hours of sunshine
there is very little in it.[1]

Throughout its history the wine trade has been harassed or protected by a host of regulations. Various motives, mercenary or
moral, have inspired these rules. In the Middle Ages there was a
strong feeling that it was wicked to make large profits and that
any merchant who asked for more than the just price was no better
than a usurer. Constant efforts were therefore made to fix a just
price for every commodity. This was not easy in the case of wine,
of which the supply varied greatly from year to year according to
the size and quality of the vintage, political circumstances and
the conditions of transport. Numerous regulations were made to
fix the price of wine, but more often than not they were ineffective.
King John, for instance, who was personally interested in making
large purchases of wine, had sometimes to pay more than the maxi-

[1] Add. MSS 32639 records a tradition that Henry I gave a vineyard
at Lincoln to the bishop there.

mum allowed by his own laws. The regulations were often inspired by local vested interests or by an exaggerated protectionism and they sometimes contradicted each other. When the legal price was set too low, either the law was ignored or trade was hindered. Sometimes the government insisted to a point where trade was so reduced that a remedy had to be found and the law modified.

For the first century after the conquest most of the wines imported into England, whether from the Ile de France, the Loire or Bordeaux, were bought at the annual Rouen fair. After the marriage in 1152 of King Henry II to Eleanor of Aquitaine the whole duchy came under the Angevin dynasty and wine ships came directly from Bordeaux, from the mouth of the Loire and from La Rochelle. The loss of Normandy in 1203 further diminished the trade through Rouen. In 1212 King John was still buying wines from the dominions of the French king as well as from his own dominions, but the amount was much less. In that year he received eighty-six tuns as prisage and bought 262 tuns at a cost of £507 11s. Of this total fifty-four tuns came from the Orléannais and the Ile de France and 267 from Gascony. Three tuns came from Germany. London was already the largest port for the import of wines, though a good deal came to Sandwich and Bristol. The royal depot for storing wines was at Southampton.

The seal was set on the predominance of Bordeaux wines by the loss of La Rochelle in 1224. They already had a better reputation than the wines of La Rochelle or Poitou, which were sold at 6d a gallon, while the legal maximum for Bordeaux was 8d. Nevertheless the wines of Aunis or Poitou were considered to be one degree better than those of Picardy or the Ile de France. In Ponthieu the former were allowed to be used for the Communion from Easter to All Saints' Day, but the wines of Picardy went off in the spring and were considered unfit for use after Easter.

Noblemen who grew wines for their own use consumed them within a few weeks, or at most months, of the vintage. Even the Bordeaux wines, which were especially grown for export, lasted with difficulty until the next vintage. For this reason it was essential to ensure the sale and shipment of export wines as soon as possible. The Bordelais did their best to secure this and also to ship their own wines before the wines from what was known as the High Country, that is from points beyond Bordeaux higher up the River Garonne or any of its tributaries. Wine coming down

the Garonne or down the Dordogne to Libourne were subject to
a duty called the Grande Coutume, which was payable by all
wines passing Bordeaux or descending the Dordogne (which joined
the Garonne a little below Bordeaux) unless they belonged to
citizens of Bordeaux enjoying the freedom of the city. At first
exemption from the Grande Coutume was the principal privilege
of the citizens, but from the middle of the thirteenth century or
perhaps earlier they arrogated to themselves the right to deny
shipment to the High Country wines before St Martin's Day on
11th November. At certain periods they succeeded in postponing
this date until St Andrew's Day on 30th November or even until
Christmas. The High Country people protested and the kings of
England were by no means anxious to countenance privileges
which benefited one section of their subjects at the expense of
another. Later when the kings of France advanced their frontiers
down the Garonne and themselves possessed some of the High
Country, they equally disliked this privilege, which interfered with
the export of their wines from the upper reaches of the Garonne
and from Langue d'Oc. There was a long ding-dong struggle
between the opposing interests, but the Bordelais were stubborn
and on the whole were successful in holding back the High
Country wines. If they succeeded in doing so until late in the
autumn bad weather often delayed the despatch of the wines still
longer, sometimes until the spring. In 1284 the King of France
secured by treaty the right to pass wines down the river, if they
were being shipped to Brittany or Paris. These in fact were a large
part of the trade. The Bordelais recouped themselves by increasing
the duties payable on the High Country wines going to England
and by holding up their shipment as long as possible. This meant
that special care had to be taken to ensure their survival. They were
racked before shipment and on account of their clearer colour and
good quality began in the fourteenth century to surpass the
Bordeaux wines. A careful selection was necessary if they were to
be in good condition and still saleable upon arrival in England in
the spring, but the additional cost was sometimes compensated
by the fact they made the voyage in better weather in the spring
and at lower freights. Possibly because he thought their quality
was better, possibly only because he had estates there, King John
had a preference for wines from Moissac and from Gaillac on the
Tarn, a river falling into the Garonne some distance above Bor-

deaux. Certainly in later centuries the difficulties to which High Country wines continued to be subject led to experiments and developments in the art of preparing and maturing wine.

No statistics of the exports of Bordeaux wine are available before the beginning of the fourteenth century, but there is evidence to show that in the thirteenth century the trade with England was prosperous. King Henry III carried a good deal of the trade in royal ships and in his search for funds often diverted or appropriated cargoes. Some wines still came from Poitou and Anjou but most of the French wine imported came from Bordeaux. There was some interruption of the trade between 1283 and 1293, when Philip le Bel occupied the city, but trade was resumed when the English regained possession. The French occupation made English merchants begin to look for wine from other sources and this was the time when malvoisie from Greece and osey from Portugal were first mentioned. There was a small but continuous import of wines from Germany. In 1293 the merchants of Lorraine were bringing Moselle wines to London. They were not allowed to sell their wines in smaller quantities than half-casks and were subject to some curious regulations. One of them was that they should not buy more than three live pigs for their eating. Rhenish wine was also imported. In 1335 King Edward III was expecting a consignment of thirty tuns and wrote to the Bishop of Cologne to ask him to safeguard its transit.

The Bordelais welcomed the resumption of English rule in 1303 and of the trade which meant so much to the prosperity of the city, and from that time the registers of the Grande Coutume provide statistics of the export of wine in the majority of years. Even in the days of greatest prosperity before the Black Death and the Hundred Years War there were great fluctuations. Exports touched a peak figure of 102,724 tuns in 1308/09, but in the following year fell to about half of this and the next maximum figure of 93,556 tuns was not reached until 1329/30.

More than half the wines exported went to Brittany and the Low Countries, but England is estimated to have taken 30,000 or 40,000 tuns in good years. This is remarkable when one considers that although the population was perhaps as much as four million, over a million more than it became after the various ravages of the Black Death, it was still less than it became at the end of the seventeenth century; nevertheless, in 1687, a record year for the importation of French wines, the imports to London were only 15,518 tuns. Yet there is no reason to doubt the substantial accuracy of the earlier figures, which suggest that wine played a much greater part in international trade and in the life of the English people than it did later. Other evidence corroborates the extent of production. The town of Colmar for instance has records showing that it exported 100,000 litres in the fourteenth century, which compares with a figure of only 500,000 litres for all the vineyards of Alsace in modern times. It is calculated that wine accounted for 31% of the imports of England and for 25% of those of the Low Countries, whereas at the present day the figure is 1% and ·56%. According to another calculation the average Englishman drank annually at least eight pints of wine in the middle of the fourteenth century and before the Black Death a good deal more. Quite recently in 1935-6 his average was as low as 2·8 pints, though in 1966 his consumption regained its fourteenth-century level. The average consumption in the Low Countries has always been higher, so there is nothing out of the way in these figures, and there is no reason to doubt that at the beginning of the fourteenth century, which was an age of rising subsistence and of improvement in government, resources and communications, more wine was drunk proportionately in England than today. The surplus available to pay for imports was growing, but as yet the choice of commodities available and viable for trade between one country and another was limited. Wine was at once a foodstuff, a luxury and a fashion, and as long as Bordeaux and England were under one crown could easily be imported, particularly as it could be carried the whole way by water. There was less competition from other commodities, and as there was more money to spend and comparatively few things on which to spend it, wine absorbed a high proportion of the available spending power. Also this power was in the hands of a small class whose prestige was linked to conspicuous expenditure. It was right for a churl to toil and sweat, but an earl had to live in appropriate splendour and to be seen at his high table quaffing wine from a golden cup. Moreover this splendour had not only to be seen but to some extent to be shared. The common man could not often afford wine, but he could sometimes push forward to have a taste of it from a fountain at a coronation or a royal wedding, and if he were a dependent of a nobleman or a prelate he did not have to climb far up the social ladder to enjoy some share of the luxuries of his betters. Custom decreed that kings, great men and church dignitaries should be generous hosts and liberal purchasers of wine. Kings gave the example. In 1317 2,600 tuns were ordered for the use of the royal army in Scotland. In 1320 the royal butler bought wines to the value of £1,545 18s 3d from twenty-four merchants of Gascony and Guienne. Edward II bought 1,000 tuns of wine to celebrate his marriage with Isabella of France, and his father Edward I in 1300 bought two lots of wine totalling 1,567 tuns. Though kings were the largest purchasers, bishops and peers were not far behind. In the thirteenth century the household of the archbishop of York consumed eighty tuns annually. In 1295 over fourteen tuns were used for the enthronement of Archbishop Winchelsea; at the same period the Bishop of Hereford made numerous purchases, including twelve pipes bought in Bristol, while in 1289 he had seven tuns from the vintage of his vineyards at Ledbury. Noblemen were accustomed to dispense wines on a handsome scale in the course of day-to-day hospitality as well as on special occasions, and dignitaries great and small drew their allowances of wine from their king or overlord. Edward III's chaplain was given two grants of wine, one of three tuns, the other of a cask of wine annually. Chaucer, who was a minor official but had good connections through his sister-in-law, the mistress of John of Gaunt, was awarded on different occasions a pitcher of wine a day and a cask a year. At the monastery of Ramsey in the thirteenth century the monks had an allowance of half a gallon each on feast-days, while distinguished guests had wine daily. Mayors and municipalities also treated themselves liberally. One cannot rely upon the accuracy of figures, but there is no doubt that it was customary to provide wine on a generous scale, and that although it was a privilege of the tables of the rich, it was dispensed to a number of people dependent upon them. Until the late Middle Ages kings and nobles used to dine in public and to keep open house. In 1213 the Earl of Lancaster spent £7,300 a year on his household, and at the end of the fourteenth century the entourage of King Richard II on a progress numbered thousands rather than hundreds.

At the apogee of the Bordeaux trade in the first three decades of the fourteenth century, exports of wine for the seven years for which statistics survive averaged 82,710 tuns. Of this amount

B

13,000 tuns were contributed by the privileged citizens of Bordeaux and over half came from the dominions of the king of France in the High Country. All wines except those of the Bordeaux citizens paid the Grande Coutume and the resulting revenues gave the king a larger income than the whole of his realm of England. At first the trade was mostly handled by Bordeaux or foreign merchants, who often escorted their wines in order to look after their sale in England. They were allowed certain privileges to facilitate their stay and the disposal of their goods, but were regarded with a jealous eye by the citizens of London.

After a good year of 74,054 tuns in 1335/6 there was a threat of war and the exports from Bordeaux fell to 16,577 tuns. For the next nine years no figures are available, but trade presumably languished. In 1346 the victory of Crécy reduced the power of France and freed the Bordeaux district from the danger of invasion, but in 1347 the vintage failed and in 1348 the first onslaught of the Black Death wrought such havoc that the exports of wine fell to 5,923 tuns. Trade revived during the Black Prince's government of Aquitaine between 1355 and 1368 but never rose above 30,000 tuns. After war broke out again in 1369 the Bordeaux exports dropped to an average of 11,000 tuns, though there were occasional good years such as 1376 when 23,820 tuns was reached. The credibility of these figures, so much lower than those attained before, has sometimes been questioned, but the studies of Carus-Wilson (*Mediaeval Merchant Venturers*, 1957) have shown that there is no good reason to doubt them and that the figures for English imports of wine, which now began to be available, tallied more or less with those for exports from Bordeaux. The trade with the Low Countries had now greatly diminished and most of the wine exported went to England, so the English trade suffered less than that to other destinations, but the decrease in it was still very great.

War was not the only trouble. Some of the loss of trade was due to the jealousies of the merchants between themselves. The struggle between the High Country interests and those of the citizens of Bordeaux went on, while both in London and Bordeaux citizens and foreigners contended with each other for privileges. After a quarrel with the city of London on this subject in 1302, Edward I offered his protection to the merchant vintners of Aquitaine in return for a customs payment of 2s a tun. In the following year he issued a charter called the Carta Mercatoria promising favourable treatment to the Gascons and all foreign merchants visiting England. But the king died in 1307, and already in 1309 the London merchants took advantage of the weakness of his successor to claim that the charter had lapsed with the death of the reigning monarch. In response to the complaints of the Gascons and in return for the promise of a subsidy, King Edward II eventually renewed the charter, but its terms were no longer respected and the quarrel continued. In 1327 the London merchants obtained an exemption from prisage, which was to be permanent, and from that time the English took a much greater part in the trade. The Gascon colony in London diminished. As many English merchants as Gascon imported wines, and some English went themselves to reside in Bordeaux. A multitude of regulations were issued to cure the dissensions in the trade, but for the most part their only effect was to cause an increase in costs. Currency difficulties also arose. The export of gold or coin from the kingdom was prohibited. Various attempts were made to induce foreign merchants to bring their goods into England but they were disinclined to do so while they were prevented from taking out their profits. Consequently the king, his nobles and the vintners all had to send their own agents to Bordeaux to buy wine. In 1368 the king tried to put a stop to this by forbidding English merchants to go to Bordeaux; in response to protests this regulation soon had to be revoked. Attempts were made to revive it from time to time and the hope of attracting the foreign merchants to resume their visits to London was not given up. In 1391, in the reign of Richard II, a new enactment was issued assuring the foreign merchants of courteous treatment and of the right to take home with them half of the money for which they had sold their goods. But this was not enough and the Gascon merchants never resumed their former role in the Bordeaux trade.

Although the Bordelais had taken a major part in the handling and sale of their wines they never owned many ships. Between 20th January 1303 and 18th August 1304, 982 ships sailed from Bordeaux with wine, but only six of them belonged to Bordeaux. 40% of the ships were English, 22% Breton, 10% Norman, and 9% came from the neighbouring city of Bayonne. The Basques were fine seamen and Bayonne always possessed a surprising number of ships for her size. As time went on the proportion of

English ships in the wine trade increased and towards the end of the period of her suzereignty England acquired almost a monopoly of the diminished trade and about three-quarters of the shipping.

From the time of Henry III onwards, the perils from enemies in time of war and from pirates at all times made it dangerous for ships to sail singly. With such a cargo as wine it was profitable to be first in the market and merchants were tempted to take the risk, but the majority accepted the protection of a convoy and in some years they were forbidden to do anything else. At the best of times sailings tended to be bunched, because long delays were imposed by the need to wait for a favourable wind, but when the ships sailed in convoy they often numbered a hundred ships or more at a time, which left England in the late autumn and returned in January or February or later. This meant that when convoys were compulsory the distinction between the autumn fleet which took the wines of Bordeaux and the spring fleet which took the High Country wines was apt to disappear, and the citizens of Bordeaux to lose the advantage of their monopoly.

Very few galleys were seen in Bordeaux and almost all the wine ships were round ships; that is they were not long and narrow but broad in the beam and stood high out of the water. Most of them were small and few were larger than 100 tons. Nevertheless quite a large crew of twenty men or so was needed to handle the heavy square sails of the 100 tonners and to defend the ship in case of an enemy attack. Their speed was much the same as it was to remain for several centuries. In fair weather they could reach the Channel from Bordeaux in four or five days and London in ten, but they seldom had a fair wind the whole way, and if they were delayed, waiting for a wind or by bad weather, the short crossing could take weeks. A month was normally allowed for a single voyage, but three round voyages in the whole year was good going, and this was seldom exceeded even in the eighteenth century. In the Middle Ages most of the wines were discharged at a few principal ports, of which the most important were London, Boston, Hull, Sandwich and Bristol. The ships themselves, however, were based on a number of small ports round the whole coast of England but particularly in the west country. The first twenty-two ships sailing from Bordeaux in 1308 included six from Channel ports, twelve from ports westward of Wareham, and one each from Bristol and Chester. A long list of ships present at the siege of Calais in 1346 tells much the same tale. London provided 25 ships and east-coast ports 103; the figures for the Channel ports were 103 and for the west-country ports 154, including 47 from Fowey and 31 from Dartmouth.

In the thirteenth century and the first half of the fourteenth century Bordeaux wines dominated the English market. They had little competition to fear from other French wines except perhaps those of Auxerre. The only other wines of reputation were those of Germany, which enjoyed the advantage of a long tradition and of cultivators whose industry and care successfully overcame the disadvantages of climate. A few hundred tuns of rhenish were regularly imported. King John liked rhenish and moselle and the latter, sometimes known as 'oblinquo' was bought by Henry III. They continued to enjoy royal patronage and, when the sweet wines were first introduced in considerable quantities at the beginning of the fourteenth century, to be sold at a higher price than Bordeaux wines, German wines were classed with them for customs purposes. German wines were not quite as dear as sweet wines, but they were considered, evidently, to be on a par with them and better than bordeaux.

The sweet wines originated in the Levant and must have been familiar to the crusaders early in the thirteenth century, although there are few references to them until later. Malvoisie or malmsey, the best-known of the sweet wines, was originally grown in the Peloponnese but was mostly imported from Crete. Romeney, originally wine of Romania, was a similar wine though less esteemed; it came principally from Zante and the Ionian islands. After a time wines of this type were grown in Spain, and ultimately in Madeira and the Canary Islands. Spanish wines are not mentioned before the fourteenth century; a little may have come from northern Spain and Navarre, but the Mediterranean coast was occupied by the Moors or within reach of their incursions. Wine growing was not entirely unknown even in the time of the Moors, but Jerez and Cadiz were not taken from them until the close of the thirteenth century and were close to a disputed frontier for a century longer.

Crusaders returning by sea probably brought an occasional sample of Levant wine, but regular trade in such wines began with the coming of the Genoese galleys to England at the end of

the thirteenth century and of Venetian galleys in 1317. Such a
voyage took five months and had to be well organized. Ships built
for the Mediterranean found navigation in the Atlantic difficult
and the Strait of Gibraltar not easy to pass. Cadiz afforded a port
of refuge, when the Levant wind barred the return passage, but
when wind and current hindered the exit from the Mediterranean,
Christian ships were in danger from the surrounding Moors. However, the Venetian galleys of the fourteenth century overcame these
obstacles. They were of similar build to the light galleys of the time
but exceptionally large, attaining five or six hundred tons. They
were narrow ships, six times as long as they were broad, but still
a little beamier than the normal galley, which was eight times as
long as it was broad. They carried a large crew of 170 oarsmen,
together with twenty or thirty crossbowmen who took up their
stance on the side of the ship between the thwarts to repel attackers.
The rowers were freemen, often Dalmatians, and not slaves. They
were paid and had the right to take with them a small allowance
of trade goods. They sat three to a bench but each man worked
at a separate oar, a very heavy affair of 120 lbs. Only a third of the
oar was inside the ship and it had to be weighted to give it leverage.
Even in the early days the galleys relied largely on their sails and
used their oars mainly for entering and leaving port and for
emergencies. When the wind was unfavourable they had to wait
in port like any sailing ship. They were not good sailers, but
towards the end of the period their sailing was improved and
they even left some of their oars behind. But the oarsmen were
still useful to help the defence of the ship and for general purposes,
and the ability to enter and leave port under their own power
saved much time and helped them to keep a regular timetable.
The oars could also help the ship past awkward points or to progress a little in calm weather. The galleys for Flanders left Venice
in the spring and usually reached their destination in November.
They sailed in a convoy of four which split up at Sandwich, two
going to Flanders and two to London. Later goods for London
were transshipped at Sandwich or Southampton, but Southampton
soon fell out of use until the fifteenth century when it again became
the terminal of the Italian trade, of which it had for a time the
monopoly. At the outset the galleys made few stops at intervening
ports until they reached the Channel, though later such stops
became frequent; this protracted the voyage to a point where the

next convoy often had to leave Venice before the last convoy returned. Nevertheless, the galleys acquired a good reputation for regularity and safety, and although the freight was high they inspired such confidence that merchants could save money by dispensing with insurance. In the last days of the service a galley with special orders to return speedily made the voyage from Southampton to Otranto in thirty-one days, but this was exceptional.

On their annual voyage the galleys could take 140 tons of freight and later as much as 170 tons. Space was limited and they concentrated on spices and other valuable goods. They only accepted wine to fill up, and these must have been sweet wines, for they sailed long after the vintage, and the normal Italian wines would not have kept. The same principle applied to the Genoese galleys, whose most paying cargo was alum, a substance used in the cloth-dyeing process. In their later days the long ships were less different from the round ships, but it was still the latter type which was mainly used to carry wine. The sweet wines were more valuable than those of Gascony as well as more durable, and could bear the increased cost of freight.

Largish round ships were already being built in the thirteenth century. They had high superstructures fore and aft which gave them a superiority in defence against the long low galleys, though they were little use for making an attack. So when a number of Genoese galleys attacked the Venetian ship *Rocaforte*, a ship of 500 tons with two or three decks, in 1264, she successfully beat them off. The Mediterranean ships had lateen sails of various sizes, which could be changed in bad weather, while the round ships of the north had heavier square sails which could be reefed. Both types of sail required a number of men to manage them, the former because they had to be manhandled to the opposite side of the ship in order to tack or gibe, the latter because they were very heavy. From the fourteenth century Mediterranean seamen also took to using some square sails in imitation of the Basque pirates from Bayonne, who had become a familiar sight in the Mediterranean. The Mediterranean and the Atlantic continued to specialize in their own type of ship but they both began to use additional small sails, which were distributed over more masts. The Mediterranean ship with one mast and large sail stepped well forward had the disadvantage that it was liable to be pooped by a following sea in a gale. These developments added little to a ship's speed but they increased its manoeuvrability and enabled a smaller crew to be employed. As competition became more intense the Venetians and Genoese tried to meet it by building larger ships for long voyages. They had always had ships of 400 to 500 tons, and in the fifteenth century the Venetians experimented with ships of 1,000 tons, but found that so great a size did not pay. The northern countries seldom built such large ships, but they developed their navigability and sea-going qualities, which enabled them to enter the Mediterranean with success and in the fifteenth century to undertake the first oceanic voyages.

As mentioned above, sweet wines became popular in England in the fourteenth century and at that date had already been for some time known there. An early reference is to a purchase of malvoisie by the Archbishop of York in 1295. In the following decades this wine began to be imported in fair quantities from Crete by Italian traders. The Archbishop also bought some osey. One cannot be sure that the osey in this particular case was not aussois or osoy from Auxerre, but in later times osey was definitely a peninsular, probably a white Portuguese wine from the neighbourhood of Lisbon of Setubal. England had maintained friendly relations with Portugal from the time of the crusade in the twelfth century, when a combined force containing an English contingent had helped to take Lisbon from the Moors. The Treaty of Windsor was concluded between the two countries in 1386, but a previous alliance dated from 1372, and a trading agreement had been made with the cities of Lisbon and Oporto in 1353. Doubtless some wines were included in the trade in the thirteenth century, though no record survives of them. The wine of Osey was popular in the fourteenth century. The monks of Battle used to buy it at Sandwich and it was known to Chaucer and later mentioned by Shakespeare. Another wine mentioned by Shakespeare was charneca. It has been suggested it was a kind of bucellas but 'charneca' meant a sandy place and there were several villages of that name. It could well have been a colares for colares is grown, on particularly sandy soil. A wine unmistakably from Portugal was that from the Algarve, and in the fifteenth century references to Portuguese wines coming from Lisbon are not infrequent. Bastard is another wine heard of in the fifteenth century; in the *Libelle of English Policy* published in 1436 it is called a Spanish wine, but it was sometimes Portuguese. It was regarded as a <u>kind of sack</u>. There was a kind of cloth called bastard and it is tempting to surmise that the name arose from the acceptance of wine in payment for cloth, a type of transaction which appeared later in peninsular trade. These wines were classified as sweet wines.

In the fifteenth century a first reference is found to a Portuguese wine which could perhaps claim to be a remote ancestor of port-wine. It was made by a Czech nobleman named Rozmital and his party, who made an extensive tour of Europe, including France, Spain and Portugal, and eventually the court of King Edward IV. In 1460 he reached the Upper Douro from Spain by way of Moncorvo and Lamego. He had to pass through a wild frontier region full of bandits and of legends of worse terrors, including even dragons. But he mentioned that at the foot of the mountains there were plenty of wine, almonds and figs. He also noted the strawberry trees, which are still a feature of the district. He mentioned that wine called Vinho de Grecia was made of over-ripe grapes dried like raisins. This was a method used later for the wines of Jerez and he was evidently speaking of a sweet wine. He also spoke of the wines of Evora, which were strong and sour and scarcely drinkable unless mixed with water. Such in the early nineteenth century was alleged to be the nature of port-wine, if it was not carefully treated and given a judicious dose of brandy before fermentation was completed to preserve some of the sugar. It is unlikely that Douro wine or Evora wine reached England at this period but Portuguese wine was not uncommon. In 1465/6 six ships brought 500 tuns to Bristol, probably from Lisbon.

The sweet wines from the Levant were at least a year old by the time they reached England, and it would have been useless to import them if they had been liable to go off as soon as some of the Bordeaux wines. They were allowed to be sold for about double the price fixed for Gascon wines and the wines from Spain and Portugal also fetched higher prices. Items of wine imported in Italian ships were sometimes described as butts of sweet wine and sometimes as barrels of wine; this suggests that some of the wine from Spain and Portugal or Italy was not sweet wine, for the Italian galleys seldom called at French ports.

The best malvoisie came from Crete, a little from Chios and other Greek islands and perhaps from Asia Minor. There are references to wine of Tyre, which could have come from the

Lebanon, where wine was still being produced in the fourteenth century and perhaps later. At first the sweet wines were only imported in Venetian, Genoese or other Italian ships. They at once attracted the attention of legislators, who devised a multitude of regulations to ensure that they were kept separate from the native wines of Aquitaine, sold as foreign wines at a higher price, and neither mixed nor adulterated. Rhine wines and French wines from the Langue d'Oc were also subject to higher duties. In 1353 the retail sale of sweet wines in the same taverns, with the exception of Portuguese and Spanish wines, was forbidden, but afterwards this rule was modified, and from 1378 the sale of sweet wines was made free. Occasional English ships went as far as Portugal or Seville; for instance in 1382 a Dartmouth barge brought 150 tons of merchandise from Seville, but it was not until the end of the fifteenth century that English ships began to venture into the Mediterranean.

The merchants of Bristol led the way. The *Trinity of Bristol* was quite a large ship of 300 tons and capable of carrying 200 tons of cargo. As early as 1455 she brought back sixty-six tuns of wine from Lisbon and other southern products including oil, fruit, wax, and 'grain' a predecessor of cochineal used in dyeing scarlet. In a voyage made in 1479 she brought back as much as 270 tons of cargo including seventy-six tuns of wine. She took out cloths, which were bartered for the wine, described as sack, beverage, or bastard. This ship, or a name-sake, for twenty-five years seems quite a long life for one ship, went as far as Oran and Puerto de Santa Maria, where she was beached and overhauled for the return voyage. She also made a voyage west of Ireland to look for Brazil. She discovered nothing, but at Huelva her captain was in touch with the monks of Santa Maria de la Rabida and it is believed that the Bristol men had discussions about the possibilities of Atlantic navigation. Columbus is supposed to have visited Bristol, but whether he did so or not, some of his ideas are thought to have been derived from the experiences of Bristol navigators.

The fact that Bristol was not a port of call for the Italians perhaps encouraged the Bristol merchants to venture in ships of their own. The Portuguese themselves at first handled the trade with Portugal, but the Bristol merchants had established themselves as the principal carriers by the end of the fifteenth century, so that in 1479/80 only two Portuguese ships and two or three

Breton ships brought goods from Portugal, compared with eleven Bristol ships. The trade with Bordeaux had by this time declined and was rivalled by that from Portugal and the Mediterranean.

As so often in the history of the wine trade, the imports of wine from the Levant were introduced by shipments connected with the wool or woollen cloth trade. It was a Bristol shipowner named Robert Sturmy who made the first recorded venture to the Levant in 1446 with the cog *Anne*. The export of wool otherwise than through the staple at Calais was subject to licence, and the licence given the *Anne* to take forty sacks of wool and 100 pieces of tin weighing 26,000 lbs to Pisa survives. Sturmy intended that his ship should proceed from Pisa to the Holy Land to pick up a cargo of spices. After calling at Seville and Pisa she safely reached Joppa with 237 men on board including 160 pilgrims, but on the return voyage she was wrecked on the island of Modon near Chios in Greece and became a total loss. But the fact that so many pilgrims ventured on such a voyage showed that there were no insurmountable obstacles. Constantinople fell to the Turks in 1453 and the Venetians were driven out of Egypt, but it proved easier to trade with lands under Turkish rule than it had been with the Venetians, or with the Genoese who had dominated the trade of Constantinople from their colony at Pera. Sturmy tried again in 1457 with a ship called the *Katherine;* she, too, successfully reached the Levant and loaded a cargo of green pepper and spices, but on the return voyage was despoiled by the Genoese. This led to stern reprisals in London, where a number of Genoese were imprisoned. Both Venetians and Genoese fought hard to keep their monopoly but they had many difficulties. Their efforts to preserve their trade with the English Channel by building larger ships was not successful for they were defeated by the challenge of the new types of northern ships, which were smaller but handier. In 1465 a breach was effected in the Mediterranean monopoly when Florence opened her ports, including Pisa, to foreign vessels. By the end of the century there was already an English consul at Pisa. Even so only occasional English ships penetrated further than the western Mediterranean. In 1468 a London merchant named William Heryot was licensed to ship wool through the Strait of Gibraltar to Pisa on a ship named the *Antony* belonging to the king, and to have men impressed for the crew. The *Antony* made several voyages and in 1482 another king's ship, the *Martin la Towere*, was licensed

to take wool to Genoa from Southampton for a merchant named
Richard Cely. Records of these early voyages are scanty, but they
were numerous enough by 1488 to be discussed by the Venetian
Senate with anxiety. Probably all the ships returning from the
Levant had brought a little wine but by this time foreign ships
were loading malmsey wine in Crete even for Venice herself. The
Venetians were obliged to permit the trade but they imposed a
special tax of three ducats on wines loaded by strangers. Henry
VII retaliated by trying to transfer the wool staple to Pisa and
ignored the protests of the Venetian ambassador. He fixed a maximum price of £4 a butt for malmsey and subjected wine imported
by foreigners to a new duty of 18/- a pipe.

Although the trade of the Italians was threatened it was still
flourishing in the middle of the fifteenth century. From 1434
Southampton had again replaced Sandwich as the rendezvous and
port of discharge for England of the galleys and as the entrepot
for merchandise from Italy and the Levant and for sweet wines.
The total import of wines, including sweet wines, had fallen since
the beginning of the century. The total for London and fifteen
principal provincial ports in 1415/16 had been 17,562 tuns, but in
1480/1 was only 6,851 tuns. London led the way with 8,790 tons
in 1414 and some 3,000 tuns in the later decades of the century,
but by no means predominated over the provincial ports. Early
in the century the Venetians were said to have exported 1,000
casks of sweet wine from Crete annually to England. When the
trade in other merchandise began to languish the Venetians began
to attach importance to the wine trade and to endeavour to keep
foreigners out of it. In 1488 they went so far as to forbid the export
of malmsey from Candia except in the regular Flanders galleys. In
1491 King Henry VII retaliated by imposing a tax of 18/- a butt
or pipe on malmseys brought in foreign ships. This tax was
reduced but the rival interests continued to bicker and the Levant
wines had now to compete with Peninsular wines. The Spanish
policy was to export wool to Flanders and not to protect the
Spanish cloth industry. England was therefore able to obtain a
lead in the export of cloth to Spain, which provided a basis for
the return trade in wine.

The Italian wine most often mentioned was vernage or vernac-
chia, which came from the neighbourhood of Florence. Some
Spanish wines, including river or ryvère, came from the north of

Spain, from the neighbourhood of Logroño. Occasional Catalan galleys brought wine from Barcelona to Southampton, and Cadiz and San Lucar were already exporting wines. In 1517 the British community in Cadiz claimed that the English merchants in San Lucar de Barrameda had been granted privileges by Don Alonso the Good in 1297 not long after the conquest from the Moors and the first grant of the town of San Lucar to the ancestor of the dukes of Medina Sidonia. Certainly there was an English judge conservator appointed by the duke to look after the interests of the Factory in San Lucar early in the sixteenth century. There are references to the export of wine quite early in the fifteenth century and Chaucer referred to the strength of the wine of Lepe, the wine of Spain that 'creepeth subtilly, of which there riseth such fumositee, that when a man hath drunken draughtes three, and weeneth that he be at home at Chepe, he is in Spain, right at the town of Lepe, not at the Rochelle, nor at Bordeaux town'. Lepe is a village some miles from the coast between Ayamonte and Huelva known for producing white wines used for blending with sherry but in later years of no particular reputation. In 1491 some regulations published in Jerez referred to foreign merchants resident in the district and also to the export of Rumney wine. This was a type of wine originally grown in the Greek islands but it and wines of a malmsey type were already being cultivated in Spain and were competing as sweet wines. The new wines were stronger than the wines previously grown, for already stronger wines were in demand in northern markets both for their potency and because they were more durable. The Spanish authorities took some care to encourage the careful preparation of export wines, which were red as well as white. In 1492 the expulsion of the Jews from Spain left a gap in the commercial community, which was filled by an influx of Genoese, Bretons and English. These men were naturally drawn to the trades with their own countries and gave to the wine trade a new impetus.

Meanwhile the Bordeaux trade had been sadly interrupted by the loss of the city to France in 1453 and by the disturbed years which preceded this event. La Rochelle was already French and the English dominions had long been shrinking, so the loss of Bordeaux itself was only the culmination of a long process. The exports of wine to England had fallen to some ten or eleven thousand tuns; after the loss of the town they fell to five thousand tuns for a time, but after the treaty of Picquigny in 1475 they recovered to something like their level before 1450, that is to some ten thousand tuns. The Bordelais forbade the entry of High Country wines until after Christmas and then only permitted them for export. They tried to find alternative markets for their wine to compensate for the diminution of that in England; they were unsuccessful in selling much wine to Paris or Spain, but found a better market in the Low Countries and the Hanse towns. Helped however by some Bordeaux merchants who had taken refuge in England, the diminished wine trade still remained in English hands and there was still more bordeaux consumed than other wines. In contrast with the sweet wines, which could survive two or three seasons, the Bordeaux wines were seldom good for more than a year. The price of new wine was fifty livres a tun, but as soon as it came in the old wine could only be sold for six livres. Nevertheless, some distinctions of quality were already mentioned. The graves wines grown on gravelly soils were already better reputed than the Palus wines grown in alluvial soil.

After the treaty of Picquigny some shadow of the former relationship was restored and trade revived, but it must be remembered that until 1532 Brittany was a country independent of France. Therefore when Edward IV at the beginning of his reign banned wines from Aquitaine the prohibition did not apply to wines shipped from Nantes or wines which had reached Brittany. Breton wines were not immune from frequent seizure, but they were less molested than French wines and trade was able to continue. The fall in the trade with Bordeaux at the end of the Middle Ages was therefore compensated to some extent by the growth of the importation of wines from other parts of France, of sweet wines from the Levant and of sweet and other wines from Spain, Portugal and Italy, though the total trade remained much less than it had been in the hey-day of the trade with Bordeaux.

CHAPTER II

Wines in the Sixteenth Century

THE end of the Wars of the Roses and the first years of the reign
of King Henry VII saw some revival in the wine trade, but international difficulties in the latter years of the reign caused a recession. The first years of Henry VIII were however a prosperous
time during which imports of wine were believed to have risen to
30,000 tuns or more. The most careful statistics that we have for
the trade of the time were drawn up by Professor George Schanz
some ninety years ago upon the basis of the customs statistics.
They give the total imports for the fifteen principal ports of England and confirm that the first twelve years of the king's reign
were the most prosperous. They were followed by a slump of
four years and then by good years alternating with bad until the
last five years of the reign, when four years out of five were bad.
They do not confirm that the imports were as large as they had
been represented. The average for the fifteen ports for the years
from 1515 to 1521 only adds up to 13,027 tuns, of which 1,500
tuns were malmseys or sweet wines. The actual totals were undoubtedly larger, but how much larger it is impossible to tell.
London trade was gaining at the expense of the out-ports and took
about half the total trade. Besides London only Bristol and
Southampton imported over 1,000 tuns. Nevertheless some wine
was imported by almost every small port and allowance must be
made for this. In addition it is not clear whether allowance for
prisage was included in all the customs returns and it is probable
that a good deal of wine, in particular the small white wines
from Poitou carried in small ships to western ports, eluded the
customs. There were also the special licences granted by the king to

individuals and the exemptions enjoyed by nobles and other privileged people. The Tudor kings and the Stuarts after them often found it convenient to give with one hand what they had taken away with the other. They tried to encourage trade and for a consideration were sometimes prepared to treat foreigners on a par with their own subjects, but on the other hand they were constantly imposing new rules, restraints and taxes. Exemptions from these were a tempting way to show favour or to obtain payment in cash in anticipation of taxes payable in the future. The collection both of prisage and customs duties were farmed out in return for immediate receipts. Licences were also sold or awarded to individuals to import wines in considerable quantities. For instance in 1516 Francis de Barbi of Florence was licensed to import 1,061 butts of malvoisie. In the same year John Eaton, cooper of London, had an authorization for 1,000 tuns of Gascon wine and Robert Loward or Lord the exceptionally large amount of 2,000 tuns. Everything to do with wine involved privilege. Taverns could only according to the law, sell it in small quantities and, under a law of Edward VI made in 1553 to curb the illicit sale of wines, no ordinary citizen could keep more than ten gallons in his cellar unless he had an income of 100 marks or £66 13s 4d, which was a substantial sum. On the other hand, though the nobles had been much diminished during the Wars of the Roses, a circumstance which contributed to a fall in the consumption of wine, for they could no longer entertain as lavishly as had been their custom, wine was still an essential feature of upper-class life. Not only royal persons but all persons of consequence owed it to their dignity to dispense wine liberally on all proper occasions and it was recognized that they must be encouraged to do so. Ambassadors were naturally entitled to such courtesies and until the reign of Charles I were in theory entitled to be kept at the king's charge. This custom early fell into desuetude, as embassies ceased to be brief visits for a special purpose and tended to be prolonged and finally to become permanent institutions, but ambassadors continued to be granted a personal allowance of ten or twelve tuns of wine custom-free. Sometimes they asked for more, one suspects for a commercial purpose. A French ambassador once asked to import 600 tuns. Other dignitaries were also given the privilege of duty-free wine; their number was gradually whittled down but in the reign of Queen Elizabeth still included judges, bishops, privy councillors, peers, knights and even one esquire. The quota for them amounted to 1,000 to 1,250 tuns. By various means therefore much wine must have entered England, which was not included in the customs returns. At the end of the reign, in 1551 when imports were lower than in the earlier years, the Venetian ambassador estimated that these amounted to a value of 100,000 ducats, a sum probably excluding the out-ports and the duties on sweet wines. This would have worked out at 16,000 tuns which is not altogether out of keeping with Professor Schanz's calculations. The same Venetian source reported that although England had no wines of her own, wines were very generally drunk, and all kinds of wine, Spanish, French, Rhenish and Cretan were used, but he thought that French wines were the most preferred. The sweet wines indeed fell out of favour at this time though they recovered in the reign of Queen Elizabeth.

Some indication of the trend at the beginning of the century can be gathered from the purchases of King Henry VIII himself. The king's butler no longer bought 1,000 tuns at a time, but King Henry was magnificent and hospitable and the royal purchases were still large enough to colour the picture. In 1518 for instance, at a feast given in honour of the Queen of France at Greenwich, three tuns of wine were consumed. It is interesting that six tuns of beer were also used. In the time of Rozmital's visit to the court of King Edward IV ale was the drink of the English people, but wine was the staple at court. Now beer was coming into fashion and competing to some extent with wine. Beer at this time was a term applied exclusively to liquor made with hops. This was an innovation. The old rhyme went:

> Hops, Reformation, carp and beer
> Came into England all in one year.

Actually hops were already being imported into King's Lynn in 1503, so their use began a little earlier, but in any case the introduction of an alternative beverage which was good enough to be used on social occasions by the nobility must have detracted from the exclusive prestige of wine.

At the festivities for the Field of the Cloth of Gold, 3,000 butts of the choicest wines of France and Flanders and of Malmseys were provided. This was a special occasion, but wine was a regular feature of noble households and, at a lower level, of the rations of

C

the common soldier. In 1544 when the English army went to help
the emperor in France and ran short of wine for three or four days
the emperor's ambassador wrote that 'this was a sort of privation
which military men could seldom endure without despair'. In the
same year the emperor's troops were at Epernay, where the stocks
of wine were plentiful; they proved so exhilarating that the troops
got out of hand and 2,000 casks of wine had to be destroyed before
they sobered up.

The wines of Champagne so much liked by the imperial soldiery
were not then much distinguished from those of the neighbouring
province of Burgundy. King Henry bought Beaune and Auxerre
and possibly wine from Ay near Epernay, where Cardinal Wolsey
owned a vineyard and the king was reputed afterwards to own
property too. When he occupied Tournai, one of the advantages
of the place was considered to be its possibilities as a good centre
for the wine trade. King Henry was anxious to have the best wines
and was pretty catholic in his tastes except perhaps for Spanish
wines, against which for reasons personal or political he seems to
have had a prejudice in his later years. After his divorce he refused
to allow Queen Catherine of Aragon to procure a cask of old
Spanish wine, which she fancied, and ordered her to be content
with the wine which he provided and to drink only new wine for
her health's sake. He bought sweet wines and also some rhenish,
although his largest order, one for rhenish wine such as was
drunk by the emperor and the Duke of Cleves, was probably
inspired by politics. Generally he preferred Gascon and other
French wines. He used to send his agents to the Rouen Fair,
where they bought Orléans wines, famous then and until the
seventeenth century for their strength. He also bought in Rouen
burgundies from Beaune and Auxerre which came down the Seine.
These were to be found also at Antwerp, which was the principal
market for Rhine wines, largely consumed locally, but also for
sweet wines from the Levant, and for Peninsular and French
wines. The wine did not reach Antwerp directly but for the most
part came by barge from Middelburg, where the staple for wines
was situated. It is noteworthy that Antwerp had a considerable
trade in valuable merchandise with Italy by land and that some
wine from as far as Champagne and Burgundy came by land to
Béthune or Tournai and thence to Antwerp by barge. In later
years the cost of transport barred the importation of burgundy

and champagne wines into England, but at this time the trade routes to Antwerp both by Rouen and by Béthune flourished sufficiently to overcome this obstacle.

The first three-quarters of the sixteenth century saw the rise and decline of Antwerp as a great commercial centre. In order to understand the influences affecting the wine trade one must look at the trends of commerce as a whole from America to the Persian Gulf. Wine was an important commodity and predominated in the Bordeaux trade, but elsewhere it was only one of several commodities.

To begin with it was the Bordeaux trade which was most important for wine. It too was subject to many strains and stresses but it was strong enough to withstand them. Anglo-French relations suffered many vicissitudes, but the English imports of non-sweet wines never fell below 4,000 tuns, and Bordeaux supplied about three-quarters of the total imports. At the beginning of his reign Henry VII banned the import of Gascon wines in foreign ships in retaliation for the bad treatment English merchants had been receiving in Bordeaux. This did not kill the trade, as except in time of war the share of foreign ships had already fallen. In 1495 King Charles VIII was persuaded to order the Bordelais to restore to the English some of their traditional privileges and in the first years of Henry VIII treaties were concluded to restore the *status quo*. But there was war in 1513, an alliance in 1514 and again in 1542, the Field of the Cloth of Gold with its gorgeous but inconclusive fraternizing in 1520, and war in 1522-3 and 1543. In 1531, to ring another change, the importation of wine was prohibited before 2nd February, a measure which penalized the Bordelais who counted on selling their wines immediately after the vintage and on preventing the shipment of the High Country wines from the hinterland until after they had disposed of their own wines. The High Country wines, sometimes known as wines of Guienne, had been popular and one supposes that on account of the delays to which they were subjected, special care was taken to select wines which would last. Perhaps these were 'the high and mighty wines', preferred by the Earl of Suffolk. On the other hand Graves fetched a higher price than other wines as early as 1528, so possibly they came from Bordeaux itself. Most Gascon wines were expected to go off in a few months, but no doubt some selected wines, particularly in a good season, were more durable. In 1528 Graves was one of the wines bought by Henry VIII at Bordeaux at an average price of £5 16s 5d a tun. The wines of Poitou and La Rochelle were not always distinguished from Gascon wines until later in the century, when they were allowed to be sold at a lower price. These wines comprised those of Aunis, Oléron, the Charente and Cognac and were exported to the Low Countries where they were used for blending. They also found their way to England, principally to west country ports in small ships. The Rochelle trade was different to that of Bordeaux for the wines were not grown by wealthy people who specialized in wines for sale at high prices but were small wines grown by peasants. Many of these only grew a little wine as a side-line. Often they were short of money and had to contract loans on the security of the next vintage. Sometimes they would take trade goods in payment. Shipments to England were mostly in the hands of British merchants who took them in small ships to Bristol, Southampton and west country ports. After the Reformation contacts were stimulated by the fact that La Rochelle was a Protestant centre during the religious wars in France. A few High Country wines were perhaps imported direct from Bayonne. Other French wines were bought in Rouen or sometimes in Antwerp.

Antwerp at this time had large foreign communities, or Factories, of Portuguese, Spanish and Italian merchants. The Portuguese Factory, which was the most prominent, had already been established for nearly a century in Bruges when it moved to Antwerp in 1499, and soon afterwards it was followed by the whole Portuguese colony. The number of Portuguese and Spaniards was much enlarged by Jewish immigrants, who had been expelled from Spain in 1492 and, often after an interval in Portugal, where at first they had been welcome and then tolerated, gradually found their way to every port in Europe. They kept up their connections with their brethren and formed an enduring network, which through its experience and connections fostered international trade for centuries and could often find ways to defeat the obstructions of governments. In 1540 Antwerp was a great market for sweet wines, which were largely carried by the Genoese. These included wines from Provence, as well as malmseys from the Greek islands. The bastards and romneys of Greek origin were now beginning to be grown in Spain. We hear of romney coming from Lepe and Port St Mary and bastards and romneys from San Lucar. English merchants could find in Antwerp all the goods that they needed for return cargoes such as spices, sugar, fruits, sweet wines, dyestuffs, oils and manufactured products of Italy or the Orient.

Formerly these commodities had been brought to Flanders by the Venetian or Florentine or Genoese galleys, which had also taken them to London or Southampton. But in the first quarter of the sixteenth century the Portuguese developed their direct trade with the east by way of the Cape of Good Hope. The price of spices fell and Lisbon became the best market in which to buy them. At the same time alum, formerly the staple commodity carried by the Genoese from the Levant, was discovered in Italy and Spain. Large deposits were in papal territory and this gave the Pope an interest, which prompted him to discourage the Levant trade and to excommunicate merchants who traded in alum with Turkish infidels. At the same time sugar, which had hitherto been a product of the Levant or at nearest of Sicily, began to be produced in Madeira and Morocco. All these developments contributed to kill the old officially sponsored trade of the Venetian galleys. In many years they now missed out their annual visit; there was a gap of nine years from 1502 to 1511. In the latter year they appeared again in Southampton Water in response to a cordial invitation from Henry VIII. The king himself went on board and was received in great splendour with many fireworks. But this was only a flash in the pan. Cardinal Wolsey was soon complaining that the galleys no longer brought precious merchandise but only trifles. They came again but brought few spices, which were now sometimes in short supply even in the Levant. In 1518 they carried camlet cloth, oil and raw silk, the latter products perhaps from Italy or Spain, but their principal cargo was 238 tuns of wine, a commodity which in their hey-day they had only taken as a second choice. Their next visit was a failure and after a last call in 1532 they sailed away never to return. Private Venetian ships continued for a few years, but also soon disappeared. The Venetians tried for a time to recover their trade by building large ships of a thousand tons or more, but the supply of free labour from Dalmatia for the galleys was drying up. The galleys were more and more rowed by slaves, but this was not satisfactory and the large ships proved too expensive to run. For voyages to the north the galleys were replaced by round ships, though they were still retained for military use and for a few special purposes in the Mediterranean.

In the 1530s English merchants of Bristol, London and Southampton began to sail to the Greek islands. Their first efforts had largely been defeated in the previous century by the hostility of the Genoese and the Venetians, but Venice was no longer strong enough to insist on her monopoly. She retained as much as she could of the trade in Greek wines with Italy but was obliged to modify her ban on foreign ships taking wine from Crete to north European ports or sometimes even to Venice herself. In the 1530s Hakluyt relates the voyages of two English ships of 160 and 300 tons going to Crete, Chios, and Cyprus. They no longer looked for spices. The Portuguese trade in them was nearing its peak and the Venetians were driven to beg to carry them in the opposite direction from Lisbon to Italy. The English ships brought back some Middle East goods ranking as spices, but their principal freight was malmseys and muscadels. For a few years Hakluyt spoke of divers tall ships making similar voyages, but towards the middle of the century they ceased, so that the voyage of the great barque *Aucher* to Crete in 1550 was exceptional. This ship failed to secure a Turkish safe-conduct in Crete, but resolved to risk pushing on to Chios after selling her goods to Turks visiting Candia. She was successful, but sighted the Turkish fleet off Chios on its way to attack Malta and was lucky to avoid capture. Turkish power was now nearing its apogee and Hakluyt attributed the cessation of voyages by English ships to the Levant to the fact that the Turks had grown so high and mighty. Although they contented themselves with accepting tribute from Chios and Cyprus and did not occupy the islands until 1566 and 1571, nor Crete until the seventeenth century, they were extending their influence through the Mediterranean as far as Morocco, and were even threatening Spain. The governor of Algiers was in touch with the Moriscos, who were still holding out in the mountains behind Malaga. The threat was not perhaps serious, but the Turks were masters of the eastern Mediterranean and it was not until 1568 that the Moriscos were finally expelled from Spain, while in 1571 the Turks suffered their naval defeat at Lepanto.

The Turks were not however really enemies of English, Dutch, or French trade in the Levant. They had no interest in trade themselves and were content to leave it to Greeks, Italians, and other nationals, many of them Christians resident in their empire, to trade for them, and to take some of the profit. They were indeed quite ready to receive civilly overtures from Queen Elizabeth, who saw an opportunity to ingratiate herself with the Grand Turk by drawing his attention to their common hatred of the Pope and of his idolatrous practices. Turks, British and Dutch, also had a common interest in stirring up a reaction against Portuguese hegemony in the east. The Portuguese held Ormuz in the Persian Gulf from 1515 to 1562, but after they had failed to take Aden in 1538, and after the Turks took Basra in 1548, the Turks remained masters of the Red Sea. The Portuguese could not keep Muslim traders out of the Gulf, partly because the Turks and Arabs were too strong for them, and partly because they could not afford to fall out with Persia. The demand for spices was still increasing, and as the trade in them with Asia from Goa was as important to the Portuguese as that with Europe, they were willing in order to retain it, to allow the Turks to open the back-door up the Red Sea for their own use and even to allow Venetians to buy goods in Goa to be carried in Portuguese ships to Ormuz and thence by Arabs or Turks to the Mediterranean. So although the Turks ceased to advance westwards, and did not finally occupy Crete until the seventeenth century or the Morea until even later, they dominated the Persian Gulf and the eastern end of the caravan route to Aleppo. In this way the Venetians regained some trade in the Levant from Asia in the third quarter of the sixteenth century both in carrying to Italy eastern goods brought up the Red Sea to Egypt and in fetching them from Lisbon. They were also helped by several years of famine in the Levant, which brought them a good trade in Sicilian and Apulian corn.

One result of these developments was a cessation or at least a slackening for a time of English direct voyages to the Levant. Spices, sugar, sweet wines and dried fruits could all be found more easily in Portugal, Spain and Morocco, and English ships entering the Mediterranean were tempted to go no further than Italy. There was trade enough at Malaga, Cadiz, Pisa and Leghorn, where English merchants were beginning to reside and English Factories to be established. Those who felt the pioneer spirit were now more attracted by oceanic voyages, but on the whole the English were more interested in the export trade, in the sale of their cloths, than in what they brought home in return.

For their purposes Antwerp, during her period of prosperity, offered a sure market next door, attainable after a short sea passage. The Company of Merchant Venturers, who dominated the trade of London, were by no means as venturesome as their name indicated. On the contrary they were a conservative body looking for sure profits. They were handling 70% of the cloth trade and were diverting an increasing proportion of it from the out-ports to London. Antwerp could take all the cloths that London could offer and English manufactures represented a third of her imports. Furthermore Antwerp was a better market even than Lisbon for goods from any point in the trading world and unlike her immediate successor, Amsterdam, was not herself a competitor for shipping. Antwerp had few ships of her own and only limited wharfage. A high proportion of goods reached her by inland waterways. Most of the wines went first to the staple at Middelburg, which in 1565-6 for instance received 162 ships with wine from France including 95 from Bordeaux and 42 from the Charente and La Rochelle. Also, on account of the danger from war and piracy by sea, much valuable merchandise was still sent to Antwerp by land. To assure their defence, ships needed guns and large crews. For this reason, in the middle of the sixteenth century the emperor, Charles V, decreed that ships sailing to the Mediterranean should not be less than eighty tons and should sail in convoy with four or five ships of 200 tons. So Spanish and Portuguese merchant fleets began to comprise a number of large ships of two or three hundred tons. The Dutch also had some large ships but in the second half of the century began to build carracks, known as *naos* by the Spaniards and Portuguese, which were lower and lighter in build. They had multiple sails and were easier to handle but tended to be too fragile for the winter trade. The wine trade was an exception to this fashion for bigger ships at least as far as the Rouen and Bordeaux trade were concerned, for the wine ships rated only forty-five tons on the average. The English also were conservative and kept their taste for smaller ships. They mostly went to Bruges or Middelburg and stopped short of Antwerp itself; in 1553 the figures for Antwerp were 90 Dutch, 80 Spanish and Portuguese, 12 Antwerpers, and only 5 English.

Another advantage of Antwerp was a good postal service which could take letters by land to the European capitals comparatively quickly. Commercial voyages by sea were still slow. Although an official fleet with a favouring wind could reach Lisbon in fifteen days or go from Flushing to the Bay of Biscay in nine days, it might have to wait a month in Antwerp to unload, or if ready to sail, be held up for an equal period by the lack of a good wind. Although ships could attain a maximum speed of eight or nine knots their average speed was one knot only. So the normal time for a return voyage to Catalonia was estimated to be five or six months, to Genoa six or seven months, and to Venice eight months. Large ships were laid up for three or four months in the winter, so they seldom reckoned to make more than one voyage in the year, even to Andalusia. With prevailing westerly winds England, and especially the west country ports, enjoyed a considerable advantage for all southerly and westerly voyages, but even from them one voyage a year was usual, except to France, northern Spain and Portugal.

The prosperity of Antwerp was short-lived. Already in 1551 troubles were beginning there. A boom in the cloth trade had saturated the market and was followed by a slump. In addition there was an outbreak of sickness and the increasing embitterment of the religious question began to endanger the position of Protestants residing in the city. The Marranos from Spain and Portugal began to be persecuted and to depart on the next stage of their flight to Amsterdam or London, or wherever they could find a refuge. Monetary troubles followed and in 1576 Antwerp was sacked by a Spanish army. In 1585 after a long blockade by the Dutch the Scheldt was closed to traffic. The Spaniards had destroyed much of the city and Antwerp's glory was passed. The Dutch, who had already become principal carriers, took over the trade. and Amsterdam became the largest northern European trade mart.

Owing to its lack of native shipping Antwerp had never been a trade rival of London. Amsterdam was, but the Dutch were international carriers, while the English were primarily exporters and their ships went in the first instance to ports where a market was to be found. This favoured the purchase of wines in the big international ports such as Amsterdam, Lisbon and Cadiz. There was no bar as yet to French or Peninsular wines being brought in English ships from the Low Countries, but there was already a tendency to restrict the importation of wines in foreign ships.

At the accession of Queen Elizabeth these restrictions were eased, and wine could come in foreign ships upon payment of alienage duties. The sale of Spanish wines, both sweet wines and an increased amount of table wines, was helped by the fact that they paid a lower duty and also by the expansion of the tavern trade. Malaga wines proved a good substitute for the Levant wines and Southampton tried without success to claim that because they came from beyond the straits they should be classified as malmseys and be included in their monopoly. For a time merchants taking Greek wines to London or other ports continued to pay fines for infringing Southampton's monopoly, but by the end of the century little was left of Southampton's privilege except a diminishing return, as the fines ceased to be enforced.

Throughout Tudor times the wealth and spending power of the upper classes fell, relative to that of the middle classes. In the reign of Henry VIII this was shown by the increased outlay on wine of the civic authorities. They dispensed wine on their celebrations and their right to do so was recognized by a customs-free allowance of six, four, and one tuns respectively of wine to the Lord Mayor, sheriffs and twenty-four aldermen of London. The merchant class was growing in wealth and the number of taverns selling wine was increasing. Taverns were supposed to be for the refreshment of travellers only, and there was an outcry against their undue multiplication; a limit was put on the licences to be granted for them, but the limit of forty taverns for London was not kept. The sale of wine was subject to the control of the vintners company and they fought hard to retain their privilege. They exercised a certain restraining influence but they were naturally interested in expanding their province. The freemen of London in 1530 successfully asserted their claim to the right to sell wine freely, and after this all freemen seeking to sell wine became vintners. Many regulations were made to prevent the abuses arising from the too free sale of liquors, but they seldom had much practical effect.

With regard to Spanish wines, the dukes of Medina Sidonia, who had held San Lucar de Barrameda as an appanage from the time of the expulsion of the Moors, were benevolent patrons of trade. The demand for wines was stimulated by the growth of trade in Cadiz resulting from the discovery of the New World, and the expulsion of the Jews and New Christians had created a vacuum in the trading community which was filled by foreigners. In 1517 there were enough English residents to cause the duke to grant them privileges and help to build a chapel. King Henry VIII licensed the chapel and gave the English merchants the right to elect a governor, and to levy imposts for the benefit of the community which were known as consulage. The authority of the governor or consul to act as judge in civil cases between English subjects and even between Englishmen and Spaniards was also recognized by the duke, who gave a plot of land and a donation for the chapel, which was to serve also as a meeting-house for the Factory. The system by which resident foreign merchants were allowed to organize themselves as Factories with a measure of self-government and of freedom from interference by the local authorities was well known in Spain and Portugal. Both nations had long had Factories at Bruges, and when the cloth staple was moved to Antwerp the Portuguese Factory became the most powerful and best organized there, though the Spaniards became the most numerous. The head of the Factory was usually called the consul and was elected by the merchants. In the Portuguese Factory at Antwerp there were at first two consuls elected annually. Later the King of Portugal appointed the consuls. In English Factories the consuls received a royal commission, but they were usually persons recommended by the merchants. In Portugal the judge conservator was recommended for the approval of the King of Portugal; in Cadiz he came to be directly appointed by the King of Spain and in San Lucar was originally the same person as the governor or consul. In both countries the conservator had jurisdiction over civil cases concerning English subjects, though there was an ultimate right of appeal to the supreme court. In Portugal there were Factories at an early date at Lisbon, Oporto, and Viana. In Andalusia the principal Factory came to be at Cadiz, but at various times there were communities at San Lucar, Jerez, and Port St Mary. As we have seen, San Lucar was recognized at an early date. At one time or another Factories existed in most continental ports, but they did not always attain a legally recognized footing.

Henry VIII not only recognized the authority of the consul at San Lucar; he also granted a charter to the Andalusia Company. The divorce of Catherine of Aragon was already souring relations with Spain, but English merchants were still able to evade the religious issue and to treat the quarrel as a purely political matter. They argued that King Henry VIII was as good a Catholic as any man, and this was proved by his regular devotions and by his willingness to proceed against persons guilty of heresy, so the unfortunate differences with the King of Spain were royal matters and not for merchants to judge. For a time this point of view was accepted. The King of Spain needed English help and was inclined to agree with the Duke of Medina Sidonia that the inclination of the Inquisition to interfere should be curbed. Gradually the tension rose, and Englishmen trying to be loyal to their king and to the Roman Catholic Church found that they were obliged to choose, and if they chose their own king they ran the risk of arrest and persecution. A time came when the King of Spain no longer needed help against France and, when Henry VIII gave help to German Protestants, the religious issue was given a freer rein. In 1539 an Englishman named Thomas Perry was arrested. He had just loaded 100 tuns of bastard wine for the Duke of Bejar, who bailed him out. He was re-arrested but after an interrogation was allowed to go home. In 1540 the Factory, consisting of the governor William Ostrych and twenty-two merchants, complained of Perry's case and of the persecution of English merchants by the Inquisition. The situation was still eased a little, when England's alliance was needed but the time was coming when the King of Spain could no longer protect the Factory against the Inquisition. Some of the English in Spain returned to Catholicism; others remained Protestant but were much embittered. In 1645 there was a famous incident when Thomas Reneger of Southampton, formerly a merchant in Spain, took to privateering, and capturing the Spanish galleon *San Salvador* off Cape St Vincent despoiled her of her valuable cargo. He sent her empty to her destination at Seville and was careful to give her master a receipt for what he had taken and to maintain that he was only compensating himself for the loss of goods confiscated from him at San Lucar. The Spanish ambassador lodged a furious protest, but Reneger was regarded as a hero in London, and the English courts, affecting to take a correct legal line, contrived to establish that the goods taken had not been registered with the Spanish authorities and were actually Genoese property. They managed to obtain Genoese agreement to the sequestration of the property and to create a division of interest between the King of Spain and the Spanish merchants, both of whom claimed the ownership. But in spite of such incidents trade went on and in 1548 the total Spanish exports of wine from Cadiz were computed to be 60,000 butts of which 40,000 went to England and Flanders. Fundamentally it was to the interest of all parties not to stop trade and there was a residue of good feeling. Some old established merchants such as Hugh Tipton, who survived as consul from 1537 to 1570, managed to steer clear of trouble. Many of the English and Irish were Catholics and had less difficulty. Even in 1590 the Duke of Medina Sidonia, returned from commanding the Armada, showed no ill-will, but helped to restore the chapel at San Lucar which had fallen into ruins and to give it a new lease of life under the patronage of the Spanish Church. It survived as a charitable institution into the eighteenth century and as there were always many Catholics among the British merchants resident the wine trade never became a Protestant Factory interest, as it did in Portugal.

At an earlier date the trade at the English end had been in the hands of Spanish merchants, of whom a number were resident in London until about 1540. The increase in the English share of the trade was led by Bristol, which in the early years of Henry VIII was already importing 500 tuns of Spanish wines, mainly by British merchants in British ships. By the latter half of the sixteenth century aliens played only a minor part in the trade. Sweet wines, including Greek muscadine from Venice, were being brought in by Dutch as well as English ships from Amsterdam, but English ships predominated. They were already favoured by navigation acts which from the time of Richard II onwards had been passed to restrict the importation of wine in foreign ships and to penalize its importation by aliens. Another act in the same sense, directed principally against the merchants of Aquitaine, had been passed in the reign of Henry VII. This act forbade the importation of wine, and also of Toulouse woad, a principal export of Bordeaux, in foreign bottoms. Later it was realized that foreign princes must be humoured, and this legislation was modified and at the beginning of the reign of Queen Elizabeth specifically repealed. Foreigners were then allowed to import goods in English ships without paying alienage, and the principle recognized and for some time adopted that free ships meant free goods; in other words the nationality of the ship and not of the owners of the goods determined the status of goods shipped. Wines could still be imported from anywhere in foreign ships on payment of alienage duties and not as in later years only from their place of origin. The tunnage and poundage payable on Gascon wines continued through Tudor times to be 3/- a tun and 6/- a tun on sweet wines, though in the latter years of Queen Elizabeth the average total duties were said to amount to £2 13s 4d a tun, for tunnage and poundage were not, as they became later, the main part of the duties.

The competition of Spanish with Levant wines was helped by the fact that, though many Spanish wines were coming to be regarded as sweet wines, those coming from Cadiz did not pay duty as such. Their success was attested by the enormous popularity of sack. References to sack first become common in the reign of Queen Elizabeth, but as early as 1480 the accounts of John Balsall, purser of the ship *Trinity of Bristol*, described consignments of sack and bastard from Lisbon, which were bartered for cloth. This provided evidence for the origin of the term 'sack' in the Spanish use of the word 'sacca' for goods 'sacados', or set aside for export and often for exchange against exports.

To compete with sweet wines sacks needed to be strong. Some sacks came from Portugal, but they were not considered as good as those of Spain or of the Canaries. The natural wine of Andalusia, preferred by the Spaniards, was light, but the English looked for stronger wines, and by blending, and by using the same kinds of grapes as those used for the sweet wines, they conformed to the English taste. Some wines had been grown in the Canaries at an early date, but it was not until the middle of the sixteenth century that they replaced sugar as the main crop and that canary wine began to be exported in bulk to America and also to England. English voyagers and those with contacts in Andalusia became familiar with the malmseys grown there and also began to speak of the good wines grown in Madeira. In the middle of the century there were already English residents in the Canaries and one, John Hill of Taunton, owned the only vineyard in the island of Hierro. Canary wines first reached England by way of Lisbon, Cadiz or Antwerp, but by the end of the century they were so popular that they were worth a special voyage to the Canaries. In 1597 sack was also imported from Cadiz and St Mary Port, and red tent from Marbella and Alicante.

It must not be forgotten that in the sixteenth century Spain still had a large merchant fleet and Bilbao had only just yielded to Cadiz the first place among Spanish ports. Some wines had been imported from northern Spain and these shaded into those from Viana in northern Portugal, where there was an English community until it was expelled in 1580. From 1580 until 1640 Portugal was a Spanish province, though still separately administered, and the English customs seldom distinguished between Spanish and Portuguese wines. In the 1588 King's Lynn port book for example, consignments of three or four tuns of wine are mentioned, but are described as wines of Spain and Portugal. In both countries the English had a thriving trade in fish, and the ships carrying it naturally took in wine, which became familiar in their home ports, largely in the west country, and in America. Such Portuguese wine as was imported commercially seems largely to have been sweet wine, or wine passing as such, from Lisbon or the Algarve. Oporto is seldom mentioned, though in 1597 a Spanish fleet was reported to be loading 1,000 tuns there, probably of beverage wine, for the use of the Spanish army at Ferrol.[1] Law suits in H.C.A. 1/44 at the P.R.O. referring to wine show there was some traffic between Oporto and London in 1593.

From the records of the Portuguese chronicler Rui Fernandes we know that in the early sixteenth century the Lamego district in the lower part of the future port-wine district had a reputation for wine. Beverage wines for the consumption of the lower classes and also table wines for Oporto and the neighbourhood were shipped down the Douro, but there was also a limited production, amounting to about 1,000 tuns, of stronger 'aromatic' wines, which would mature for three or four years. These were sold at four or five times the price of the table wines and represented about a tenth of the total production. They were not entrusted to the river but were sent on mule-back to Castile and to Lisbon for the use of the court and of the nobility. There is no record of this ancestor of port-wine having reached England, though some may occasionally have done so by way of Lisbon, and some of the table wines from the Douro probably came to England from Oporto.

Naturally during the war with Spain trade with Portugal was

---

[1] London and Kings Lynn Port Books E 190/10/4 and 430/5.

interrupted (but less so than might have been expected on account of the sympathy which existed with England and of the opposition to Spain centred in the Portuguese Pretender Dom Antonio), and in a general way the Spanish occupation of Portugal encouraged English traders to seek outlets elsewhere, in the Far East and in the Levant among other places. It has already been mentioned that both Venice and the Turks reacted against Portuguese domination of the spice trade. The Venetians put it about that the peppers brought by the long and dangerous route round the Cape lost their savour and the Spaniards were inclined to meet them half-way by diverting some of the Lisbon trade towards Venice in order to exclude the English and to have more ships in the Mediterranean and fewer in the Atlantic, where the English and the Dutch made navigation hazardous. At the same time the great banking houses of Fugger and of Weiser were having difficulties in Lisbon, and were not only negotiating there to safeguard their trade, but were even talking of moving some of their interests to Venice or even to Constantinople.

In order to preserve their valuable trade between Goa and Ormuz the Portuguese were content to forgo any share in the trade of the Persian Gulf and the Red Sea, so that in 1584, a year following a great shortage of eastern goods in the Levant, the Dutch merchant Van Linschoten saw Venetians openly bargaining in the Goa market. At the same time some English emissaries were investigating the possibility of trade with Ormuz; they were apprehended, and though the sympathies of some Portuguese with the cause of Dom Antonio and therefore with England saved them from any serious consequences, no direct trade ensued. No back door for the export of English cloths was opened into the Middle East, nor did the strong wine of Shiraz, which was soon to find favour with the earliest English Factories in India, find a vent in the English market. But the English took their cloths to Aleppo and there was a general activation in the Levant, where the Turks were interested in the profits of trade but not in handling it themselves. They were content to let the Venetians, the Arabs, or the English, Dutch or Greeks handle it for them. In this way some far Eastern luxury products reached Venice and perhaps Germany, again through the Levant. English traders got these from Lisbon or began to fetch them themselves from India, but they marketed English products in the Levant and took in return Middle Eastern products, including currants and some spices and at first a considerable quantity of wine.

Though the Turkish defeat at Lepanto had surprisingly few direct results it gave the Turks food for thought and a new respect for Christian power. In 1580 they signed a treaty with Spain and the last flicker of Morisco resistance was translated to North Africa, where some of the Moriscos became the most ardent of pirates. The enmity of Islam was however concentrated against Spain and the Pope and his idolatrous practices. This enabled the English and Dutch to suggest that they too hated all these and deserved to be regarded as friends. These arguments won a certain hearing. In the last part of the reign of Queen Elizabeth, England achieved a good trade with Morocco, where the skills of English artisans were also appreciated by the local rulers and a number were employed. In Turkey in 1580 London merchants exchanged letters with the sultan and obtained an assurance that they would be protected. Queen Elizabeth followed this up with a royal letter stressing her common interests with the sultan against Spain and sent five ships loaded with tin, a commodity of which the Turks stood in need. Her ambassador William Harborne was accredited to the sultan in 1583 and succeeded in obtaining capitulations which assured the traders of good treatment. In 1586 good relations were reinforced by the return in ships of the Turkey Company of a number of Turkish prisoners captured from the Spaniards by Drake in the West Indies. The Turkey Company was founded in 1581 and was succeeded by the Levant Company, with which the Venice Company was merged. It began to send fifteen or more ships annually to the Mediterranean and to gain an influence in the city of London which lasted into the eighteenth century and affected government policy even after the Levant trade had begun to decline.

By sailing in convoy the Turkey or Levant company's ships were able to face the corsairs and to establish a *modus vivendi* with the North African powers. English ships were seen again in the Greek isles, in the ports of Asia Minor and even in Egypt. They took passengers as well as goods, and conveyed Christian pilgrims to the Holy Land, where they were tolerated by the Turks, and Moslem pilgrims to Alexandria on their way to Mecca. The Dutch, English and French now won back a share of the Levant trade from the Venetians and Genoese. The Levant Company, founded

D

in 1605, acquired some thirty ships of 100 tons or more which were better found than those of their Mediterranean competitors and included several of two or three hundred tons. The company was primarily constituted for trade with Turkish and Venetian ports but was allowed certain rights of consulage in other Mediterranean ports as far west as Malaga.

The terms muscadel, muscadine, or malmsey were still used for Greek wines, but the name malmsey began to be a generic term for all sweet wines and to be applicable to similar wines from Malaga and soon from Madeira. An act of the first year of Queen Elizabeth alluded to the great affluence of sweet wines during recent years and to the evasion of duty by many of them. In particular it laid down that malmseys from Malaga, which were made of the very same grape as Greek malmseys, should be counted as sweet wines. The importers objected to this, and after several years during which the point remained in question seemed to have won their case. The merchants of Southampton, however, petitioned for Malaga wines to be regarded as sweet wines. The reason for this was that they had been granted a monopoly of the trade in sweet wines by Queen Mary as a reward for the welcome they gave to her husband King Philip of Spain. This monopoly did little to restore their trade but for a time they collected the fines levied on sweet wines landed in London or elsewhere for infringing the monopoly. The fines were increasingly evaded, but some continued to be paid at least until 1637, when the farm of the moiety of the fines, which were due to the king, was sold for twenty pounds. In that year therefore the monopoly was still in force though not many fines were collected and the trade in sweet wines had greatly declined. In theory Southampton maintained her right into the eighteenth century, for it is mentioned in S. Baldwin's *Survey of the Customs* published in 1770.

In the first years of the century the trade still flourished and sweet wines were the most expensive wines, fetching 4/- a gallon as against 3/8 for sack. Most of the wines came from Crete or Zante, still in Venetian hands, though some came from Turkey, where Greek vineyards were still tolerated. Much came in English ships, but some came by way of Venice or Livorno. The extent of the trade in the last years of Queen Elizabeth was shown by the considerable stocks kept in London and by the keen competition for the farm of the duties. In 1612, which was a prosperous year, the imports of sweet wines were still high and computed to be 12,700 butts. By 1621 the figure had fallen to 7,200 butts, but in 1619 the farm of sweet wines for eight years was sold for an increased rental of £10,873, so the trade must still have been valuable, though it had lost ground compared with that in French and Spanish wines. In 1612 Sir Frank Swinnerton had offered £9,000 a year and a down payment of £8,500 to farm them for eight years. A few years earlier he had not offered more than £15,000 a year to farm the French and German wines together. By 1613 the farm of the French and German wines had risen to £19,000 a year plus a down payment of £10,000.

The trade in Spanish wines had not altogether disappeared during the war with Spain and many prizes of Spanish wine had been taken. These included 2,000 butts at Cadiz, when Drake singed the King of Spain's beard, and some at Corunna before his landing in Portugal in 1589. He found no wine in Portugal, but only some barrel staves which he looted near Lisbon. However, the sympathy in England for the Portuguese pretender Dom Antonio kept the Portuguese connection alive and there was always some clandestine trade. In records of lawsuits in 1593 there is mention of traffic with Oporto. Dom Antonio visited England and afterwards set up his headquarters in the Azores for a time. English seamen and traders found wine there, but more important were their talks with Portuguese navigators who divulged to them some of their knowledge of unknown seas.

The English wine trade had now spread to Alicante and Malaga, and to Italy and Sicily as well as the Levant. The wines of Florence were well regarded, but were inclined to go off quickly and needed to be shipped promptly through the Strait of Gibraltar before the late autumn winds from the Atlantic held them up. The Bordeaux trade remained the most important single trade and after the turn of the century exported from 4,000 to 7,000 tuns to England, while nearly as much again was exported from La Rochelle and the Loire. The Bordeaux wines were subject to heavy French export taxes, but sold more cheaply than they had twenty years before and than the Spanish and sweet wines. They fetched 2/8d a gallon compared with 4/- asked for muscadine and muscadel, 3/- for rhenish, and something between 3/- and 4/- for sack and canary. At the end of the sixteenth century the wine ships from Bordeaux sailed immediately after the vintage and reached London at the end of the year. In January 1597 for instance there were twenty-six ships from Bordeaux in the port of London, one from Rouen, and thirty-four from the Low Countries. The negotiations for the farming of the customs give some idea of the scope of the trade. In 1556 a licence had been given to import 10,000 tuns. This was over a year's supply and was a good deal more than was imported in 1603. An alternative to French wine was rhenish, which could easily be got from Antwerp, or after the demise of Antwerp, from Amsterdam. But although rhenish was appreciated and a good deal was imported into East Anglia, it never rivalled French or Spanish wines. A fair idea of the wines current at the close of the queen's reign in 1597 can be gathered by the spoils taken by the Earl of Cumberland from the capture of 143 ships of various nationalities. The wines taken comprised 225 pipes of bastard, 142 pipes of canary, 579 pipes of sack (presumably from Cadiz), 26 butts of alicante, 65 butts and 40 pipes of malaga, 81 pieces of rhenish and 814 tuns, two hogsheads and ten tierces of Gascony wines.

CHAPTER III

Towards the Civil War and the Restoration

THE first years of the reign of James I were years of peace and of comparative freedom for the wine trade. For some time to come the retail prices of wine were still in theory governed by a law of Henry VIII, but the law of 1553 regulating prices had been repealed and for a time prices remained fairly stable without much government control. The importation of Bordeaux wines rose again and in 1612 Sir John Swinnerton made a much higher bid for the farm of the French wines than he had in the days of Queen Elizabeth. The king, in spite of the protests of Parliament, persisted in selling monopolies to get ready cash. In 1610 the death of one of the monopolists, the Lord High Admiral, offered an opportunity for a commercial agreement about wines to be made with Venice, but it was not followed through. In 1618 the Thirty Years War began in Germany. The war was to destroy many vineyards, to produce a shortage of rhenish, and to encourage the fashion for beer and the Dutch taste for Hollands. In England the result was the imposition in 1620 of a duty of 40/- a tun on all wines, to pay for King James's intervention on behalf of his son-in-law the Elector Palatine. In 1624 war with France and Spain led to a temporary prohibition of French goods and of the importation of wines in foreign ships. Trade was less hindered than it might have been, because the king's chronic need of money drove him to sell many exemptions.

Spanish wines at this period equalled French wines in popularity, but wines from Bordeaux and also from La Rochelle still predominated. Graves wines, usually red, and later to be called

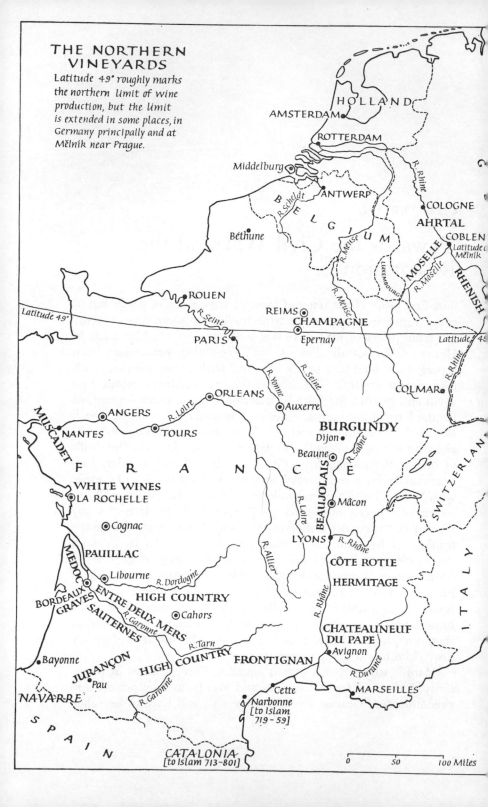

THE NORTHERN VINEYARDS

Latitude 49° roughly marks
the northern limit of wine
production, but the limit
is extended in some places, in
Germany principally and at
Mělník near Prague.

HOLLAND

AMSTERDAM

ROTTERDAM

Middelburg

R.Scheldt

ANTWERP

R.Rhine

COLOGNE

AHRTAL

B E L G I U M

Béthune

COBLEN

Latitude
Mělník

R. Meuse

LUXEMBOURG

MOSELLE

R. Moselle

RHENISH

Latitude 49°

ROUEN

R. Seine

REIMS

CHAMPAGNE

R. Meuse

Latitude 49

PARIS

Epernay

R. Rhine

R. Yonne

R. Seine

ORLEANS

COLMAR

ANGERS

R. Loire

Auxerre

MUSCADET

NANTES

TOURS

BURGUNDY

Dijon

F   R   A   N   C   E

Beaune

R. Saône

SWITZERLAN

WHITE WINES

LA ROCHELLE

BEAUJOLAIS

Mâcon

Cognac

R. Loire

LYONS

R. Rhône

PAUILLAC

R. Allier

CÔTE ROTIE

MEDOC

Libourne

R. Dordogne

HERMITAGE

BORDEAUX

ENTRE DEUX MERS

HIGH COUNTRY

I T A L Y

GRAVES

Cahors

R. Garonne

SAUTERNES

R. Rhône

CHATEAUNEUF
DU PAPE

R. Tarn

Bayonne

JURANÇON

HIGH   COUNTRY

FRONTIGNAN

Avignon

Pau

R. Durance

NAVARRE

R. Garonne

Cette

MARSEILLES

Narbonne
[to Islam
719 - 59]

S   P   A   I   N

CATALONIA
[to Islam 713-801]

0   50   100 Miles

Haut Brion, had already won a reputation and were better considered than the Palus wines. The white wines of La Rochelle were cheaper, and as has been mentioned, were grown in a small way by peasants, much as in later years the green wines of the Minho in Portugal were grown. There was no permanent community of British merchants in La Rochelle, but there were frequent connections with England, and La Rochelle possessed a number of small ships, which took wine to Brittany and also fetched High Country wines and brandies from Libourne above Bordeaux. La Rochelle also traded with Ireland and was the base for some of the French Newfoundland fishing fleet. Some of the latter called at Madeira, the Azores or Cadiz, though seldom at Lisbon or Oporto, on their homeward voyage, and loaded wines for England. After the failure in 1627 of the Duke of Buckingham's attempt to raise the siege of the Huguenot city by King Louis XIII the links with England grew weaker. The war with France also destroyed a few vestiges of the old privileges which English merchants still enjoyed in Bordeaux. The Charente, which was part of the hinterland of La Rochelle and had produced some substantial wines, now turned to brandy. Cognac became the brandy capital and the country north of Bordeaux towards the Loire began to produce more brandy than wine. This helped the peasants, who could sell their grapes even when they were not good enough for export wines, but the manufacture of brandy required larger operators and more capital.

Some wine from the Loire and from as far as Orleans reached England by Nantes, but no more is heard of burgundy for some time. On the other hand James I had a taste for Frontignan. This came by way of Leghorn and was seldom imported directly from Marseilles.

Otherwise Spanish wines and particularly sack were the most popular. Somewhat belatedly the fashion received official recognition at court and allowances of sack for various officials were approved. We have seen that already in the reign of Henry VIII malmsey had become a collective name and covered sweet wines, though there was still a separate customs heading for these. Now most of the malmseys came from Spain. When classified as sweet wines, an extra duty of 2/6 a butt was added to those paid, and between Michaelmas 1641 and May 1643 £26,695 was collected on 23,443 butts. The term sweet wine had become confusing, as it was applied equally to wines from the Mediterranean and to wines from Cadiz or elsewhere which were strong and sweet. Lewes Roberts, whose *Map of Commerce* was published after the Civil War, but whose experience abroad dated from some time before it, even referred to wines from the High Country of Bordeaux as sweet wines. Howell, who published *His Familiar Letters* in 1638, left some account of them. He said that sherry was often used to make sack but was inferior to canary. Of late years more canary had been brought into England than into all the world besides. Formerly it had been drunk in small glasses, but latterly either the wine had weakened or Englishmen's stomach had strengthened, for old and young now lapped it up like milk. Sack was certainly a great favourite and the most praised by Shakespeare and contemporary writers. One of them wrote:

'Sack is their chosen nectar; and they love it better than their own souls; they will never leave it off, until they have sacked out all their silver; nay, nor then neither, for they will pawn their fiddles for more sack'.

There have been many arguments about the origin of the term 'sack'. It was sometimes spelt 'secke', and this has been alleged as evidence that the name was a variant of 'sec' or 'secco' and meant dry. Cyrus Redding backed up this suggestion with a quotation from a writer named Venner dated 1628. Canary was often called 'sweet sacke' and Venner said that it should not be called sack at all, for the real sack was a paler, thinner wine from Jerez or Malaga, which many people like to take with sugar. This was a usual practice with rhenish and other white wines which were not sweet, and although sack became a very comprehensive term covering almost any white Spanish wine, there seems no doubt that canary sack was initially a different type of wine to sherry or Malaga sack, but that the English taste was always for sweeter and stronger wines and therefore the mainland wines sought to imitate the stronger wines of the islands.

On the other hand it is doubtful whether the term 'dry' was applied to wines before the eighteenth century and another explanation is that sack was wine made from dried grapes, called Greek wine or vin d'Espagne. This was a method we have mentioned as used on the Upper Douro at an early date and was also used in the Jerez region. The issue is confused however by the fact that 'sacca' also meant export and 'vino de sacca' meant wine which had been 'sacado' or set aside for export. In order to obtain an import permit merchants were often obliged to accept export goods for a similar value in return. We have already referred to this procedure as followed by the *Trinity of Bristol* in 1480. Eight whole cloths were exchanged for eleven tuns of sack wine, and one red cloth for oranges and one tun and one hogshead of sack. Other transactions were the bartering of seven whole cloths for nine tuns of bastards and 'a sad blew darbbyn cloth' for two tuns of beverage. The term 'sack-boats' was also applied to small ships carrying codfish to the Peninsula. They took wine for their own needs and sold any which was left over. The masters of such craft, who were also often the owners, were small people likely to lack proper bills of lading or documentation for any goods they had picked up, and to have customs difficulties which could best be solved by *ad hoc* barter arrangements with the Spanish or Portuguese authorities. Perhaps several meanings of the word 'sack' converged. The 'sack' goods would be a general term covering all kinds of goods but ending by meaning all kinds of wine. It looks as if this was the original meaning, though the connection with the word 'secco' or dry may have arisen afterwards.

The real Falstaff, of course, lived before canary was known and before Spanish wine was called sack, but he could well have drunk an early sherry. Before port or champagne were known no wine so caught the English fancy as sack. Shakespeare therefore celebrated it, and described Stephano, when his ship was wrecked, swimming ashore with the help of a cask of wine thrown overboard by a sailor. He made a bottle from the bark of a tree and from it he gave some to Caliban, who swore on the bottle to be his true subject, for the liquor was not earthly. So wherever Englishmen penetrated, whether it was to Virginia or the East Indies, they took sack with them. We find Tom Coryate, the famous Odcombian legstretcher, so named from his native village in Somerset, being welcomed by English merchants after his overland walk from Aleppo to India with drafts of sack in Surat.

Howell's statement that canary had in earlier times been drunk only in small glasses suggests that it had been a concentrated liquor but that with the expansion of the trade the merchants had tended to dilute it. There seem to have been two trends at work. On the one hand, as soon as a wine became popular, the shippers tended to use it for blending with other wines. On the other hand, while the strong wines were diluted, other wines were strengthened to imitate them. By the time of Howell the fashion for Greek malmseys had passed; he said that few wines in Greece had body enough to stand a long journey and only a few muscadels and malmseys were brought over in small casks. Whatever the truth of this, malmseys now came mostly from the Canaries and romneys from San Lucar or Cadiz. Tom Coryate in a letter to the High Seneschal of the famous Mermaid Club hoped that his friend the Rev. Peter Rogers would be regaled with the pure quintessence of the Spanish, French and Rhenish grape but made no mention of Greece. For some reason the virtue had gone out of Greek wines; the East India Company experimented with muscadine and other white wines but found that they went sour and were not popular. They lamented that the consumption of too much sack lengthened still more the death-roll of their employees but reconciled themselves to the fact that it was an indispensable provision for their ships and their Factories. They allowed half a tun to the commodore of their fleet and provided a pipe of canary for the entertainment of a returning Persian ambassador. They grumbled at the expense, and finding that only sack or canary would do, bought their stocks wholesale when possible. In 1633 they purchased forty butts at £18 a butt. When the Factories ran out of sack they drank Shiraz instead. This was a strong white wine. An interesting feature about it was that it was sold in bottles and apparently shipped from the Persian Gulf in bottles packed in chests. Perhaps these were really earthenware jars, such as were used in places where no wood was available for making casks.

In competition with the Canaries, Madeira was also turning from sugar to wines, and by 1646 was said to be exporting 2,000 tuns. Most of it went to America and not much is heard of Madeira in England at this time, but in 1625 the Duke of Buckingham thought of taking his fleet there after the unsuccessful attack on Cadiz, so it was evidently thought of as a place worth plundering. He had however found plenty of wine in Cadiz and it had played the same unfortunate part as it was to do in the next seige nearly a century later. In 1625 the inner harbour of Cadiz was more open and less strongly defended than it was to become later and the fleet was able to sail past the city and occupy the isthmus behind it. The troops found warehouses full of wine and by sacking them suffered much in health and discipline. After failing to take the town they were obliged to re-embark. They only reached the Irish port of Kinsale after many weeks of delay and much trouble with sickness and wintry weather.

The surprising feature of the Duke of Buckingham's fleet was the size of a number of his ships. One has been brought up on the legend of Drake with his handy ships defeating the clumsy Spanish galleons, but by 1625 the Royal Navy had gone some way to follow suit. There were eight ships of over 500 tons including the *Royal Anne*, the flagship, which was rated at over 1,000 tons. Her seagoing performance was poor and she seems to have been more of a liability than an asset. Of the remaining seventy-one ships, eleven were over 300 tons, fifty were of 200-300 tons and ten under 200 tons. Not all the fleet were royal ships: many were merchant ships on charter. The average size is unusual, for English merchant ships were small and there was even in the earlier part of the seventeenth century a reaction against large ships. Spanish ships in the American trade averaged 400 tons and Dutch ships tended to be larger than English merchant ships, which at the end of the century averaged little more than 100 tons.

With the extension of trade over the oceans and back into the Mediterranean from the north, there had been a great development of ships in the sixteenth century. The Portuguese led for a time. Their famous caravels were long and low-built and at first only carried lateen sails though they soon had square sails too. Their merit was that they were speedy and handy and easily defended. Before the beginning of the sixteenth century their influence was already showing itself in English and Dutch ships; they made good privateers and were used in England for the Bordeaux and Spanish trade. However, they were not strong enough for winter weather and were replaced by carracks, which were stronger and beamier and better adapted for carrying cargoes. By the middle of the sixteenth century the galleys had disappeared from northern waters and had largely been replaced in the Mediterranean by carracks with two or three masts and ample cargo space. They were not built in the north, though many were acquired, but somewhat similar ships were built and were styled hulks. The north and the south influenced each other, but on the whole the north went in for ships built for speed and aggression, while the Spaniards and Italians preferred ships which were easily defensible and were often larger than northern ships. The galleons, though not necessarily large, were roomy and had high castles fore and aft for men and artillery. They were slow and unwieldy but strong in defence. The development of ships was not so much in size, capacity or speed as in ease of handling. With more sails of different types, which were lighter to handle than the old square main-sails, they sailed better into the wind and could be worked by smaller crews.

Wine was a bulky cargo requiring a good deal of stowage space but not a very valuable one except perhaps where malmseys and canaries, and later the choicest wines of Bordeaux, were concerned. On the other hand wines were perishable and the vintage preceded or even coincided with the season of bad weather. Except for the Levant trade in which wine was seldom a major item, large ships were rarely used for wine. The ships using Bordeaux were nearly always small, many of them under 100 tons. Often they had to sail in convoy and their return was dependent on the availability of warships to protect them as well as on the date of the vintage, which in the seventeenth century varied between 24th September and 13th October. When there was no delay due to bad weather or other causes the wine was shipped as soon as possible.

Formerly the malmseys had been sold for twice as much as Bordeaux wines. The difference in price diminished but did not disappear. In 1632, when wholesale prices for wine were again established by law, the price of bordeaux was set at £18 a tun and of La Rochelle and small French wines at £15, while muscadel, canary, and alicante were £32. Sacks and malagas or sherries (the term sherry was just coming into use) were first priced at £26 then at £32. In other words sacks and malagas were tending to be canaries rather than the other way round. Although the distinction between sweet and other wines was preserved in the customs tariff it was now a distinction according to country of origin rather than according to quality, for some Spanish and Portuguese wines were sweet and strong, while others resembled French table wines. It is not clear when precisely peninsular wines became officially classified as sweet wines, but it must have been some time after 1624 when an order in council laid down that although malaga was not subject to the tax on sweet wines landed elsewhere than at Southampton the question remained open and must be settled by a court of law. The sweet wines had formerly been retailed by apothecaries and after some vigorous disputes between the apothecaries, the distillers, the grocers and the vintners, the apothecaries retained the right to sell cordials and liqueurs as tonics, as well as medicines and drugs. Such liqueurs as ratafia and hippocras were sold discreetly in small sealed bottles. There is a tradition that port-a-port, the first strong wine from the Douro, was sold in this way as a medicine in the seventeenth century before ever it was imported in quantity or became well-known. But if the apothecaries retained a small corner in the wine trade the vintners naturally aspired to govern it. They still retained their privilege to control the licensed sale of wines in the city of London and they strove to enlarge this at the expense of other companies. They protested in the early years of the century against the increases in duties, and when after an interval the impost of £2 a gallon was reimposed they countered with a charge of 1d a gallon on the retail price of wine.

For a time during the war with France French trade was prohibited. In 1626 a number of English ships were sequestered in Bordeaux. But in spite of wartime difficulties the amount of prize-wine seized and of licences to trade with the enemy granted kept the wine trade going, so that in 1629 there was a positive glut, which inspired John Taylor, the so-called water-poet to write:

> For now our land is overflowing with wine
> With such a deluge or an inundation
> As has besotted and half-drowned our nation,
> Some that are scarce worth forty pence a year
> Will scarcely make a meale with ale or beer.

Taylor had more than a literary interest in wines. The city of London was quit of prisage to the king but levied its own prisage of a few gallons on every incoming cargo and Taylor held the concession for this. No doubt he had been impressed by the unusual influx of ships. Both the government and the vintners were dismayed by the fall in prices, so there must have been a temporary surplus, though in 1630 there was a dearth which produced anxious enquiries from the Lord Chamberlain as to where he could stock his cellar, and orders from the king to the vice admiral in Devon to appropriate any wines he could find on English or Scottish ships and to pay the market price for them.

In 1641 Parliament raised the questions of the extra impost of £2 a tun on wines originally imposed to help the Elector Palatine and of the increased prices, and also took issue with the vintners over their extra 1d a gallon. The vintners were accused of making undue profits and also of adulterating their wines and falsifying them with unwholesome mixtures, 'such as rotten figs, raisins, bilberries, blackberries, aloes, allome, izinglasse, deale, sawdust, cyprus wood, lymewater and sugar, cider, milk, stoome and other unwholesome ingredients, by which it is manifest that the nobility and gentry are greatly deceived and abused both in the price and condition of their wines, oftentimes to endangering their health'. The vintners indignantly denied the charges and blamed the Court for their readiness to grant exemptions and monopolies, saying that these were the root of the trouble. Nevertheless Parliament decided that the vintners extra charge of 1d a gallon had been too much and was in any case illegal. This was a matter which greatly interested the public, and many pamphlets and broadsheets were published. But England was now moving towards the Civil War and had other things to think of. So far from men of forty pence drinking wine many gentlemen were soon to be reduced to going without. The ballad-mongers sang the praises of good ale:

> The old renowned Ipocrist
> And Raspie doth excel;
> But never any wine could yet
> My humour please so well;
> The rhenish wine, or muscadine,
> Sweet malmsie is too fulsome;
> No! Give me a cup of barlie broth
> For that is very wholesome.
> Twill make me sing, I cannot go home,
> 'Its long of the oyle of barley',
> I'll tarry all night for my delight
> And go home in the morning early.

The court may have been venal and bibulous, but King Charles I himself showed an example of moderation. In his father's day court functions had sometimes turned into orgies. A spirit of emulation was perhaps responsible for the drunken scenes which marked the visit to Theobalds of the King of Denmark; His

Danish Majesty was a toper whom few Englishmen could safely challenge, though strangely enough it was Gonzaga, the ambassador of abstemious Spain, who was reputed once to have done so and to have emerged the victor. But the court of King James lapsed from sobriety on other occasions when they had not the excuse of the visit of a bibulous monarch. King Charles behaved better and cut down the expenditure on wine. In 1625 he allowed about £1,300 for French wines and £1,581 for sweet wines for the necessary provision of his household. Personally he only took a glass of wine at dinner which he mixed with water. At his last hour on the scaffold he consented to take a small glass of claret to fortify himself.

Naturally during the Civil War the wine trade was reduced. Many of the nobility and gentry were now deprived of their estates, driven into exile or reduced in circumstances. A new heavy excise tax was introduced and the total duties payable, which a few years before had been £3 a tun, rose to £9. In 1651 a new Navigation Act was passed which was to remain in force for more than a century. It was stricter than any of its predecessors and prohibited the importation in foreign ships of goods which were not the product of the nation concerned. So even after the war with the Dutch ended in 1654 they were debarred from the trade in French wines which they had followed since 1628, the date of the last prohibition. Several petitions were addressed to Parliament for French wines to be made free of this ban, but they were all rejected, though special licenses to import were still sometimes sold to individuals. So when fresh legal prices for wines were established in 1657 they were higher. They were 1/6 a quart for Spanish wines, 1/- for Rhenish and 7d for French wines.

Nevertheless the wine trade recovered in the last more settled days of Cromwell's government. Conspicuous expenditure had declined and the Puritans abhorred drunkenness and high living, but they were by no means abstainers. Cromwell's court was run modestly, but it was modelled on that of a king. In the early months of 1654 it was provided with prize and other French wines to a total of 135 tuns. Cromwell bought also Spanish and Rhenish wines, and on his state visit to Bristol willingly accepted the gift of a pipe of sherry. The shape of things was much as it had been before. Ambassadors, and noblemen who had enjoyed the privilege of importing wines, were confirmed in their rights, and though the royal right of prisage had been declared contrary to the law, the farmers of prisage were allowed to carry on. Nor was wine altogether confined to the upper and middle classes. Beverage wine was still supplied to Cromwell's fleet in place of beer, whenever it cruised in southern waters and called at southern ports, and prize wine was set aside for this purpose. It was perhaps through purchases of wine by the fleet that Portuguese wine, which had declined as a result of the Spanish occupation of Portugal, began to be known again. The fleet supplied itself from Portuguese, as well as from French or Spanish ports, and in 1657 took on board 400 tuns of madeira.

The attitude of the King of Spain, while until 1640 he ruled over Portugal, had varied. He had recognized the appointment of an English consul at Lisbon in 1607, but the English merchants expelled from Viana in 1580 did not return, and trade with Lisbon was interrupted for long periods, though some clandestine trade always continued. In time of war the clandestine trade had been largely in the hands of Irish or pretended Irish Catholics but in the reign of James I in time of peace this had come into the open. Treaties were made with Spain in 1604 and 1640 but were not always observed. At the end of the reign of James I there were considerable imports of sugar, salt, tobacco, oil and southern fruits from Portugal. Some wines under the names of sack or bastard were probably imported too, but they were not distinguished from the wines of Spain, so there is no record of them.

After the liberation of Portugal from Spain in 1640, and a period of hesitation, King Charles recognized King John IV of Portugal and in 1642 signed a treaty of friendship and alliance with him. This recognized the right of England to trade with Africa and above all the privileges of the English Factories and their consuls in Lisbon and Oporto. It did not grant any increased facilities for trade with Brazil. The English were still legally obliged to trade with Brazil only through Lisbon, though in fact they continued to have an appreciable clandestine trade, mainly in Brazilian sugar. The English Factories in Portugal began to prosper. The company of merchants trading to Spain and Portugal had appointed consuls in the sixteenth century, and after the company's demise in 1606 the appointment of Hugh Lee as consul in Lisbon had been recognized.

The institution of Factories of merchants with an organization and privileges recognized by the authorities of their place of residence was familiar enough to the Portuguese, who had had their own Factories. English Factories had existed in Portugal in the sixteenth century and it was claimed that in the disturbed conditions of the seventeenth century the existence of such bodies was essential for the safe conduct of trade. They had suffered something of a hiatus during the Spanish régime, but in 1642 they were again adequately recognized. They were exempted from persecution by the Inquisition and largely from interference by the Portuguese authorities; above all they were given the right to appoint their own judge conservator. The conservator was a Portuguese citizen, whose appointment was subject to the approval of the King of Portugal. He exercised jurisdiction over all ordinary trade matters arising between British subjects, or British subjects and Portuguese, and of most other cases involving British subjects except cases of crimes in which the offender had been caught red-handed. The treaty of 1642 also recognized as heads of the Factories British consuls chosen by the Factories and commissioned by the King of England. The consuls were allowed to collect consulage, a levy of a ducat or about 5/- on every English ship coming to Portugal and of a $\frac{1}{4}\%$ on the value of all goods imported by Englishmen, to meet their expenses and the cost of relieving distressed British subjects. Provided that they did not obtrude their religion the English were allowed to practise Protestantism. In Lisbon, where services could be held in the embassy, this caused no great difficulty, but in Oporto, where there was no diplomatic privilege, the activities and even the presence of a chaplain were contested. The privileges granted by treaty were often only grudgingly recognized and from time to time disputes arose about the burial of British subjects, about the kidnapping of British children to be brought up as Catholics and about customs and taxes. But the consuls were permitted to take charge of the estates of deceased British subjects and to administer them, and on the whole the Factories were left alone to lead a self-contained existence. There were some interruptions during the English Civil War, during which the King of Portugal naturally had royalist sympathies, which caused him to allow Prince Rupert to make use of Lisbon as a base for his piratical activities. But until then the Factories had prospered, for when the King of

E

Portugal sequestered the English merchants' goods they were valued at £10,000 in Lisbon and at £12,500 in Oporto and the Western Isles.

Portugal was not strong enough to sustain a war against Oliver Cromwell and was obliged to sign a new treaty of alliance in 1654, which dotted the i's and crossed the t's of the privileges of the Factories. The right of the English to be tried by their own judge conservator in all except criminal cases with a right of appeal only to the Portuguese Supreme Court, was specifically reaffirmed. New concessions were won for trade with Brazil and above all a secret article guaranteed that no higher duty than 23% should ever be levied on English goods imported into Portugal and that in case of dispute the valuation of the goods should be decided by arbiters chosen by the English consul and the customs house officers. The Portuguese were reluctant to ratify so onerous a treaty and were only forced to do so, two years afterwards, by a demonstration of Admiral Blake's fleet. They often disputed the interpretation of individual articles but henceforward the treaty was in the main observed, and perpetuated as the Factories' charter and guarantee of their privileges and prosperity. The wine trade was not to begin on any scale for another generation, but it was the presence of large British communities on Portuguese soil which enabled it to follow the requirements of English taste and eventually to acquire so lasting a predominance.

The jubilation which marked the restoration of King Charles II in 1660 was significant for the wine trade. Pepys described the scene on the royal flagship, where the sailors, recently so loyal to the Lord Protector, spared neither cash nor credit in drinking loyal toasts. On entering London the king was greeted by fountains flowing with wine and many citizens went down on bended knees in the streets to drink his health. A few celebrations were not enough to alter the wine trade, but the return of the royal court and of so many exiles, who had become used to the wines of France and Flanders and were determined to enjoy themselves after having endured so many lean years, created a great change of atmosphere, particularly in London. The greatest spending power was concentrated in the capital and around the court, and the evils it produced were vividly described or anticipated in the king's own proclamation to the navy soon after he reached London. It condemned drinking, swearing and debauchery and 'a sort of men of whom we are sufficiently ashamed, who spend their time in taverns, tippling houses and debauches, giving no other evidence of their affection to us, but in drinking our health and inveighing against all others who are not of their own dissolute temper; and in truth have more discredited our cause by the licence of their manners and their lives than they could ever advance it by their affection or their courage. We hope all persons of honour, or in place and authority, will so far assist us in discountenancing such men that their discretion and shame will persuade them to reform what their consciences would not; and that the displeasure of good men towards them may supply what the laws have not, and it maybe cannot provide against, there being by the licence and corruption of the times and the depraved nature of man many enormities, scandals, and impieties, which may by the example and severity of virtuous men be easily discountenanced and suppressed'.

King Charles no doubt gave his name to these splendid sentiments without reluctance. He was fond of pleasure, but he was a man of taste, sometimes drunk but no drunkard. His proclamation appealed to the Puritan conscience and was welcomed by the sailors. But he was not the man to give an example of abstemiousness and the vices he decried became all too typical of his court. But a Puritan court would not have sponsored the introduction of choice wines and of new refinements, which offset to some extent the commercialization of wine. This commercialization had nothing to do with the Restoration or the court but was the result of the gradual growth of the middle classes and of the decline of feudal hospitality. Taverns continued to multiply; this could become an abuse but they were also becoming an essential social institution, places where all classes of people met, though in the eyes of the law they were still supposed to be only places of refreshment for bona fide travellers. Wine, which had been the privilege of the rich and noble, who occasionally regaled the poor with it, was more generally drunk. This tendency had already shown itself in England during the hey-day of the possession of Aquitaine but had since receded. Now when economic conditions improved wine became more popular among all classes in England save the lowest, who made up for it by drinking more beer and spirits. It is interesting however to note that in the region of Bordeaux itself the peasants drank little wine before the end of the eighteenth century and cultivated their vineyards for the sake of the ready cash they produced without being able to afford to drink much of the wine themselves.

After the Restoration the duties on wines were heavier than they had been but were still much lower than they soon were to become, and for the time being simpler, because the new tariff replaced a number of out-moded regulations. Only two principle duties were chargeable on wines under the 1660 Act, namely the Old Subsidy and the Additional Duty, or New Subsidy. The gross duty chargeable under the Old Subsidy was £4 10s od a tun on all wines except Rhine wines which were taxed by the awm (about 40 gallons) and paid about £6 a tun. For Additional Duty all wines except sweet wines paid £3 a tun. Portuguese wines were classified as sweet wines for the Old Subsidy but not for Additional Duty. The sweet wines for this purpose were Spanish and Levant wines, and they paid £4 a tun. In addition all wines had to pay a charge of 10/- a tun called coinage, which was used to defray the cost of the royal mint. Thus the gross charge per tun amounted to £8 on French and Portuguese wines, to £9 on Spanish and Levant wines, and to £9 10s od on Rhenish wines. Various allowances could be claimed, so that the net duties amounted to about £6 8s 11d on French wines, £6 2s od on Portuguese wines, £6 17s 3d on sweet wines, and £8 os 9d on Rhenish wines. Wines imported by aliens or in foreign ships paid more. Wines landed at the out-ports paid less, but were subject to local dues, and had to pay the difference if they were forwarded to London. In spite of the attempt to simplify the law it remained complicated. There were always two sets of books, one kept by the searchers who boarded ships and verified the quantities of dutiable goods carried and the other by the customs officers, who entered the amount of duty actually paid. In due course several other duties were added, but the two subsidies imposed in 1660 remained for the next century or more the foundation of each customs transaction.

The Navigation Act was also renewed in 1660 in stricter form with regard to trade with the colonies. Aliens were prohibited from engaging in trade in the dominions overseas or from exporting their goods in any but English ships. The definition of an English ship was made more precise and the prohibition of the carriage of foreign goods except in English ships of the country of origin was extended to prohibit them being carried in English ships to foreign ports. The only exceptions were in favour of

Rhine and Levant wines, and of wines from Madeira or the Azores. Rhine wines could be imported in any ship and English ships could load Levant wines at customary ports in the Mediterranean. Madeira could be shipped from Madeira directly to America. This meant that Levant, Italian or any southern wines could be loaded in Italy or in any Mediterranean port, but not in Cadiz or Lisbon. Salt for the Newfoundland fisheries could also be taken directly from Europe or Scotland. This was of importance to the wine trade, in so much as fishing vessels engaged in the triangular trade between England, America and the Peninsula often carried Spanish or Portuguese wine. Any remaining doubts whether French or Peninsular wines could be imported in Dutch ships were removed by a specific article in the Act banning them.

Soon after the Restoration, in 1661, a new treaty was signed with Portugal. Under its terms Catherine of Braganza was betrothed to King Charles, and Bombay and Tangiers were ceded to England as part of her dowry. There were now as many as two hundred merchants trading to Portugal, who had petitioned in favour of renewing the alliance, and the new treaty confirmed all previous treaties and alliances including Cromwell's treaty of 1654. A letter written in 1672 shows that there were then about 100 members of the Lisbon Factory and about twenty-one in Oporto[1]. Quite a number were said already to have gone back to England, their fortunes made. Even at this early date the writer remarked that some of the merchants were very ingenious men, and many had made a good living, but others were battening on their privileges, and knew so little of the customs or humours of Portugal that he was able to learn very little by conversing with them. The same writer mentioned that a Lisbon resident named Barnaby Crafford made very good wine and one can surmise that then, as later, a number of Englishmen made a vineyard their hobby and sent presents of wine to their friends. The sugar from the West Indies was spoiling the market for Brazilian sugar and the trade with Portugal in the next years was to depend for return cargoes more on Portuguese products and less on those of the Portuguese colonies, but wine still played only a small part in Portuguese exports. Lacking the money to pay for Queen Catherine of Braganza's dowry of two million crowns, the Portuguese loaded the ships escorting her with jewellery, sugar, and as much

[1] H.M.C. Dartmouth. 1st series 111-23.

Portuguese merchandise as they could collect, but wine was conspicuously absent. Madeira is the only Portuguese wine to which we find occasional references. Some madeira no doubt found its way to England, though the main trade was with America. In 1676 Christopher Jefferson, who called at Madeira to load wine for the West Indies, spoke of an export of 25,000 pipes. Similar statements were made about Madeira exports in the eighteenth century and seem to have been exaggerated. Nevertheless there was a substantial trade. The seaman Edward Barlow, who in the course of his long career at sea visited and described almost every known port, said in 1663 that madeira was the best wine for keeping and for carrying to a hot climate. In that year his ship took 500 pipes to Rio de Janeiro and a number of half- and quarter-pipes; fifty of them leaked, to the great loss of the merchants. In 1678 his ship was again in sight of Madeira, but finding that the wind was taking her past the island and that a call there would have meant a long delay, she sailed on to the West Indies. Barlow noted that there was a glut of wine in Jamaica and it was fetching very low prices, so he was glad that his ship had not loaded any wine. It is easy to understand how similar occasions led to madeira being taken back to England.

The trade in wine, mostly in English ships, with the West Indies and the American colonies had begun early. Naturally the colonies followed the fashion in England, so in the earliest days, in 1609, we hear of Captain John Smith in Virginia drinking sack. Towards the middle of the century the taste turned towards French wines and these were the cheapest. The legal maximum price for French wine was twenty pounds of tobacco the gallon, while malaga and Spanish wines cost thirty pounds. The island wines of Fayal and Madeira, which could be imported directly without infringing the Navigation Act, cost only twenty pounds. The gentlemen of Virginia retained a taste for claret until the end of the century. In 1689 for instance, the attorney-general William Byrd ordered twenty dozen of claret, and six dozen each of canary, sherry and rhenish, to aid the deliberations of the legislative council. But before this there was already a thriving trade with Portugal, the Atlantic islands and Spain, encouraged by the many fishing vessels, both English and American, which took fish to southern Europe and carried back salt, southern products and often wine. They welcomed return freights in addition to the provisions they took for their own consumption, and although the Navigation Act forbade the carriage save by way of England of mainland wines, the colonial customs were not unduly particular. The Portuguese wines perhaps became popular in America before they did so in England. By 1688 the legal maximum price for claret was 8/- a gallon, but only 5/- for madeira, and 4/- for other Portuguese and for Spanish wines. Canary wines continued to enter directly in spite of the Navigation Act and French wines became rarer, as much because there were few direct ships as because of legal impediments. So when southern planters aspired to grow their own wines, as they sometimes did, they were inclined to bring over dressers and experts to help them from southern Europe rather than from Bordeaux.

The profusion of wild vines found growing in America encouraged settlers to suppose that native wines could be produced there. Indeed such an aspiration was specifically mentioned in the first charter for Pennsylvania granted to William Penn. There were many attempts to produce wines, sometimes not unsuccessful. In 1686 a French traveller, visiting one of the finest plantations in Virginia, met with a vine which he described as a claret from Portugal, so strong that to the amusement of his hosts he insisted on adding water to it. If this was not an early specimen of a Douro wine it was certainly a precursor with a strong family resemblance. It is probable that some mainland Portuguese wines and even Oporto wines reached America at an early date, but if so we have no record of them.

In England, however, in spite of the prosperous trade with Portugal, Portuguese wines were little heard of at the time of the Restoration. The Lord Steward's accounts give a good idea of the wines used at the court at this time.[1] The concessions for the supply of Gascon wines, of sweet and Spanish wines, and of distilled liquors were given separately. In 1664 Joseph Batailhe (or Battalia) was commissioned to purvey good, wholesome and serviceable Gascon and Graves wines. His name was often to recur in this connection until the time of William III, when he or a man of the same name supplied champagne. In the same year Richard Dalton contracted to supply sweet, good and wholesome Spanish wines. Batailhe took on the Spanish wines in 1666 and Dalton often dealt in French wines, so neither man confined

---

[1] Lord Steward's Books L.S. 1/6.

himself to a particular branch. The king also received presents of wine, for instance from Louis XIV, and sometimes ordered wine directly, for instance four tuns of Bordeaux through David English the consul there.

Canary and sack and other sweet wines were still the luxury wines and were bought in small quantities. Bordeaux was the favourite table wine and was beginning to be known by special names such as Graves, Haut Brion and later Pontac. The cheaper white wines from La Rochelle were not mentioned in the Lord Steward's accounts specifically but were no doubt used; they probably made up the two dozen bottles of white wine issued to the King's Players in 1663. Later they were given an allowance of four gallons of French wine and one gallon of sack for each night they performed, together with twelve fine manchets of bread and eight gallons of beer. The daily allowance of the king, when he rode abroad, was a quart of sack, two quarts of claret, two bottles of ale and three manchets. Ale and beer were much consumed and there is a mention of Lambeth ale for the queen. Cider was also drunk, and when he played a game of tennis the king liked a bottle of metheglin, which was a kind of mead. Champagne and burgundy were also beginning to compete as luxury wines with the sweet wines, but they still figured in the form of presents rather than of regular purchases. The wines were also racked and treated at court and the expenses for doing this were included in the accounts. The icing of wine was customary, for Simon Monselli was given an allowance of £50 for the gathering and cooping of ice and snow and the preserving of the same in the king's snowhouses from 1st October 1664 to the last of September 1665.

At a lower level on the fringes of the court, the impact of the Restoration on the tastes of up and coming citizens is nowhere better reflected than in the pages of Pepys' diary between 1660 and 1667. Wine was a regular feature in the life of men who followed the train of the court. Pepys was at first somewhat ashamed of drinking in taverns on Sundays, but he saw that many of his Puritan friends had got over their scruples and he then took it as a matter of course. He soon invested in a cellar, though he still felt such a grand thing was a little above his station. His first venture was to join with three friends in an order for two butts of wine from Cadiz. He divided it up and after taking his share of a hogshead topped it up with four gallons of malaga. Afterwards his heart failed him. He was afraid that the wine might go bad or be pilfered from his cellar, and he welcomed an opportunity to dispose of it to his friend Sir William Batten. But he soon plucked up courage again and began to keep a regular provision of sack, sherry or canary, and other wines. On one occasion he had raspberry sack, which could have been a posset flavoured with raspberry juice or a domestic raspberry wine. He did not aspire yet to champagne or burgundy though he became familiar with them in later years.

Pepys bought Spanish wine by the tierce, the third of a hogshead, and besides sack and sherry drank malaga and tent. Malaga was becoming a favourite in England as a substitute for sack. The contemporary ballad by John Baltharpe called *A Straits Voyage* gives a good picture of a seaman's life in the Mediterranean and often celebrates malaga and other Spanish wines. He praised sherry which he hoped to drink with Peg and Moll, sweet Sue and Nancy, when he at last reached a home port. He paid a tribute to the strong wine of Alicante known as bull's blood, but malaga was his favourite:

> That day unto Malhago road
> By reason fair wind we had got
> At that same time we anchored not;
> But there our boat she went ashore
> And sack she brought aboard full store;
>
> That night there was some drunk, some sober,
> And some were also half seas over;
> Some men would prate beyond their skill,
> When of this sack they got their fill.
> And when you tell them on't next day
> They do not know then what to say,
> Nay, that same time, if but a swabber,
> He'll swear he'll rig the whole ship over.

Although Malaga was not much more than 100 miles farther from England than Cadiz the voyage there involved the passage of the straits which was often difficult. On the other hand, as a Mediterranean port Malaga could claim for wines shipped from there a drawback in England not applicable to those from Cadiz, while the Spanish customs were less exacting than those of Cadiz. Tent wine also came from Malaga, though this red wine originally came from a small area between Rota and San Lucar, where the limestone soils, good for sherries, were replaced by sand. The name tent came to be applied to any heavy Spanish wine and it was a favourite wine for use in the Communion. At the beginning of the eighteenth century some tent was grown in Madeira, and this was a strong dark wine often shipped in small quantities to America to be used, if required, for deepening the colour of canary wines.

In 1665, before the disasters of the plague and the fire of London diverted Pepys for a time from the care of his cellar, he owned two tierces of claret, two quarter-casks of canary, a smaller vessel of sack, a vessel of tent, one of malaga, and another of white wine. There is no mention of rhenish though he often drank it at taverns. He was already well-versed in claret. As early as 1660 he drank some strange and incomparable good claret at the Rumbells and in 1663 at the Royal Oak he partook of a sort of French wine called Ho Bryan, which had a good and the most particular taste he ever met with. In his own house he served wines with some style, decanting them from bottles with his own crest on them into the appropriate glasses. Glasses were now generally replacing the multitude of cups of wood or leather, or of ivory or precious metals, which had previously been used. Glass-works for their manufacture were springing up around London and in some provincial towns such as Bristol. Already in 1667 Pepys found it rather shabby and old fashioned that earthenware cups should still be used at the Lord Mayor's banquet.

Before closing this account of Restoration manners we should have a look at the wines drunk at the select supper parties of royal mistresses and of high society, where champagne and burgundy were making their entry. Their great ambassador was Marguetel de St Denis, Count of St Evremond. He first came to court in 1660 as a member of the French embassy sent to congratulate King Charles upon his succession and returned in the following year after a disagreement with the French court to spend the forty remaining years of his life as an emigré. He became a great favourite with King Charles and other leaders of society such as the dukes of Buckingham and of Ormonde and with Hortense Mancini. The king gave him a sinecure as governor of Duck Island in St James's Park with a salary of £300 a year. Famous as a moralist, a wit and a gastronome he survived as a well-loved but, it must be admitted, as an increasingly grubby old man until

1703. He is particularly credited with having introduced champagne to the beauties of the court. The word champagne originally meant an open stretch of country and was applied to the products of the vineyards of the open plateau or *montagne*, as it was called, in the neighbourhood of Epernay, in contrast to the wine of the *coteaux* grown on the sides of the hills sloping steeply down to the valley. The term occurs in other contexts and is still used for certain cognacs presumably originally grown in similar country. The champagne district produced wine in the Middle Ages and has been mentioned above in connection with Cardinal Wolsey and King Henry VIII, but was not much known in England in Stuart times until the Restoration. Originally champagne, and particularly the wine of the *montagne*, was a red wine not very different from the wine of the neighbouring province of Burgundy or indeed from claret, except that claret was originally a lighter colour. There was a great rivalry between burgundy and champagne, but the latter won a reputation for taking greater care with its wines and was one of the several wines to which Henry of Navarre pledged his allegiance. It was only at the time of the Restoration that the term 'champagne' began to be limited to an effervescent white wine. One of the earliest references to champagne in seventeenth-century England is to a small quantity of wine described as *shampaigne* imported by the Earl of Bedford in 1665. A year earlier he had imported three pieces or casks of *Sillery*, but although this came from the champagne country and was a famous name later, this appears to have been a still wine.

St Evremond was well-known as a gastronome before he came to England. He belonged to a coterie which prided itself on its gourmandise and good taste. In 1654 St Evremond wrote of the three knights of the order of the St Esprit de Cordon Bleu, the Commandant de St Souvé, the Compte d'Olonne, and the Compte de Bois Daufins. They carried their gourmandise to extreme lengths. They could not touch veal if it were not of La Rivière, partridges other than those of Auvergne, or rabbits except of La Roche Guyom. For wine they drank the products of the three *coteaux* of Ay, Hautevilliers, and Avenay. They became known as the 'three coteaux' and St Evremond in a letter to the Compte d'Olonne advised him to spare no expenses to procure champagne even if he were two hundred leagues from Paris. He added that if he had to name the wine which he preferred, he would choose

Ay because it was the most natural of all wines, the healthiest and the freest from all earthy flavour, with an exquisite taste and an added aroma of peach most special to it.

This wine from the *coteaux*, also known as river wine, was a pale straw-coloured wine, which was unstable and became effervescent in the following spring. The pleasure of the beaded bubbles in the glass was not altogether a new one or confined to champagne. Andrea Bacci, who published in 1596 a massive work in Latin about wines, described a wine which he called claret as 'a wine so endowed with true spirit that, when after a few months it was taken from the cask and ready to be drunk, it rose in beautiful golden bubbles above the rim of the cup and had such a fragrance and delicious flavour that the partakers were enraptured, and their spirits were wonderfully comforted though their heads sorely turned'. From the mention of the golden bubbles the wine was evidently pale in colour or at most a *rosé*; claret usually meant a bright red wine but in early days was not necessarily red. The attraction of the bubbles must have been greatly increased as soon as there were glasses transparent enough for them to be seen mounting all the way up the stem. The Venetian glasses first in fashion were opaque, but by 1674 special glasses were being made by Ravenscroft in England for claret, sack, brandy and champagne, and some of them were perhaps of glass thin and clear enough to allow something of the colour and texture of the wine within to be seen. St Evremond himself is credited with the first introduction into England of the flute, the tall tapering glass used for champagne, though some early seventeenth-century Dutch paintings show something much like it. So in 1663 Butler in his play *Hudibras* was already talking of brisk champagne and in 1676 in *The Man of Mode* Etherage endowed champagne with its favourite epithet 'sparkling'. By the end of the reign champagne had spread beyond intimate court circles and Pepys was being accused of accepting hogsheads of champagne as bribes from ships' captains. He undoubtedly by this time knew and liked champagne, for he took some with him to Hyde Park for a picnic, and provided it for an official dinner he had to organize for the brethren of Trinity House. A decade later it was beginning to be sold through commercial channels and could be got at fashionable places of resort such as Garroway's coffee house, Pontac's and Lockett's. Yet such choice, delicate and perishable wines were not good business for the ordinary merchant and tended to be ordered more often than not privately by the rich and noble through their personal connections in France. Nevertheless the bubbling wine had captured the public fancy and was already celebrated by poet and playwright as the symbol of wit, gaiety and love. St Evremond in his old age began to feel that it had become a little vulgar. In 1701, when he was ninety years of age, he wrote to his old friend the Earl of Galway and deplored attempts being made to increase the production of the *coteaux* wines of Ay by growing them on the *montagne*, the province of the still wines. He even went so far as to suggest that the *montagne*, which had been the original champagne and was a still wine, was to be preferred, for it was reliable and could be depended upon to improve for at least two years, whereas the wine of Ay was only good for a few months in the spring.

The invention of sparkling champagne is often attributed to Dom Perignon, cellarer of the monastery of Hautevilliers from 1668 to 1715. He is also credited with the first introduction of proper corks to replace the old-fashioned stoppers made of tow dipped in oil and sealed with wax. But the development of corks was a gradual process and cannot be attributed to Dom Perignon or any individual. St Evremond was talking of Hautevilliers in 1671, and even of champagne in the same breath as oysters. The pleasures of the bubbles were already known and much of the traditional legend of champagne was already in being when Dom Perignon first took office. But this does not detract from the notable contribution he made to the development of the wine during his long and devoted years of service. These were to be found in his studies of the growth of vines, of the nature of the soil in the various vineyards and of the best methods to blend the grapes.

Burgundy, the other new luxury wine, had long been known in England. Formerly it had been taken down to the fair at Rouen, but while Burgundy was an independent duchy much had gone to the Low Countries. Since 1482 Burgundy had been part of France, but the wealth of Antwerp and then of Amsterdam had continued to provide a principal market for the wine. Indeed, in the days of the prosperity of Antwerp the wines of Burgundy and Champagne had gone quite often by land to the headwaters of the Scheldt as well as by way of Rouen. Normally the carriage of casks of wine for any distance by land was too expensive, but although burgundy could come to Paris mainly by water, the fashion for it seems to have died in the early seventeenth century, and Paris drew most of its supplies from the Loire valley and the neighbouring Ile de France until the latter part of the reign of Louis XIV, when champagne and burgundy became popular again. In England, owing to the Dutch wars and the increasing stringency of the Navigation Acts, there was little profit in importing either champagne or burgundy commercially. On the other hand, as soon as the wines became fashionable, noblemen were in a position to take out a licence to import wines personally and to ask friends in France to look after their despatch. Earl Russell imported a puncheon of burgundy to Woburn in 1658 in this way and in 1664 the Earl of Bedford imported sixty-two bottles of 'Shably' also to Woburn. The earl and his sister also took out a licence to import champagne with the help of Lord Crofts and of the Marquis of Sillery. King Charles regularly bought burgundy; he imported six tuns in 1664, and in 1665 received a present of burgundy, hermitage and champagne from King Louis XIV. King Louis used to take a glass of champagne with his meals but in his later days he switched to burgundy. This may have been on doctor's orders, but a pleasant story attributes it to the initiative of a peasant of Pouilly Fuissé, who after a specially good vintage loaded up his cart and trudged with it all the way to Versailles. When he got there he asked to see the king. He was laughed at for his pains, but was not to be denied, and somehow or other the king got to hear of it and ordered him to be brought in. The king tasted his wine and liked it and afterwards he made a habit of taking it. A glass or two was enough. The king was a tremendous trencherman but a very moderate drinker. Claude Arnoux, a Frenchman who spent some time as a tutor to an English family in London, and in the reign of George I wrote a book in praise of burgundy, said that King Louis' wine was Nuits and not Pouilly Fuissé, but still a burgundy. The fact that he sent burgundy to King Charles suggests that he developed a taste for it quite early and set the fashion, though after 1685 the Huguenot exiles are also given credit for doing so. In his book Arnoux mentioned that wine from Upper Burgundy only had to be carted ninety miles to reach the Seine; wine from Lower Burgundy could be sent by water from Auxerre all the way, so the decline in consumption in Paris is hard to explain, though political differences could be held responsible for the decline in the trade by Rouen.

CHAPTER IV

The Closing Years of the Reign of Charles II

THE closing years of the reign of Charles II were a time of great development of wines in society and also of the political pressures which were to distort and hamper the wine trade. The principal obstacle latterly to the free traffic of wine had been the Navigation Acts. These hit at the trade of the Dutch and stopped wines other than rhenish being imported by way of the Low Countries. Levant wines from places occupied by the Turks were also affected, but in any case their importation had been largely replaced by that of Spanish wines of similar type. Wars and restrictions and the loss of Aquitaine had all affected the wine trade at various times, but hitherto the natural laws of supply and demand had been able to reassert themselves. For the time being it was the trade with Bordeaux and La Rochelle which enjoyed a favoured position but this situation was soon to be reversed.

Bordeaux was already specializing in quality wines for the English market and Haut Brion fetched £14 a hogshead while ordinary Gascon wine could be had for £12. The difference in prices tended to widen, and during his travels in France in 1678 John Locke noted that the English were ready to pay half as much again for Haut Brion and Pontac. The Dutch, who had an even bigger trade with Bordeaux than the English, specialized in the cheaper wines and often went to look for them in the High Country. They bought Jurançon, described as very white, very sweet and very good, from the foothills of the Pyrenees near Pau. This was a wine which had enjoyed some reputation since the days of Henry of Navarre. The Dutch had already taken to fortifying it lightly with brandy to enable it to stand a journey which would probably be long. The wine had to face not only delays in Bordeaux but a further voyage from the United Provinces to the Baltic, where most of the wine was re-exported. Possibly, however, some of the wine escaped the restrictions in Bordeaux by being shipped from Bayonne. In a work published in 1646, according to Enjalbert, Jean Eon Nantais spoke already of these Dutch practices. There were then two or three Dutch families who had naturalized themselves as citizens of Bordeaux and were able to exercise the privilege of buying High Country wines and shipping them without delay. They sometimes paid higher prices for them than for the Bordeaux wines, and in order to imitate the sweet wines of the Levant they bought 'vins pourris', wines made from grapes ripened to the point of rotting, and 'mistelles', slightly sweet wines of which the fermentation had been arrested by a dose of brandy. In 1675, after there had been Huguenot disturbances in the city, Colbert abolished the Bordeaux privileges for a time, and until they were partially restored the High Country trade must have benefited.

The production of brandy in the neighbourhood of Bordeaux had greatly increased in the course of the seventeenth century. Formerly wine which could not be sold soon after the vintage could only be used for turning into vinegar. The peasants now found that if their wine was not very good it could be burnt for brandy and fetch a good price. In 1672, when there was war with Holland and nothing was being exported there, England took 7,313 hogsheads; as early as 1646 England had taken 3,000 hogsheads and as much again from the Charente. According to English sources the trade only grew up after 1660, but the imports were 4,000 tuns in 1675 and 8,000 tuns in 1689. In 1712 Charles Davenant believed that the friends of the French trade had blown up these figures in order to enhance its importance, but there is no doubt that brandy was popular, and spirits as well as beer were challenging the pre-eminence of wine. The taste for spirits was first imputed to Elizabethan soldiers, who had learnt to drink gin in the Low Countries. It became a common practice to strengthen beer with a dose of gin to make the mixture known as 'purl'. According to legend the young King Charles in the course of his adventurous escape after the battle of Worcester was given at a country inn a pot of beer well laced with strong waters. By the

1670s spirit drinking was taking hold and there were already complaints that London citizens on holiday were drinking too much
brandy.

There is no record of Jurançon reaching England, but King
James II liked the wines of Cahors, which were rather strong red
wines, and also as Duke of York had recommended Navarre
wines, which were similar, to Pepys. As king, he also bought Bar-
bentane, which may have come from the Pyrenees, though it
could have been a Rhône wine from another place of that name
near Avignon and the Hermitage vineyards, which also contributed
to King James's cellar. In the last years of King Charles Portuguese wines also made their first appearance in the Lord Steward's
accounts. Nine barrels of Algarve were bought for 26/8 a barrel.
A barrel could be large or it could be as small as five gallons. At
the same period the king was paying 23/- and 31/- for hermitage
and 53/4 for burgundy; the Algarve wine was probably cheap but
it is also possible that the barrels were small.[1]

As the government regulation of wines became more onerous,
experiments with new wines became more difficult. Wines had
always been the darling of the tax-collector and from 1670 onwards
they became almost an obsession which governed the trade and
eventually even taste in wine. We have seen that the need to find
a market for English wool and then for English cloth was historically a primary motive. It had been the reason for the Levant trade
after the Levant monopoly of Eastern spices and other luxuries
had been broken. It was now the trade with France which was in
jeopardy. As early as 1572 a French edict had banned the importation of foreign textiles, so French attempts to protect their industry
were no new thing, but the tariffs brought into force by Colbert
in 1664 and in 1667 were worse than anything that had gone before.
Already in 1663 John Fortrey, a gentleman of the king's bedchamber, had published a work entitled *England's Interest and
Improvement* which was designed to arouse English opinion on the
subject. He argued that the trade with France was exhausting our
treasure, and was unfavourable to our interests to such a degree
that, on being shown statistics demonstrating the extent of the
balance of trade in his favour, Louis XIV himself had decided
against any further restriction on a trade which was so profitable
to him. Fortrey did not go so far as to recommend a cessation of

[1] L.S. 1/20 and 30.

F

trade with France, but he proposed that all French goods requiring no further manufacturing or processing after their importation should be subjected to heavy duties. A second edition of the book was published in 1673, and before that, in 1667 when there was war with France, Parliament resolved to prohibit French wines. At the same time canary wines were prohibited because they were expensive and had to be paid for with specie. With two principal sources of wine cut off the market would have fared badly, but the prohibition was made ineffective by the numerous special licences granted to import both sorts of wine and not long afterwards was brought to an end by the speedy conclusion of peace in 1668. At the same time the *de jure* recognition of the independence of Portugal by Spain, which had been hanging fire ever since Portugal's *de facto* assumption of independence in 1640, was at last obtained through England's good offices due to Portugal under the terms of the Anglo-Portuguese alliance.

The wine trade was not however to escape further penalization. Parliament decided to raise £100,000 by the imposition of new duties and later raised this target to £310,000 and then £400,000, to be spread over eighteen months and then two years, or until such time as the target was reached. The rates of the new duties were 4d a quart on French wines, sixpence on sweet wines and 1/- on brandy, so in spite of the unpopularity of trade with France French wines were given the most favourable treatment.

The intention was to charge the new duties by means of an excise duty on the retail sale of wine rather than through a customs duty. This would have entailed the employment of excise officers, who in order to enforce the law would have needed special powers to search private houses and premises where wine might be stored. Such police powers would have infringed the right of all true-born Englishmen to be masters in their own houses and any such proposal was calculated to arouse passionate opposition. After a long discussion whether the proceeds of the new revenue should be earmarked for expenditure on the equipment of the fleet for the summer and for no other purpose except the payment of seamen's wages, the bill passed two readings by a majority of only one or two votes. But it was never implemented and at the end of 1669 the idea of collecting an excise duty was given up and an additional customs duty entitled an impost on Wines was substituted. At first some remainder of the original proposal was left, in that the buyer could pay instead of the importer, but soon this option was abolished and the impost was laid squarely on the shoulders of the first importer. In the course of time several attempts were made to replace customs duties by excise duties, but they invariably foundered on the rooted objection to the grant of special powers to excise officers. Excise officers in spite of this were often to be denounced as tyrants infringing English liberties, but their powers were not sufficiently enlarged before the end of the eighteenth century to make the collection of an excise tax on wines administratively possible, although the additional powers given to customs officers in 1670 were scarcely less vexatious.

The impost on wines was supposed to be a temporary measure to raise a specified maximum sum, but it was given an extension and then made permanent. From 1670 it was prolonged for seven years at half-rate, and after that was renewed periodically at a rate of £8 a tun for French wines, £12 for sweet wines including Portuguese wines and £9 for Rhenish wines. The clothiers complained that their trade with France was being strangled by Colbert's legislation, but for another seven years the wines of Bordeaux and La Rochelle continued to enjoy an advantage. It was only in 1678, soon after the seven years renewal of the impost, that the news of the Treaty of Dover and the revelation that King Charles II was a pensioner of Louis XIV spurred Parliament to impose an embargo on French trade, a measure which at once satisfied their resentment against France and promised to reduce a lucrative source of revenue on which the king leaned heavily to enable him to carry on without further recourse to Parliament for money.

It was now at long last the turn of Portuguese wines. As has already been mentioned, England had been sympathetic to Portugal during the first years after the loss of her independence, which corresponded with the Elizabethan war with Spain. Dom Antonio, the Portuguese pretender, had visited England and negotiations had been set on foot on his behalf. These resulted in an armed landing in Portugal and before that played a part in the provocation which inspired King Philip II to send his Armada against England, but had little effect in Portugal itself, except that a great deal of clandestine trade and some feeling of sympathy persisted between the two countries. The Azores for a time became the centre of resistance to Spain and feeling there was strong for the pretender. English ships often called there and at times the islands escaped the embargo on English trade with the mainland. One important result of the existence of a dissident Portugal was that much information about Portuguese navigational discoveries, which had been kept secret, leaked to English and other non-Portuguese quarters. Hakluyt relates that the English merchants Newbery and Fitch, who were arrested as spies for Dom Antonio and taken from Ormuz to Goa in 1583-4, took the opportunity to learn much about Portuguese trade routes and methods on behalf of their employers, the Turkey Company. This information applied to the Indian Ocean and the Persian Gulf and Far East, but much was also learnt in the Azores about the West Indies and America. The Azores were inhabited by settlers of whom a number were of Flemish origin. The fellow-feeling with the islanders encouraged English ships to call there on their way to the West Indies, and both in the Azores and in Madeira they provisioned themselves with wine. Ships also took wines for their own use from the mainland of Portugal, but in spite of the revival in the middle of the seventeenth century of the English Factories in Lisbon and Oporto and of the frequency of communications with England, little Portuguese wine was imported through commercial channels. Undoubtedly small consignments of wine found their way particularly to west country ports, and members of the Factories often sent presents to their friends. But neither the boom in Anglo-Portuguese trade nor the marriage of King Charles II and Catherine of Braganza promoted any interest in Portuguese wines. As will be explained, little wine was drunk at the Portuguese court and as a princess Queen Catherine would have had little opportunity to learn to appreciate wine. She soon lost any prejudices she may have had on the subject, for during her widowhood she imported some port-wine to England and accepted presents of wine from Avignon.[1] But if the few barrels of Algarve ordered in his last years are excepted, King Charles, as far as is known, never ordered any wines from his wife's country. The truth was that Portuguese wines had no reputation: nothing was heard of wines from Oporto, and the Lisbon wines, which were soon to be well thought of, were described by the seaman Barlow as indifferent. Lady Fanshawe, the wife of the English minister at Lisbon, called them rough but wholesome. When in 1712 Parliament required a full report on

[1] London Port Book E 190/137/8.

the back history of the whole Portuguese trade and Charles
Davenant, the inspector-general of the customs, caused a survey
of the available customs returns to be made, he concluded that
imports of Portuguese wines before 1675 were confined to a few
presents and in the years 1675-8 the imports to London amounted
to 43, 178, 378, and 427 pipes respectively. One of the earliest
references to 'Portugal wines' at this time is to $5\frac{3}{4}$ pipes imported
by the Spanish Envoy on 18th January 1677, who surprisingly
paid £58 3s 0d duties upon them.[1]

Small as these figures were, they indicated a progressive increase,
and a few English merchants in London must have been looking
into the subject. In 1678 they were especially anxious to find new
means for promoting trade, because many English ships were idle
after the end of the Franco-Dutch war on the Continent and of the
favoured position which they had been enjoying as neutrals. They
now had to face a vigorous renewal of Dutch competition. It
appears that the Dutch had already shown the way towards trading
in Portuguese wines. From 1672 when their trade with Bordeaux
had been cut off they had gone to look for the white wines in
which they were principally interested at Lisbon and Jerez. According to the French historian Enjalbert they also bought wines
in Oporto and in 1675 acquired wines from Lamego, Vila Real,
and the Upper Douro. England was also turning again to Spain
for wines, and according to the same authority imported 17,000
hogsheads from there in 1675 as against 35,000 pipes from France.
According to the English statistics the figures for 1675 and 1676
were 7,495 and 9,665 tuns French wines and 4,012 and 5,095
Spanish wines. The Dutch interest in trade with the Peninsula
was encouraged by the arrival in Holland of refugees from Bordeaux, some of whom were Huguenots but others of Jewish origin
and originally from Portugal or Spain. The latter found in
Amsterdam many co-religionists originally of Spanish-Portuguese
origin.

The Portugal merchants, as the London merchant trading with
Portugal styled themselves, submitted in 1677 a memorial to
Parliament recommending the importation of Portuguese wines.[2]
In it they pointed out that the English cloth trade with Portugal
was estimated to be worth £400,000 a year, but was in grave danger

---

[1] Cal. of Ty. Books, 18th January 1677.
[2] Copy in Burney Coll. 806/m/11.

of being utterly lost. It had already been diminished by Portuguese protectionist legislation and would disappear altogether if these laws were made more severe. They thought that the best remedy would be to mollify the Regent of Portugal, Prince Pedro, by offering him customs concessions for Portuguese products. They claimed to know of a variety of good wines produced in Portugal, whose production could easily be augmented. They said it would be very advantageous to import such wines in exchange for English manufactures, as it would not be necessary to pay for them in specie as was the case for the purchase of French wines. They added that at present the total importation of Portuguese wines amounted to thirty-three tuns, whereas that of French wines was 7,000 tuns. Trade in Portuguese wines was prevented by the new impost, under which they paid £4 a tun more duty than French wines, but if the duties were equalized, a thriving trade could be begun.

These arguments sounded fair enough and Parliament gave them serious consideration, but they concluded that any reduction in the duties on Portuguese wines would involve making similar concessions for Spanish wines and that there was no need to think of any such thing, for the Spanish textile industry was thoroughly decayed and could not compete in any way with the sale of English cloth in Spain. The Spaniards in fact, like the Portuguese, were trying to reduce their importation of foreign manufactured luxury goods; the Earl of Arlington told Pepys that the King of Spain and his grandees were showing an example by wearing plain clothes of Colchester Bays, while the ladies in winter were wearing mantles of white flannel. But if the clothes were simpler they were still of English manufacture; no serious steps were being taken to revive Spanish industry and no lobby of traders to Spain was molesting Parliament. The Portuguese on the other hand appeared in earnest; they were making serious efforts to set up their own industries and in the near future the Portuguese minister in London, Luis da Cunha, was going to recommend to his government that they should extent their restrictions on the import of English cloth to include bays as well as luxury cloths. But Parliament was not prepared to make any concessions, though they were eager enough to obtain them, and they sent Francis Parry and Charles Fanshawe to Lisbon to negotiate a new commercial agreement with Portugal, or a reaffirmation and redefinition of the 1654 treaty. Meanwhile the question soon lost its urgency, for Parliament enacted a prohibition of the importation of French wines, which lasted from 1678 to 1685 and gave to Portuguese wines the opportunity for which the merchants had asked.

The Lisbon negotiations were still taking place when the prohibition of French wines began to operate, but the English plenipotentiaries did not find that the Portuguese became any less stubborn. They retained their conviction that the 1654 treaty favoured England too much and that they were justified in trying to whittle away the privileges granted by it or to find means to circumvent them. The rights of the English chaplain in Lisbon, and still more of his colleagues in Oporto, were always a bone of contention, as indeed was any concession allowed to the English to follow their own religion. These questions were perhaps even more intractable than those of trade and customs duties. Consequently, although the Prince Regent replied politely to the English representatives, and promised that he would religiously observe the treaty and would examine sympathetically any claims that its terms were not being observed, the negotiations dragged on without achieving any positive concession. When at last a definite answer was wrung out of Prince Pedro, it was only a refusal to modify the treaty which he said was perfectly satisfactory and had endured in its present form for twenty-five years. The only change to which he would agree was the removal of the 'indecency' resulting from the naming in the treaty of the usurper Cromwell by inserting the king's name in place of that of the Lord Protector.[1]

The Factories would themselves have been satisfied with the 1654 treaty and nothing more, if they could have obliged the Portuguese to accept their own interpretation, and the Portuguese preferred the treaty they knew to a new one which might bind them with more precisely worded commitments. In this way the 1654 treaty remained the basis of the privileges of the English Factories in Portugal and more important than even the Methuen Treaty of 1703. The question of a revision often came up, but nothing ever resulted, though there was a constant struggle on the part of the Portuguese to find loopholes in the provisions of the old treaty or excuses to neglect its requirements, while the English strove with equal fervour to bring about its strict observance. In 1680 Prince Pedro saw no reason whatever to yield to English

[1] For these negotiations see Add. MSS 31501.

demands after political causes in England, having no connection with Portugal, had brought about a prohibition of French wines and had opened up a market for Portuguese wines without the need for any move on his part whatever. On the other hand the new trade relieved to some extent Portuguese economic stringency and the restrictions on the import of English cloth began to be applied less severely than before.

For an understanding of the situation some account of the Portuguese background with regard to cloth and wine is necessary. For several years past a series of laws, known as the Pragmatical Decrees, had been promulgated with a view to the restriction of the consumption of luxury goods and the repair of Portugal's economy, which had been sadly run down as a result of the expense of the war of independence, the loss of trade and colonies in the Far East and other causes. These decrees owed much of their original inspiration to the Counter-Reformation, and the language in which they were framed still emphasized their moral and religious aspects as much as their economic significance. Similar enactments were common in other Catholic countries and in Protestant countries too. In Portugal the first decree dated from early in the seventeenth century, though the decrees affecting English trade were not issued until the 1670s. Their first declared aim was to inculcate sobriety in dress and social habits. Although the Portuguese loved to dress up and liked nothing better than a gorgeous ceremony, they were forbidden to use gold or silver lace, embroidery or bright fashions. A decree of 25th January 1675 prohibited silk, silver or gold thread, silver buttons, and even the wearing of cloth not manufactured in Portugal. These restrictions were applied with some severity to appearances at court, but the Pragmatica did not at first specifically forbid the passage through the customs of the articles in question; the ceremonies of the Church were exempt and foreigners and visitors wore what they liked. Portuguese ladies seldom in any case appeared in public and when they did so it was mostly well wrapped up on their way to or from church. Nobody questioned what they wore in their own houses. In the streets all classes began to wear the same drab clothes and the King of Portugal was scarcely distinguishable by his garb from a cobbler. At the time when the decrees were most severe the wearing of all coloured cloth and even of black cloth was banned, but although new decrees spasmodically ap-

peared, and others were threatened, the situation gradually relaxed
through the 1680s and the Nine Years War which followed. The
ban on certain types of cloth left a good deal of latitude to Customs
officers to turn a blind eye when the question of classification
came up, even when the prohibitions under the later decrees began
to apply to the entry of cloths as well as to the wearing of them.
Lisbon played a predominant part in the trade of Portugal, and
it was in Lisbon that one would expect the Pragmatica to be most
rigorously applied, but Lisbon was also the most international city
of Portugal with a large foreign community, and supplied the
greatest opportunities for evasions.

Although the Pragmatica were religiously inspired, the Church
itself was the greatest user not only of luxury materials for vest-
ments and ecclesiastical finery but also of cloth for the ordinary
voluminous robes worn by priests, monks, and nuns. The Pragmatical Decree of 1677 expressly allowed judges, clergy and
students to wear full length gowns. The Church gave the Portuguese a legitimate outlet for their taste for magnificent display.
Also the main purpose of the decrees came to be more economic
than moral, and to seek inspiration in the doctrines of Colbert
regarding the need to promote native manufactures. Both the moral
and economic motives were popular in a country which was above
all things devoted to religion and was also exhausted by her
struggle for independence and the loss of much of her empire.
The spice trade had largely been captured by the English and
Dutch and in the second half of the seventeenth century the
Portuguese trade in Brazilian sugar and tobacco faced increasing
competition from the English and French West Indies. Economic
nationalism was growing up everywhere and the French king was
reputed to have refused to wear mourning because it would have
entailed using English black cloth. In England there was a movement to make Englishmen wear only English cloth while they
lived, and some Acts of Parliament enjoining that they must be
buried in English wool when they died. Portuguese nationalism
was sharpened by the continued Spanish threat to her independence, and the fear that the English or the Dutch or the French
would take from her the remainder of her empire. The Pragmatical
Decrees aimed in the first instance at luxuries such as French
ribands and laces turned afterwards against coloured cloths and
superior fabrics, which mainly came from England and could not

be manufactured in Portugal. Later Portuguese statesmen such as the Count of Ericeira and Duarte de Ribeira de Macedo, Portuguese minister in Paris, aspired, as disciples of Colbert, to set up manufactures which would enable Portugal to dispense with imports from abroad. The building up of a cloth industry was an obvious priority. Communications in the interior of Portugal were so bad that some inland districts tended perforce to be self-sufficient and provided a certain foundation in the form of cottage industries. Therefore the new factories were for the most part established in towns in the interior like Covilhã or Porto Alegre. To assist their foundation New Christian artisans were brought in from Seville and craftsmen were sought in England, France, and the United Provinces. In the sixteenth century many Jews or New Christians, expelled from Spain, had found a refuge in Portugal and had given Portugal the benefit of their skills until the Spanish policy of intolerance spread to Portugal. In the seventeenth century many New Christians remained in Portugal and helped to keep up a tradition of excellent craftsmanship, but a number were driven out, particularly from the upper classes of commerce, and the Portuguese were obliged to turn first to Italians, and then to English, Dutch, French or Germans to carry on the trade, especially foreign trade, for which they had little liking or aptitude. Enlightened men, some of them churchmen like the Jesuit Antonio de Vieira, denounced the folly of extirpating the New Christians, but although some of them continued to work for a time in the new factories their presence was hateful to the Church and they were gradually eliminated. On the other hand the hiring of Dutch, French or English artisans to work in Portugal was vigorously opposed by their home governments. An attempt in 1669 to set up a workshop in the Alentejo province to manufacture serges and druggets with eight workmen under the superintendence of a French draper named Lambert moved Colbert himself to order the French ambassador to entice Lambert back to France. In 1679 it was the turn of the English Secretary of State Coventry to complain. He wrote 'I have been long and constantly importuned with complaints from Portugal and the king's ministers there concerning the late ambassadors spiriting our men from hence to teach weaving and making bays and other stuffs. It seems the practice still continues and men of that trade on every passage went over, so that one Condé pretends to the setting up of 150 looms himself, which if he succeed in, will set up a trade there, that will not only lose us our Portuguese trade but in all probability our Spanish trade too. His Majesty has considered this (and so have some of the Council) and has commanded me to write to you what legal means he has either to recall those that are gone or to forbid more to follow'.[1]

The attempt to set up Portuguese manufactures obtained only a limited success and was not pursued with vigour for long. A contributory reason, as far as England was concerned, was that the English craftsman did not acclimatize himself very well. He was apt to go to seed in a strange country and to do more drinking than teaching of his craft.

Failing the production of new manufactures Portugal had, in order to balance her trade, to create new exports or to pay the balance in specie. Before the discovery of the gold mines of Brazil at the beginning of the eighteenth century Portugal made do as far as specie was concerned with the Spanish silver which filtered in from Cadiz, with a little silver from Venice, and a little African gold. Brazilian sugar and oriental spices had been the basis for a flourishing trade with the Mediterranean, but these trades were flagging and she now required something more. The return trade from Portugal in oil, dyestuffs and southern fruits could be expanded a little, but it was not enough, and English merchants looked with covetous eyes on the trade with Brazil. There was always trouble about this, and even the favourable 1654 treaty provided for the preservation of the monopoly of the Portuguese Brazil company in wines and some other commodities and for the exclusion of English ships from trade with Brazil except by way of Portugal and as part of the regular annual Brazil fleet sailing from Lisbon. Under the marriage treaty of 1661 four English merchants were allowed to reside in each principal Brazilian city, but there were always difficulties about this and the limited concessions for direct trade allowed by the treaty. Nevertheless by one means or another England took part through Lisbon and Portuguese intermediaries in the Brazil trade and this was to be a principal factor in the prosperous development of Anglo-Portuguese commercial relations. England's share in the slave-trade, for which Portuguese possessions in Africa provided the raw material, also counted for much. The Dutch now controlled the Gold Coast, but the Portu-

[1] Calendar of S.P., 5th September 1688.

guese still participated in the profitable trade between Whydah and Bahia and obtained a large quota of slaves from their own Angola territory and some from Portuguese Guinea and other African posts still in Portuguese hands. The English obtained little or no part in the Spanish slave trade but trade with the West Indies and America was profitable and there was some clandestine trade between the West Indies and the Spanish colonies.

The wine trade was however to be the principal new feature in the Portuguese economy. For a long time it depended more on political factors than on its own merits and some explanation is required for the reasons why a country so suitable for the cultivation of vines was so backward in taking advantage of the fact. The Portugal merchants in their memorial anticipated that the trade would develop on very much the same lines as that of other wine-growing countries. Their friends in Portugal saw vines growing everywhere in a benign climate and found they could grow wines themselves which were adequate and sometimes excellent. Small quantities of various qualities and sorts could be produced easily but the production of thousands of tuns for export presented a very different problem.

The climate of Portugal near the coast is damp and particularly in the north is not very good for wine, but it rapidly improves inland, while in the Algarve it resembles that of Cadiz, and wine can be produced well enough around Lisbon and in central Portugal. Wines from Lisbon and the south were exported to England in the Middle Ages and were largely regarded as sweet wines; in the seventeenth century they were driven off the market by Spanish wines. In the north of Portugal an infinite amount of wine was grown in the Minho, but it was green wine and not suitable for export. Some wine was grown in the valleys of the Lima and Minho, and is believed to have reached England through Viana, where there was an English Factory in the sixteenth century until the English merchants were expelled in 1580. The wines from the district resembled those of Galicia and northern Spain, which also reached England in greater quantities while Bilbao was a principal port before the development of Cadiz after the discovery of America. The wines of Lamego on the Upper Douro have already been mentioned. In the early sixteenth century about 1,300 pipes of the best quality had been produced but all this had been taken by land to Lisbon or Castille. By the seventeenth century this trade had diminished. There is no mention of such wines being well-known in Madrid though they may still have gone to Salamanca and the frontier provinces of Spain. Their desuetude in Lisbon will be explained. No doubt some table wine continued to go down the Douro to Oporto and as has been mentioned the Dutch discovered this in the 1670s apparently before the English did.

A curious change had taken place in the status of wine in Portugal. In the Middle Ages the upper classes were of north European origin and the court at Lisbon had similar customs to those elsewhere. Wine in the Middle Ages was a part of conspicuous spending; until the eighteenth century it was not the normal drink of the people, even in the districts of France where it was grown. This was largely the result of the expansion of Islam, which had infiltrated most of the wine-growing regions of Europe, stopping short at the summit of its power not very far from the northern frontiers of wine. In their great days the Saracens did not exclude wine, and later the Turks did some drinking on the quiet, but it was either conspicuous expenditure as at Seville or backstairs drinking of the strongest wines for the sake of getting drunk as by some Turks. The love of wine was deepest not in the lands where the climate favoured it most, but on the northern fringes and beyond, where except in very prosperous times it could only be drunk by the rich. Exceptions to this are perhaps Germany and Italy; only the latter country had a large area which was easy for wine growing and at the same time untouched by Islam. In Italy wine was generally drunk but perhaps for that very reason no very ardent effort was made to improve or export it. In Spain and Portugal and the south of France, on the other hand, wine was drunk at court but there remained from the days of the Moors a strong feeling of aversion towards any excess in it.

In the Middle Ages Portugal perhaps felt less Moorish influence than Spain, where the conquest was completed later and left for some time a large undigested Morisco element. The expulsion of the Moors from Portugal took place more than a century earlier and was more complete. Later there was a backwash of Moriscos, who established themselves in pockets as far as the valley of the Vouga, where they left villages with Arab names and great water wheels of Moorish design. The final expulsion of Moriscos and New Christians and Jews from Spain brought many to Portugal, while the destruction of King Sebastian and a whole Portuguese army at Alcazar Quebir in Morocco in 1579 decimated the Portuguese upper class. Before this the great period of discovery and colonial expansion had drawn off many and brought in return exotic strains and many children of Asiatic, Brazilian or African mothers. The many widows and grass-widows, created by the absence or death of their husbands, and their growing children were left to the care of servants often of mixed blood. So although towards 1700 the Portuguese nobles in Lisbon were great sticklers for their purity of race and blood, they struck casual visitors as a swarthy lot. Since that time the situation had been changed again by the arrival of so many Englishmen, Frenchmen, Dutchmen and Germans, but in 1702 William Bromley thought as many as a third of the inhabitants of Lisbon were of Mozarab blood. Visitors were also struck by the oriental aspects of the Portuguese court.

The development of eastern manners in the upper classes was perhaps due more to their decimation and exhaustion, to the absence or death of fathers and the relegation of children to the care of servants, than to any actual admixture of blood. The Prince Regent Pedro, from 1683 King Pedro II, had a Spanish mother, a daughter of the house of Medina Sidonia of Andalusia, but had many characteristics recalling those of his contemporary Muley Ismael, the bloodthirsty emperor of Morocco. Though personally violent sometimes, King Pedro was not bloodthirsty in any large way and he was naturally better informed on European affairs than his Islamic colleague, but he equally thought of himself as a warrior king and saw himself leading his troops to battle on a fine horse. The attitude of the two rulers to wine, women and religion was much the same. Alcohol was anathema, women an obsessive passion, religion a matter for careful outward observance but also for constant and devoted piety. Ismael was the stronger character. He led his armies, he massacred his enemies, he governed his harem, he collected pistols, he ruled his domains with austerity and fervour for a number of years. King Pedro was as conscientious in following his devotions as Ismael was, and in his public life tried his best to do what was expected of him, though he was somewhat haunted by a consciousness of sin and often found it hard to make up his mind. Privately he had a liking for mulatto women and for low company and he would have confined his wife to a harem if he could. The liking for low company was a

common reaction among monarchs against the restraints and for-
malities of their lives, and the fact that this society in Lisbon contained many men and girls of mixed blood was perhaps accidental,
but his suspicion of wine and attitude towards women was usual
in Portuguese society of the time. The average Portuguese lady
seldom went outside her house except to Mass and was as jealously
guarded as the inmate of a seraglio. Mats and carpets were used
to sit on more than chairs. The king dined alone and nothing upset
him more than to notice someone near him whose breath showed
that he had taken something to drink. Such a man was banished
from court, and although wine was a staple product of Portugal
very few Portuguese in Lisbon kept wine in their houses. Many
of them had never tasted it pure in their lives and would go for
as long as a month without tasting wine at all. Above all they
abhorred drunkenness. In the height of anger they could use no
worse reproach than to call a man an English sot.

Some Portuguese noblemen, several of the first rank, had French
wives and were cosmopolitan, but most of them lived in the Portuguese fashion. Many of them had fine vineyards in the neighbourhood of Lisbon surrounded by substantial walls, and understood
the culture of the vine very well, but few took any trouble with
their wine or sought to improve it. They would plant twenty kinds
of vine together promiscuously, and when the time came for the
vintage they would pick all the grapes at once, green, ripe, over-
ripe and stalks together, and throw them higgledy-piggledy into
the vat. They scarcely distinguished between one wine and another except that to give colour to red wine they added the husk
of the grapes to the must after treading. Their methods throughout
were rough and ready. They sometimes tried to remove the taste
of the wood from the casks by burning brimstone in the casks,
but the wines usually had a strong taste from the skins with the
hair turned inwards, in which they were habitually carried from
the vineyards. Such was the description by a young Englishman
named Cox, who spent some time in Lisbon in 1700 and was well
acquainted with the principal members of the Lisbon Factory.[1]
A little earlier, in 1693, John Methuen, the English minister in
Lisbon, who took a keen interest both personal and official in
wine and the wine trade, remarked that the Portuguese, having

[1] Sloane 2294, *Account of Portugal*, and Add. MSS 23726, *Diary of
Thomas Cox.*

an interest in quantity rather than in quality, would never begin the vintage early if there was any prospect of rain to swell the grapes, even though it would ruin their quality.[1] Indeed many of the citizens seemed to esteem wine more as a medicament than as a drink; they sometimes took a bath of wine which was supposed to be very good for a pain in the limbs.

Hitherto most of the wine of any quality exported from Portugal had come from the centre or south. Some of the Douro wine carried to Lisbon on mule back may have been exported, but the trade in this had diminished. This was partly due to the change of taste and consequent lack of demand by the upper classes, but also to the jealousy of the Lisbon wine growers, who obstructed the entry of wines from anywhere outside the Lisbon district. This was a common phenomenon. The attitude of the citizens of Bordeaux to the High Country wines has been described. Marseilles tried to keep out wines from the Rhône Valley and in Portugal Oporto fought to exclude wines from Coimbra, and Beja, a town in the Alemtejo, would not suffer the wines of Montemor. In 1678, the very year in which Portuguese wines began to enter England in bulk, the Lisbon Senate debated raising the rate of duty on wines entering by sea in order to reduce to its former level the amount of wines coming from other districts of Portugal, but principally of Douro wines embarked at Oporto. This shows that in addition to the special wines brought by land there had also been a trade in table wines of the Douro brought down the Douro and then by sea. But in 1700 Cox knew nothing of them and spoke of Oporto as having been until very lately a producer of green wines and small wines only.

In Lisbon, therefore, English merchants found a certain local production of wine and a few enlightened noblemen who served wine in their households for prestige and appreciated the benefits that would accrue to their rent rolls from the export of wine. Methuen was to discover the merits of Barra Barra, a red wine from the opposite bank of the Tagus, but the carriage of wine from outlying districts was expensive and most of the land was owned by large proprietors. There was no large class of peasant proprietors from whom wine could sometimes be bought at bargain

---

[1] Althorpe MS: Methuen to Halifax, 21st September 1694; and Chevening MS U1590 at Kent Record Office: Paul Methuen to Stanhope, 6th October 1699. Rain spoilt the 1698 vintage.

prices, as there was in the north of Portugal. Labour was also scarce and hard to find for any new work on the land. In the north the situation was different. There were a number of small proprietors who grew wine for their own needs, and though the wine was poor it was generally consumed. The prejudice against wine was much less than in Lisbon, but good wine was hard to find, and though some was grown on the Upper Douro it was little known. Such stocks of good wine as existed soon ran out, but there was a shortage in England and the shippers hoped they could do with any wine. Vines grew on every house and their product could be bought cheaply from the peasants, who were delighted to receive a little cash. Around Oporto and in the idyllic countryside of the Minho vines grew in Virgilian fashion on arbours and up the trees in picturesque confusion; their roots were in the rich soil around the edges of the maize fields. They grew in green valleys in the shadow of moorlands or chestnut-studded hillsides, and produced without stint or overmuch labour. At best the wines they produced were fresh and had a slight effervescence; the champagnes in their origin were no more; natural wines with an effervescence in the year following the vintage; perhaps the merchants dreamed of becoming new Dom Perignons. But the Minho wines were too thin to travel well and soon went sour. Hunger was the only inspiration of the peasants who grew them and they would never sacrifice plenty for the sake of quality. They were industrious but intensely conservative, as they still are, and capable of great improvidence in sacrificing the future for immediate needs. Luis da Cunha, the Portuguese minister in London who had been a magistrate in Oporto, related that when the King of Portugal was trying to promote a Portuguese silk industry the peasants would cut down the mulberry trees to save themselves the trouble of picking the leaves for the silkworms.

So when their opportunity came in 1678 the English merchants found Portugal a peculiar place. They only had to walk a few yards in any direction to see a vine, but there was no established export trade as there was in other wine-growing countries, and few who appreciated wine for itself. In Lisbon the great landlords could not be dragooned and there was a shortage of labour; in the north wine of a kind was to be had cheaply but the whole industry had to be organized from the beginning. Labour could be had, and although the peasant was resistant to new ideas, good material for

G

coopers and for all kinds of artisans was to be found. Otherwise the merchant had to fend for himself. He had to take the wines as he found them, the bad with the good, to make such improvements as he could, and to create an industry which appeared to have few roots in Portuguese culture.

In 1678 the official importation of Portuguese wines to London was 427 pipes and the export from Oporto to all destinations according to Portuguese sources was 408 pipes. In the same year 15,435 pipes of French wine entered London, but in the next years and until 1686 no French wines were imported through the customs at all. In 1679 the total imports fell from 14,000 tuns to 9,000 tuns, but were resumed at about 14,000 tuns for the remainder of the seven years of prohibition of French wines except for the years 1682, 1683 and 1685, when Portuguese wines were imported in fantastic quantities and the total was higher. In the remaining years Spanish wines and in some years Rhenish wines led in making up the total. The import of Portuguese wine in 1679 rose to 1,013 tuns, but in the bumper years 1682, 1683 and 1685, the totals were 13,860, 16,772 and 12,185 tuns respectively, though the next highest figures were 1,718 and 1,611 tuns only.

In 1679, when the official imports were so low, there was a great deal of smuggling. A harassed official wrote that the roads near Southampton were jammed with wagons laden with French wine and that scores if not hundreds of tuns of wine were being brought in in almost open defiance of the law. Smuggling was less easy in the home counties in the immediate vicinity of the principal market of London, but was common enough in Kent, Sussex and Hampshire. Further afield numerous creeks and havens, and the convenient bases of the Channel Islands, Ireland and the Isle of Man, not to speak of Scotland, made contraband easy, but there were not the same markets available. However, after 1679 a higher proportion of wine came through the customs though often on false declarations. Even before the first outstanding influx of Portuguese wine in 1682 French wines in disguise were coming in. On 13th January 1681 Daniel Finch, later the 2nd Earl of Nottingham and Secretary of State, wrote to his uncle Sir John Finch that the House of Commons had been unexpectedly prorogued but that before they were so incontinently dismissed they had found time to pass several votes in a great rage. One of these was a resolution that the commissioners and officers of the customs had wilfully broken the law prohibiting French wines, and if they did so thereafter wilfully or negligently they must be questioned therefore in Parliament.

As Parliament did not meet again for the rest of King Charles' reign except for a very short session at Oxford, the House of Commons had no further opportunity to harass the commissioners of customs during the king's reign. Finch had explained to his uncle that the anger of the House arose from its anxiety to prevent the king enjoying an adequate revenue, and to force him by the pressure of expenses and charges to come to them for money and to submit to their wishes. Finch estimated that Portuguese wines paid twice as much duty as French wines. In fact according to the tariff French wines paid £16 10s od a tun gross while Portuguese wines paid £20 10s od and Spanish wines £21 10s od. When so many thousands of tuns paid duty as Portuguese or Spanish or Rhenish wines the king benefited; so far from losing money by the prohibition of French wines imposed on him by Parliament he made a substantial gain.

The statistics for the wines imported into London were compiled from the entries in the London port-books and were submitted to Parliament in 1712 in a report made by Charles Davenant. the inspector-general of customs. They cannot be taken as gospel, but they were based upon the amount of duty actually collected and presumably give a fair idea of the amount of wine which passed through the customs. The books give the name of the importing ship and of her master, and of the consignee and place of shipment, but are often vague about the latter. The usual name for Oporto was Port-a-port, but the term port could mean Oporto or any place in Portugal, or port-wine or just Portuguese wine. One would have expected most of the wine to have come from Lisbon in the first instance, as Lisbon wine was better known, but the evidence suggests that most of the wine came from Oporto.

There are no official figures available for exports of Lisbon wine at this date, but there is a continuous series for the exports from Oporto to all destinations from 1678 onwards. These are a puzzle, for in 1682, 1683 and 1685, the three bumper years for Portuguese wines according to the London statistics, the totals in pipes are 700, 1,251 and 391 pipes only. In later years it was officially accepted that most of the so-called Portuguese wines imported at this time were really French wines. Whig commentators easily believed this, but the lack of comment either in Lisbon or in Bordeaux on any remarkable switch from French to Portuguese suggests that there was a good deal of truth in it. Certainly John Locke, who was travelling in France in 1678 and went from the valley of the Loire to Bordeaux in the late summer, noted that the Bordeaux people were apprehensive about the turn things were taking in England and that in anticipation of the prohibition the price of wine had fallen by about half in Bordeaux, and in Saumur and Angers even more. But there is no subsequent evidence to show that these fears were realized. The wine-growers in Bordeaux and other districts of France voiced various grievances in the following years but made no particular complaint about the prohibition. Contemporary French statistics for the year 1682 indeed represented that in that year 203 ships loaded wine in Bordeaux for the United Kingdom and a further twenty-one ships took wine and brandy for the same destination for totals of 12,970 tuns of wine and 5,478 tuns of brandy. These ships must have been Dutch or some other nationality than English though a few of them may have been Scotch, and from information provided by the conservator of the archives of the Gironde it appears that the records for the year show no obvious signs of any interruption of the traffic in non-French ships from Bordeaux. Equally in England the complaints about the badness of the Portuguese wine and the shortage of claret date from 1691 and not from a decade earlier.

In later years the intendants of Bordeaux spoke of circumventing the prohibition by sending wine to Bilbão or San Sebastian in Spanish or Portuguese casks or in French casks counterfeiting them. They claimed that the system worked well until about 1694, when the English customs sent agents to Spain to investigate and put a stop to the practice. But one searches in vain in the port-books for any confirmation of any considerable trade in wine with ports of northern Spain. They show only a small trade with San Sebastian and a few ships calling at Bilbão to load wool and iron and very little wine. However, there are contemporary references to the carriage of wine in Dutch ships and this is probable. The evidence is scanty and conflicting and a careful and lengthy search would be necessary to determine how much French wine reached England and what proportion it formed of the total. In the years 1679, 1680 and 1681 there was a marked increase in the importation of Rhenish wines, and as the Navigation Acts allowed the importation of Rhenish wines in Dutch ships it would have been a comparatively simple matter to pass French wines off for these for shipment from a Dutch port. But 1678 and 1680 were good vintage years for Rhine wines and 1679 though indifferent in quality was plentiful, so stocks of rhenish may have been available. The importation of Spanish wines was unusually large only in 1680 and 1684, in which years they were perhaps used as cover. Some of the French wines may have come by way of the annual fair at Rouen, which was an easy port of call for small ships from the Channel and west country ports, and later French wines were sometimes mixed with Rhenish wines at Dunkirk and shipped on Dutch vessels.

The absence of any outcry against the quality of the Portuguese wines suggests either that the first imports were carefully selected or that they were skilfully blended so that there was no marked change or deterioration in the wines marketed. Further, the total importation in the three Portuguese wine years was greater in other years, which suggests that after all a proportion of the declared wine was actually Portuguese. Although the archives of the British legation in Lisbon are reticent on the subject, they do contain one scribbled note, which appears to have been written in 1684 by someone recently returned from Lisbon, on a Lisbon despatch as a comment for the guidance of the secretary of state in his current negotiations with the Portuguese. It reads 'upon a report of ye farming of the customs, the customs of ye English goods imported were valued at more than ye customs of all ye foreign nations, and ye English do ship off more of ye products of Portugal than all other nations'.[1] Wines would scarcely have been worth mentioning in this context unless a substantial start had been made with the trade. Even the Oporto export figures show some increase in the years concerned, and the remarkable slump from 16,000 tuns in 1683 to 1,600 tuns in 1684 is due perhaps both to an over-shipment in the previous year and to a bad vintage, for at least in Lisbon wine was scarce in that year. Although a number of entries in the port-books are vague and describe the wines as 'port' or 'from port', others give a definite port of origin such as Lisbon or Oporto, or sometimes smaller ports like Viana or Aveiro, or occasionally Madeira. These entries sound genuine, and as there were a number of ships bringing other

[1] S.P. 89/16, fo. 192.

goods from Portugal it is unlikely that they did not take such wine as was offered at a time when the market for it was so good. One can pick on a few entries which sound likely to have been faked, for instance the ten gallons of declared Portuguese wine imported expensively overland from Dover by the French ambassador on 19th March 1683. But Samuel Pepys imported half a hogshead of port-wine on 5th March 1685 just after the death of King Charles and ten gallons again in March 1686 after the prohibition was ended.[1] Some wine as good as the French wines was probably imported, and the 289 tuns imported in the year after the prohibition ended doubtless represented these. About 100 tuns came from Oporto and Lisbon and a little less from Madeira. They included a couple of tuns imported by the Lord Bishop of London, probably for the Communion, and two hogsheads of port and half a cask of Lisbon for the Queen Dowager Catherine of Braganza. During the time of the prohibition, purchases such as that of two hogsheads of port-wine figuring in the private accounts at Woburn of the Earl of Bedford probably referred to genuine Portuguese wine. The earl was a regular purchaser of wines bought directly from friends abroad and had already bought Lisbon in 1676; the port was purveyed by John Houblon, a leading Portugal merchant. It must all be guesswork, but it is not unreasonable to surmise that the 1686 English import figures and the Oporto export figures represent the quality wines. The total production of these in Portugal was very limited; there was some in Lisbon and the south, a little perhaps came from the Upper Douro, more from Viana and the neighbourhood of Coimbra, and from Madeira. When the good wine, supplemented at first by a few stocks, ran out, which it soon did, the merchants would have been tempted to buy green wine, which was in plentiful supply and could be had cheaply. Such wine was apparently not at first taxable or included in the Oporto customs figures, though it became so when the Portuguese saw that foreigners were making a big profit out of it. At first the customs officers could probably be squared but in a year or two the regulations were tightened and the merchant also found that they had to go slow on the green wine, which was unsatisfactory, and that they must step up the production of better wine. They looked farther afield for better wines, and the increase of demand naturally in the course of a few years produced an expansion of

[1] London Port Book E 190/88/1 and 137/8.

vineyards in the inland districts with a better climate for wine growing. The records show that old Portugal hands like the diplomatists Francis Parry and Charles Fanshawe and the consul Maynard bought Portuguese wines, presumably for their own consumption as they were not merchants, and this suggests that wines of quality were already to be had in Portugal by those in the know. In the interval between the end of the prohibition of French wines in 1686 and its renewal in 1690 the imports of Portuguese wines were very low, but they were still higher than before 1678 and slowly growing, while the discrepancy between the Oporto figures and the English customs figures lessened.

LISBON AND CADIZ
WINE DISTRICTS

CHAPTER V

Port and Claret

THE four years 1686-9 saw more French wines imported than there had ever been since the separation of Aquitaine or were to be again until the twentieth century. Yet the total imports of wine were somewhat less and the maximum figure for French wine imported into London, 15,518 tuns in 1687, was less than that for Portuguese wines in 1683, which reached 16,772 tuns. But the predominance of French wines over other wines was greater than before. Anthony Wood remarked that whereas claret had hitherto principally been drunk in the form of burnt or mulled claret at funerals, now claret was the fashion for all occasions and even sack was seldom preferred. Therefore the price of claret was rising while other wines including canary could be got cheap. French wines were no longer the fashion only at court but were commonly used in taverns. This was not to last. The vintage of 1689 was not affected and some French wine was brought in in 1690, but by 1691 the new prohibition consequent on the revolution and the war with France was fully operative. The official imports for the year Michaelmas 1690 to Michaelmas 1691 were only fifteen tuns, and the total import of wines was 9,552 tuns, about half of what it had been before. The chief increase was in Portuguese wines, from 1,115 to 2,964 tuns, while Spanish and Rhenish wines showed a slight increase and Italian wines jumped from 156 to 593 tuns. The upper classes liked the Italian wines, but they did not travel well, and at the end of the century John Croft believed that their scarcity was an important factor in promoting the growth of the Portuguese trade. Some noble lords, including Godolphin and Nottingham, consoled themselves with rhenish but for some reason, probably war conditions and the difficulty of transport, the imports of rhenish never rose to more than a few hundreds of tuns or equalled those of the years between 1678 and 1685.[1]

The new prohibition affected the trade of Bordeaux much more than the previous one and Bordeaux had also been suffering from other difficulties. Owing to the efforts of Colbert, French merchant ships were more numerous, but the Dutch represented about a third of the tonnage using Bordeaux and the city itself still owned few ships. The ships in the wine trade were small, averaging 140 tons. The English ships taking wine from Bordeaux were smaller still, particularly those from the out-ports, and averaged less than 100 tons. The Bordelais were fighting to preserve their privileges and the advantages allowed their wines over those of the High Country. Until 1675 they had been successful and there had been a decline in the export of High Country wines only offset by the increase in the industry for turning them into brandy. Colbert then abolished the privileges, for he was more interested in the prosperity of the export trade in general than in that of the Bordeaux citizens. He was personally interested in the wines of Quercy on the Tarn, which perhaps accounted for the appearance of Cahors wines in the cellars of King James II and of the Earl of Rutland. Later he was persuaded by the obstinate opposition of the Bordelais, and by their arguments that the protection of their wines helped to preserve the quality of the export wines in general, to make some concessions. He made them pay the same tax as everybody else, but he allowed them again to exclude High Country wines from export until Xmas. Although, as John Locke mentioned in his letters, Bordeaux was the natural port of exit for goods coming as far as Montpellier, the restrictions on wines were only occasionally lifted, for instance in 1698 when there was a good vintage in Langue d'Oc but a shortage in Bordeaux. In that year wines were allowed to be brought in and barrel staves for Langue d'Oc allowed to be sent out. Colbert also frowned on the mixing of Bordeaux wines, until 1683 when he was persuaded that some blending was beneficial and agreed to condone the practice in the case of wines being prepared for export, provided that it suited the taste of English or Dutch purchasers.

---

[1] London Port Book E 190/151/9: Duke of Devonshire five casks of one awm (awm = about forty gallons); Godolphin 6 casks. E 190/154/1 gives imports by Nottingham.

While the policy of Colbert worked in favour of the High Country wines against the monopoly of the city of Bordeaux, other vicissitudes were disturbing its commerce. The whole region suffered from the disabilities to which the large Huguenot element residing there was exposed. Bordeaux also harboured a number of families of Jewish or Portuguese origin, who took a leading part in the trade and finance of the city and equally with the Huguenots were subject to persecution. In 1674 ninety-three Jewish families left the city to swell the numbers of those who ever since the first expulsion of the Jews from Spain and their subsequent exclusion from Portugal, had been finding new homes in more tolerant countries. Particularly in Amsterdam the New Christians among them often reverted to their Jewish faith and formed the nucleus of a network of contacts extending though the ports of Europe and the Mediterranean, beyond the limits of Christendom to Salonica, Smyrna and Constantinople. From the time of the Reformation these communities had been joined by Protestant refugees including Huguenots from La Rochelle and Bordeaux. After the revocation of the Edict of Nantes in 1685 Huguenot families were not allowed to emigrate, but many still succeeded in doing so, and these included more families from Bordeaux. The refugees did not lose touch with the places whence they had fled and these connections were important to trade, which often followed clandestine channels when it was impeded by embargoes or by wars. As all the principal ports exporting wine had contributed to the flow of emigrés this was also helpful to the wine trade.

Although the wine trade of Bordeaux had come pretty well through the first English prohibition it was to be considerably shaken by the second prohibition during the Nine Years War. During the peace that followed, one of the intendants deplored the mad planting of vines everywhere and the undue dependence of Bordeaux on a single export. In the early years of the war as many as four vintages had been held up, largely unsold, and had accumulated until they were spoilt, although the demands of the French navy took off some of the stocks and the best use was made of every wile to ship wine in neutral ships or on false bills of lading.

In England the situation was much more difficult than it had been, because the new government was no longer inclined to countenance the making of false declarations. Nevertheless, at least at first, a number of frauds continued. In 1689 the intendant at Bordeaux asked for permission to export wines under the Spanish flag and claimed that the despatch of wines in Spanish casks was working well. The importation of French wines in Spanish or Portuguese casks was a subject of common talk in England, and Farquhar introduced into his play *The Constant Couple* a character named Smuggler, who brought in 5,000 tuns in this way from San Sebastian. He explained that his cargo was worth £5,000 to him and well worth 5,000 perjuries. All would have been well, if he had not been given away by a tide-waiter. Such rascals were more trouble to a merchant than a fleet of French privateers and he would have to pay an enormous bribe to escape being denounced.

Gossip no doubt exaggerated the extent of these malpractices. The intendant is unlikely to have invented the story and the port-books do reveal an occasional suspicious shipment from San Sebastian, for instance one of fifty tuns in 1695 by a former shipper of French wines named Fred Groening. But in the port-book, few ships were entered as coming from northern Spanish ports at all and the majority of ships carrying Spanish wine came from the Canaries, Cadiz or the Mediterranean. There is more evidence of the possibility of this traffic in the years after the war, when owing to the high duties on French wines their clandestine introduction was still profitable. According to export figures compiled in Bordeaux, 807 tuns of wine were exported to north-west Spain in 1698-9 and 4,543 tuns in 1699/1700. At the same time there was a sharp rise in the imports of Spanish wines into England, particularly into the out-ports.

The Bordeaux trade suffered so much that wholesale evasion must have been less than during the previous prohibition, which it must be remembered took place in time of peace, when communications were easier. Nevertheless, some French wine was smuggled or came in by way of the Low Countries, and a little entered in the form of prize wine. There was some doubt whether prize wine was not included in the general prohibition of French wines, but this cannot have been the case, for there are occasional allusions to prize wine. For instance, in June 1695 John Mansell purchased about fifty tuns of prize wine in Weymouth and shipped it to London and another merchant brought in thirty tuns of prize wine from Dover.[1] Most of the prizes were taken into western ports, and the difficulties and legal delays were such that any wines which did not mysteriously disappear before reaching an English port more often than not officially or actually went bad. A large Swedish ship of 400 tons for instance was captured five days out of Bordeaux with 210 tuns of white wine on board. By the time she was brought into port 68¾ tuns of wine had vanished and after deduction of 3¼ tuns for leakage 138 tuns were left. This was rather a good balance, but it was appraised as 'eager', that is turned sour and worth only £2 10s 0d after payment of duty, though the captain, as was only natural, claimed more.[2] In London there were many complaints about shortages of wine, so although contraband existed, it must have been considerably reduced.

The lovers of claret had been spoilt during the reign of King James when it had become so fashionable, and high prices had been paid for choice wines. When the price of ordinary Graves in Bordeaux was 84 livres the tun English buyers had paid 400-450 livres for Haut Brion. Such wines were already sometimes sold in bottles and were often blended with other wines and counterfeited in various ways. Tory noblemen deprived of their good claret were spurred by their annoyance to declaim even more loudly against the government of William and Mary. Port-wine became a symbol of the Whigs and claret of the upholders of divine right and of the Stuarts. The dialogue between port and claret became part of the propaganda war between Whig and Tory.

A leading defender of claret was Edward Ward, editor of the popular periodical *The London Spy*. Ward was a publican who liked to pose as a gentleman and a philosopher. He spiced his work with bawdiness, but he had talent and painted a vivid picture of the London taverns, coffee-houses and brothels, mingling in it loyal Tory sentiments and praise of claret with risqué stories. A number of ballads and broadsheets were also published on the subject and the most famous of these were *In Search of Claret* and *A Farewell to Wine*, published in 1691 and 1693 by Richard Ames. Ames described a long pub-crawl round the favourite resorts of the town. He combed the taverns in search of claret, but everywhere he was offered port instead. At the Mitre they

[1] Port Book E 190/155/2.
[2] High Court of Admiralty, 2 and 32.

were too busy mulling red and white port to pay any attention to him. At another well-known tavern he was offered Barcelona, at a third Navarre, at a fourth so much Florence that he imagined he had been transported to Leghorn. Indignantly he rejected the port as spiritless and flat. Finally he was shown a long wine-list including 'the Lisbon wine Calcavella so much in use'. This wine was generally esteemed as a cut above port. He decided that he would have to make the best of the situation and to give up any hope of claret; he resigned himself to drink anything provided that it was not port, and gave his order to the waiter:

> Hold, you prating whelp, no more,
> But fetch a pint of any sort
> Navarre, Galicia, or anything but port.

This preference for Navarre suggests that Navarre wines, like their neighbours from Galicia and from the Viana and Monção districts of Portugal, were regarded as the next best to claret. Besides there was always the hope that they might prove to be claret in disguise or at least blended with claret.

The reaction to port and Ames's description of it is also significant. When confronted with a bottle of port the poet burst out:

> Mark, how it smells, methinks a real pain
> Is by its odour thrown upon the brain,
> I've tasted it, 'tis spiritless and flat,
> And has as many different tastes
> As can be found in compound pastes.

This description calls to mind the later criticisms of port-wine, that when young it was fiery and had a strong smell, and that instead of mellowing it was likely to turn muddy, spiritless, and flat. It was a long time before a remedy was found for these defects.

The claret for which Richard Ames thirsted was a 'good old dry orthodox claret'. It had a bitter tang in it and this was a quality which was sought in the claret substitutes grown in the north of Spain and Portugal, and perhaps in the Azores. French officials following the new developments in the English market with anxious interest were inclined to attribute to the government a positive policy in the matter. In 1701 Casaux de Hallay, the deputy representing Nantes in the new council of commerce sitting at Versailles, reported that English consuls in Portugal, Catalonia and Galicia were encouraging the planting of vines in their districts, and were recommending that the grapes should be picked early when they were scarcely ripe and their sugar content was low, so that the wine from them would resemble French wine. He went so far as to suggest that gourmets had been sent to places where the warmer climate produced sweeter wines in order to encourage an earlier vintage of wines diminished in strength and possessing an acidity to correct their natural sweetness. This was in any case the opposite of what the wine shippers were soon to seek to do, as the future demand was to be for sweeter and stronger wines and not for dry or acid ones. In any case there is no evidence that official solicitude went so far, though most ministers and consuls had a keen personal interest in wine apart from their official interest in it as an article of commerce. They also appreciated that gifts of wine were a good way for a representative abroad to curry favour with his superiors at home.

Alexander Stanhope, minister at Madrid, arranged in 1697 to send some claret type wines to the Duke of Newcastle through Consul Parker of Corunna. He described the Galician vintage and told the duke he was sending him two excellent hogsheads, one of white Ribadavia, the other a wine like a pale claret not inferior to champagne. The same minister complained that his son James, the future earl and prime minister, like the rest of fashionable circles in London, was crazed about champagne, and refused to appreciate the carefully selected wines he was sending him from Spain.[1]

At the same period John Methuen, minister in Lisbon, was looking out for good Lisbon wines and was sending them to important people, while his son Paul, who had become a friend of the Stanhope family and had served Alexander Stanhope for a time as attaché in Madrid, also used to speak of wine in the regular correspondence which he kept up with Alexander Stanhope. Methuen at this time was also seeking light wines, such as he believed conformed to the English upper-class taste, and although his son-in-law Humphrey Simpson dealt with Oporto as well as Lisbon, there is no record that Methuen ever tried out the heavier wines from the Douro or even knew about them.[2]

[1] H.M.C. Portland, ii-377.
[2] Kent Archives, Chevening, MS U1590.

George Stepney, minister in Vienna, had merchant cousins trading abroad, as Stanhope had, and was interested in wine. Like John Methuen he held an appointment as commissioner of trade for a time, and in Vienna he anticipated Methuen by proposing an agreement for the exchange of cloth against wine. His project for the sale of English cloth in Hungary in exchange for the sweet Hungarian wine known as Tokay did not materialize, but his influence may have helped to encourage the fashion for Tokay, which prevailed for a time in select circles in Queen Anne's time.

John Methuen's treaty of commerce with Portugal, concluded in December 1703, was brief and to the point. By it Queen Anne undertook the Portuguese wines should never pay more than two-thirds of the customs duties chargeable on French wines, while in return King Pedro promised to repeal the restrictions on the entry of certain types of English cloth. Methuen himself had close connections with the trade, for his father had been a pros-perous clothier at Bradford-on-Avon and his brother Anthony carried on the family business. As soon as he became minister in Lisbon he acquired a house and garden on the outskirts, and ordered a long list of fruit-trees and flowers and plants from England, which he tried to acclimatize. He also took a great interest in his vineyard and often gave news of the vintage to his friends. His friends or patrons, the Marquess of Halifax, Earl Godolphin, James Vernon, and the dukes of Shrewsbury and of Marlborough, all at one time or other received presents of wine from him. He hoped that the wines would be good. One at least of their comments has survived. His daughter's father-in-law, Sir William Simpson, wrote to him 'I dyned with my Lord Tr. (Lord Treasurer Godolphin) on Wenesday [sic] last where his Lp. dranke yr health & tasted yr wine which was much commended'.[1] As the friends of ambassadors were likely to belong to the claret lovers, who at the top were by no means confined to the Tories, it is not surprising that Methuen looked for claret-type wines, though sweeter wines might have been easier to find in Lisbon. In 1694

---

[1] MS C 163, Kenneth A. Spencer Research Library, University of Kansas; Sir William Simpson to John Methuen, 24 April 1704; and Earl Spencer's MS at Althorp; John Methuen to Marquis of Halifax, 2 May 1693, 4 September 1694: and S.P. 89/17 John Methuen to Sir J. Trenchard, 3 March 1694. Sends pipe of Barra Barra from the *quinta* of that name consigned to Humphrey Simpson. For Halifax correspondence MS at Althorpe, quoted by courtesy of Earl Spencer.

he was looking for small and delicate wines for the Marquess of Halifax and promised to send the best he could find. In 1696 he was sending Barra Barra to his friends;[1] this was not a Lisbon white wine but a fuller red wine from the vicinity of Lavradio on the opposite bank of the Tagus. Its nearest modern equivalent is perhaps Periquita.

In the 1690s the English customs did not record any imports of Portuguese wines approaching the fantastic quantities of the three boom years in the 1680s. In 1690, the first full year of the war, the imports to London were 1,115 tuns only; they grew to 6,052 tuns in 1692 and to a peak figure of 9,454 tuns in 1694. The merchants, trying to build up the Portuguese trade, began by looking for wines capable of replacing clarets and competing with Spanish wines. In previous years, while imports were small, they had begun to take the best wines from Lisbon, Oporto, and Madeira. Now they had to find much larger quantities to supply the tavern trade and to satisfy a thirsty public. But Portugal had no established export trade in wines and could not suddenly produce so much wine of good quality, although at first there may have been some stocks of better wines left over from a previous vintage. Oporto had a flying start on account of the mass of green wines grown in the Minho, which peasant proprietors were glad to sell cheap. Some of the nobility also seem to have realized the opportunity offered to them and to have developed vineyards on their properties in the valley of the Tamega, a tributary of the Douro joining the river some twenty miles above Lisbon. They made money and built a number of country houses named *soleras*, which are their memorial. The Tamega valley is outside the wine district of the Upper Douro and on the seaward side of the massif of the Marao, but it is far enough inland to have a fairly dry climate. Probably it produced some tolerable table wine, which flowed into the port for blending as the Tamega did into the Douro.

In a good year the green wines were viable for a time and for want of any other the shippers used them freely for blending. They also resorted to positive adulteration. Even in Bordeaux such practices had become common, often quite legitimately, in order to meet the requirements of Dutch and other customers. Some of the Portuguese wines so mixed proved viable but many

---

[1] Althorpe M.S.: Methuen to Halifax, 4th September 1694. S.P. 89/17, Methuen 2nd May 1963 and 13th March 1694, and bills of lading.

H

of them went bad and justified the diatribes of Richard Ames. Nevertheless the trade grew rapidly at first, but the 1693 vintage was spoilt by a long wet summer, while even when shipped the wines spent long weeks waiting for a convoy; as they were sour and watery in the first instance many of them soon fretted and went entirely off. The English importers suffered great losses, and in 1695 the English imports fell from over 9,000 tuns to 3,983 tuns. The decrease must have largely arisen from a shortage of Lisbon wines; as the export of Oporto wines showed a comparatively small decrease; 4,610 tuns passed the Oporto customs outwards, which confirms that a high proportion must have been condemned before it passed the English customs.[1]

In 1696 the English imports recovered to 6,668 tuns but tended to remain lower for some years. However, for the time being Oporto wines held their own against Lisbon wines. Some particulars of the convoys appointed for Portugal in the autumn of 1696 are known. The Lisbon convoy consisted of thirteen ships of from 40 to 200 tons; the Oporto convoy was for the same number but of ships mostly of 100 tons. Several ships were going to smaller ports, one to Setubal, one to Faro, one to Figueira, a largish ship of 160 tons to Viana and three small ships of 40, 60 and 70 tons to Caminha near Monçao. One James Gardner claimed to be the only importer from Madeira and asked for a convoy of three to six ships. The Madeira cargoes would be mainly wine, while wine would also be carried by the other ships but in company of other goods. Soon after this the Portugal merchants were protesting to Parliament against a proposal to increase the duties on wines, and complaining that they had made great losses through their wines turning sour and through the high cost of wines, which prevented them selling the stocks they had accumulated, particularly of canary. They feared that if the market for Portuguese wines failed, the restrictions on the importation of English cloth would be increased. On the other hand the Portuguese minister Luis da Cunha asked for an abatement on the customs duties and promised that if this could be granted, a relaxation of the Pragmatical Decrees might be considered.

The merchants did not lie back and confine themselves to protests. They made active efforts to find in Portugal wines which would please both their customers who liked their claret and those

[1] C.O. 388/3. Oporto Factory Memorial.

who looked for a sweeter stronger wine. It is interesting that Luis da Cunha, although he was well acquainted with Oporto, thought that the English public were now forgetting about claret and preferring the sweet wines of Portugal. He spoke of the Algarve as a possible district where vineyards should be encouraged, so was not thinking of the Douro.

Although the green wines of the Minho had been a disappointment the wines of the Lima valley above Viana and of Monçao on the River Minho on the frontiers of Galicia were proving hopeful. These were red wines, often rather thin, but in a good year they could pass as claret. By 1703 there was a small British community at Viana complete with a vice-consul and a chaplain. There were also several English merchants living at Monçao. They had brought in English coopers to make casks out of the local oak or chestnut wood and to teach their trade to the Portuguese. For a time several hundred pipes were exported from this part of Portugal, but the discovery of the virtues of the Upper Douro wine and the development of Oporto soon eclipsed Viana, which also suffered from the silting up of the harbour. In 1711, English, Dutch and Portuguese residents of Viana addressed a memorial[1] to the King of Portugal on the subject and begged for an engineer to be sent to save the harbour. The records continued to show an occasional ship entering Viana, but it does not appear that any substantial work to improve the channel was ever done.

In later years even the Portuguese were inclined to agree that the English had been responsible for the development of the vineyards of the Upper Douro and to believe that before their coming nothing had grown there but broom and furze. This was largely true of the Upper Douro above Regua, which was only taken into the port-wine delimited area in the time of Pombal, but not of the Lamego and Regua district itself. The production of quality wines had declined, but table wines were still going down the river to Oporto though they were little known. Thomas Cox, a well-informed young Englishman residing for some time in Lisbon, wrote in 1700 that the wines of Oporto were almost all green wines, smaller than the wines of Lisbon.[2] He said that since the beginning of the Nine Years War the Oporto wines had become popular in England and about 14,000 pipes were exported from

[1] Add. MSS 38153, Fo. 194.
[2] Add. MSS 23726.

Oporto against 6,000 pipes from Lisbon. Allowing for wastage and exports to Ireland, Scotland, etc., this estimate of about 10,000 tuns did not differ greatly from the figure of total imports from Portugal to London and the out-ports amounting to 8,703 and 7,657 tuns in 1699 and 1700; the figure for Oporto exports to all destinations in the same years was given as only 6,254 and 7,287 pipes, but to make up the total the exports, not only from Lisbon but from Viana and the smaller ports and Madeira and the Azores, would have to be added, plus the wines from Spain falsely declared. The first authentic account of the trade in wines from the Upper Douro is perhaps that given by the English merchant Thomas Woodmass of Kettering, who visited Viana and Monção at the time of Methuen's commercial treaty and was at Regua near the time of the vintage in 1704.

The tradition in later years in Oporto was that the two sons of a Yorkshire shipper, who had been sent out to learn the wine trade, were the first English to explore the Upper Douro. Another story credited with the discovery Peter Bearsley, son of a merchant named Job Bearsley who settled in Viana in the 1680s. He was said to have found some uncommonly good wine in a monastery not far from Regua and to have bought some to send down to Oporto. It is not unlikely that something of the kind occurred, for the Church was a principal land-owner and in the sixteenth century a monastery near Lamego had been famous for its vineyard, which produced 15,000-16,000 almudes (about 600 pipes) of wine of the best quality. The Bearsleys were authentic enough; Woodmass was met by Job Bearsley when he landed at Viana. Afterwards the family moved to Oporto and founded a firm of wine-shippers which after nineteen changes of name carried on recently as Taylor, Fladgate and Yeatman. Most of the vineyards round Lamego were on somewhat heavier soil, but some perhaps had already spread to the thin schistous soil of the mountains where the full wines to be known as port were later grown. It is noteworthy that the three classes of wine described in the early sixteenth century were still spoken of in the eighteenth century. The green wines, table wines and Factory or port-wines of the later period corresponded to the green and other ordinary wines, table wines and aromatic wines described by the geographer Rui Fernandes in 1531. The table wines had always been shipped down the Douro, which was navigable as far as San Jõao de

Pesqueira some distance above Regua, and evidently were still reaching Oporto in 1678, the year in which Portuguese wines began to be exported to England and in which the Lisbon Senate obstructed the export of Douro wines to Lisbon. The English shippers must have come across such wines in Oporto, even though they did not at first know precisely where they came from.

Woodmass had set out from Liverpool in the brig *Bonaventura* which belonged to his father, and had several adventures. The sea was stormy and the captain often drunk; in addition the ship was captured by a French privateer in the Channel, rescued by a British ship, and taken back to Falmouth. After being repaired she set sail again and at last reached Viana safely in time for Christmas 1703. After his visit to Viana and Monçao Woodmass travelled along the coast on horseback towards Oporto but the country was in a very disturbed state owing to the passage towards the Spanish frontier of the allied army commanded by the Earl of Galway, and was full of deserters and of soldiers who had turned into brigands. He was captured by a party of them and spent the night tied to a tree, but was rescued in the morning and taken to Vila de Conde where he was befriended by an English resident and by a kindly Portuguese priest. So he reached Oporto, where he found a well-established English and Scottish community and the English consul John Lee. The latter told him that the English enjoyed many privileges under the treaties and had good relations with the Portuguese farmers, who were honest men, but they had trouble enough with the government officials and with the land-owners, who were determined to gain complete control of the wine trade. These remarks were significant in their suggestion of the shape of things to come. The English usually got on well with their work-people; they were inclined to treat them well by local standards, and the small farmers were only too happy to receive money for wine which had previously fetched little or nothing. But the big land-owners were soon joining together to put up prices and to try to win the upper hand in an industry which seemed only to be making foreigners rich. In one way the Oporto Factory was better off than that of Lisbon, for although it lacked the support of the legation diplomatic privilege, it only had the local authorities, the bishop and the municipality of Oporto, and a few nobles and land-owners confronting it. These could be tough but were less formidable than a king and his government.

As a foreign community of some wealth it was more important relatively in a provincial town than the Lisbon Factory was in the capital. But as soon as the Factory ceased to buy wine locally and sought stronger wines from the Upper Douro new problems arose. The wines often had to be taken considerable distances by cart to the point of embarkation on the Douro. They could not be sent by land because the route led over a considerable mountain and the transport would have been too expensive and difficult. Even the journey down the river took several days and was subject to accident and to the whims of unpredictable boatmen. It was also easy for the Portuguese to subject the traffic to many regulations and to hold up the wines until the Factory paid higher prices. The land-owners were well-placed to hold the Factory to ransom, for they knew that shippers wanted to ship the wine before the worst of the winter season and in time of war to sail in time to join up with a convoy. After Christmas the entry over the bar of the Douro was often impassable in stormy weather, while the Douro itself often had dangerous floods. The shippers ran heavy risks by delays with a perishable cargo, apart from the cost of holding back ships or sending them away empty. It was only after years of experience that both sides learnt that too much obstinacy might result in their both being losers. A sort of gentlemen's agreement was then reached by which the wine was shipped down the river as soon as it was ready and a fair price was settled afterwards in the light of the vintage and the current circumstances of the year's trade.

The Oporto Factory in 1703 was smaller than it had been in the years following the 1654 treaty, but they nevertheless managed to lead very self-contained English lives. In Oporto, as opposed to Lisbon, the men at least had to deal with the Portuguese farmers and to be closer to the soil, but Woodmass remarked that the English families kept very much to themselves and employed English-speaking negro servants, so that they had no need to speak Portuguese even to their cooks. This prosperous and segregated way of life was to be the pattern for the English Factories in Lisbon and Oporto throughout their existence. In so far as their aloofness kept them out of local politics their manner of life had its merits, but the existence of an alien body in their midst, who kept a much higher standard of living, naturally provoked Portuguese jealousy. Many of the English worked very hard and won the respect of Portuguese officials and the devotion and loyalty of their work-people, but in times of prosperity there was an idle element, who thought only of quick profits, took no trouble to make themselves acceptable, and afforded justification for local resentment.

The founders of firms were often rugged men of energy, competence and integrity, who established good contacts with the Portuguese and sometimes won the esteem of the Catholic hierarchy. Their sons and grandsons were not always of the same calibre and there were new men coming in who were jealous of the old-established firms, and only wanted to make quick profits easily. As long as they commanded respect the members of the Factory passed muster in Portugal and could afford to be stand-offish. When some of them became idle, pretentious or vicious the jealousy of rich foreigners in a poor country gained strength, and the troubles and quarrels arose which plagued much of the history of the Lisbon and Oporto Factories.

Woodmass found that the Oporto shippers had a high opinion of the wines of the Upper Douro and for the most part took a pride in the quality of their wines. Some of them had established their own contacts with Upper Douro growers, but they were very discreet about these and reluctant to betray knowledge of them to their competitors. The good fellowship, which was a feature of the life of the Factory, was always to be tempered by a natural disposition on the part of every man to keep his own trade secrets. Woodmass noted this on his ride up to the Douro. The way lay over a rough road taking three days or so. Above Oporto the Douro is at once lost among steep hills, which give the character of a gorge to much of the valley. The only road until very recently lay over several ranges of hills and between Amarante and Regua over the Quinhão pass about three thousand feet high. This must have been a goat-track in 1704, for even the road based on that built in the later eighteenth century was very steep. Woodmass and his friends crossed the pass without mishap or suffering anything worse than the discomfort of the dirty Portuguese inns. Another party of English were following the same road but the two parties tried to give each other the slip, for they wanted to keep their contacts and their knowledge of good places to buy wine to themselves. Woodmass himself gave no hint of these secrets, so we do not know exactly where they went. He mentioned that the vintage was a small one but that the wines were going cheap, fetching only 13 milreis (about 4/6 to the milreis) a pipe, which was less than the price being paid at Monçao. He said that in Monçao the wine was bought from small farmers who seldom had more than five pipes to sell. In so much as the best wine was grown on the worst soil it is quite probable that the squatters on the hillsides on the fringes of the big estates of the Douro often by accident produced better wines than the big land-owners, but although we have no evidence on the subject it seems likely that Woodmass's friends, who had also to make arrangements for the transport of the wine down the river, preferred to buy their wine in bigger lots. The original port-wine was often called priest's port and it is probable that the tradition of good wine was best preserved by a few monasteries or large estates and it was there that the best wine was to be found.

Much of the better wine was no doubt used for blending and to make up the rest the Oporto shippers had to shop round as best they could. Records of what actually happened to the wine in Oporto are scanty, but the original port-wine from the Douro seems to have had some of the characteristics later associated with the name. One of the earliest specific descriptions of port is to be found in the *Compleat Physician*, a sort of medical dictionary published in 1693 by Dr William Salmon. He described port-a-port as a very strong-bodied wine and a strong stomatick, but not very palatable and therefore not so much drunk as other wines. Very probably it had been sold in small bottles as a cordial. The characteristic of the heavy Douro wines was that the grapes were thrown, stalks and all, into the press and trodden for as long as seventy-two hours to make the wine stronger, deeper-coloured, and more stable. John Locke in 1678 described a similar process used in the Langue d'Oc for a similar purpose. When successful such wines had strength and sweetness, but the port-wines tended to have a strong tarry flavour from the resin-treated skins in which they had been carried, and the stalks made them bitter; in their efforts to mellow the wine the vintners often ended with something bitter and turbid and the addition of green wine cannot have helped much.

After reading these dismal descriptions it is heartening to look at another side of the picture. In 1697-8 we find John Richards, a Dorsetshire gentleman, cosseting his port-wine as fondly as his claret or his malaga. He had bought a quarter of a cask of malaga in Lyme Regis which he drew off into nine dozen quart bottles. In March 1698 he still had some old port left, but he bottled the cask of port he had received from London the previous autumn and drew off eleven dozen and three bottles. It is fair to add that in 1700, when the war was over, he invested in a hogshead of claret and sent two carts with five horses to fetch it. This yielded 244 bottles and eight bottles more. Claret was not unknown in Dorsetshire even during the war, for in July 1697 Mr Penny bet him two bottles of claret that the French had taken Barcelona and six bottles more that the Duke of Saxony would not remain King of Poland. Claret was welcome, but this did not mean that port was not appreciated as well. In 1702 he was again drawing off eleven dozen large quart bottles from a cask of red port-wine. His cellar also contained canary and white port, the latter perhaps from Lisbon.

After the end of the war French wine could be imported freely again, but it was subject to two heavy duties additional to those paid by other wines, one called for the impost of £8 a tun, the other the second 25% on French goods, which amounted to £25 a tun. This meant that the gross duties on French wines, according to *Saxby's Customs*, amounted to about £58 a tun and on Portuguese wines to about £30, £5 or £6 less in each case if all deductions were claimed; Spanish wines paid a few shillings more than Portuguese wines. As Bordeaux also had a bad vintage in 1697-8 it is not surprising that the French trade was slow in picking up. In 1701, which was one of the best years, it amounted to 1,732 tuns for London and 319 tuns for the out-ports. For the year ending on 30th September the Bordeaux export figures were 1,852 tuns to England, 2,605 tuns to Ireland, and 1,036 tuns to Scotland. Exports to Brittany were 26,636 tuns and to the Low Countries 43,733 tuns. English merchants still believed that claret would be restored to favour if the duties were reduced, but Luis da Cunha, the Portuguese minister, thought that the English were now converted to the sweeter Portuguese wines and the intendant in Bordeaux agreed with this view. The preference for sweeter wines was apparently not a phenomenon peculiar to England, for Dr Martin Lister visiting Paris in 1698 observed that there was a growing liking for sweetness and strength in the wines fashionable there.

Although the Tories clung to claret, King William was showing an increasing interest in Portugal and did not encourage French wines at court except champagne, of which he was fond. This was bought and paid for in Holland. The consignments of champagne were regularly entered in the books but were not charged in them. The king's old friend, the Duke of Zell, used to keep two or three dozen of the best champagne, five years old, for the king's visits to him. It is interesting to note that champagne could be matured for five years and could do so in the bottle. The king's bottle porter always had a flask ready for him when he went hunting. The list of wines for such occasions had not altered much since King Charles's day. The principal change was that port-wine now headed the list with 24 flasks for the party. Other wines numbered rhenish 11 flasks, sherry 11, palm-wine 2, canary 11 and champagne 2. By way of solids 54 manchets of bread and 234 loaves were provided. Port-wine was issued for the Communion service at St James's chapel, and sweet wine or sherry as perquisites for the clergy at the ceremony of the washing of the old people's feet. The issue for the Communion service was thirteen bottles of port and three quarts of sherry. There was also an allowance of 6d a day for nuts, but this was for the queen's parrot and not to go with the port.[1]

[1] L.S. 1-36.

CHAPTER VI

The War of the Spanish Succession, 1702-13

THE pattern of the wine trade set by the Nine Years War changed comparatively little during the years that followed or even at the end of the war of the Spanish Succession. Portuguese wines predominated and were followed not far behind by Spanish wines. In view of the heavy traffic between England and the United Provinces, Rhine wines might have been expected to play a part, but their imports never rose to more than a few hundred tuns. The higher English customs duty on them was scarcely enough to be a decisive factor or even the disturbances of war in the Rhineland; the fundamental reason probably was that their initial cost was high owing to the marginal climate in which they were grown and they already had a sufficient local market to absorb them. Italian wines on the other hand, for which a fashion had begun immediately before the war, were imported in most years in quantities of from one to two thousand tuns. They were often criticized for their failure to keep, but in spite of this Thomas Pitt received 4-5 dozen bottles in India and found it good, though the French wine sent to him proved to be mostly port. In England the prohibition of French wine was somewhat less rigorous than it had been in the previous war and there was no further doubt about prize wines from condemned cargoes being sold upon payment of the duties. In the closing years of the war, when the Tories were in power, there was talk of revoking the prohibition of French wine and of reducing the duties. This led to an increased demand and to French wines or wines described as such reappearing in the market. Nevertheless the long prohibition was

taking effect and the public were gradually losing their taste for
them.

Privateers in the Channel and the vicissitudes of war limited
supplies, and there were times when there was little wine to be
had in London except from persons with their own cellars. The
Oporto trade suffered more than that of Lisbon on account of
the vicinity of Vigo with its enemy privateers and the difficulty of
obtaining convoy protection. Lisbon did better, but in the later
years of the war, when there was a fleet in the Mediterranean and
an army to be supplied in Catalonia, the constant traffic offered
as many opportunities to Spanish as to Portuguese wines. Some
accounts of a London firm named Curzon and Skelton for the
years 1710-12, which have survived, show that wines did not come
directly from Cadiz but from all other Mediterranean ports such
as Alicante, Valencia and Barcelona and even from Galicia, also
from the Canaries.[1] In the knowledge that there was a shortage
of wines, most men-of-war brought back a little wine and supplemented the imports of regular merchants. Owing to the danger
from privateers in the Channel, the out-ports sometimes took as
much as 3,000 tuns of wines, but London still accounted for 70%
of the trade. Most of the prizes were taken to west-country ports,
but the wines on board often went bad owing to the delay before
their sale was authorized; they stood a better chance if they evaded
the customs, which they often did. The wines reaching western
ports were Spanish or Portuguese or French prize wines; the
Italian wines went to London and the rhenish to London or North
Sea ports.

At the abortive Siege of Cadiz in the first year of the war in
1702, Spanish wine and brandy were to play a conspicuous but
unfortunate part. It was not the first time they had proved a pit-
fall at Cadiz; in 1625 the discovery by the troops of large stocks
of wine as they approached the city contributed to the breakdown
of discipline and the disaster which befell the English army. This
had been on the Isle of Leon on which Cadiz stood. In 1702 the
channel into the inner harbour was barred and the fleet could not
sail into it past Cadiz as it had done in 1625. The landing-force
had to disembark on the opposite side of the bay near Port St
Mary.

The sequel as regards wine was similar, for Port St Mary was

[1] Chancery C. 103/68.

full of warehouses where the wines and brandies and other goods
for export were stored. As the town had been abandoned by its
inhabitants, the army soon found its way into the storehouses and
after sampling the contents began to loot indiscriminately. The
navy had not been implicated at first, but they were soon involved,
for there was nowhere to take the plunder except on board ship.
The sailors were not slow to follow the example of the soldiers
and to appropriate all they could find both for their own consumption and to take home for sale. Some officers quarrelled with each
other about the spoils and Captain (later Admiral) Norris had to
be court-martialled for striking a fellow-officer in the course of
a dispute about some casks of wine. Some of the goods were
claimed to be the property of allied merchants and were appropriated for safe keeping, more or less legitimately. A few consignments were alleged to have been legitimately purchased, for instance
three butts of sherry and $3\frac{1}{4}$ casks of red tent allowed by the Duke
of Ormonde to his secretary Jezreel Jones.[1] Such incidents supplemented the normal channels of trade but were disastrous to the
morale of the armed services and to the reputation of the allies in
Spain. Similar events on a smaller scale followed the capture of
Gibraltar. The navy disputed with the army the possession of any
liquor that was to be found; the garrison needed supplies and the
navy had been placed on half-rations, so there was genuine need
as well as a thirst for gain. But such quarrels caused much ill-
feeling and the bad behaviour of the allies placed a valuable weapon
of propaganda in the hands of the enemy.

In 1703 the future of the Portuguese trade had been assured
by the entry of Portugal into the war on the allied side and by
the subsequent commercial treaty concluded by John Methuen.
Ever since 1693 King William had been making tentative efforts
to renew or refresh the old alliance with Portugal, but had not
offered any inducements sufficient to persuade the Portuguese. It
was actually the Emperor who took the most positive step to win
over Portugal, by sending an ambassador to offer an alliance and
the hand of an archduchess for the King of Portugal's elder son,
but Louis XIV forestalled the Emperor by concluding an alliance
with Portugal in July 1701 in which Spain took part. The desertion
of Portugal had not been expected by the sea Powers and came as
a shock to them. They were being hard pressed by the Emperor

[1] H.C.A. 32/48.

to send a fleet to Italy and realized that if Portuguese ports were closed to them by the French, it would be risky for an allied fleet to enter the Mediterranean and ships going to the West Indies could be attacked from Portuguese bases. King William decided that he would send a special ambassador to Lisbon to try to win back the Portuguese. He chose for this purpose John Methuen, who had already served at Lisbon from 1691 to 1696 and had left his son Paul there as his successor in the legation. King William died before Methuen left England but his policy lived on. Methuen had to concert his negotiations with the Dutch minister and with the imperial ambassador, and also from October 1702 with the Almirante of Castile, who represented dissident Spain. The Dutch on the whole had the same motives for seeking an alliance with Portugal as did England, but they were reluctant to pay a heavy price in men or subsidies and, as international traders rather than exporters of their own manufactures, took a more liberal view of trade with the enemy than did the English and were inclined to suspect England of trying to appropriate an unduly large share of trade at Dutch expense. The imperial ambassador favoured an alliance in principle but was doubtful of the capacity of Portugal to give much material help and was most reluctant to undertake any share of the burden or to risk offending Spanish opinion by making concessions of Spanish territory to Portugal. The Almirante of Castile at first made a great impression in Portugal by the splendour of his entourage and by his convincing promises that all Spain would rally to the Austrian cause. But the Almirante had no resources except his personal fortune, which was large but was soon spent, and the promised insurrection in Spain was dependent upon the supply by England and the United Provinces of the money and troops to set the Archduke Charles upon his throne. His promises of Spanish support proved far too optimistic, but the allies were influenced by them and Methuen took the lead in the negotiations by making very handsome offers to the Portuguese. There were some misgivings about these, even in England, but he was supported by Nottingham, the secretary of state, and by Godolphin, the lord treasurer who held the purse-strings. Methuen's diplomatic colleagues all alleged that he was too soft with the Portuguese. It was true that the allies ended by promising to Portugal more than they could perform and Portugal herself undertook more than her capacity allowed. The Methuen treaties had several loose ends and proved in many respects unsatisfactory, but the allies had to contend with a very strong French influence in Portugal and it is doubtful whether any agreement could have been reached within any reasonable time if Methuen had not taken the initiative and the responsibility for offering very favourable terms.

If it had not been for Methuen's personal interest in the wine and cloth trades, the two political treaties might not have been followed by a commercial treaty. The principal treaty, which was known as the quadruple treaty and included the emperor, dealt with the measures required to invade Spain and to place the arch-duke on the Spanish throne. The second treaty, known as the triple treaty, included Great Britain, the United Provinces and Portugal only, and dealt with more general and long-term questions affecting the three allies. Methuen intended to include some commercial provisions but these were largely cut out on account of the danger of Anglo-Dutch disagreement about them. Although England had long been anxious to persuade Portugal to modify the restrictions hampering her cloth trade, Portugal had always insisted that any concessions must be dependent upon England improving the balance of trade by importing more Portuguese goods, for instance wine, but the question was not very urgent for either party at the moment, because the banning of French wines during the war assured the Portuguese wines of the English market, and the Portuguese market for English cloth was also assured as long as the war lasted. Therefore for the time being the Portuguese were disinclined to administer the Pragmatical Decrees strictly. So although Methuen had discussed the question of a new treaty with the Portuguese minister in London in King William's time and still had it much in mind, he possessed, as far as the record shows, no specific instructions on the subject, nor was he given any, when the commercial question was omitted from the two political treaties. Methuen had left Lisbon for London before the actual conclusion of the treaties, which were signed by his son Paul. He returned to Lisbon as ambassador with the ratifications, and it was then that he took the initiative. His previous discussions in London had been halted by his inability to offer any acceptable concessions or to see a way to persuade Parliament to agree to any reduction of the duties on Portuguese wines. He now devised a means to overcome the difficulty.

Portugal had faced the hazards of a military alliance with reluctance, but its actual conclusion and the hope of settling old scores against Spain had produced a certain enthusiasm. The disillusion caused by the failure of the Cadiz expedition a year before was forgotten and there were still great hopes of a pro-Austrian rising in Spain. Furthermore Methuen found himself in an exceptionally strong position, because he alone of his colleagues had cash in his pocket to begin paying not only the English share of the subsidies due to Portugal under the recent treaties, but also the emperor's quota of a third, which, when the emperor was unable to pay, England was obliged to advance. Methuen was on good enough terms with the Portuguese court to be able to discuss the question of a commercial treaty with the Marquis of Alegrete, who had been his commissary for the previous treaty negotiations and as president of the council of finance was at the receiving end for the subsidies. Da Cunha in London still felt that better terms could be obtained but Methuen succeeded in pushing his proposal through before the minister's objection was received.[1] Methuen took it upon himself to promise that the duties on Portuguese wines would never exceed two-thirds of the duties payable by French wines, if the restrictions on the import of certain kinds of English cloth were removed. At the same time he impressed on the Portuguese nobility the advantages that would accrue to them from an increase in the export of Portuguese wines. Although Methuen suffered too much from gout to circulate in society, his son Paul was on good terms with the sons of many of the nobility and Alegrete himself was the owner of large vineyards, as indeed was the Duke of Cadaval, the leader of the pro-French party. Even those who followed the abstemious Portuguese tradition with regard to wine were not insensible to the advantages of an increase in income from their vineyards. It was in fact the Lisbon trade with its better shipping facilities and its many large estates which benefited in the first instance rather than that of Oporto.

Even so it was a risky thing to send home the agreement for ratification without first having obtained specific authority, but Methuen felt reasonably safe because his concession in the matter of duty was more apparent than real and would not cost Parliament a penny. There was nothing to prevent Parliament increasing the duty on all wines, Portuguese included, and before the year

[1] Add. MSS 20817, fo. 400. Da Cunha's Memoirs.

1704 was out it did so, though not quite so quickly as had at first been intended. The treaty was agreed without discussion and ratified in a comparatively short time to the relief of Methuen, who in spite of everything could not help feeling a little anxious. In the next few months the enemy were going to invade Portugal and to destroy some vineyards, but these were in the Beira and the Alemtejo, where wine was grown but all consumed locally. Neither the vineyards near Lisbon nor those supplying Oporto were to be seriously affected.

Another danger to Methuen's treaty was the possible reaction of the Dutch. Indeed, as soon as the Dutch minister Francis Schonenberg heard about the treaty he claimed most favoured nation treatment for his country. The Portuguese with some backing from Methuen refused to agree and it was not until Schonenberg offered somewhat better terms for Portuguese wines imported into the United Provinces than they had been given in England that in the following year they signed an agreement with the Dutch on similar lines. However, the agreement was only important as a matter of principle, for the Portuguese-Dutch trade in cloth and wine never developed as the English trade did.

In December 1703, the month of the Methuen commercial treaty, Queen Anne gave a good example by buying eight pipes of red and two pipes of white port-wine. One cannot be sure that these wines came from Oporto, but it is likely, for the other Portuguese wines she bought were specified as Lisbon, or Carcavella, or madeira. These latter wines were esteemed by Tories as well as Whigs and continued to be bought for the royal cellar, though in the later years of the reign purchases of port-wine did not often figure. Prince George of Denmark was dedicated to drinking and during his life-time his faithful wife saw to it that her cellar was plentifully and variously stocked. She bought palm-wine and canary, rhenish and moselle, and gratefully accepted a sizeable gift of florence from the Grand Duke of Tuscany. Her patriotism did not however extend to the exclusion of French wines. French wines were indeed the favourites, and the Archduke Charles, when he left Portsmouth for Lisbon on his way to claim the throne of Spain, received on the flagship for his voyage a pipe of canary, but also eleven dozen and nine bottles of hermitage. Perhaps the hermitage could have passed muster as wine from Orange, a principality to which the house of Nassau still laid claim, but in

I

the same year of 1704 the queen sent her cellarer to Holland to buy Graves, Haut Brion, Puntack or Pontac, burgundy, champagne, and also hermitage. Even in 1702, the first year of her reign, she had bought from Mr Chaigneau, who had been King William's supplier, eighty hogsheads of Haut Brion and of Margaux or Margoux, and a second lot of thirty-one hogsheads of the same with a hogshead of French navarre and a tun of white Bayon (perhaps Jurançon). Afterwards regular supplies were brought from Holland, where to the vexation of English merchants the Dutch refused after 1704 to review the embargo on French trade which they had been persuaded to join England in declaring, and henceforward traded freely in French wines. As for the queen, it is not surprising that she had to spend over £4 on the purchase of a large book on royal paper, ruled with red lines and bound in vellum, for the entry of the Dyetts, and a second large book for the entry of the Extra-Dyetts.[1]

Where the queen led, those who had the means followed, and there was a good deal of evasion of the law. Before the war, in 1698, an English visitor to Calais, named Thomas Bowrey, found that he could buy burgundy there for 1/8 a quart, claret for 10½d a quart and champagne for 1/-. This was not cheap, but it was inducement enough to smuggle even small quantities across the Channel. During the war advertisements for French wine still appeared in the papers. In 1705 for instance, claret was being offered at 5/- a gallon, which was no more than the regular price of port. This may have been prize wine, which presumably made up the average of 1,000 tuns or so of French wines imported through the customs every year to London and the out-ports. Nevertheless, in 1708, when prize wines were less common, the account book of a London merchant shows claret offered for £15 and £14 10s 0d a hogshead, at a time when a hogshead of port was fetching £15 and of sherry £10 10s 0d. A number of sales at Lloyd's Coffee House in various years during the war included French wines and brandies, usually unspecified but occasionally named, as in 1705 when Haut Brion and Pontac were offered. There were two sales of French claret in 1707, two in 1708, two in 1710, four in 1711 and seven in 1712. Probably some of the seventy-four entries of wines unspecified and of entries of cargoes unspecified from ships with French names also referred to French

[1] For Queen Anne's wines see Lord Steward's Books, L.S. 13/46 etc.

wines, and under the Tory régime towards the end of the war these sales were more numerous. Some of this may have been run-down wine, like the twelve hogsheads bought by Curzon and Skelton, a firm dealing mainly in Peninsular wines, in 1710 at the low price of £9 a hogshead. But it appears that knowledgeable men such as John Harvey could produce claret throughout the war, though they sometimes had to pay dear for it. Harvey paid £48 for a hogshead in 1709.[1]

Meanwhile the highest in the land saw no wrong in doing some personal smuggling. Lady Sunderland tried to bring in some wines from Holland, but was caught, and in spite of her rank had to pay £256 19s 6d in fines. Robert Walpole engaged in smuggling ventures and enlisted the help of Philip Stanhope and of the secretary of the Admiralty Josiah Burchett. The consignment was intercepted on the way to King's Lynn and another was only saved from a similar fate by a timely gift of brandy to a customs officer. Another lot was nearly caught and had to be brought up the Thames in the Admiralty launch. In this way the wheels of state were lubricated with claret, burgundy and champagne. There was also more general smuggling. The House of Lords enquiry into the clandestine trade in 1704 examined witnesses who declared that they had seen as many as fifteen ships in Bordeaux, mostly from the west country, Scotland and Ireland, loading brandies and wines; there was a suggestion that the government discouraged informers and was inclined to hush the matter up. However, although the favoured few could still stock their cellars, the efficiency of the customs was gradually stepped up and for most of the time the lesser folk went short. Even Congreve, who had a post as commissioner for wine licences and presumably knew his way about, complained towards the middle of the war in 1706, 'if I have the spleen, it is because this town of London affords not one drop of wine outside a private house'.

This picture of the situation is supported by accounts from Bordeaux which show that although some of the loopholes for wine to enter England were larger than they had been in the previous war, the trade was badly hit. At first the French navy had consumed an appreciable proportion of the Bordeaux production, but in the later years of the war, when the fleet was often laid up, this outlet for the wines failed. In 1704 the fleet

<hr />

[1] Accounts of Curzon and Skelton, Chancery 103/68.

could still give protection, and one convoy escorted as many as
fifteen ships from Bordeaux to Dieppe, but in 1705 things were
bad and wine was reported to be so cheap that the price scarcely
paid for the taxes. The intendant complained that the peasants
were ruined, and he despaired of finding means to raise his tax
quota. The Rochelle trade was also hard hit, but except during
the Dutch embargo on 1703/4, trade with the United Provinces
carried on. The French gave passports to Dutch ships, and although their Spanish allies did not always respect these, Bordeaux
ships went up the Channel to Dutch ports without too much
difficulty. Only at the end of the war in 1711/12 the French themselves embargoed trade with the Dutch. On the other hand the
1712/13 vintage, which was hopefully loaded in the expectation
that the English market would be thrown wide open, had to be
diverted to the United Provinces.

In the reign of Queen Anne the newspapers began to provide
a new source of information about the wine trade. The days when
noblemen were accustomed to take out licences to import wine
on their own account were passing. Many of them still made their
own arrangements, and although these were handled by merchants, they continued throughout the eighteenth century to be
conducted on private and personal lines, but most wines, even
many of the best quality, were bought by merchants for sale
through ordinary commercial channels. Wines were much advertised and more of the general public began to buy wines to
put in their cellars rather than a few bottles at a time for
immediate use. The advertisements made frequent mention of
Spanish wines such as mountain, malaga, canary and palm-wine,
also barcelona, ribadavia or galicia. Florence was often mentioned,
but the pride of place went to Portuguese wines, to red and white
port, to Lisbon and the red Barabar from the opposite bank of
the Tagus, to Viana and the red Monçao, and also to Figueira and
Anadias wines from the central part of Portugal. In the face of
Spanish competition the Portugal merchants were trying to live
down the reputation of bad muddy port complained of in the
taverns and to capture the high-class trade. They recommended
their port-wines as right and true wines, pure and unadulterated.
Other favourite descriptions were deep, bright, and fresh. For
Oporto wines strength was prized and always claimed. A pleasant
notice in a 1712 number of the *Courant* read 'Red port, red lisbon,

deep, strong, fresh, and of excellent flavour, thought in the judgement of men of sense and experience to be good and better than any of those wines which have been adverised by the bouncing merchants of London and Westminster; and the better to preserve it neat and in its purity we do not design to hawke our reputation in the sale of our wines at little eating houses nor coffee houses, being resolved to sell none at any other place but at our vault aforesaid under Leather Sellers Hall in Little Street, Helen's within, Bishopsgate Street, the new lisbon at 6/-, the neat port at 5/6 a gallon.'[1]

Whatever the port of the tavern trade had become, the port for gentlemen's cellars aimed to be a new and natural wine, clear in colour and of some strength. When Vanbrugh called port-wine thick muddy stuff and Matthew Prior exclaimed 'it was a dismal thought that our warlike men might drink thick port for fine champagne', they must have had in mind the tavern ports, which were often confected with a little wine from the Douro and much else. Prior, despite his humble origin, had much experience of entertainment in embassies and good houses, and should have known what he was talking about, but his remarks nevertheless may have been pure Tory propaganda. The Whigs told another tale. The port that they praised sounded as if it had a little brandy added, but was purer than the general run of tavern wines. In 1711 Steele spoke of good edifying port such as was to be had at honest George's. He added that it made night cheerful and threw off reserve, whereas the plaguy French wine not only cost more but did less good. Addison described the good, honest, hard-drinking yeoman Will Funnell, who drank beer and cider helped out by innumerable nips and whets, but had also imbibed three or four tuns of port in his life, not to mention two or three glasses of champagne. In the *Guardian* he depicted the case for Portuguese against French trade under the guise of a lawsuit between Count Tariff and Goodman Fact. Count Tariff, the advocate of France, appeared in a fine brocade waistcoat curiously figured with fleurs-de-luce, a broad-brimmed hat, a shoulder-knot and a pair of silver-clocked stockings. He abounded in empty phrases, flourishes, violent assertions and feeble proofs. Goodman Fact, on the other hand, was arrayed in a suit of British broadcloth, plain but very rich. His cane, it was true, was from the East

[1] *The Courant,* 8th January 1712, Burney Collection.

Indies and he had one or two superfluities from Turkey and other parts, but in the main his garb was truly English, and it was said that before coming to the trial he encouraged himself with a bottle of neat port. He won his case of course, and it was incredible how general a joy his success caused in the city of London.

The dialogue between port and claret continued at this time to be a matter of great political interest with the result that references to it in literature, plays, and pamphlets were common. Good wines had become a luxury afforded by only a limited class, but as long as the memory of French wines lasted, the vintners had to exert themselves to find an acceptable substitute. In the report which the inspector general of customs, Charles Davenant, submitted at the request of the House of Commons in 1711, he gave statistics of the French and Portuguese trades and pointed out that although wine was the principal product of France, England now only imported Italian, Spanish and Portuguese wines, and these had been found satisfactory, at least by the middle classes 'who are now the greatest consumptioners'. Nevertheless he thought that the high duties on French wines and French goods had not been profitable and that if they were reduced France would offer a good market for several English products. England, he suggested, could do with fewer imports from France than she had taken before the war and he did not recommend an open trade with France as practicable, but a substantial trade with her could be developed if the duties were reduced and trade was allowed to take a more natural course. Davenant was a Tory, but the views he expressed were moderate. He had seen from the statistics that the trade with Portugal was important and appreciated that it would be unwise to risk losing it. The Tories in Parliament, who now had a majority, felt that there was little danger of this and that in any case the Methuen treaty only benefited the Portuguese. Already in 1708/9 they had proposed a bill to allow the importation of claret and the unanimity of the opposition, and even of the Junto Whigs and of the followers of Robert Walpole, had been shaken on this question. Another proposal had been made to allow the Maryland and Virginia merchants to accept French wines in exchange for tobacco. The views of those who desired a renewal of French trade were expressed positively in a petition to Parliament in 1713. The petitioners represented that the existing laws had been ineffectual in preventing the entry of French wines, yet the woollen trade and the Portuguese trade in general had not suffered. On the other hand the interference with the wine trade had led the vintners to a general practice of adulteration and to make use of malt spirits, sweets and other viler liquors to lengthen out the common draught. They therefore asked 'since many people in Great Britain will not drink port, but rather find means to get in French wine though paid for in specie, whether such practices, or the exchanging of tobacco, fish, etc. for French wine, will most conduce to the true interest of the kingdom and its plantations? Why should British subjects be under a necessity of drinking worse wine than the neighbouring nations at four times the price?' This was the opposite view to that put forward by Steele. Undoubtedly French wines were infiltrating in some quantity during the last years of the war, and war-time difficulties had favoured the further progress of adulteration, but the Tories exaggerated, and there was still enough competition in the trade to prevent the deterioration of wines, which for a time accompanied the complete monopoly of port in later years. On one point they were definitely mistaken; the Portuguese were very determined on the subject and would not have allowed the duties on French wines to be equalized without abrogating the Methuen treaty.

The Portuguese, Spanish and Italian merchants had protested vigorously in 1710 that any bartering of French wines for Maryland and Virginia tobacco would be enough to ruin the Portuguese wine and fish trade and to drive Portugal to reintroduce the restrictions on the importation of English woollen cloth.[1] When under the influence of Bolingbroke the introduction of the treaty of commerce with France threatened the whole basis of the Methuen treaties, their arguments were strengthened. They were frequently set out in the *British Merchant*, the Whig periodical supporting the Portuguese trade. The *British Merchant* freely admitted that if the duties were reduced, Englishmen would prefer to drink claret, and left it to literary gentlemen to write up the excellence of port-wine in itself. *The British Merchant* confined itself to economic arguments in favour of the Portuguese trade and maintained that the benefits were such that English gentlemen should regard it as a patriotic duty to drink port-wine and to sacrifice

[1] House of Commons Journal 21st February 1710.

the gratification of their palates for the sake of the trade. In other words, as the poet put it:

> Be sometimes to your country true,
> Have once the public good in view;
> Bravely despise champagne at court
> And choose to dine at home on port.

It is noteworthy that the controversy was confined to port and claret. Nothing was said about the merits or otherwise of Spanish wines compared with French wines, or even of those of Lisbon or Madeira. Latterly Spanish wines had made great progress. In 1703, the first year of the war, only 345 tuns had reached London and the out-ports compared with 9,267 tuns of Portuguese wine. In two of the last years of the war, 1710 and 1712, the figures for London and the out-ports for Portuguese wines were 6,712 and 6,703 tuns and for Spanish wines 5,914 and 4,652 tuns. The merchants trading to Spain never feared for their cloth trade as the Portugal merchants did. They maintained that there was no need to make concessions to Spain, because Spain had no native textile industry to threaten the English sales of cloth. It was true that the Spanish industry had declined and it was a long time before the government's efforts to resuscitate it were successful. Therefore Spanish wines unlike Portuguese wines never became a subject of controversy linked to the fortunes of Whigs and Tories, and even of Hanoverians and Jacobites.

Towards the end of the reign of Queen Anne it looked as if the Tories would restore the trade in French wines. An act permitting their legal importation subject to certain conditions was indeed passed on 17th March 1711; it only had a modest effect on the customs returns but there was nevertheless a reaction in favour of claret, as was reflected in the popular plays of Suzanne Centlivre. In her play *Gotham Election* published in 1715 she described the behaviour of the inn-keeper Scaredouble, who was anxious to keep on the right side of his customers whether Whig or Tory. Asked by the election agent Friendly to bring the best wine his house afforded he replied: 'The best my house affords, ha, ha, ha, that is as you think it, Sir; now most of your gentry for the past vour [sic] years, do you mind, will touch nothing but French claret; there are some that like your port-wine still, but very few, and those of the poorer sort, as my barboard will bear witness.'

Friendly then tried to find out what Scaredouble's real inclinations were by saying, 'Bring such as you like yourself.' Scaredouble evaded this question by telling the bartender to bring up a bottle of the best lisbon wine, a wine which was acceptable to both Whig and Tory. In another scene Tickup, a Tory agent who hated a Whig, tried to draw a fellow-customer named Mallett by asking him what wine he would drink. When Mallett replied ' 'Tis all one to me, Sir', Tickup ordered a bottle of French red, and asked Mallett how he liked it, adding that he thought it was pretty good. Mallett replied, 'I think so too, Sir, but second thoughts is best.' This was perhaps an allusion to the sudden *volte-face* of Parliament in favour of port-wine.

The revival of claret was to be only temporary. For a time Italian wines stole some of the scene and, while Barcelona was in the hands of the allies, benefited by an increase of shipping facilities and of convoys from Livorno. Their import attained an appreciable total of 2,520 tuns in 1710 and helped to make up for the shortages of supply from other quarters. But in spite of the initiative of the Grand Duke of Tuscany in promoting the trade these wines, which did not travel well and required speedy transport, soon went out of fashion. Rhenish wines might have competed and were popular with the nobility, but no more than 500 tuns were ever imported and the future lay with Portuguese wines with Spanish wines coming in a good second. But while the field of the wine trade was growing narrower in England the prospects were widening somewhat elsewhere and British ships were beginning to carry wines all over the world.

The first new market for wines had been America, and for England the American colonies. In the earlier years they naturally followed the English fashions. In 1609 Captain John Smith in Virginia was drinking sack, but after the middle of the century French wines were the best liked and the cheapest. The taste for claret in the colonies perhaps persisted longer than in England, for although direct communications with France were few and were prohibited by the Navigation Act, the American customs were lax during most of the eighteenth century and some French wine still reached those who were prepared to pay for it.

On the other hand the relatively easy communications with the Iberian Peninsula, and still more so with the Atlantic islands which lay very near the direct course to America of sailing ships,

gave the Peninsular wines the advantage. By the end of the seventeenth century they had become a good deal cheaper than French
wines. In 1688 the official maximum price for claret was 8/- a
gallon, whereas madeira was 5/- and other Spanish and Portuguese
wines 4/-. Ships loading wines after the vintage in Spain or Portugal also faced winter weather at first, but once they were clear
of European waters they could count upon the trade winds to
take them safely and rapidly most of the way to their destination.
In addition canary, madeira, sherry and port travelled better than
the delicate French wines. So even the Virginians with their taste
for French fashions tended to turn to madeira.

The same factor encouraged the growth of the trade in salt fish
between England, America and the Peninsula, and in the salt for
curing the fish, which came from Portugal. The consumption of
salt fish in England had declined since early Tudor times. Various
laws aimed at arresting this decline failed in their object. People
in England ate less fish on account of the desuetude of the Friday
fast after the Reformation, but also because the standard of living
was rising and there was more meat available in the winter months.
In southern European countries good Catholics still ate fish on fast
days, and few of the common people could afford to eat meat on
any day. Little of the gold or silver from the New World reached
their pockets and in Spain the fast days numbered 120 days in
the year in Castile and 160 days in Aragon, while Saturday was
also a meatless day. So the English cod-ships, and soon the
American ones, did a good business plying a triangular trade
between England, Newfoundland and Portugal. Some ships made
as many as four direct voyages in the year between Newfoundland
and the Peninsula. They did not at first engage in other trade but
naturally took in ship's stores, including wine. In 1693 William
Bromley, an English visitor to Portugal, saw English ships loading
fruit and wine for the return voyage to America. They also took
Portuguese salt from Aveiro or Setubal and this was specifically
exempted from the restrictions of the Navigation Act. Sometimes
they had more wine than they needed in Newfoundland and they
brought it back to England. There was a tradition that the west
country firm of Newman brought back port-wine in 1679 and
found that the voyage had greatly improved it. There are some
contemporary records of wine entering England in this way; for
instance the ship's company of the *Ian Kendall* imported sixteen

gallons of port-wine to London from Jamaica in 1683.[1] Robert
Newman brought seven casks totalling 140 gallons for private use,
plus a further twenty gallons for sale, to Dartmouth from Newfoundland in his ship the *Margaret* in 1727; a year later entries
appeared in the port-books of small lots of Spanish wine coming
from Newfoundland. There is no reason why Robert Newman's
predecessors should not have done the same. Towards the end
of the eighteenth century the custom of taking port, sherry or
madeira to the East or West Indies to mellow them with a long
buffeting became very well-known.

The island trades began in a less casual way. In early Spanish
colonial days Canary wines were exported to the West Indies and
Mexico, and even over the Isthmus of Panama to Peru. The
Madeira trade began later, but Madeira wines were going to Brazil
in the sixteenth century and by the time of the English seaman
Barlow in the 1660s often travelled in English ships. Although
the trade in madeira was principally with America the special
mention of madeira in the 1660 English customs law suggests that
it was already well-known in England. By a special exemption
from the Navigation Law, madeira could be shipped in English
ships directly to America. This privilege was also extended to the
Azores. The founders of the Pennsylvania Company paid a tribute
to Madeira in their charter of 1693, giving as one of their aims
the cultivation of wines in America more generous than those of
Madeira. This aim was never achieved. Madeira became a favourite
wine in the colonies but faced little competition from native
growths. A good idea of the madeira trade can be gathered from
the correspondence between 1695 and 1714 of an English merchant
named Bolton in Madeira with his English principals. Most of the
wine went to America but some went to England. On 28th March
1695 William Bolton received in London by a warship three
quarter-casks; this was just a present, but in the same year a
merchant ship took three consignments totalling 188 pipes and
seven hogsheads. By 1700 shipments to the West Indies were
considerable; a small island like Nevis could take fifty pipes and
in 1701, in anticipation of the outbreak of war, Bolton thought it
was safe to reckon on Barbados absorbing 500 pipes. In 1702
there were consignments of 200 pipes for Antigua and 100 pipes
for Jamaica. Barbados also imported mainland Portuguese wine,

[1] London Port Book E 190/114/4 and 118/7.

for in 1704 Bolton mentioned a ship calling on its way to Barbados
with 200 pipes of lisbon on board. There is no mention of Bolton
shipping wine to Brazil, but in 1707 five large Portuguese ships
took 2,000 pipes, a quantity which caused an appreciable rise in
the market price in Madeira.

Bolton was only one of several English firms, and he estimated
the total production of madeira as 30,000 pipes. In 1707 he
reckoned that he had in October about 3,000 pipes of the last
year's vintage left; he used to rack the new wines in the New Year
and to begin to ship them in the spring. Although madeira had
such a good reputation for keeping he aimed to dispose of his
wines before the close of the year, that is about twelve months
after the vintage but no longer. His firm traded with the West
Indies and Virginia, also with New York, Boston and Philadelphia.

Bolton's estimate of 30,000 pipes gave Madeira an equivalent
production to the exports from the whole of the mainland of
Portugal. It is difficult to say whether this was an over-estimate
or not. Only half that figure was claimed in the mid-eighteenth
century, and although some other estimates were equally large,
there is no confirmation of them in any customs statistics of
receipt. But undoubtedly much wine was lost or used on board
ship, or failed in other ways to appear in the customs returns,
while some was consumed in the island itself or exported to
Portugal or Brazil. Probably Bolton's estimate was on the large
side, although the Madeira trade flourished, and so did that of
the Azores or Western Isles, which also sent occasional shipments
to England. In 1705 the French director of finances, Monsieur
Desmarets, received in France a couple of cases of wine from the
Azores and pronounced it to be choice and of good quality, so it
must have passed muster.

Wine followed the English flag to the East as well as to the West
Indies. A century earlier Tom Coryate had been delighted to find
sack to drink in Surat and from the beginning the ships of the
East Indies Company carried wine. They did not always call at
Madeira or stop long enough to take any cargo, but Bolton some-
times shipped consignments of forty to eighty pipes by them.

Some light on the East Indies trade at the turn of the century
is thrown by the papers of the *Mary Galley*, a ship built for a
London ship-owner named Thomas Bowrey in 1704. On her
maiden voyage to Calcutta and the Dutch East Indies in October

she was licensed to carry three chests of thirteen dozen quart bottles of claret. Actually she carried more, for five chests totalling a little more than sixty-four dozen were sold in Sumatra, while at least one more chest was disposed of in presents. Captain Talson, the commander of the *Mary Galley*, had intended to sell his liquor in Batavia in Java, but he was put off by the news that the market was glutted and took it to Fort York, Bencoolen, instead. He also had with him a stock of beer, which he succeeded in selling in Batavia though it was threatening to turn sour.

Thomas Bowrey, owner of the *Mary Galley*, evidently had some taste for wine and food, for he gave a dinner for the launching of the ship, for which he provided fifteen flasks of Florence and a gallon of rhenish. It is interesting to note that the claret was shipped to the Indies in bottles and not in casks. Italian wines were imported into England in flasks, often covered with straw like the chianti bottles of today, but it is usually accepted that other wines were kept in the cask until shortly before they were drunk. Nevertheless there are fairly frequent instances of wines being sold in bottles by the chest. In addition to the wine the *Mary Galley* carried for sale 121 'spires', wine glasses with spiral stems, which shows that there was a market for luxury products in the East Indies.

On the *Mary Galley* only an allowance of a daily quart of arrack was mentioned for the captain's table. However, for general consumption three tuns of beverage wine and three tuns of other wines were taken on board. These were purchased from Thomas Hammond, a Portugal merchant who was a part-owner of the ship. The interest of wine for the East Indies trade was also shown by the purchase of six leagers (300 gallons) of cape wine at Cape Town. Some of this was sent to England in twelve-gallon casks, but most of it was taken by the ship and sold at Bencoolen. Although little was heard of cape wine before the end of the eighteenth century in England, it was one of the earliest colonial wines to be exported. It shared this distinction with Peru, which began to grow enough wine for its own needs in the sixteenth century and even exported wine to Mexico until the Spanish government put a stop to it. At first wine was exported from Cadiz, regardless of cost, to the remotest places, so that one of the minor hauls of the Elizabethan seafarers was 300 tuns of wine, described as wine of Castile, found in 1586 by Thomas Candish buried in the sand near Arica in Chile. Later wine for local consumption was grown in Mexico as well as Peru, and the self-sufficiency of part of the Spanish main was one of the reasons why Spanish wines looked for new outlets in Europe. Cape wine was the only other colonial wine which was ever exported in sufficient quantities to be of commercial importance.

The name 'galley' borne by the *Mary Galley* draws attention to another development of some interest to the wine trade. Eighteenth-century galleys were designed to be fast sailers to enable them to outstrip enemy privateers and to carry valuable or perishable goods. They were built in fair numbers during the Nine Years War and the War of the Spanish Succession to meet the needs of those merchants who preferred to take a chance than to suffer the infinite delays which were the price of going in comparative safety with a convoy. Those ships were lightly built and narrow, and although they did not depend on oars they carried oars for use in an emergency. The *Mary Galley* carried eight large galley oars in addition to the smaller oars required for the ship's boat. Oars could be a great help in time of need, and on her maiden voyage the *Mary Galley* used them to escape from some French privateers she encountered off the Sussex coast.

Galleys carried a large crew and less cargo than the average ship and were therefore expensive to run. Their light build also made them vulnerable to bad weather. But they were speedy and easy to manoeuvre and in case of need could fall back on their oars to enter or leave an estuary or port or to make a little progress in calm weather. They could thus take a chance and sail without convoy in the hope of running through an enemy blockade. Where a cargo of wine was involved it was important to arrive quickly in order to minimize the risk of deterioration and if possible to catch the first of the season's market.

True galleys, in which oars played a major part, had remained longer in service in the Mediterranean, where it was always possible to hug the coast, winds were fitful and light in summer, and there were no tides to take ships in and out of port. The so-called galleys of the north in the early eighteenth century were usually quite small ships. The *Mary Galley*, though intended for a long ocean voyage, was only 141 tons. Her original specifications were for a length of 79 feet 6 inches by 21 feet 6 inches, but she was actually completed on beamier lines to measure 63 feet only along her keel with a width of 21 feet 6 inches as originally ordered. Such galleys were far from being real galleys, but they were narrower and lighter than other ships. Some larger ships called galleys were built for the British navy. The *Charles Galley* of 525 tons was an example. She was built in 1676 as a fourth-rater with a length of 122 feet and a width of 28 feet 6 inches. She was a fast sailer and at least until she was rebuilt in 1693 made good use of her oars. She used them in a light wind in the Channel and exercised with them in the Tagus. In 1687 she entered an Italian harbour with her oars and used them again for some hours off Cape Spartel, near the entrance to the Strait of Gibraltar, when the land breeze failed. After her refitting the oars were no more mentioned and in 1704 she had to be towed down Portsmouth harbour to join the fleet. The oars seem to have been abandoned, for she made no use of them when she was pursued in a very light wind by French galleys near the French coast and had to be towed by the ship's boat into the harbour of Villafranca. But she retained the sailing qualities of the new galley type and was constantly employed to carry urgent despatches. For instance in May 1704 she carried from Lisbon to Admiral Rooke's fleet off the Provençal coast the news that the French fleet from Brest was entering the Mediterranean. She also took Rooke's despatches with the news of the capture of Gibraltar to England.[1]

Clearly the galley type of ship was useful for the wine trade. Many such ships made speedy and profitable voyages. They were fast at sea and could steal in and out of estuaries and small harbours quickly and unobtrusively. Many venturing on their own made profitable voyages. Others were taken and retaken, and became the subjects of lengthy proceedings in the prize-courts. The navy disliked the galleys, because they were unamenable to convoy discipline and were always having to be rescued from enemy privateers, which meant trouble but no prize money. Despite the vigorous criticisms to which it was exposed the Admiralty on the whole did its best to provide an adequate programme of convoys. The Board of Trade consulted the various bodies of merchants about their needs and worked out a schedule with the Admiralty. There was a constant battle, not only for ships but for men, and the Admiralty was hard pressed. The merchants reported the number of men they needed for the various trades, West Indies, Baltic,

[1] Adm 51/184, Logbook of *Charles Galley*.

Mediterranean, etc., and tried to obtain for them exemption from being pressed. The navy kept their men on board to avoid losing them and raided merchant ships without mercy to obtain their essential crews. Seamen earned higher wages in the merchant service, which were scarcely offset by the occasional winnings of prize money in the navy. They did their utmost to avoid being pressed, though they deserted often enough from merchant ships too. The *Mary Galley* lost three out of her crew of 26 in her 1704/5 voyage and five in her next voyage. As regards the wine trade, there was in theory a dove-tailing of interests, for the season for loading wine was in the winter after the vintage, when the larger ships of war were in dock and their crews laid off. But it did not always work out that way, and while the navy was refitting there were fewer ships available for convoy duty. The convoys themselves gave rise to many complaints on account of the many delays and of the discipline they entailed. Merchant captains often angered the navy by ignoring orders, and captains of warships sometimes lost patience and abandoned their charges. Nevertheless, in spite of all the grumbling and difficulties the convoys operated pretty regularly, and although the nature of the wine trade tempted the individual to take a chance in order to deliver the goods before his competitors, its seasonal nature resulted in a number of ships being ready at the same time and this was convenient for a convoy programme.

Merchants carrying perishable goods had to take exceptionally heavy risks in time of war, but the demand for wine was always keen and the trade always proved very resistant to impediments. Except for a few ships of 300 or 400 tons going to the Mediterranean, wine ships were usually small, many of them of 100 tons or less. The six tuns of wine carried on the *Mary Galley* as stores was presumably a larger quantity than usual on account of the length of the voyage, but in southern latitudes wine replaced beer as an essential part of the sailor's rations, so the aggregate of beverage wines taken for this purpose was considerable. In the navy the usual ration was a pint a day, but the seamen seldom received as much as this and most pursers mercilessly watered the beverage down. However, in this way Portuguese wine became familiar to the English sailor at a time when the general consumption of wine in England was falling off. In the log books of the navy there were many references to wine being taken on board in amounts ranging from seven or eight butts on frigates to forty pipes or more on the larger ratings. A fleet could take a thousand or even two thousand tuns.

Towards the end of the succession war, even the defenders of Portuguese wines began to doubt whether they could hold their own against French wines. After peace had been concluded at Utrecht, a commercial treaty was made between Britain and France, and when this was ratified by Queen Anne on 24th March 1713 it seemed that the demise of Portuguese wines was assured. But the specific assent of Parliament was still required for the implementation of articles 8 and 9, in which the two countries reciprocally granted most favoured-nation treatment. The bill to approve the treaty passed its first reading without any difficulty, but although the Tories were anxious to have their claret at less expense and painted a glowing picture of the advantages to be won by a renewed trade with France, the commercial world, both Whig and Tory, began after consideration to make reservations and to feel that the Portuguese trade in the hand was worth more than the French trade in the bush. There were a number of interests which stood to lose by the competition of French products and these included not only the importers of Portuguese and Spanish wines but also the distillers, who were threatened by the importation of French brandy, and the silk manufacturers and others who handled products with which the French could compete. Trade was not confined to the Whigs, and even the country gentlemen, who were regarded as essentially Tory, were not unaffected, for they sold corn to the distillers and some of it for export to Portugal. The merchants trading to Portugal, Italy and Spain were up in arms and a flood of petitions against the bill poured into Parliament. The second reading passed by 202 votes to 135, but the opposition spread to unexpected quarters, including Sir Thomas Hanmer, the member for Suffolk, who had been regarded as Right-Wing Tory, possibly with Jacobite leanings. He explained that his constituents, many of whom were clothiers, had protested against the possible loss of their Portuguese trade, and that the interests of the silk and woollen industries and of the labouring classes must come first. Many felt like him and responded to his lead. In this way a number of Tory votes were won for the opposition and at the third reading the bill was thrown out by a majority of 194 votes to 185.

K

If this was the feeling of Parliament when the government was in the hands of the Tories and of Bolingbroke and all seemed set to favour the renewal of trade with France, it stood to reason that the death of Queen Anne and the coming of the Whigs to power would remove all doubts of the preference of the English people for the trade with Portugal. Da Cunha Brochado, the Portuguese minister while Luis da Cunha was absent as plenipotentiary at Utrecht, had been much tempted to use his final argument, the threat that if the preference for Portuguese wines guaranteed by the Methuen treaty was abolished, the restrictions on the imports of English woollen cloth would be reimposed. He found that he had no need to do so and congratulated himself on having re-frained, particularly as he had been tempted to play his last card, for there had been rumours that the approval of the treaty of commerce was linked with plans to bring over the pretender and to send to France discharged soldiers from Marlborough's army to help the building up of an invasion force. Brochado was jubilant at the upshot and wrote that all the fair hopes that the court had given to the people of the great advantages of their mysterious negotiation were turned to smoke, and they were left without a treaty of commerce, it being understood that it was better to have no treaty than to keep one which did so much harm to England and so much good to France. He added that the general joy ex-ceeded even that of the peace.[1]

This was probably a fair impression, though it was premature to say that the treaty had been cancelled. Defoe told Harley that a mistake in tactics had been responsible for the *volte-face*. If the government had not allowed the issue to become a party question and had bided their time, Parliament in its search for funds would automatically have taxed Portuguese wines and would have obliged the Portugal merchants to resign themselves to the treaty. Boling-broke did not in fact give up. He hoped to frame some revision of the 1654 treaty which would be agreeable to Portugal, and was still discussing the question with Brochado at the end of 1713. Since the Methuen treaty, the expansion of the output of the gold-mines of Brazil had introduced a new factor into the situation, which Brochado fully appreciated. Trade with Brazil was much more important than before, and English commercial interests were anxious to win an increased share of this by trading directly

[1] Coimbra MS 2974.

with Brazil, by the easing of the restrictions on British participation through Portugal and by the revocation of the prohibition of the export of Brazilian gold. These subjects offered scope for a fresh negotiation. Brochado reported to Lisbon that Portugal could not afford to apply the embargo on gold strictly, for the English and Dutch were hungry for gold, and if they could not acquire it by legitimate trading would be likely to take it by force. On the other hand they were not by nature conquerors. They would insist on favourable terms for their trade, but if they were allowed these, there need be no apprehension that they would lay hands on Brazil. Bolingbroke's alternative was swept away by the march of events and Portugal was able to continue as before. But Brochado's advice to go gently in the matter of the embargo on the export of gold was on the whole followed.[1]

Meanwhile a French delegation headed by de Fénélon, a deputy of the Bordeaux chamber of commerce, had been in England discussing the implementation of the treaty of commerce. They went home when articles 8 and 9 were rejected by the House of Commons, but later returned for a time at the invitation of Bolingbroke. The wine exporters of Bordeaux had been anxiously waiting for the upshot and had begun loading their wines in the expectation that they would sell them in England. But the government in Paris did not share the interest of Bordeaux. Matthew Prior, writing to Bolingbroke to console him for the set-back, was obliged to admit that the French were growing colder and were for the most part indifferent to the fate of articles 8 and 9. Even the citizens of Bordeaux were reconciled, for they diverted the wines intended for England to the United Provinces, and the increase of the Dutch market in the succeeding years did much to make up for the loss of English trade, to which in fact for over twenty years they had become accustomed. In 1721 the export of Bordeaux wines amounted to 34,138 tuns, more than had ever gone to England except in the early fifteenth century. Most of this wine was consumed in the Low Countries but a substantial part went on to the Baltic, first in Dutch then in Scandinavian ships.

Some historians down to Lecky in Victorian times thought that a great opportunity had been lost, but it is unlikely that the

[1] Coimbra MS 2974. Da Cunha Brochado to Diogo de Mendonça Corte Real, May, June 1713, and C.O. 391/24 for Bolingbroke correspondence.

French would ever have in practice allowed the free entry of English manufactures. On the other hand the Methuen treaty, which had counted for little during the war, now came into its own. The English even tended to exaggerate its benefits, and although the Portuguese complained, they realized that it was bound up with England's commitment to respect the integrity not only of Portugal, which other interests might have obliged her to do in any case, but also of Brazil, which could easily have been torn apart otherwise by the French, English and Dutch.

CHAPTER VII

Wine in England in Early Hanoverian Times

THE reign of George I was a time of peace and prosperity in which the wine trade shared. In 1728, the first year of George II, 29,956 tuns were imported, a figure which was not exceeded until the end of the century. The port-wines, which predominated, did not however progress in quality as they did in quantity. On the contrary a dark age was beginning for wine, during which, as under prohibition in the United States, taste languished and liquor was only valued for its intoxicating qualities. This was remarkable in view of the increasing refinement of the age and the development of all the appurtenances of drinking. It was true that the court no longer led the fashion. If it had done so there might have been a vogue for German wines which were less and less imported. The Georges drank French wine too, as did the aristocrats who led the fashion, but after reaching in the first year of peace in 1713 a comparatively high figure of 2,551 tuns, French wines gradually declined and after 1728 less than 1,000 tuns were imported annually. The value of trade was however much higher proportionally because these wines imported by a limited set were very expensive. Also, as long as any widespread taste for French wines lingered, the smugglers did their best to remedy the situation. As late as 1738 a writer named Joshua Gee claimed that they brought in not only brandy but great quantities of claret, which near the coast could be bought for 4/- a gallon. Possibly this happened temporarily and locally, but the better-class Englishman would scarcely have paid 5/- a gallon for port if good claret had been available cheaper. The seizures by the customs, which in aggregate were large, revealed a good smuggling trade in brandy, tobacco and silks, and some wines, but not very many of them. Despite the influence of the great aristocratic houses and the growth of a numerous middle class only too anxious to imitate their betters, the taste for good wines became rarer and rarer.

Nevertheless, good old wines were not entirely unknown. They existed in classical times and their memory was preserved in the Rhineland where they matured in the enormous tuns which were a source of local pride. In a German anthology appears a saying dating from 1560, 'avoid new wine like the plague', and in the fifteenth century the Czech traveller Rozmital, the same who left an account of a possible early ancestor of port, saw a huge vat belonging to the Bishop of Angers, where wine had been kept for fifty years. Much later, in 1678, John Locke saw a vat holding 200 tuns at Marmoutier, also on the Loire. The wine in such vats was refreshed annually with young wines as the *soleras* of Jerez came to be. Most of the vats were ecclesiastic, for only monks and canons had the labour and the leisure to give such constant care to their wines. Otherwise the sweet wines from the Levant were the first as a class to attain often a certain maturity. To stand the long voyage to northern Europe they had to be durable. They kept this characteristic when they or similar wines began to be grown nearer at hand in Spain and Sicily, and then in Madeira and the Canaries. Canary won an early reputation for maturing, and Queen Anne already paid more for old madeira than for young. Some old wines were also prized in Spain much earlier, for Andrea Bacci in his history of wines published in Latin in 1596 spoke of Spanish fathers laying down wines for the coming of age of their sons.

Occasional references to age in other wines are found at the beginning of the eighteenth century. King William's five-year-old champagne has been mentioned. In 1706 Robert Walpole sometimes bought old burgundy at 4/- a bottle and this was the most expensive wine he had. He also bought Hocheimer, and in 1704 the British resident at Hanover, Poley, wrote to his colleague Henry Davenant at Frankfurt to enquire after this vintage, saying 'if it is not easy to get Bacharach I leave it to you to choose a Hocheimer of 4/5 years old'.[1] In 1706 George Granville, later Lord Lansdowne, wrote to a friend to suggest a meeting with a

[1] Add. MSS 34727. Poley to Daventry, 1st August 1704.

young poet, newly inspired, actually the eighteen-year-old Alexander Pope, saying also 'I can give you no Falernian that has outlived twenty consulships, but I can offer you a bottle of good old claret that has seen two reigns'. A little later the saying that the four most desirable things in life were 'old wood to burn, old wine to drink, old friends to talk with, and old books to read' was attributed to Lord Bathurst in conversation with Lady Suffolk, but it has been credited with equal probability to St Evremond, who died in 1703.

There is little doubt that old wines, though not unknown, were rare, and were always matured in the cask, or nearly always, though Levant and Mediterranean wines were early shipped in bottles because wood for casks was scarce where they were grown. But the first wines to be kept commonly for longer than two seasons were port-wines. As soon as brandy began to be added to them at the time of the vintage they needed to be mellowed before they were palatable. This process only became common in the second half of the eighteenth century so that by the end of the century most port-wines were at least three years old. Maturing wine in the bottle, particularly port and claret, was unusual before the nineteenth century. Glass bottles were in common use in Holland in the early seventeenth century but in the time of Pepys, and indeed later, they were made of dark coloured glass and were squat and tubby articles with long necks. Their shape saved them from being easily knocked over, and they could be quite ornamental, but they resembled decanters rather than wine bottles as we know them. In the eighteenth century their necks became shorter and they became onion-shaped, as Hogarth depicted them. In his picture of an election feast he showed a number of such bottles with white collars round their necks to describe their contents. These were required, as the colour of the wine could not be seen through the dark glass; these labels evolved into the wine labels of enamel or silver still used today. Jonathan Swift possessed some and mentioned them in his will.

The early bottle with its long neck looked not unlike a chianti bottle. It may well have been derived first from Italy. About 1690 bottles with shorter necks came into use. In the days of long-necked bottles and early corks it was easier to crack a bottle by breaking off the neck than to risk damaging the wine in the course of extracting the cork. Swift in his *Directions to Servants* ridiculed

clumsy butlers who had not yet learnt the proper use of a corkscrew and broke them by using them to nick the bottle's neck.
The term 'cracking' a bottle survives; the practice has its merits,
for it ensures a clean break and a clean wine with no cork in it.
The author has seen it used for a very old bottle of perhaps pre-
phylloxera port from the cellar of the Portuguese descendant of
an old Hamburg Oporto firm.

Prototypes of the modern claret bottle with a marked shoulder
and almost straight sides were made in 1713 at the time of the
Treaty of Utrecht, but did not come into general use before the
end of the century. It is probably an exaggeration to say that wine
could never be matured in the old type of bottle because it could
not be laid on its side. Even Pepys spoke of the wines old and new
ranged in bottles in the cellar of his friend Povey. Italian wines,
which did not last long, but also sherries and other Spanish wines,
which sometimes did, were imported in flasks or bottles with flat
sides, and these would have presented no difficulty. But other
types of bottle, though less convenient, could also be kept on their
sides in frames or in sand or straw, or in niches in a wall, or in
running water. From the mention of cisterns Povey may have
used the last method. John Houghton in 1683 spoke of bottles of
cider being matured in this way, laid on their sides so that the corks
were kept damp. King William's five-year-old champagne was
bottled, and Swift in 1730 spoke of his friend, the Rev. John
Walsh, who always kept a hogshead of the best claret in bottles
well corked and laid upon their sides. Normally wine was bottled
at a later stage, when it was thought to be fit for drinking, but
some wine was kept in the bottle longer. On this point one can
quote Swift again. He was not perhaps so great a connoisseur of
wine as he liked people to believe, but he reflected the current
ideas in Dublin, where in the 1720s good wine could still be more
easily got than in England, and the standards of England's
Augustan age lingered longer. Among the wines in his cellar was
hermitage imported from Rouen at some expense. He had a
disappointment with one consignment which turned sour, but the
next lot, though not ready to drink for two years, improved steadily,
and after seven years Swift still had a few bottles which tasted
better than ever.

However, the importation into England of wines in bottles,
other than Italian wines, which in any case had fallen out of

fashion, was prohibited by an act passed in 1728. This measure was intended to put a stop to smuggling and also prohibited the importation of wine in small boats or in containers smaller than sizeable casks. In later years a few bottles seem to have been allowed in for private importers, but the severe restrictions hampered the movement of wine in bottles and the development of the bottle as an instrument for maturing wine. But in the latter part of the century there are references to port-wine being carried in hampers and bottles from one coastal port to another. The heavily fortified port-wine was scarcely drinkable until it had mellowed, and this led to a general belief that no wine was really good until it had been kept for some years. No doubt some wine matured incidentally in bottles before the practice arose of putting it expressly into bottles for the purpose.

A book published by Claude Arnoux in 1728 gives some idea of how far enlightened wine lovers had got in maturing wines in the early part of the century. Arnoux spent some time in London tutoring the sons of a Mr H. J. Freeman and he wrote his book in the hope of popularizing the wines of his native Burgundy in England. He spoke of the care that was given to the preparation of burgundy. Only one type of grape, the round black 'noirine' was used. The grapes were not picked before the dew was dry, and required to be pressed carefully in three stages of two hours each with an interval of six hours between the pressings. They were matured in casks, from which the excess was allowed to escape from time to time, but were also put into small bottles in which the progress of the wine could be followed. He divided the burgundies into three classes, *vins de premier*, *vins de garde* and white wines. The *vins de premier* such as Volnay, which he described as the best wine from Champagne, mostly lasted for only a year, though Pommard lasted a little longer and Beaune could last for two years. The *vins de garde*, such as Nuits, which he said had been a favourite of Louis XIV, were rough at first but had the reputation of lasting. He rated Chambertin as the best of burgundies, and said it could be drunk up to the age of six years.

Arnoux recommended Chassagne as a *vin de premier* which could stand travel well and could be safely left in bottles. He went so far as to recommend that the wine should travel in the bottle rather than in the cask, saying it could be sent overland to Calais in carts carrying 1,000 bottles. The cost for Volnay would be £20

the queue (according to Henderson the queue of burgundy was
108 gallons, of champagne 72·6 gallons; other accounts make it
larger) and £13 for freight, so would cost only 14-15 sols (about
1/-) the bottle c.i.f. London. He thought that the wine sent by
cart would travel better in bottles and in any case the wine from
Beaune should be bottled, but if sent in the cask it should be sent
to Auxerre, a journey of only ninety miles, whence it could be
shipped to Rouen by water.

Something should be said at this stage about the development
of corks. Corks were the natural corollary to the glass bottle, but
it seems unlikely that such a useful substance was not used in
the countries of its growth as a stopper before bottles were made
of glass. Shakespeare referred quite often to corks and Celia told
Rosalind to take the cork out of her mouth, so that she could
drink her tidings. The poet clearly had a bottle in mind, but his
phrasing suggests that his cork was to staunch as much as to contain. The question is confused by the existence of two similar
words 'cork' and 'caulk' with converging meanings but different
origins. According to the Oxford Dictionary the word 'cork' is
derived from a Latin word meaning the bark of the cork tree, the
work 'caulk' from a different word meaning to tread, and so to
stop up and in particular to stop up the seams of a ship by driving
in oakum. Shakespeare perhaps had the northern nautical usage
first in mind. Indeed, early references to cork mention it as being
used for floats for fishing nets rather than as stoppers for bottles.
On the other hand early bottles, whether of glass or of some other
material, were often caulked not with corks but with wisps of tow
soaked in oil and capped with sealing wax. Wooden stoppers and
of course glass ones in the earliest bottles or phials were also
common. However, a comic pamphlet entitled *Philacothonista*,
published in 1635, described corks shooting out of a number of
beer bottles, which indicates that corks were already sometimes
used for stopping bottles closely. Apothecaries used corks for the
small bottles in which they sold cordials or liqueurs, and the noble
family of Russell were ordering corks for their wine bottles before
the Restoration. Most of the corks at first were the long tapering
corks used for loose bottling, and Dr Lister, describing the wines
of Paris in 1698, said that most of them were loose bottled. This
meant that some of them were not loose bottled, and we know
from John Houghton's *Collected Letters*, dating from 1693, that

cider was put into close corked bottles, for he said that cider could be kept until it came to the strength of canary, if the bottles were laid on their sides so that the corks swelled in them. He also recommended that French wines should be kept well bunged, and although the first edition of his letters was published in 1693, the earlier letters were dated 1683 and were based on the works of James Worlidge, a recognized authority on gardening who flourished from 1669 to 1698 and recommended that bottling was the only way to keep cider. As early as the 1630s the records of the East India Company mentioned that cider, which came from France at that time as much as from the west country, was normally matured for twelve months before it was fit for drinking.

Further evidence of the development of the close-corked bottle for the keeping as well as the serving of liquor, whether wine, cider or beer, was given by the first appearance of the corkscrew. The late Herbert Warner Allen found a scholarly reference to some prototype of this splendid implement in the Dark Ages, but the corkscrew as we know it, or bottlescrew as it was at first called, made its appearance at the end of the seventeenth century. There is no reference to the king possessing a bottlescrew in the seventeenth century, and the first reference so far found to anyone buying one was to the purchase of a bottlescrew by a Devonshire doctor in 1696. They must have been quite common by then, for only four years later Edward Ward in the *London Spy* gave a good description of the use of a bottle screw which is worth quoting. He was describing a dinner party at which two country parsons and a Quaker were present.

'At last we came to a good-looking soldier's bottle of claret, which at least held half a pint extraordinary, but the cork was drove in so far that there was no opening it without a bottle-screw. Several attempted with their thumbs to remove the stubborn obstacle, but no one could effect the difficult undertaking; upon which the donor of the feast: "What, is nobody amongst us so provident a toper as to carry a bottlescrew about him." One cried "No", another "No, poize on't, he had left his at home"; a third never carried one, and so t'was concluded no screw was to be had, the parsons being all this time silent; at last says the lord of the feast to his man, "Here, take it away, though I protest," says he, "it is a fine bottle, and I'll warrant the wine is better than ordinary, it's so well corked. But what shall we do with it? We cannot open it. You must take it down, I think, tho I vow 'tis a great deal of pity, but prithee bring us up some more bottles that may not puzzle us so." The oldest and wisest of the parsons having observed the copious dimensions of the bottle and well knowing by experience that sound corking is always an advantage to good liquor, "Hold, friend," says he to the servant going out with the bottle, "I believe I may have a little engine in my pocket that may unlock the difficulty", and fumbling in his pockets, after he had picked out a common prayer-book, an old comb-case full of notes, a two-penny nutmeg grater, and made a great move of such kind worldly necessaries, at last he came to the matter, and out he brings a bottlescrew, which provoked not a little laughter throughout the whole company. "Methinks, friend," says the Quaker, "that a common prayer-book and a bottlescrew are improper companions, not fit to lodge in the pocket together. Why doest thou not make thy breeches afford them separate compartments?" To which the parson made answer: "Since devotion gives comfort to the soul and wine in moderation preserves the health of the body, why not a book that instructs in the one and an instrument that makes way for the other, allowed as well as the soul and body to bear one another company." "But methinks," says the Quaker, "a bottlescrew in a minister's pocket is like *The Practice of Piety* in the hand of a harlot. The one no more becomes thy profession than the other does her." To which the parson replied: "A good book in the hand of a sinner, and an instrument that does good to a whole society in the hand of a clergyman I think are both very commendable and I wonder why a good man should object against it here." '

From this story it is clear that in 1700 corkscrews were a new fashion, but that the advantages of a good cork to preserve and mature the wine as well as to prevent it from spilling in a bottle carried in the pocket were well understood. All the same, the cork described could not have been flush with the neck of the bottle; it must have projected a little for otherwise no one would have tried his thumb on it. Elsewhere Ward described the train-bands marching through the city, the tall men with pikes and the short men with guns, but everyone of them with a quartern of Nantz brandy in his pocket which he occasionally fingered to see if the cork was as close as could be. This too sounds as if the tightness of the corks was subject to doubt, but corks and bottles were evidently evolving and there was no talk of cracking the famous claret bottle, so it probably had a short neck.

A generation later a bottlescrew still seems to have been thought of as something rather special. Swift had a little gold runlet with a bottlescrew, which he kept in his pocket and could produce to open a bottle of claret. He valued it enough to mention it in his will together with silver and enamel bottle labels, which he bequeathed to his friend the Earl of Orrery.

Swift during his later years was a good example of a moderate drinker, who yet took pride in his cellar. He took a daily bottle of wine for his health's sake but seldom more. He was able to afford French wine because it was comparatively cheap in Dublin, and although his habit of putting sugar in his wine seems odd it was usual in his day. On the whole he gave an example of civilized drinking. Sometimes at Dr Delany's he would drink no more than half a pint, but if he liked his company he would sit for many hours over it, 'unlocking all the springs of policy, learning, true humour, and inimitable wit'. Although it was the age of Robert Walpole and Lord Bolingbroke, and of topers who equalled them, excess was not universal. Another friend of Swift, Mrs Pendarves, described the innocent gaities of their literary set among whom she shone under the name of Aspasia. She was to marry Dr Delany and to survive to become in her old age a favoured friend of George III and an object of veneration because she had once known Swift. She spoke of a profusion of 'peek and booze' at her parties, of mulled wine, a variety of liquor and the finest sillabub she had ever tasted. But conversation and music and a little dancing, but not drinking, were the high points. Mr Wesley played the harpsichord and on another occasion they entertained Handel.

Swift told Aspasia that in the old days in London he had roughed it without horses, servants or conveniences, and had made shift with port-wine or porter's ale to save charges. Actually in those days he had confided to Stella that champagne and burgundy did not agree with him and he preferred a little Portuguese wine. As dean of St Patrick's he changed his tune. In his letters to his wine-drinking friends such as Lord Bathurst or Sheridan there was little mention of port-wine, though he did suggest once that when there was a cold wet summer in France the wines from the warmer countries such as Spain and Portugal were better than French wines. But most of the talk was about French wines, and when Sheridan asked him to dinner and described the wines he would offer, there was no mention of port or lisbon. Sheridan spoke of Tokay costing a pistole (18/- or so) a quart, Margaux red as a ruby, Lachryma Christi, Côte Rôti, and Cyprus. Sack still figured on the list, but it is not clear whether canary or sherry were meant. Such was the range of a good cellar in Dublin about 1730 and perhaps an indication of what an English gentleman would still have liked to offer if conditions had been easier.

In England Spanish wines were still well to the fore and still more so in Scotland. Scotland was a poor country and perhaps smuggled more than paid customs duty, but in these years it took over 1,000 tuns of Spanish wine, about 90% of its total imports of wine. In London the city companies, who were a conservative body, were faithful to canary and still gave it pride of place at their dinners though its general consumption had much declined. But their staple wine was already port. The Haberdashers used to buy an annual pipe of what was already described as old red port, paying for it a price ranging from £33 in 1729 to £38 in 1733 and £32 in 1734.[1] They also served white port and lisbon which cost a little more than the red port. Unlike most of the city companies they did not serve canary or rhenish or sherry or mountain, though they did in 1729 buy some expensive palm-wine at 8/- a gallon which could be counted as canary. They seldom bought claret. This contrasted with the choice of a great nobleman, such as the Earl of Bristol, at the same period. He spent £276 on claret, champagne and burgundy, much smaller amounts on Spanish wines, and £115 on port, madeira and white lisbon. For modest households French wine had become too expensive. In 1738 for instance, Sarah Bynge Osborne, a country gentlewoman, described the arrival of the great Winchester waggon with a hogshead of two-year-old port-wine for herself and her mother. She hoped it would serve, as the wine from Southampton was usually good, and if it did she would order more. She liked to have the best wines possible, but she could not afford to pay for the more expensive ones. A little earlier the Purefoys, another county

[1] Archives of the Haberdashers Company.

family, were buying the best port-wine and paying a good price for it of 7/- a gallon. But in 1740, the last year before the war with Spain, they were still buying as much canary, sack and mountain as red port. The restriction on bottles apparently did not apply to canary, for it arrived in pear-shaped bottles, wrapped in straw, called bettes, which sometimes burst. The mountain came in a cask and was usually bottled some time before drinking, but on one occasion it was already brisk and had to be drunk at once. Both canary and mountain, as advertised in 1731 in *Reed's Journal*, were often matured for three or four years and were then able to command a higher price.

Port-wine was also often advertised at a higher price because it was two years old. This could mean that it had begun as a naturally generous wine or that it had been fortified. Strongly fortified wine often needed to be kept longer than two years to become palatable. By now the tradition of port-wine was well established and in 1730 even the Portuguese geographer Antonio de Oliveira Freire, following the fashion, though as a Lisbon man he had probably never been near Oporto, talked of the generous wine of the Douro, the ambrosia of the north. In England port-wine had been adopted by the Whigs as a symbol of the solid virtues of old England to be opposed to French fripperies and Jacobite treason, but it was now coming to stand for the establishment whether Whig or Tory. Even Pope, who was a Tory, a Roman Catholic and no tippler, followed the fashion. In 1725 he wrote from Twickenham to his learned friend Humphrey Wanley in London to ask him to send him twelve quarter-casks of good and wholesome port-wine, such as they used to drink together at the Genoa Arms.[1] In spite of the outcry against the tavern wines some port was evidently good enough. Hogarth, who painted so many convivial scenes, appreciated port very much. On his famous excursion to Rochester a high point was the splendid meal eaten at Gravesend. It consisted of 'a dish of soles and flounders with crab sauce, a calve's head stuffed and roasted, ye liver fryed and the other appurtenances minced, a leg of mutton roasted, with good small beer and excellent port'. Port-wine inspired conviviality and good talk and had become the favourite of dons and clergymen. Richard Cumberland left a picture of the drinking of dons in his amiable portrait of his old schoolmaster of Bury St Edmund's school, who

[1] Add MSS 4163 fo. 100, from Pope to Wanley, 1st July 1725.

loved his friend and had no antipathy to the bottle. He liked to prime himself with priestly port. He used to hold a kind of public day to which his friends and neighbours resorted. On that day he drank a bottle of port and played a game of backgammon after which he came in gaiety to evening school for one hour only. At a higher academic level the famous character and Homeric scholar Richard Bentley was a lover of port. Pope celebrated it with a verse and a delicate allusion:

> As many quit the streams that murmuring fall
> To lull the sons of Margaret and Clare Hall
> Where Bentley late tempestuous wont to sport
> In troubled waters but now sleeps in port.

So much for the legend of port, first set up by the Whigs, which was becoming a truly national institution. The tradition of port as a generous but natural wine was still preserved, and though port as sold to the tavern trade tended to be more and more fortified or adulterated, a more natural wine continued to be purveyed by the private trade to the more select and favoured customers.

The fortification of wine was not anything new, though the process by which port-wine was fortified during the vintage by the addition of brandy to arrest fermentation was a new development. The adoption of the method by the Oporto Factory is often ascribed to the year 1727, when an association of shippers was founded to consider what could be done to improve the trade. There is not much contemporary evidence to confirm this story, which became current later. There was probably some basis for it, as the shippers had to face the serious problem of supplying a public with an increasing taste for stronger wine from sources which were inadequate. The primary reason for adding the brandy was to arrest fermentation and to preserve a sufficient proportion of the natural grape sugar, which was high in the Upper Douro grapes but was rapidly lost if fermentation was not arrested. By this means a body of stabilized wine was obtained with which cheaper wines from elsewhere could be blended. Applied with discretion the method had merit, but it was easily abused and not yet sufficiently understood. The addition of brandy during the first fermentation was a different matter to the additions made at later stages to strengthen the wine, which had always been made and still continued to be made after the wine reached Oporto or

in England. Various forms of adulteration, blending and treatment had always been practised.

The taste for brandy in England dated from at least a century
back and tended to increase. There were complaints of the abuse
of brandy drinking in the reign of Charles II, particularly at
Dulwich where the citizens went to drink the waters but were apt
to drink brandy in addition. The use of spirits was such an every-
day habit that it came in for comparatively little mention, but
there are many incidental references. Tettersell, who captained
the ship in which Charles II escaped from Shoreham to Dieppe,
heartened himself with a bottle of spirits as well as the clean shirt
which warned his wife that he was taking no common passenger.
Pepys made no mention of keeping spirits in his house but he
sometimes resorted to their use. On a crucial occasion when he
had to defend his administration in the House of Commons he
related that on his way down to the House he dropped in at Mrs
Hewlett's and took half a pint of mulled sack followed by a dram
of brandy. With the warmth of the brandy he found himself in
much better order as to courage truly and spoke for four hours
to such effect that the king complimented him and many members
said he was fit to be Solicitor-General.

Even in abstemious Portugal alcoholism due to brandy became
an evil among the peasants of the Upper Beira, where no doubt
production increased to supply Oporto and the Douro. In England
whets of brandy were a common habit at all times of the day and
in polite circles also became a female weakness. Every large house
had its still-room, where the lady of the house made herb wines.
These were often harmless enough but they could be potent. So
when the ladies were banished from the dining-room to leave
their lords to serious drinking the ladies were not left entirely
without resources. For sociable drinking they had chocolate,
coffee and tea, but some of them acquired a taste for stronger
liquors and progressed from their still-room wines to usquebaugh
and exotic pick-me-ups. In early times the apothecaries sold sweet
wines and after their dispute with the grocers' company and the
distillers' company at the beginning of the seventeenth century they
kept the right to sell medicines and drugs. These included ratafia
and the original port-a-port. A discreet way to buy strong liquor
was to visit an apothecary, as it was in later days to patronize a
grocer or to have the bootleg hooch delivered at the back door.

L

Great ladies such as the Duchess of Grafton and Hortense Mancini kept a bottle of usquebaugh by their bedside. The Earl of Galway used to send Hortense whiskey from Ireland. Such foibles did not escape comment. Edward Ward described a dram-drinking lady of fashion in *Adam and Eve Stripped of her Furbelows.* 'It would make a man smile to behold her figure in a front box. Her twinkling eyes by her afternoon drams of ratafia and cold tea sparkle more than her pendants. Her closet is always well stored with juleps and restoratives and strong waters as an apothecary's shop or a distiller's laboratory, and she herself is so notable a housewife in the art of preparing them that she has a larger collection of chemical receipts than a Dutch mountebank. As soon as she rises she must have a Salitary Dram to keep her stomach from the cholick, a whet before she eats to procure appetite, a plentiful dose for concoction, and to be sure a bottle of brandy under her bedside for fear of fainting in the night.'

In the male world, when they were not whets, spirits were mainly consumed in the form of toddy or punch; they were not offered for themselves in quite the same way as wine or beer. The same restrictions which shut out French wines in favour of port substituted native spirits made of grain or colonial rum for French brandies. It happened that the country gentlemen had more corn than usual at their disposition. There were only three bad harvests between 1715 and 1730 and there was enough grain to export to Portugal as well as to support thriving distilleries and breweries. It was a prosperous time for the whole country and even the labouring man need not have gone short of his daily bread. Unfortunately the surplus of corn tended to go to the distiller rather than to the baker. Even so matters might have gone on well enough if the distilling trade had been controlled, but upon payment of a low excise duty any man could set himself up as a distiller and sell spirits without hindrance. The small operators did not make high-grade spirits from malt as the big distillers did, but used all manner of ingredients to make vile liquor. By 1726 a committee of the justices of the peace was complaining that gin was being retailed by weavers and chandlers in one house in five in some London parishes and was causing misery and pauperization. Although the industrial age is not usually reckoned to have begun before the end of the century, working men were already pouring into London and the larger towns in search of employment. Their prospects and their average wage were perhaps slightly better than they had been before, but whereas their subsistence had often been paid largely in kind, they now worked away from home for a weekly wage. Their housing was perhaps no worse than it had been in a rural slum, but no longer afforded room for a pig or a vegetable patch. They received their wages all together at the end of the week in the neighbourhood of a ginshop or sometimes actually on licensed premises. Finding themselves among friends, with money in their pockets and little alternative occupation or distraction, they naturally turned to the nearest tavern or drink-shop.

For practical rather than for moral or humanitarian reasons there was an outcry against the demoralization of the working classes. Hogarth painted a lurid picture of Gin Lane, but it was the loss of strength to work for their betters or to fight for their country which struck the governing classes as important. There was a move to subject the liquor trade to control but there were powerful vested interests involved to oppose any increase in the excise duties on spirits. If Walpole's Excise Bill of 1733 had been successful, it might have brought about an improvement. In the first instance his plan aimed only at transferring the control of certain imports from the customs to the excise so that the duties would be paid by the vendor in the form of an excise tax rather than by the importer in customs duties. Walpole believed that his new system would be more economical, efficient and lucrative, and would help to bring smuggling under control, for the division of powers between the customs and the excise, and the keen rivalry between the two departments, widened the loopholes for the entry of contraband. He planned to apply his scheme in the first instance to tobacco but had in mind to extend it to wines and brandies afterwards. He hoped to reconcile the country gentlemen to an increase of the excise duty on spirits by convincing them that any loss to the distillers would be offset by gains in the sale of beer and perhaps in the Portugal trade and the sale of port-wine. But for its administration the Excise Act required the grant of increased powers to the excise officers to enable them to carry out their duties of inspection. They would probably have to be given licence to enter private houses in their searches for contraband. The possibility of such an infringement of their liberties was utterly repugnant to the electorate. The opposition roused against

Walpole's proposals was so vehement that they had largely to be shelved. Some steps were taken to restrain the small distillers but these largely failed and it was not until the 1760s that the abuses of the gin trade began gradually to be brought under control and to diminish.

It was mainly the lowest classes who were the consumers of gin, and gin did not compete directly with port-wine, though the general habit of drinking spirits and the popularity of colonial rum, which was imported at a comparatively low rate of duty, did so. Also the taste for spirits affected generally that for wines and encouraged the fortification of wines. This was a general phenomenon which also had an effect on claret. Claret was often blended with strong Spanish Beni Carlo or with hermitage or even fortified. Port-wine was however the greatest sufferer, and in spite of its popularity informed opinion still held that port could not maintain its place in the English market without the support of a preferential rate of duty. This was the opinion in 1727 of Arthur Stert, one of the most esteemed members of the Lisbon Factory and one of a west-country family with members resident in Oporto. A few years earlier, in 1715, the Portuguese minister in London, da Cunha Brochado, had expressed a similar view. He had been receiving a number of complaints that both the English customs duties and the Portuguese export duties were too high. He reported to Lisbon that he considered the complaints to be unjustified. He said that the Portuguese dues were very modest and in England, though Portuguese wines had formerly been classified as sweet wines and had paid higher duties, they were now favourably treated and had no prospect of being given a further advantage to enjoy the same preference over Italian and Spanish wines that they already had over French wines. He blamed the Portuguese growers for charging too much and for not taking enough pains with the quality of their wines. For this reason he had found that no guest at his table had ever asked for Portuguese wine a second time.[1] One must make allowance for the fact that Brochado like most ambassadors had formed his tastes in Paris and that those who frequented diplomatic circles were inclined to be snobbish and in any case were glad of an opportunity to enjoy French wines, which when they had to pay duty, were very expensive, rather

---

[1] Coimbra MS 2974. Da Cunha Brochado to Diogo de Mendonça Corte Real. April/July 1715.

than the port they could have every day. But it is true that both growers and shippers in Portugal tended to be corrupted by easy money, and that while good wine was short great liberties could be taken with the tavern trade. Wine drinking was seeping a little downwards in the social scale, but the further decline of French wines shows that apart from their cost, the taste for them was being forgotten.

The Hanoverian court did not lead the fashion but it reflected international taste, and it is interesting to find out what George I and George II were drinking. As might be expected they were fond of hock and moselle, but these wines were bought abroad and were not charged in the English accounts, so that the wines figuring most in them were French wines. Claret headed the list with 140 hogsheads in 1719/20 and was already listed under the names of the famous growths of Pontac, Laiet [sic] and Latour. The wines next most consumed were palm-wine, thirty-four hogsheads, and champagne, thirty-one hogsheads. The other French wines named were hermitage, Côte Rôti, burgundy and Frontignan. The white wine, of which only four hogsheads were bought, was probably also French. Sherry accounted for only fourteen hogsheads. Sack was considered good enough to be given as a present to the King of Prussia for a value of £170, but was not a favourite.[1] There is a curious reference to German sacks, so perhaps a rhenish substitute was preferred. Presumably port-wine was drunk by the underlings but there is no mention of it or indeed of any Portuguese wine except a few bottles of madeira. Lisbon, though going out of fashion, still had a good reputation. A poem of the time entitled *Lament for an Empty Cellar* by Leonard Welstead and dated 1725 confirms the picture of wines in vogue given by the Lord Steward's book and fills it out a little more.

> The cellar; rather say the frame
> That but usurps a cellar's name
> Lo! a sad void! and void of cheer
> No Bellarmine, My Lord, is here;
> Eliza none at hand to reach,
> A Betty called in common speach!
> Nor muscats, nor Frontignan's treasure
> To ensnare kind girls to pleasure;

[1] L.S. 13/267.

Nor Margou, stored in priestly cells
That on the palate gratefully dwells;
Nor yet the grape matured by suns
O'er glittering lands where Tagus runs
Is here; Pontac, nor Hermitage,
In rusty bottles, pledge of age!
Nor Cyprus soft, the lovers balm
Is here; nor vine surnamed the palm,
That does to mind bright Windsor call!
But all is blank and empty all.

A Bellarmine was a pot-bellied jug called after a cardinal of
that name. An Eliza was also a jug. A Betty was a Florentine or
pear-shaped flask wrapped in straw. Windsor, surprisingly enough,
was Windsor ale.

CHAPTER VIII

Spanish Wines

BEFORE turning to the development of the wine trade in Portugal during its apogee in the second and third decades of the century and towards its crisis in the time of the Marquis of Pombal, some account should be given of Spanish wines, which rivalled Portuguese wines in England until 1741, when their importation was interrupted by seven years of war.

In the eighteenth century comparatively few wines reached England from the north of Spain, and the importation of canary greatly declined, but Cadiz remained an important centre of export though it was rivalled by Malaga. The English Factory at Cadiz, or perhaps it would be more correct to say in Andalusia, for at some periods the communities at Jerez, San Lucar or Port St Mary played a greater part, had as long a history, or longer, than that of Oporto. From the beginning however it had been less independent. In its origins it had owed much to the dukes of Medina Sidonia. Its judge conservator was appointed directly by the King of Spain and not chosen by the members of the Factory, subject to the king's confirmation, as was the case in Portugal. The privilege of having a judge conservator was confirmed by the treaty of 1713 but somewhat vaguely. The King of Spain merely undertook to issue special decrees on the subject as called for by the circumstances of the various courts of law. The privilege lasted through the eighteenth century but was not written into any further treaty. From the time of the Reformation the numbers of the Factory had been reduced and many Catholic British subjects had ceased to be members. These were largely absorbed into Spanish society and the Factory itself played a much humbler part than in Lisbon, where Protestants could afford to be independent and not to mix with the Portuguese. In Cadiz the Catholic British element predominated and the Protestants had to keep on good terms with them.

In the eighteenth century sherries and malaga wines had largely replaced sack. In so far as sherry was a kind of sack and sack was primarily a canary wine it seems strange that the canary and palm-wines, the prototypes of sweet and generous wines, fell from fashion when strong wines were in such demand. After 1721 the imports of canary wines into England, which had averaged some 1,300 tuns a year, declined rapidly, and towards the end of the century in 1785 only sixty-five tuns were imported although Spanish wines were otherwise returning to favour. A principal reason for this decline was the competition of Cadiz and Malaga, where wines of a sweetness and strength had been developed which could hold their own with canary wines, though formerly the latter had been held pre-eminent for these qualities. Also the Canary Islands had the disadvantage that they offered no sufficient market for English exports. Even in the 1670s there had been complaints that the wines had to be paid in bullion, and this difficulty grew no less. Faced by increasing costs and competition, the merchants trading in canary wine tried to recover their market by turning to cheaper wines and so increasing their turnover. But the Spanish authorities were conservative and disapproved of any reduction of quality or price. The attempts of the merchants to recoup themselves by increasing the export of canary wine to America were also obstructed. Both the merchants and successive Spanish ambassadors in London pleaded for canary to be allowed the same privilege of direct export to the English colonies as madeira, but were unsuccessful. However, the absence of the privilege was qualified by the fact that the American customs in the earlier part of the century were far from strict. In 1718, for instance, the Boston customs would usually pass consignments of canary up to fifty or sixty tuns provided that they were declared as madeira. Canary continued to find a certain outlet in America, and Vidonia, a type of canary also grown in small quantities in Madeira, became very popular there. As the Canaries lay on the route to America some trade in wine continued, but the wines were no longer worth fetching by a special voyage from England.[1]

[1] C.O. 388/22. Consul Cross. 28th December 1718.

In 1724 the Spanish economist Geronimo Ustariz wrote a book about commerce and trade which was not actually published until 1742. He claimed that the English benefited more by trade with Spain than by trade with Portugal, because in Spain they received payment for their goods in bars of silver as well as in wine. This had been true in the past. In the sixteenth century the Dutch had even found it worth while to carry silver overland to Toulouse and Navarre, and some of this trade continued into the seventeenth century. As late as 1691 silver was easily to be had in Spanish Mediterranean ports. Writing to his father in Madrid from Valencia, James Stanhope said that the situation was quite different to that in Madrid, for silver dollars were common currency there.[1] But by 1720 the gold mines of Brazil were in full production, and after the annual fleet came in, English merchants in Lisbon could obtain payment in gold with relative ease. Spain therefore no longer offered this particular advantage.

Uztariz said that the most important production of Spanish wine was in the south and for about twenty-five years past at Malaga. The Malaga trade had been promoted by the discovery towards the beginning of the century that sweet wines grew very well on the barren mountains and high grounds behind the city. It had also been helped by improvements of the harbour made in 1717 and by the fact that the several dues levied on wines were much less onerous than those exacted in Cadiz. He said that the Seville duties had been lately increased to a degree which hindered the export of sherry. This statement was confirmed in 1732 by the English consul at Cadiz, William Cayley; he complained that the English trade in the past two years had been subjected to great oppressions and that the treaties had been infringed.[2] At about the same time a commission of three members, consisting of Benjamin Keene, English minister at Madrid, Arthur Stert, a Lisbon merchant, and John Goddard, who acted as Spanish secretary, were treating with the Spanish government about commercial questions. Their time was largely taken up by old claims, many of which went back to the War of the Spanish Succession, but they aimed at a discussion of Anglo-Spanish trade in general. They exchanged many courtesies and sat until 1733 but made

---

[1] Stanhope MS from Chevening at Maidstone Record Office 36/1. James to Alexander Stanhope, 27th April 1691.
[2] S.P. 94/219. Consul Cayley, July 1729.

little real progress, and Anglo-Spanish relations remained unsatisfactory until they were interrupted by the outbreak of war in 1741.

In their feelings about wine Spaniards were not unlike the Portuguese. They inherited something of the same puritanical attitude derived from the Moors. Uztariz condemned the adulteration of wines and the fashion for strong wines and for spirits. He observed that the Italians had spoiled their wines by adulterating them and measures should be taken to prevent this happening in Spain. The distilling of aniseed and strong waters should also be discouraged. Spain had plenty of wine and its export should be encouraged; there was no need to reduce the export duties, as the foreign demand was enough to support a good trade. There was little danger of exports causing a shortage for wine in Spain, but even if it were to do so, it would be preferable for Spaniards to put a little water into their wine, and to export their wine and brandy rather than to risk drinking too much themselves.

Spanish tastes in Andalusia were such that they did not care for the strong sherries in demand for the English market, but only liked the light *finos* which they drank cold and diluted with ice. On the other hand Madrid differed from Lisbon in that wine was still an essential feature of the prestige of entertainments at court. For this reason there was a large demand and the officials of the court exercised a close control on the production of wine in the Madrid district. They had the right to buy up each year all the wines they required, first for the use of the court, secondly for the consumption of the people of Madrid; wine could only be sold in the open market after they had taken what they wanted. Most of the wines consumed came from within five leagues of Madrid and some of them had a good reputation. The wine of St Martin was said to be the best white wine in Spain. Moscatels were brought from a little farther afield, and Lucena, a sweet wine used for blending, came from as far as Cordoba. But this was exceptional, for communications with the south of Spain seem to have been very bad. In the 1690s Alexander Stanhope took great pains to procure Ribadavia from Galicia and even Barabar from Lisbon, but never spoke of sherry or malaga.[1] In the 1750s Benjamin Keene, who prided himself on his good table, took

---

[1] H.M.C. Portland, ii-377. Alexander Stanhope, and Chevening MS. Paul Methuen to Alexander Stanhope 19th October, 26th December 1694 and Alexander to James Stanhope 21st May, 3rd December 1699.

much trouble to provide himself with French wines by way of Bilbao, and with Carcavelos from Lisbon, but he never purchased Spanish wines even from Alicante, the nearest southern port to Madrid and enjoying an excellent reputation for its wines. Neither Stanhope nor Keene ever mentioned the local Castilian wines.

The inaccessibility of Madrid and the lukewarm interest of the Spaniards themselves meant that the export of wines from southern Spain was largely dependent on foreign trade. In the early colonial days the wines had found a sizeable market in the Spanish-American vice royalties, as the use of wine was essential for Church and court. The ecclesiastical use of wine for the Mass could be considerable. According to Gonzalez-Gordon, Seville cathedral at its apogee had twenty-four altars celebrating 400 Masses daily and used 10,750 litres (2,500 tuns) of wine annually. The wines for America could be borne safely and easily by the trade winds if advantage was taken of the right season, but in practice they were subjected to many delays and vicissitudes and did not usually reach their destination quickly. The shippers therefore had every inducement to develop wines which were generous and durable. Until the middle of the eighteenth century most of the wines going out from Cadiz were new wines; this mattered less when they were intended for immediate lay consumption, but the Church needed wine which would last in an unaltered state for at least a year. In the last years of the eighteenth century no one in Cadiz knew when the solera system had begun or whether wines had been matured in the old days. Gonzalez-Gordon suggested that it began in San Lucar in the year 1706. Gonzalez-Gordon is a great authority, but one cannot help surmising that something like the solera system may have been practised at an earlier date in the monasteries and convents, which had the land, the time and the money, and also the cellars or storehouses enjoying comparative security in time of war or civil disturbance. Large tuns, which had a little wine taken out and a little added each year, were known at Angers in the Middle Ages. At a later date, in 1685, Gilbert Burnet, Bishop of Salisbury, saw a tun of Valtelline wine, which seemed to have some of the characteristics of both port and sherry. He described it as an aromatic wine tasting like a strong water drawn off spices and, though a natural wine, as strong as brandy. The grapes were left on the vines until November to ripen thoroughly and then kept in garrets for two or three months before pressing. The liquor was then put into an open vessel, where it threw off a scum twice a day for a week or a fortnight, after which it was put into a closed vessel and for the first year was very sweet and luscious, but at the end of the year about a third was drawn off and replaced with newer wine and so on every year. Every March it fermented and for a long time became undrinkable, but each year it slowly became stronger. Burnet met a lady named Madame de Salis who had kept such wine for forty years. It had become so strong that one could not drink more than a thimbleful. Burnet spoke of the Jesuits in Naples and Apulia as great dealers in wine and said that the Minims (an order of mendicant friars) were very active and sold wine retail. At Jerez there was a Carthusian monastery with vast cellars which specialized in wine for centuries. The sons of the Church appreciated wine for its own sake as well as an essential for the Mass. At Cadiz in the early seventeenth century Thomas Gage, before sailing to Guatemala, spent happy evenings drinking the good sherry with the friars. Also, in the early days, Catholic churchmen, unlike their Protestant colleagues, gave first priority to the conversion of the heathen in the new conquests. This entailed the provision of a sufficient supply of wine to the remotest corners of the world to uphold the faith. It is very likely therefore that the monks of Cadiz and Jerez were interested in developing something like the solera system to produce a durable and uniform wine for export.

To avoid the hazards of bringing wine from Spain, the settlers in the New World soon began to try to grow wine themselves wherever the climate allowed, principally in Mexico and Peru. At first the government encouraged the planting of vineyards in Peru, and they were so successful that wine was even exported to Mexico. Subsequently measures were introduced to protect Spanish wines and this trade was forbidden, but Peru remained self-supporting, as did Mexico also to some extent. Spanish wines could be brought to the ports and local wine-growing curbed near the principal centres, but of necessity the remote mission stations had to provide for their own needs. So the missionaries, and especially the Jesuits, took vines with them wherever they penetrated, to Mexico and California, to Argentina and Chile. Sometimes in North America they grafted their stock on to native vines. So the colonial market for Andalusian wines fell off, but

the Dutch and English filled the gap and after the beginnings of
their wars with France in the seventeenth century did a good
trade with Cadiz and San Lucar. At first the malaga wines were
thought to be sweeter, but the English and Dutch found that by
blending the sherry wines they could bring them up to the strength
of canary. At the end of the sixteenth century the survival of the
English Factory at Cadiz had been threatened, but there were
always a number of English or Irish Catholics resident to keep
up the connection in times of stress. Some of them took out
Spanish naturalization papers, and the presence of resident foreign
merchants kept up the interest in the export trade in wine, which
the Spaniards themselves were prone to lack. In spite of the fact
that foreigners, and even Spaniards, who were not Castilians or
possessed of a resident qualification, could not take part in the
colonial trade, the Dutch and to a lesser degree the English managed
to conduct a trade with America under Spanish names and this
practice continued until the war of the Spanish succession. Although neither Cadiz nor Malaga were occupied by the allies,
except Cadiz which was besieged for a short time in 1702, the
allies had command of the sea and occupied Catalonia and for a
time Valencia. In the closing years of the war Spanish wines were
imported in quantity to England and after the peace attained a
high level. Among the articles of the Treaty of Utrecht was a
provision confirming the privileges of the Anglo-Spanish treaty
of 1677. Nevertheless the British consul at Cadiz complained that
trade was on a worse footing than it had been before.[1] It was true
that in the reign of Phillip V there was a revival of Spanish
government, and of Cadiz as a port for the colonial trade. About
the year 1730 the Spanish government took up residence for a
time at Seville, and Cadiz was the headquarters of the rebuilt
Spanish fleet. The propinquity of the government perhaps increased local consumption and reduced interest in the export of
wine. The fleet supplied itself locally. In 1740 it took on 400 tuns
at Cadiz, brought in this instance from Malaga.[2] The English were
not influential enough to play the part they acted in Portugal, and
since the war had become less numerous than the French and less
important in the Mediterranean trade. There were more English
Catholics resident than Protestants, and though negotiations were

[1] C.O. 388/22 Consul Russell, 23rd January 1719.
[2] S.P. 94/225 Consul Cayley, 30th October 1740.

set on foot in 1731-33 to place Anglo-Spanish trade on a better footing, little progress was made except to settle a few old outstanding individual claims.

Nevertheless the English shared in the general prosperity of Cadiz, and the wine-trade flourished until war broke out in 1741. It was helped by the number of ships which brought fish, corn and butter to Cadiz and sought outward freights. The butter and some of the corn came from Ireland, and this was an additional factor which encouraged the Irish and Catholic element in the British community. The Factory regarded all British subjects as coming under their authority and in particular required that they should pay the consulage dues authorized by an English act of Parliament, which went to pay the expenses of the Factory and the consul and for the relief and repatriation of distressed seamen and other distressed British subjects. From 1736 the rate of consulage was one real (3·2d) per ducat (11 reals) on outward freight and two reals per ton on inward cargo, the latter charge for the relief of distressed British subjects. The Irish refused to pay consulage and received the backing of the Spanish authorities, who maintained that an English act of Parliament had no significance in Spain. After some dispute the Factory gave in, and it was agreed that any payment by the Irish should be voluntary; those who found the services of the Factory helpful continued to pay and for a time a system of live and let live was adopted. But the Spanish authorities interfered in other ways, and the foundation in 1734 of a *Gremio de vinhateira* or chamber of commerce for the promotion of the wine trade proved a hindrance rather than a help. The *Gremio* promulgated a series of regulations, which included a prohibition of the introduction of wines for blending. This applied particularly to the Lucena wines of Cordoba, already mentioned in connection with Madrid, which although grown on a cold mountain-side were generous wines used for strengthening. It also applied to malaga wines, which were only allowed entry for re-export, and were subject to a heavy duty as indeed were all wines exported, including those locally grown. The friars, who hitherto had in most cases evaded the payment of duty, were made to pay the same dues as other people, and the storage of wine was prohibited on the ground that it gave encouragement to a proliferation of middlemen, who made too large profits. The policy of the *Gremio* diminished the interest of the export trade and encouraged

the sending out of wines as new wines immediately after the
vintage. The rigour of the regulations was however tempered by
exemptions and evasions. The activities of the *Gremio* meant that
much of the wine not exported immediately was sold at once to
retailers for consumption by the local people, who only demanded
light wines, but exemptions were granted for storing some wine
both for export and for distilling, and the monks and friars retained their warehouses. The Carthusians and Dominicans, who
had considerable storage facilities, remained in business until the
end of the century. Also the customs administration at Cadiz had
a traditional reputation for venality, and although the revival of
Cadiz and the actual residence of the government for a time in
Andalusia possibly stiffened the administration for a time, old
ways did not change much, and the wine-trade did not suffer
unduly until the war interrupted it almost entirely between 1741
and 1747.

At the time of the conclusion of peace there was an acute shortage of corn in Spain and this brought a rush of shipping to Cadiz.
English ships brought corn from Sicily, from Ireland and from
all the smaller English ports, and even one or two cargoes of
wheat from Boston and New York. This trade created good opportunities for return freights and in 1749 the trade in wine with
England, which had been resumed gently in 1748 with a total of
2,706 tuns, rose to 7,344 tuns. From this date a minute book and
accounts of the Cadiz Factory are available until 1825.[1] In time
of war the Factory ceased to operate and at other times the
minute book consists mainly of a record of the annual meetings
and elections of officers, but the accounts of expenditure on relieving seamen and other British subjects and of the consulage collected on the inward trade give some idea of the progress of the
Factory in the years of peace up to and after the Napoleonic wars.

The first meeting of the Factory recorded after the war was held
in 1749 and was attended by sixteen members, including some
Irish. Unfortunately the consul, who presided as chairman and
was named John Colebrooke, was not a man of long experience of
Spain as his predecessor William Cayley had been. The minister
in Madrid (Sir) Benjamin Keene described him as 'a mighty busy,
bustling, projecting kind of important puffy city man'. He tried
to force the Irish to pay consulage, and when they refused to do

[1] F.O. 332 i and ii, Cadiz Factory.

so, he procured a legal opinion from the Attorney-General Sir Douglas Ryder to the effect that Irish citizens were not British subjects within the meaning of the Consulage Act and were therefore ineligible to take part in the affairs of the Factory. But the writ of Whitehall could not be invoked in Spain, and the Spanish authorities, who had never taken kindly to the idea of a foreign tax such as consulage being levied in their bailiwick, raised strong objections. Colebrooke was in due course edged out of office and was replaced by the Hon. Edward Hay, a former member of the Lisbon Factory, and a brother of the Earl of Kinnoul. The Irish were readmitted as full members of the Factory and one of them, Endymion Porter, was elected to be one of the two deputies responsible for the administration of the Factory under the consul. For a short time the Factory continued on an enlarged basis. The number of principal merchants attending the annual meeting rose to twenty-three, and the accounts showed payments to local Spanish hospitals and convents on behalf of distressed seamen and other English and Irish subjects, which indicated a higher degree of co-operation with local Catholic institutions. Unfortunately this was only a short interlude. The Spanish authorities soon issued a regulation requiring that all residents should declare their protection and come to a definite decision whether they claimed Spanish naturalization or whether they desired to remain British subjects. It was no longer possible to have one's cake and eat it and most of the English and Irish Catholics opted for Spanish nationality. The annual meeting of the Factory was thus reduced to about eight members on the average, as although about twenty declared themselves British in the first instance and 28 fresh names were added in the years between 1749 and 1778, the strictness of the regulations caused many merchants to leave and by 1754 there were only nine exporters left in Jerez. Sherry remained a favourite longer in Scotland than in England, but in the 1730s it was being advertised in England as a cheaper wine and was again being outstripped by malaga. In 1728, for instance, King's Lynn, which served a prosperous clientele of country gentlemen and gave a fair indication of the trend of the better-class trade, imported only two tuns from Cadiz, compared with fifty-four tuns from the Canaries and seventy tuns from Malaga.[1] Later in the century 'mountain' wine from Malaga retained its popularity during a period when the

[1] Kings Lynn Port Book E 190/452.

wines of Jerez declined. Malaga also had always been known for some very old wines. Pepys spoke of a bottle of Malaga sack thirty years old, which tasted more like a spirit than a wine. This was a rarity, but in 1756 references exist to malagas aged ten or fifteen years.

After Malaga and Cadiz the most important Spanish mainland port for wine was Alicante, where the local wines had a good reputation. A fair amount from Alicante went to East Anglian ports, much of it by the coastal traffic from London rather than directly. There were good wines in Spain in the north, but they were on the further side of the Cantabrian Mountains from Bilbao and Santander, and few found their way to England in the eighteenth century. An occasional ship-load went from Barcelona, Valencia and the Balearic islands, and Beni Carlo from Valencia was used for strengthening, much as wine from the opposite coast of Algeria was used in the twentieth century. An attempt was made to bring Catalan wines to Cadiz for blending but this failed, and the wines of Barcelona were largely turned into brandies, of which Barcelona developed a large export.

Much of the white wine in Jerez was made from the luscious Pedro Jimenez grape which had been known in England as early as 1632 under such English names as Peter-see-me. Vines of the same type were planted around Malaga, so that the white wines from both places were similar. The red tent wines, which were first grown in a small area of non-calcareous soil between Jerez and San Lucar, were afterwards produced on a large scale at Malaga. In the eighteenth century tent was much used as a wine for the Communion. It was also imported into France under the name of Alicante. Towards the end of the eighteenth century, when the popularity of sherry was reviving in England, a good deal of malaga was taken to Cadiz to proceed from there as sherry. In earlier years, when malaga was more popular than sherry and export from Malaga was easier than from Cadiz, the reverse trend had perhaps existed, and wine from the sherry district had found its way to Malaga for export.

After 1749 the imports of Spanish wines into England averaged about 3,000 tuns and did not reach a figure of 7,000 tuns again until 1795. In the war years between 1779 and 1782 they had dropped once to 1,031 tuns (in 1782), but never as low as in the 1740s. The activities of the Cadiz Factory were interrupted

M

between 1779 and 1783, but continued at a reduced level in other years until the beginning of the Napoleonic wars in 1793. The trade in Spanish wine did not however suffer overmuch and tended to increase after 1783. Before that, in the 1770s, the whole trade of Cadiz had been reduced and in 1771 only five members had attended the annual Factory meeting. At this time the total export was estimated to be only 15,437 butts and the trade with Spanish America to be reduced to 1,845 butts. As early as the 1750s the Factory records had referred to consignments of brandy reaching Cadiz from Barcelona and other Spanish ports. While the brandy content of the Douro wines was being reduced, at least in theory, sherry was increasingly fortified in order to find favour in the English market.

The revival of the sherry trade in the 1780s was, as so often happened in Spain and Portugal, given its first impulse by foreigners, in this case residents mainly of French origin. Some of the names famous later in the sherry trade began to appear. The honour of bearing the name which goes back furthest actually belongs to the Spanish firm of Rivero, which can trace its origin to the middle of the seventeenth century. One of the oldest names belongs to the firm of Pedro Domecq, which was founded by an Irishman named Patrick Murphy who settled in Spain towards 1730. Murphy was not a merchant but a farmer who owned good vineyards in the Macharnudo and Carrascal districts north of Jerez. He was still a bachelor when he died in 1762 and he bequeathed his vineyards to his friend Jean Haurie who was an immigrant from France. Haurie was a general merchant, but he became intensely interested in the vineyards he had inherited and fought vigorously against the restrictions of the *Gremio*, which prevented sherry shippers accumulating stocks of old wine. In 1772, as a result of a prolonged law-suit, he won permission to engage in all three branches of the wine trade, as grower, storekeeper and shipper. Like Murphy he never married, but he founded a company with his five nephews and heirs, and after his death in 1794 one of these married Pedro Domecq, a man of Basque origin, and other French kinsmen, such as Pemartin and Lacoste joined in the trade.

In 1754 an Englishman named Brickdale was said to be the only shipper of his nation. This is not altogether borne out by the Factory records, which in 1750 mention several British names, among the importers at least, including Endymion Porter, an Irishman then a member of the Factory, Richard Butler who later became naturalized as a Spaniard, Henry Pickering and John Hogan. In 1754 as many as thirty-four British residents signed a petition to the Pope regarding the appointment of a visitor to the church of St George at San Lucar. After the Irish left the Factory and most of the residents of British origin took out Spanish papers it became difficult to say who was British and who was not. Many names figured in the Factory records only as recipients of assistance long after they ceased to be members of the Factory itself. Such were the relicts or descendants of Sir Martin Westcombe, who had been consul in the war of the Spanish succession. Other British subjects represented English importing houses, and as temporary residents never became members of the Factory. Such was Samuel Goode who came out to Cadiz in 1750 and figured as an exporter; he was one of a Dartmouth and Exeter family trading with Spain. There was also some interchange between the Lisbon, Cadiz and Oporto Factories. Names like Garnier and Maine, known in Lisbon, appear also in Cadiz. Arthur Stert, who served on the commission treating with Spain in 1732, and his son of the same name, came of a family well-known in Lisbon and Oporto for a number of years and represented at home by an M.P. for Plymouth. Arthur Stert also lived in London for a time as a Portugal merchant. There was a good deal of coming and going, which kept alive the connection between the various branches of Anglo-Peninsular trade at home and abroad.

Jean Haurie, a principal pioneer in the revival of the sherry trade, bought warehouses and set up his own cooperage. In the sixteenth century native oak and chestnut had been used for making casks at Jerez, but Spain had increasingly become a treeless country, so most of the pipe-staves were probably imported. Haurie was a wine-grower as well as a shipper, and set an example which was more often followed in Spain than in Portugal, where the growers and the merchant shippers were distinct. The Spanish writer Pan Ferguson gives a list of nineteen shippers in 1774, but the total shipped only amounted to 100 tons, with Haurie the largest shipper sending six tuns only. The second- and third-largest exporters were British, being Brickdale and Piker, which is probably a variant of Pickering. The Cadiz exports were undoubtedly low at this period, but the list was probably incomplete and did not include exports from other ports in the area, such as Port St Mary, San Lucar and Seville itself. A list of eleven exporters in 1798, quoted by Julian Jeffes and taken from the papers of the old-established Spanish firm of exporters, Rivero, gives a very different picture with a total export of some 7,000 tuns. Jean Haurie, now Jean Haurie and Nephews, still led; but with an export of 2,000 tuns. James Gordon, a Scotsman, was second and the name of Brickdale still appeared with 450 tuns. Other sources give a smaller figure for Cadiz exports, and the English customs figure for 1798 was a little less for Spanish wines than it had been in 1774, but it almost doubled in the next year and as much wine, it was believed, went to France as to the United Kingdom. The 1798 figures itemized by firms sound credible and perhaps underestimate rather than exaggerate the total increase of trade.

James Gordon, whose trade already rivalled that of the Hauries in 1798, was a Catholic from Ayrshire who came to Cadiz in 1785. At about this time the British element was recruited by several new arrivals. Those who were Catholics readily intermarried with Spanish families. There were also one or two families like the Archdekins, who had lived in Spain or Portugal for some time and knew the country, but who worked in the Consulate or Factory without ever becoming prosperous merchants. Another Scotsman who became very prominent in the Factory was James Duff. He was not a Catholic, though he became related by marriage to the Gordons. He had been in Cadiz since 1767, in which he figured as a wine-shipper and also as one of the two deputy-consuls who in the eighteenth century were chosen annually by the Factory. After rendering very useful services as consul during the Peninsular War he was made a baronet and died in 1815 at the age of 81. He took a leading part in the revival of the sherry trade, and his firm Duff-Gordon & Co became one of the largest exporters. By the time of the Peninsular War the sherry trade was largely in British hands again, but the British community remained closely linked with families of Spanish and even of French descent, and never became a closely-knit essentially British body as the Factory at Oporto was for all of its history.

Although Brickdale was on good terms with the Catholics and contributed to the support of St George's Church, he does not appear to have been a Catholic himself and was even rumoured to be a Freemason. It was said that there was at one time a numerous Freemason's lodge at Cadiz. There is not much supporting evidence: Andalusia was a pious province; and in contemporary Lisbon, which was regarded as comparatively liberal, Freemasons were, after the papal ban of 1738, still vigorously persecuted. However it is not impossible, for a measure of free thought had penetrated some of the highest circles in Spain, and an occasional cardinal or viceroy were believed to have favoured the Freemasons. Certainly Freemasonry had an attraction for the Jews and new Christians, whose far-flung connections continued to play a considerable part in finance and foreign trade and in the wine trade in particular. Whether assisted by the spread of free thought or not, Cadiz in the late eighteenth century reverted to its seventeenth-century tradition, when a recognized system for evading governmental restrictions on trade was accepted. Jean Haurie defeated the *Gremio* fair and square after a long legal battle, though the Baron de Bourgoing, a visiting Frenchman, observed that the authorities made a last vigorous effort to enforce the restrictive regulations in all their rigour in 1785 but were unsuccessful.

The first effect of the French Revolution was to arouse the hostility of the Spanish government and to cause the temporary departure of a number of French residents, who since the war of the Spanish succession had formed the largest foreign communities in Spain. In Andalusia the Irish were left the most numerous, but for a time the unpopularity of the French and the improvement of trade encouraged more English, Germans, Flemish and Genoese to move in. The trade in wine with France was little interrupted by bad political relations and that with Ireland was larger than might be expected. Like Scotland, Ireland was a poor country, but in terms of population it was much larger relatively to the rest of the United Kingdom than it became later, and until the union its trade was separate. One of the largest of the new British exporting houses was that of an Irishman named William Garvey, who settled in Cadiz, married a Spanish girl and then moved to San Lucar.

Spanish wines imported into England, which had only been 2,000-3,000 tuns prior to 1786, took an upward turn and attained over 6,000 tuns in 1791.[1] It is not known what proportion of the

---

[1] 6,520 tuns according to Henderson. Schumpeter's figures are 5,782 and 77 canary, but for England and Wales only, and the 1894 parliamentary report's figure is 5,098 and 116 canary.

increase was due to Cadiz wines, but some indication of the relative importance of trade with various Spanish ports can be gleaned from the returns of seamen's sixpences. Every British home-coming ship had to pay sixpence for every seaman of its crew; the proceeds were used for the maintenance of Greenwich Hospital. The returns for London gave the name of every ship, the port from which she had come and the number of sixpences paid. They represented about half the total traffic, as many ships went to out-ports or paid their dues at another port of call. The figures in 1789 were 19 ships from Cadiz, 24 from Malaga, 6 from Alicante, 5 from Almeria, 4 from Denia, 6 from Valencia, 1 from Altea and 1 from Rosas. There were 30 ships from Seville, which presumably included San Lucar, and some ships from other ports also called at Cadiz. Not all the ships carried wines, but a majority had wine in their cargoes.[1]

Visiting Malaga in 1787, the English traveller Townsend thought that less wine was grown there than formerly. But the Malaga trade was still considerable. Much wine was sent to Cadiz for blending and also to France, where Bordeaux wines were now habitually blended with malagas, sherries and wines from Beni Carlos on the Valencian side of Catalonia. Townsend noted in Malaga that the peasants were very industrious and devoted an immense amount of labour to their vines. He said that a leading wine-grower was named James Murphy, who had found that if the grapes were separated from their stems before they were put into the press, Malaga could produce a light white wine equal to sherry. It is rather surprising that he emphasized the lightness of sherry, for it was about then or soon afterwards that the shippers from Cadiz began again to turn their attention to the heavier wines, and to fortify them with a view to making them into better competitors with port.

It will be remembered that before the intervention of the *Gremio*, sherries, like the wines of Madrid, had sometimes been strengthened by blending with Lucena wines from Cordoba. It was perhaps therefore no coincidence that the term *amontillada*, applied in the late eighteenth century to a type of sherry which had gained strength with age, was said to be derived from Montilla, a wine-growing district near Cordoba. It was also at about this time, in the last two decades of the eighteenth century, that the

[1] Adm. 68/206. Seamens sixpences.

types of sherry known as *finos*, *rayos*, *palos cortados*, *manzanillas*, *olorosos* and *amontilladas*, began to be differentiated. These names applied mostly not to wines, which were different at the time of the vintage, but to developments of character afterwards which often could not be predicted. *Manzanilla* wines, however, were made from grapes which had been picked earlier, and were taken directly under cover without being dried for a period in the sun as was the usual practice. Therefore they had different characteristics although they developed into parallel types. If the wines were *añadas*, that is unblended wines left in a vat, they developed unpredictably into one type of wine or another, but it was found that the best way to ensure the production of any particular type was to perpetuate the life of the cask by constantly taking wine from it and replacing the quantity taken. If this was done at discreet intervals and the replacement wine was well chosen the new wine would conform to the quality of the old, and once the system was well-established, the production of wines of uniform quality and type could be guaranteed.

This system, known as the *solera* system, entailed the use of a number of butts called *soleras*, containing various types of wine, which were periodically replenished from other butts known as *criaderas*. There might be as many as five *criaderas*, each containing wine a little older than its neighbour. After the wine had stayed in an *añada* for a period sufficient to allow it to declare its character, it was put into the first *criadera*, from which wine was taken from time to time to the second *criadera*, and thence by two or three further stages to the *solera*. The wines in the *criaderas* and *soleras* were all wines from which all the sugar had been removed. When the mature wine was eventually taken from the *solera*, a sweeter wine could be procured by blending. This was done by adding a sweet syrup made from Pedro Jimenez grapes, in which fermentation had been arrested by an addition of brandy on much the same lines as were adopted for making port-wine.

Even such an authority as Gonzalez-Gordon, the author of *Jerez-Xerez-Scheris*, felt himself unable to pronounce on the date of the introduction of the *solera* system or of its reintroduction at Cadiz and Jerez. Clearly it became general not long after the Napoleonic wars, but for some years references to it were scarce. The various terms for types of wine became known gradually, and it is not certain whether the meaning of some of them, for instance of *manzanilla*, was the same at first as it became later. Cyrus Redding, whose book on modern wines was first published in 1841, only referred casually to the *solera* system, though he mentioned specifically the formation of the *flor* characteristic of sherries. The *flor* is a film of yeast cells which forms a scum on the surface of sherries two months or more after the vintage if the sugar has been entirely removed by fermentation. It is a phenomenon almost unknown in other wines except in a few in the Jura. In sherries it performs a valuable function for it protects the maturing wine from outside influences and is a particular enemy of the vinegar virus which turns wines sour. The *flor* of flower drops to the bottom in the spring and autumn, but is reproduced regularly in the *soleras* whenever there is an addition of fresh wine.

Gonzalez-Gordon thought that the *solera* system was probably used at San Lucar as early as 1706. Certainly if the claim made some years ago by Messrs Pedro Domecq, that one of their casks dated from two centuries back, is true some such process for maturing wine must have been used well back in the eighteenth century. But in the eighteenth century it may well have fallen into desuetude, for the trade diminished for a number of years and was handled by a number of small exporters, who lacked the capital for *soleras* and were largely prevented by the Spanish regulations from trading in anything else than new wine. On the other hand, in earlier days the old monasteries and convents had the storehouses and the capital which individual merchants lacked, and also the need for durable wines to send to the missions in America. It is improbable that they developed *soleras* to the point of being able to produce any type of wine on demand, as occurred in the nineteenth century, but they probably did mature their wines and put them for the purpose into something resembling *soleras*, though the type of wine produced may have been much more haphazard, and a matter of hit or miss.

CHAPTER IX

Crisis on the Douro

THE Lisbon and Oporto Factories had been able to attain prosperity in the first instance without the help of the wine trade at all. They did so in the decade after the Restoration, when a number of merchants were able to make their fortunes and to return to England. From 1690 onwards, and even more so after the war of the Spanish succession, the wine trade played a major part. It was a principal factor in stabilizing Anglo-Portuguese relations, though even at its apogee in the 1720s and 1730s many ships sailing from Portugal to England carried cargoes of fruit and other southern products and little or no wine, or were engaged in the triangular trade with America and had brought fish from Newfoundland before carrying cargo from Portugal to England. The Lisbon Factory also did an increasing trade as carriers between Lisbon and the Mediterranean, and although the export of bullion from Portugal was always legally forbidden, every weekly packet-boat and most visiting warships carried homewards the gold bars representing the profits of the Factory's transactions. By 1710 or 1711 the Brazilian mines were coming into full production and the bank of England was buying gold to the value of £50,000 annually. In 1712 an Exeter merchant wrote 'we have hardly any other money current among us except Portuguese gold'. Indeed one could expect to be given it by the bank throughout the century, even in the days of William Hickey after the boom had passed towards the end of the century. Between 3rd August 1724 and 20th March 1726 the gold bought by the English mint was valued at £115,979. It was the gold, and from about 1730 the diamonds, of Brazil which paid for Portugal's unfavourable

balance of trade. The wine trade still played an important part
but a smaller one than it had played initially. Between 1701
and 1703 the value of the exports of wine was computed to be
£175,000 and the discrepancy between Portuguese imports and
exports to be £368,000. Between 1721 and 1725 the value of the
wines was £332,000 more than it had been from 1701 to 1703,
and the trade deficit had only increased £56,000 to £424,000. But
by the years 1736-40 the deficit had grown to £863,000 and was

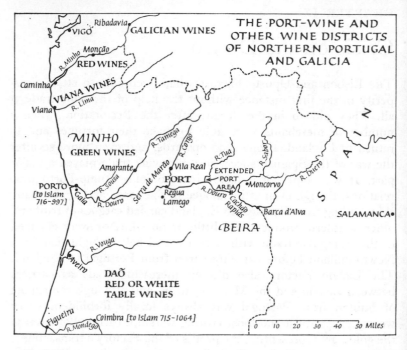

still £686,000 in the years 1741-46, though the wine trade was
worth £346,000 and trade in general was prospering. On the other
hand the export of gold and diamonds had risen from £728,000
in the five years 1711-15 to £1,371,000 in the five years 1741-45,
and English exports to Portugal from £638,000 to £1,115,000.
There have been many arguments about the exact figures of Anglo-
Portuguese trade but these figures serve to give an idea of the
general position, which is agreed by most writers on the subject
such as Borges de Macedo, E. B. Schumpeter and H. E. S. Fisher.
During these prosperous years 1741-45 the total English consump-

tion of wines was a third less than it had been formerly, but Portuguese wines, which had been freed by war of the competition of Spanish wines, represented 82% of the wines passing the English customs and 86% of Portuguese exports other than bullion.

The Lisbon Factory, followed by the Oporto Factory, were by far the largest British communities in Portugal, but at this period there were some English merchants in most of the smaller ports and there were vice-consuls at Viana, Figueira and Faro. There was rivalry between Lisbon and Oporto, and although the cities were not much more than 200 miles apart the roads between them were so bad that they had little intercourse by land. They had less by sea than might be expected, for the entry to the Douro was difficult and dangerous, and foreign ships were liable to have difficulty with the customs, even though they had already been cleared once at a Portuguese port. Away from the sea Portuguese communications were very poor and the separate provinces led self-contained lives. This should not have been the case in the open valley of the Tagus, but the metropolis of Lisbon had grown disproportionately and had drained the life from much of its hinterland. Lisbon existed on foreign trade and had to import much of its subsistance from abroad. Coimbra and the towns north of Oporto were near the sea and more in touch with the outside world, but the peasant populations were largely self-subsisting. The interior northern part of the country towards the Spanish frontier was cut off by mountains and was self-contained. It was in these areas that local peasant industries survived. They were sufficient to provide for the limited local needs and had provided some basis for the government's abortive efforts to set up Portuguese manufactures on a larger scale. The Douro valley became an exception to the general rule, for although there was no direct road down the valley to Oporto, the wine trade in the Upper Douro produced wealth and the means to buy imports. Elsewhere trade only existed on any scale where there was easy access to the sea, but as has been mentioned, not very many English ships took in both Lisbon and Oporto in the same voyage, and the foreign trades of the two towns remained largely distinct.

Towards the middle of the century the Lisbon Factory could muster eighty or ninety signatures for any memorial, and had perhaps over a hundred full members. The total community was much larger. Lord Tyrawley, looking for premises for his embassy, reported that he would need at least one very large room to serve as a chapel to accommodate seven hundred people for the weekly services.[1] Besides the members of the Factory there were a number of temporary residents and hangers-on, and also a Catholic community of English and Irish merchants, priests and members of the English college. Most of the Factory lived well but mixed little with the Portuguese. This was not altogether original sin on their part, for differences of religion and social customs made social intercourse difficult. There were of course exceptions and many of the heads of the old merchant houses, although they did not frequent the Portuguese much, won their esteem by showing patience, understanding, goodwill and integrity. The former qualities, though not necessarily the last, were essential for dealing with the cumbrous, slow-moving and often rapacious Portuguese bureaucracy. Cardinal Motta, patriarch of Lisbon at the time of his death in 1754, used to speak very kindly of the Oporto merchants he had known when he was a district judge there. The Marquis of Pombal himself told Abraham de Castres, British consul and then minister at Lisbon, that many of the elder members of the Factory were excellent people, though some of the younger generation were inclined to make trouble.[2] The former, with established fortunes, long experience of Portugal and many old connections with Portuguese officials, were inclined to leave well alone and to put up with the deficiencies of the régime, tiresome though they might be. The younger folk with their fortunes still to make, and anxious to take a short cut towards them, were less amenable. They were often brought up sharp by Portuguese regulations and their first impulse was to complain to the consul or minister, and if he was in the least unsympathetic to use backstairs influence in London to bring pressure to bear on him. Often their complaints had substance but sometimes, as Tyrawley used to complain, they were popinjays.

In the first years after the Treaty of Utrecht, Thomas Burnet, a son of Gilbert Burnet, Bishop of Salisbury, was consul-general in Lisbon. During his period of office between 1719 and 1727 he did his best to carry on the Methuen tradition of friendliness with the younger Portuguese nobility. He was a man of parts and in

[1] S.P. 89/35 Tyrawley to Newcastle, 7th November 1728.
[2] S.P. 89/48, de Castres to Claudius Amyand, 9th July 1752 and 11th March 1754.

later years advanced in the legal profession and became a competent judge, but as a young man about town he had been a gay spark and had even been rumoured to be a Mohawk, a member of one of the gangs of young people whose exploits had terrorized London. His reputation did him no harm with the younger set and as a man of fashion and the son of an eminent Whig he was accepted in Lisbon at his own valuation and almost on a level with the minister. He gathered about him a côterie of pro-British Portuguese, and posing as an expert on Portuguese affairs was rather encouraged by Whitehall to send home political as well as commercial reports. He pointed out that the nobles derived a large part of their incomes from the sale of wines and oils to the British and that it was wise to cultivate this common interest. This was reasonable enough. The Methuen commercial treaty had at first helped the wines of Lisbon rather than Oporto, and at times the Lisbon wines exported to England had equalled the Oporto wines in quantity and had probably surpassed them in value. The Oporto wines were now gaining ground, but until 1724 the Lisbon wines represented about a third of the total, while the Lisbon exports of fruits and oil were greater than those of Oporto.[1]

In the days of the Methuens the nobles had played a part in the councils of state and had been worth cultivating. King Pedro himself had appreciated the uses of the English Factories and of their trade. King John V had been young and very inexperienced when he came to the throne, but once he had overcome the diffidence of youth he determined to crush any signs of independence on the part of the nobles and to rule autocratically. The elder Arthur Stert, returning to Lisbon in 1726 after an absence in England, said that he found the king very much altered; the king now thought he was much wiser than anybody else and was pretty ungovernable.[2] It is true that he had no interest in trade, and his ministers, who in any case were given little authority, were equally disinterested. Owing to the lucky increase in Portugal's revenues from Brazil, the king and his ministers were able to indulge their distaste for commercial matters, and the foreigners responsible for them, with comparative impunity. King John himself was only interested in promoting the glories of the Portuguese Church and in building up the Patriarch of Lisbon to splendours as great as

---

[1] Add MSS 11569, reports of Thomas Burnet.
[2] S.P. 89/33, Arthur Stert, 28th July 1726.

those of the Pope. The bridge that Burnet tried to maintain between the Factory and the Portuguese was therefore perhaps less important than it had been. But in any case it was to be destroyed by an unfortunate incident.

The post of consul-general at Lisbon, carrying with it fees of over £1,000 a year, was not to be despised, but Burnet would have liked better to be minister and might have attained that ambition if his father, the bishop and Whig statesman, had not died in 1715 at the very time when he might have hoped his influence to have been restored. However, for his first five years in Lisbon he did well enough as consul-general; his first two chiefs were easy-going and took no umbrage at his cutting a dash. The case was altered when a gallant but gouty major-general named James Dormer was appointed minister. The two men soon quarrelled and Burnet asked to be transferred, but agreed to stay on at the request of the Duke of Newcastle, then Secretary of State. After some unsuccessful efforts to bury the hatchet Burnet asked again to be moved but in the autumn of 1727 was still in Lisbon. His Portuguese friends asked Burnet whether there would not be some celebration of the coronation of King George II which was then impending. Dormer showed no sign of rising to the occasion and excused himself on the ground that he had no equipment and in particular no proper liveries for his servants. Burnet's servants had liveries, which he had probably bought from the previous minister, and he let it be known that he proposed to give a coronation party. Upon receiving a warning from a member of the Factory that Dormer would regard it as a grave affront, he suggested to the minister that he might come to the coronation party and then give one himself in the following week for the birthday of the King of Portugal. Dormer replied that he regarded Burnet's letter as an intolerable impertinence, whereupon Burnet carried on, not only with the English party which might have been regarded as a proper affair for the consul-general, as head of the Factory, to conduct, but also with the party for the King of Portugal, which involved Portuguese notables. The second party only ended at 2 a.m. and later in the morning, just as Burnet was about to step into his coach to go to court to pay his respects to the King of Portugal, he was set upon by eight of Dormer's footmen led by White, the secretary of legation, sword in hand. There was a free-for-all between Burnet's adherents and those of Dormer in the course of which Burnet was knocked down and wounded, but with the help of his servants he regained the shelter of his own house. Burnet acted correctly and refused to name his assailants to the Portuguese authorities, but there were many witnesses of the affair and so the King of Portugal soon had a full account. He was angered by this disrespect to his person and declared Dormer *persona non grata*.[1] The English government accepted this and withdrew Dormer, but also replaced Burnet by an impeccable consul-general named Charles Compton, who was a brother of the Earl of Northampton and a nephew of the Speaker of the House of Commons. In addition, in order to conciliate the Portuguese, they sent out a new diplomatic representative with the rank of ambassador. This was Lord Tyrawley, who had had some experience of the peninsula. The Portuguese grew to like him, and they accepted Compton, but mutual confidence had been destroyed. The Burnet incident is of interest not only as illustrating a type of friction which occurred from time to time between consuls and ministers abroad, though fortunately it seldom became so hot, but also because it had a definite effect on Anglo-Portuguese relations. The Lisbon consul-general had often played quite a useful part, but in future the Portuguese were chary of placing much trust in him, while the Factory, who had hitherto accepted the consul as their head, began to think of him as a mere government servant, and to want to take a line independent of both the consul and the minister. Some of the Factory had backed Dormer, probably because they disliked Burnet for spending so much time with the Portuguese. Henceforward relations between the Factory and the consulate and legation, and between various factions of the Factory itself, deteriorated. There was still easy money to be made and this attracted a brasher type of merchant to Lisbon. Naturally there had always been some Portuguese jealousy of rich foreigners who seemed to lead such easy lives and to be draining Portugal of her wealth, but this had been tempered by respect for the integrity and capacity of the old merchant houses. Now there was more reason for resentment and the Factories were building up trouble for themselves. After a year in Lisbon Lord Tyrawley was moved to remark that he hoped to leave the Factory in a better position than he found it, 'tho' with great respect be

[1] Add MSS 11570, Tempest Milner to Burnet, 15th October 1727, etc. Also Egerton MS 921.

it spoken and under the rose, excepting Mr Stert and four or five more they were a parcel of the greatest jackanapes I have ever met with, fops, beaux, drunkards, gamesters, and prodigiously ignorant even of their own business'.[1]

The Oporto Factory was smaller than the Lisbon Factory and there was less scope for jackanapes in the provinces than in the cosmopolitan capital. The Oporto merchants were not of course immune from English faults, but they remained more homogeneous and united, and perforce were brought into closer touch with the local Portuguese authorities than were their colleagues in the metropolis. In Lisbon the wine trade was only one of many; in Oporto it played a greater part and was as important for the Portuguese as for the Factory.

In Oporto, though the consul held a royal commission, he was chosen by the Factory and continued throughout the century to be a local man. From 1716 to 1756 the office was held first by David Jackson for four years and then for over thirty years by his brother Robert. Both Jacksons were partners in a firm of wine-shippers. From time to time the Oporto consul appealed to Lisbon for help. Officially he was subordinate to the minister at Lisbon, and even to the consul-general there, but normally he tended to take an independent line. In 1740, when war was about to break out with Spain, the Royal Navy sent J. B. Parker, who had been serving as consul at Corunna, to Oporto as a reporting officer. During the war H.M. ships patrolling the coast and keeping a watch on Spanish ports often put into Oporto.[2] As a result the Oporto Factory saw a good deal of the navy and had the advantage of direct communication on the subject of convoys. Formerly this question had often caused disputes in Lisbon between naval captains on the one hand and the minister and the Factory on the other. The latter urgently required convoys to be provided, while the navy argued the priority of other commitments. All convoys started from Lisbon and it had been difficult to make arrangements for Oporto to be included. Ships coming out from England could leave the convoy off the bar of the Douro, but those leaving Oporto had to go to Lisbon first. The direct and cordial relations which the Oporto Factory established with the navy from 1740 onwards enabled protection to be given for the homeward voyage, and both

---

[1] S.P. 89/35. Tyrawley to Newcastle, 5th February 1729.
[2] S.P. 89/41 for Consul Parker's correspondence.

compensated Oporto for its distance from diplomatic protection and increased its standing with the local Portuguese authorities.

The Oporto district and the north of Portugal had many more peasant proprietors than were to be found in the centre and south. This was particularly the case in the Minho district. Such men were passionately attached to their patch of soil, which they cultivated intensively, but they were poor and struggling and infinitely conservative. They cared for quantity rather than for quality, as they still do. Da Cunha, the Portuguese minister in London, who had served as a magistrate in Oporto as a young man, said that it was hard to teach them anything and that when the King of Portugal tried to encourage the growth of mulberry trees for the promotion of the silk industry, the peasants would often cut down the mulberry trees in order to strip them more easily of their leaves. Every peasant had his own vines and was glad enough to sell his grapes for cash. In the Minho most of the vines were of the climbing variety and grew in shady places on the trunks of trees on the edges of the maize fields. The vines grown in the rich soil were bountiful, but the wines were mostly thin, poor and sour. Elsewhere and further inland, the peasant struggling with a small-holding on poor soil in some rocky, inhospitable spot too miserable-looking to be coveted by his rich neighbours, who took the best land in the valley bottoms, could sometimes produce a small but rewarding vintage, a bargain for any merchant who had the luck to find it.

The vineyards on the Upper Douro were largely in the hands of bigger land-owners, 'the great men of the wine country', as the Factory called them. They differed from the Lisbon land-owners in that more of them lived on their properties and inherited from former days some memory of growing wine for quality. In Lisbon the proprietors of vineyards were more often absentee landlords and, except for a few who had been educated in France and had acquired a more cosmopolitan outlook, they shared the indifferent or even suspicious attitude towards wine which was characteristic of the court and of most Portuguese in the south. The religious houses on the other hand, of which there were many, were always resident and maintained some interest in their wines. Some of the best vineyards were reputed in England to belong to the Jesuits, so that good wine in England was often called priest's port.

From the account quoted of Woodmass's ride up the Douro at

N

the time of the Methuen treaty it is clear that men from the Factory had already begun to shop around in the Douro district for wines and to make personal visits for the purpose. Often good bargains could be made, but they involved long exhausting rides on mule-back up remote valleys and steep mountain paths to buy small lots, which then had to be taken down to the river, perhaps a journey of several hours, and shipped down the river to Oporto. The Douro boatmen were tough fellows and prone to drink the wine, replacing what they had taken with water. In any case the voyage to Oporto took several days and involved a more arduous journey than anything required to bring local wine to Lisbon. It was easier for residents of the Upper Douro to organize the collection of the grapes, the pressing of the wine and the transport of the new pressed wine down the river than it was for transient visitors, and as soon as the land-owners on the spot realized that the trade had become a profitable business, they banded themselves together to take control. As early as 1711 the Oporto Factory complained that the landowners were in league with the magistracy to monopolize the control of the river traffic. This made it difficult to buy wines piecemeal from small proprietors, and actually it was more advantageous in many cases to deal with a large proprietor, who could supply a large consignment, arrange for its despatch down the river and give some guarantee of its quality. Naturally the Douro owners took advantage of the comparative ease of controlling the single route down the Douro by regulating the licences given to the boatmen. Knowing that the shippers were anxious not to lose the season, they could, and often did, hold up the despatch of the wines in order to get better prices. It was only after bitter experience of the losses caused by undue delays to both parties that a gentleman's agreement was reached to send the wine to Oporto as soon as it was ready and to leave the settlement of the price to be argued out later in the light of the quantity and quality of the vintage and of the state of the market. It would seem that the Douro owners had the best of the bargaining position, in so far as they had the best wines and the control of the route to Oporto. But there was also the 'barro de mar', the sea bar or entry into the Douro, as well as the 'barro de terra', the access down the river.[1] The Oporto authorities were

[1] C.O. 385/15/i. Oporto Factory memorial of 13th August 1711 and Add. MSS 38816, fo. 53.

as anxious to control the entry of competing wines from other provinces of Portugal as the Douro owners were to maintain the monopoly of their own wines. But some wines were grown quite near Oporto, for instance in the valley of the Sousa river, and small boats could land wines from a little farther up or down the coast without overmuch difficulty. However, the fashion for strong wines assured the predominance of the Upper Douro which principally produced them. Some wines were shipped directly to England from Aveiro or Figueira da Foz, but to earn the name of port-wine it was better to bring them to Oporto for blending. Viana, for a few years an important source of wine, fell out of the running because its harbour had become silted up and there was no longer the same demand for the claret type of table wine grown in the Lima valley and around Moncão and sometimes shipped from the small ports of Caminha and Esposende as well as from Viana. Nevertheless a good many wines from districts both north and south of Oporto were brought in to be blended with the Douro wines. Some of these in good years were of a quality to compete with the Douro wines, but on the whole the market could take anything the Douro produced and the Douro growers had little to fear from competition. The evidence about the price of port-wine is hard to assess. In 1715 the Portuguese minister in London, da Cunha Brochado, said that 38 milreis a pipe was being charged in Oporto and he thought this was too high.[1] In 1731 a Portuguese merchant living in London spoke of 36 milreis, while an estimate at about this time by an English Lisbon merchant gave prices ranging from 36 to 50 milreis. In 1731 the Lisbon wines, representing about 10% of the total Portuguese trade, were valued higher than the port-wines at 45 milreis. The figures for the value of the total trade in Portuguese wine, compiled by Schumpeter and taken as an acceptable basis by the Portuguese economist Borges de Macedo, confirm that until about 1750 the price of port-wine remained fairly stable, though even before that time the growers complained that the shippers were forcing their prices down and their costs up.

The Oporto Factory had to deal with the municipal authorities, the Royal customs, the bishop and the coopers' guild. The prosperity of the wine trade was a common interest for all of them,

[1] Coimbra MS 2974. Da Cunha Brochado, quoted by courtesy of Coimbra University.

but they bickered between each other for a larger share of the profits. The town had to meet heavy expenses, particularly for the maintenance of the Oporto regiment of the royal army. The bishop had jurisdiction over goods entering or leaving the district and levied his own dues thereon. The customs were precluded by the 1654 treaty from charging over 23% *ad valorem* on the imports of English manufactures but had other means of adding to the Factory's burdens. The export duties on wine were not heavy but they rose from ·666 milreis a pipe in 1716 to 1·270 milreis in 1732. The customs tried to insist that 20% of their dues should be paid in bullion. This was vexatious, as bullion was scarcer in Oporto than in Lisbon, but could be offset as long as imports could be paid with exports, which was practicable for merchants who set off their imports of cloth against exports of wine. Many of the shippers dealt in both textiles and wines, and, directly or indirectly, had no difficulty in doing this. The coopers from an early date organized their guild and tried to obtain control of the fabrication and distribution of casks. Some empty casks were imported, but the majority were made in Oporto from pipe staves imported from England or the Baltic or in some cases made of native Portuguese oak or chestnut. The Portuguese did not therefore take the English control of the wine trade lying down. Nevertheless the English maintained their predominance and as far as shipping was concerned a monopoly, for the Navigation Act prevented the carriage of wine to England in foreign ships, and after the war of the Spanish succession Portuguese shippers carried only a small share.

The problems of the English Factories in Portugal were generally ventilated at the time of Lord Tyrawley's arrival as ambassador in 1728. Tyrawley was an ebullient Irishman, the son of Brigadier O'Hara who was convicted for looting at Port St Mary in 1702. He had served with his father at the time and had subsequent experience of the peninsula. Personally he was something of an old reprobate and was well-known for his harem of ladies. However the Portuguese rather liked him for this. It was an old joke among them that English bishops had wives and that the Archbishop of Canterbury had several. This was almost an article of faith among them and any English minister with a name for gallantry won the nickname of Archibishop of Canterbury. Paul Methuen had qualified for this and Thomas Burnet, himself the son of a bishop, did his best to earn the title. Now Lord Tyrawley enjoyed it and it did him no harm. But he was an active and competent minister; he knew Spain and Portugal well and he earned the respect of the Portuguese by taking pains to understand them and to study Anglo-Portuguese problems objectively. When he arrived in Lisbon he found that the Factories were constantly appealing to the 1654 Anglo-Portuguese treaty and he proposed that a copy should be made available and should be displayed publicly in the Portuguese customs houses. But he found that although the contents of the treaty were well-known and had been published, the original copy had been mislaid in Whitehall and the legation files contained no documentation on the subject. The English had always claimed that they would be satisfied if the treaty were correctly observed. The Portuguese had never disagreed, but had made many reservations about the interpretation of almost every single article. There were endless disputes and, in the absence of any authoritative text, checking-up was difficult.

Nevertheless the disputes on many points had been settled by the issue of a fresh Portuguese *alvara* or explanatory decree. After the best part of a century the number of these had mounted up and it would have been possible to make a collection of *alvaras* to cover every disputed article. Tyrawley took great pains to make such a collection and after ransacking the legation archives eventually discovered a copy of the treaty which confirmed in every particular the printed version published in London. But even this was not enough and he bent his energies to obtain a sight of the original Portuguese version by bribing a clerk in the Portuguese ministry of foreign affairs. The whole business, including the cost of collecting the *alvaras*, cost him £600; King George II was most reluctant to reimburse him but eventually did so.[1]

In the course of his studies of the economic position, Tyrawley elicited in 1729 two reports from the members of the Lisbon Factory. They gave very different accounts. One of them made by Burrell, a merchant with interests in the corn trade and connections with the South Sea Company, concluded that Portugal had an unfavourable trade balance of £308,375. This was in keeping with what was generally thought, though modern writers such as Schumpeter and Fisher, basing their conclusions on contemporary eighteenth-century statistics, agree on a figure of £550,000. The

[1] S.P. 89/35, Tyrawley, 25th February and 10th April 1729.

second report made by Arthur Stert reached the surprising conclusion that Portugal had a favourable trade balance of £153,000.
Stert was also a senior member of the Factory and a much respected
character. He had been Admiralty agent in Lisbon and during the
war of the Spanish succession had taken part in several contracts
for supplies to the Portuguese army. He became a commissioner in the commercial negotiations with Spain in 1730-33 and
belonged to a well-known Devonshire family which included an
M.P. for Plymouth and members of the Oporto Factory. Another
Arthur Stert, his nephew, was equally prominent in Lisbon twenty
years later and a great friend of Sir Benjamin Keene, consul in
Lisbon and then minister for a short time in Lisbon and ambassador for some years in Madrid.

Stert achieved his conclusion by estimating English sales of
goods at a lower figure, and by omitting the Viana trade and the
profits of trade in British ships between Lisbon and the Mediterranean. The latter was important for the trade in corn with Italy,
and was estimated to be worth £100,000. He emphasized the value
of the wine and fruit trade to the Portuguese and the advantage
they won by enjoying twelve months' credit, whereas the English
had to pay in cash. He also maintained that the cloth trade had
declined lately owing to French and Italian competition and to a
falling off in quality of English cloth, but that the King of Portugal
still received more customs duty on English goods than from those
on the commodities of any other power. He denied that there was
reason to complain of the bullion exported to England and maintained that it was largely used to pay debts to foreigners.[1]

It was true that some of the bullion belonged to Dutch or other
merchants who had not the same facilities for shipping it out of
Portugal, but most of the bullion was for the English account and
the freight of that carried for others was also an appreciable asset.
The sums involved were certainly large. Tyrawley had recently
warned the Factory to be prudent about the export of bullion
which was being regularly taken out by every packet-boat and by
H.M. ships. Provided that the bullion was taken to the ships by
boat discreetly and under cover of night, the Portuguese turned a
blind eye on the practice. But the law was sometimes openly
flouted, particularly by newcomers who did not know the ropes

[1] The two reports are in S.P. 89/35 ff. 183 and 196, with Consul
Compton's despatches of 25th June and 6th August 1729.

or had not taken the trouble to cultivate the goodwill of Portuguese officialdom, and when this occurred an occasional arrest was made. Once this had happened it was difficult for the British minister to settle the incident. In May 1728 Tyrawley spoke of 100,000 moidores (a moidore was the same as 28/- then) having arrived with the Brazil fleet and being taken out by H.M. ships, while an additional 20,000 moidores had been taken out in March.[1] These figures are very credible and fit in well with a total of over £100,000 carried, according to Fisher, by the Falmouth packet-boats between January and June 1741. On the other hand very much larger figures were often quoted, and can be supported by the size of the amounts brought every year or two years by the Brazil fleets amounting, according to Lucio de Azevedo, to over twelve million cruzados (£1½ million) in 1727 and eight million cruzados (£1 million) in 1728. The total exports of specie from England and Wales for the years 1727-29 according to Schumpeter were, in thousands of pounds, 2,278, 2,924 and 3,236. It is true these figures included silver and bullion originally derived from all parts of the world but they dwarf the trade figures for Portugal, about which there was so much argument, and are puzzling to the layman.

Stert's report strengthened Tyrawley's hand in his talks with the Portuguese. English merchants were inclined to spoil their case by bragging about the extent, success and profits of their trade with Portugal, and their assertions needed a corrective. Nevertheless, Stert's statements caused surprise and his figures seemed exaggerated. His estimate of 25,000 pipes of wine for the Oporto exports was reasonable, but the value of 50 milreis he put upon the pipe was a maximum rather than an average price. The Douro wine-growers later spoke of 40 milreis as the price paid for their best wine, but according to most contemporary sources the average was nearer 36 milreis. For instance Robert Jackson, the consul at Oporto, estimated that in 1727 Oporto exported 20,000 pipes at 36 milreis a pipe.[2] Stert's estimate of 10,000 pipes at 28 milreis for Madeira was also on the high side. There were many invisible and incalculable factors involved, but it is probable that Burrell's calculation was nearer the truth than Stert's. Schumpeter's statistics give the average imports of Portuguese wines for

[1] S.P. 89/35, Tyrawley, 30th May 1729.
[2] S.P. 89/34, Oporto Factory memorial of 12th May 1727.

the years 1726-30 as 12,325 tuns (about 25,000 pipes) worth £306,849, which would be the equivalent of about 43 milreis a pipe including freight.

The English returns include the direct imports from Madeira, which only averaged 231 tuns in the years 1726-30, though afterwards they increased. They did not however exceed 1,000 tuns before 1765. The exports from Madeira to America, which were more important, do not figure in the English returns. Mention has already been made of the account of the Madeira trade given in the Bolton letters. On one occasion an estimate of 27,000 tuns was given for the total vintage for the year 1707. This was an estimate of total production including wines consumed locally, but some late seventeenth-century accounts spoke of fifty or sixty ships being engaged in the trade and of an export of from 5,000 to 10,000 pipes. Bolton's own account, except for the one very high estimate for 1707, suggests that 10,000 pipes was more likely to have been the maximum than 20,000. In the year 1800, when the trade had considerably developed, an export of 17,000 pipes was said to have been a record and to have absorbed the whole of the island's production, and in 1819, when madeira was in high favour in England, the maximum import was 5,844 pipes. Madeira was well placed to avoid the net of official statistics on account of the number of ships which sailed for world-wide destinations in America and the East Indies, and allowance must be made for exports to Ireland and Scotland and for contraband, but the production of the island was limited by its size, so very high estimates must be treated with caution.

Whatever the exact truth, the Portuguese wine trade was prospering in the 1730s and Oporto had improved its position relative to Lisbon and other Portuguese wine-ports except Madeira. Nevertheless there must have been some cause for disquiet to move Lord Tyrawley and the Factories to take such pains to study the question. Undoubtedly from about 1740 the consumption of imported wine per head in England began to fall, but the elimination of Spanish competition during the war with Spain saved the Portuguese trade for some years longer from any ill consequences. In 1746 a blow was struck at the wine trade by the first increase in duties since the reign of Queen Anne. It amounted to £4 a tun on Portuguese wines and to £8 a tun on French wines. The total importation of wines fell after 1740 from about 20,000 tuns to 15,000 tuns and once in 1744 to 10,000 tuns, but this was no doubt due to a failure of the Portuguese vintage, and during the war with Spain which lasted until 1748, the proportion of Portuguese wines to the total English imports rose from 50% to 90%, and port-wines made up three-quarters of these. For the time being therefore the Oporto trade did not suffer much, but the increase of duty no doubt increased the temptation to adulterate wines, and of the wine drunk in England a higher proportion was home-made or confected with only a basis of genuine imported wine.

In 1750 King John V died after a reign of 44 years and King Joseph I succeeded to the throne of Portugal. The reign of King John had been literally a golden age, during which the tide of gold and then of diamonds had reached its highest point and had been reflected in the fantastic golden altars of the many new and glorious churches. But it had not been enlightened. In 1744 de Castres reported from Lisbon that it was impossible to imagine how difficult it was to gain any information on political questions. The Secretary of State had no more power than a junior clerk and was ashamed to see a minister or consul. For some time the two cardinals, da Cunha and de Motta, were the only men who had the ear of the king, but even their advice was only acceptable when they told the king what he wanted to hear. De Motta personally was quite accessible, but he disliked foreigners and was convinced that their influence in matters of trade was bad. There was a strict censorship and nothing, however trifling, which in the least concerned the administration, could appear in print, unless it had been carefully examined and approved by one of the Secretaries of State. Nevertheless the wealth from Brazil had staved off any recession until now and it was only after the middle of the century that trade began to slacken.[1]

The new king was more easy-going than King John, but almost immediately he appointed Sebastião de Carvalho, the future Count of Oeiras and Marquis of Pombal to be his chief adviser, and his government, though more enlightened, soon became as autocratic as before. Carvalho had been minister in London from 1738 to 1743 and afterwards in Vienna, though he nominally retained his post in London. His second wife was a Viennese lady of good family. He had not learnt to speak English or perhaps to understand the English character, but he was fluent in French, and read

[1] S.P. 89/44 De Castres to Stone, 20th January 1744.

many English and French books. He had acquired indeed quite a
cosmopolitan outlook and a keen interest in trade problems. When
the imposition of new duties on wine was proposed in London he
at once protested to the Duke of Newcastle. His protests were
rejected and he was assured that he had no reason for complaint,
as the duties applied equally to all wines.[1] In fact French wines
paid £4 a tun more under the new duties than other wines and
Portuguese wines gained rather than lost, but Carvalho was not
convinced. He had more justification for his persistent complaint
that the Portuguese in London were denied the privileges to which
they were entitled to put them on the same level as British subjects in Portugal. He acquired a chip on his shoulder about this
and not unnaturally, when he became a minister in Portugal it
was feared that he would be anti-British, particularly as owing to
some difficulty of protocol he had not been given the customary
leaving present when he terminated his mission to London. Benjamin Keene, who had talked with him in London, described him
as 'as poor a pate from the university of Coimbra as ever I have
seen', and habitually decried him, though eventually he began to
have a better opinion of him. Keene's rating was mistaken and
Carvalho did not prove to be anti-British. He was critical of the
privileges enjoyed by the Factories, very autocratic and a great
stickler for the rights of Portugal, but British ministers admitted
that he preferred the British to the French and that he had a
genuine appreciation of the benefits of Anglo-Portuguese trade.
Indeed, in the whole of his twenty years of power he rarely, if
ever, deviated from his allegiance to the alliance with Britain or
showed serious signs of joining the Bourbon family compact. He
had some knowledge of the wine trade apart from that acquired
in official life, for he owned vineyards at Oeiras near Lisbon,
which by a coincidence produced not the usual lisbon white wine
but a generous red wine inviting comparison with port. He also
owned or acquired some properties not actually in the port-wine
district, but near it.

Before the accession of the new government, and while the war
with Spain still lasted, various disputes had arisen about ships
from Oporto putting into the Tagus being made to pay Lisbon
consulage and customs dues. Although the Oporto Factory through
their closer relations with the navy had secured better protection,

[1] Add. MSS 20799, fo. 77, etc., for Pombal's London despatches.

it was not always possible to arrange for a direct convoy from the Douro, and home-bound ships often had to go to wait for a convoy at Lisbon. If the weather was good and the delay not long they could anchor outside the bar, but they were often obliged by bad weather or a prolonged delay to enter the river, where they came within the jurisdiction of the Lisbon customs and the Lisbon consulate. These troubles were eased by the conclusion of peace with Spain but were soon succeeded by others. The English minister, de Castres, did not find that his forebodings about Carvalho were realized; indeed the latter often displayed a friendly interest, but perhaps just because the government took a greater interest in trade and was therefore more disposed to interfere, or because the Factory had grown more awkward, disputes multiplied. One of them concerned a seizure of gold from a merchant named John Burrell, the same who had submitted a report on Anglo-Portuguese trade in 1729. He did not himself demand that a very strong line should be taken and the amount seized of 344 milreis was comparatively small, but a principle was at stake, particularly as the seizure had been made at Burrell's house and not when the gold was being taken to a ship. Another prominent merchant, John Bristow junior, insisted that strong diplomatic protests should be made. John Bristow was a nephew of John Bristow senior, deputy governor of the South Sea Company and a friend of Benjamin Keene, minister in Madrid, and for a short time, before the end of the war with Spain, in Lisbon. Keene had himself been agent for the South Sea company and as a peninsula expert was often consulted by the Secretary of State. Largely through the influence of these two men Lord Tyrawley was sent out again to Lisbon on a special mission to investigate pending questions. He remained in Lisbon from April to August 1752 and was not unsuccessful. The Portuguese ultimately agreed to restore the gold seized from Burrell, and another dispute, that about the judge conservator, was also smoothed over. The Factory had taken the opportunity of the election of a new conservator to insist that he should be subject to special conditions, which would prevent the abuses they claimed had been committed by his predecessor. This conservator, named Quintinilla, had contrived to be re-elected more than once and had occupied the office for twelve years, but had been very unpopular with most of the Factory. The Factory had the right to submit the name of a successor for approval by the king but not to lay down the conditions on which he should serve, as they now tried to do.

The Factory welcomed the coming of Tyrawley and he was also well received by Carvalho. De Castres had tried to keep out of the dispute about Quintinilla and been criticized by the Secretary of State for not taking a firmer line, but Tyrawley as soon as he had gone into the matter, was himself very critical of the Factory. He reported that it was certain that the King of Portugal's officers were sometimes pretty severe upon British subjects, but that they often had some justification for it. The Factory enjoyed many indulgences which they had come in the course of time to regard as due to them of right, though no such privileges were written into any treaty he had ever been able to discover. He continued: 'A great body of H.M's trading subjects reside at Lisbon, rich, opulent, and every day improving their fortunes and enlarging their dealings. These people can properly be said to be under no government but that of their own opinions, which each man will follow, or take advice of His Majesty's Minister as best suits his present occasion there, so it is not to be wondered at, if things sometimes run into some little confusion. I am only surprised it does not happen more frequently'.[1]

With the help of de Castres, Tyrawley settled both the principal disputes. The gold was restored to Burrell and after the Factory had been persuaded to cancel the election of the new conservator and to resubmit his name without any unacceptable conditions the king approved his appointment. Tyrawley gave what support he could to British interests, but he was annoyed at being sent to Lisbon upon what he regarded as an unnecessary and paltry mission, and upon his return to London submitted a critical report of the Factory. He said that the majority of the merchants were satisfied with the position regarding the bullion and for many years had been content to let well alone, for with the help of a few judicious bribes and of the good connections which the older firms had been careful to establish with the Portuguese, they had always been able to dispose of their gold with the connivance of the Portuguese authorities. Until now de Castres had not found Carvalho unreasonable; he had made no fuss when a courier to the Portuguese embassy in London had been unfortunately beaten up and had helped the avoidance of incidents by dropping a word

[1] S.P. 89/48, Tyrawley to Newcastle, 16th April 1752.

of warning when some offending British captain was in danger of arrest when next his ship came in and he came ashore. Upon Tyrawley's recommendation he granted a request from the Oporto Factory to be allowed a convenient place for a cemetery and the privilege of bearing arms for their defence against bandits when they went on journeys up country, taking with them large sums in cash to buy wine from the peasants.[1]

However, in 1753 the Factory raised fresh complaints. Several merchants including Bristow desired to ship corn to Spain, where there was a shortage and a profitable market, but there was a shortage also in Lisbon and Carvalho prohibited the export of corn, thus in the view of the Factory infringing British rights under the 1654 treaty. Neither de Castres nor Crowle, the new consul general, supported the Factory's claim. Crowle, a former member of parliament, had been civilly received by the Factory but reported that they were full of grievances and showed an unpleasant spirit. His predecessor, John Russell, had been rather weak with them and had allowed them to elect a committee with very extraordinary powers. Crowle had felt obliged to object to these, but hoped that this violent spirit could be calmed and things brought into their proper channel. De Castres had already told Tyrawley about the committee and the doings of the faction in the Factory whom he called the Grumbletonians. He said they aspired to give orders to the minister and to the consul-general and thought themselves ill-used if they were not kept informed of every word which passed between the legation and the Secretary of State. Now in the course of a further furious quarrel about the corn, Crowle made the mistake of allowing his complaint against a particularly obstreperous Grumbletonian named William Shirley to reach the Portuguese government. De Castres supported Crowle and Shirley was deported, but the English government felt bound to lend an ear to the representations of the friends of the Factory, admonished de Castres for giving in too easily and recalled Crowle. Crowle died of apoplexy before he could leave Lisbon and the Portuguese raised no objection to Shirley's return; but this repetition of something very like the Burnet incident of thirty years before discredited British officials and was bad for Anglo-Portuguese relations.[2]

[1] S.P. 89/48, de Castres, 13th January, 12th February and 27th June 1753.
[2] These incidents are described in S.P. 89/48.

Although the home government had supported the Factory their eyes were now opened to its faults. Some two years after his return to England Lord Tyrawley wrote another report which carried the process further. He said that in spite of its appearance of prosperity the Factory had lost the esteem of the Portuguese and was rushing to its ruin. The treaties were obsolete and the decisions of the Portuguese courts now regulated procedure. This was slipshod and corrupt but more to the taste of the British merchants than a straightforward system. When he had appointed some of them as commissioners to discuss their difficulties with the competent Portuguese officials they had attended a few meetings and then had refused to attend any more, thus showing that they preferred fishing in troubled waters to a good fair agreement. The Portuguese *proveedor* (the official who decided disputes about customs valuations, etc.) had told him that he had received many complaints and that the merchants of the Factory were a set of coxcombs or 'petits maîtres', who thought more of their *quintas* (country villas), balls, masquerades and gaming than of their business. Scarcely one of them would give himself the trouble to go to the custom-house to despatch his own goods, but left it to the Portuguese clerks who were all pettifogging rascals and the worst rogues in the country. Tyrawley said he had asked them why they did not attend the custom-house themselves and had been told that it was so dirty and snobbish a place that no gentleman could set foot in it. He added that other foreign merchants did very well without the privileges the English claimed, and the Factory no longer consisted of the respectable, frugal men he remembered. They were become universal traders rather than English factors, and many houses dealt more, or at least as much, in French goods, Hamburg linen, Sicilian corn and other commodities from different countries as in English produce.[1]

Tyrawley's aspersions were not unfounded but they were influenced by his bad humour about his whole mission. He had grown old and testy and was no longer the favourite that he had been with the Factory, and still more with their wives, in his prime. Not long before, in 1747/8, Benjamin Keene had formed a very different impression, and when he wrote from Madrid felt a nostalgia for 'the jolly, free Factory'. He himself was getting on in years and admitted he was no longer a 'cupidon'. But he had

[1] Add. MSS 23634. Minute dated December 1755.

much enjoyed the society of his Lisbon Factory friends. He said more than once that he would gladly exchange all the duchesses and countesses of Madrid for the Factory ladies. In point of fact there were several duchesses who were cosmopolitan enough and willing to be kind to an ambassador. Keene had consoled himself with them reasonably well and at Lisbon, as a bachelor minister with a liking for feminine society but with a much cosier and less dangerous character than Tyrawley, he had innocently frequented Mrs Arthur Stert and wives of the other senior merchants, who were exempted from the criticisms both of Tyrawley and the Portuguese. The Factory atmosphere was of course more agree-able to an Englishman than were the ceremonious ways of the Spanish court and Keene's much-quoted description correctly interpreted his feelings, though upon consulting the context one finds that Keene made it with reference to his young secretary Peter Mallortie, who had just died, and not to himself. No duchesses were kind to Mallortie; as a secretary he was occasion-ally privileged to witness some great state function at the heels of his chief, but his usual way of passing an evening was to take his dutiful hand at whist until it was time for Keene to go to bed. Lisbon had been Mallortie's home and he had access to the com-forts of the Factory. The British there had created a world of their own, which for the inmates was pleasant enough. There was nothing like it in Spain, where Protestant English were few and the Catholics lived like Spaniards. In neither country were there any social opportunities for foreigners outside the Factories, except at the very top. The English were criticized for their insularity, but could be excused for their failure to mix and for making the best of a bad job.

While Tyrawley was a soldier by profession, Keene came of merchant stock in King's Lynn and was naturally more at home in the Factory. Not all the Factory were coxcombs, but too much prosperity had spoilt some of them and now this prosperity was threatened. It was not only that the era of gold and diamonds was about to draw to its close but that as England became a world power the Factories in Portugal diminished in importance. Hither-to the Factories had had a powerful lobby in Parliament and the city of London, and the ministers at Whitehall had been inclined to be more sympathetic to their grievances than H.M. ministers abroad. This situation was to revive to some extent during the

Peninsular War, but for the time being the British government had other interests in mind and was less disposed to press Portugal in favour of the Factories. They were reluctant to do so, even when Portugal was obliged by a renewal of the threat of a Spanish invasion to invoke the terms of the English alliance and to place themselves under an obligation.

This was the situation when the delayed crisis of the Douro at last began to make itself felt. There are fewer records at this moment of the Oporto Factory than that of Lisbon. The Oporto Factory was less internationalized and less spoilt, but had probably evolved in the same direction. After the peace with Spain the statistics of the wine trade show the usual discrepancies, but all reveal a decrease of 15% to 25% in the seven-year period 1748-54 compared with 1741-47. In a falling market the shippers were better placed to pick and choose and to buy cheap wines from outside than from the Douro growers. They had some success in beating down prices. Once they threatened to buy no wines at all, and the prices were supposed to have fallen catastrophically to 10 milreis a pipe. It is doubtful whether they bought much so cheaply from the Douro, but they provoked the growers to make a great effort to shake off the shackles of the Factory's monopoly and their dependence on the English market. An Oporto resident of Basque origin named Bartholomew Pancorvo conceived that new markets for port-wines could be found in northern countries. The Dutch had long taken French wines there, and Spanish wines too, and strong wines suited the northern taste. Only small quantities of Portuguese wines had hitherto passed the Sound into the Baltic, but even distant Russia was a hopeful market for strong crude wines and had recognized Portuguese wines to the extent of including them in their customs tariff at the lowest rate.[1] Pancorvo's ideas were therefore not without merit, but they required capital to implement them, which Pancorvo and his friends lacked. He soon went bankrupt and his failure was hastened by the prompt action of a member of the Oporto Factory named James Stuart, who outbid Pancorvo by offering as much as £17 a pipe (60 milreis) for wines of the 1753 or 1754 vintage. The year given is 1754, but 1753 seems more likely as the Oporto exports were half as much again as in 1752 or 1754.

[1] C.O. 388/32, 9th April 1731, contains a copy of the Russian Customs Tariff.

It was in September 1754 that the Oporto Factory addressed a letter, which has been much quoted, to the Douro commissaries. It is not very clear who precisely the Douro commissaries were or for whom they acted. They seem to have been agents employed by the Factory to buy wines at the Regua fair and to do other business which the Factory could not attend to itself, but at the same time to have reflected some local interests. They were probably intermediaries who included some vineyard owners among them.

The Factory told the commissaries that the port-wines, which had been held in such esteem in England, had so lost their credit that other wines and indeed any other kind of liquor were preferred to them, and that in spite of the increase of population in England the demand for port-wine was falling off and many people were saying it was injurious to health. This was an exaggeration, for although Spanish wines were competing again, 1753 had been a good year for Oporto, and Portuguese wines still represented over two-thirds of the total English consumption. But the Factory insisted that the situation was calamitous and affected both merchant and wine-grower equally, but that the wine-grower was principally to blame. In support of this charge they made three main accusations:

1. The greed and desire of the Douro proprietors to increase their stocks prompted them to buy from vineyards which were in cold country at too high an altitude or were otherwise unsuitable, and they added this inferior wine to the wine they sent to the Factory.
2. The proprietors did not tread their wine long enough, nor employ enough labourers to work the wine sufficiently for the production of a full-bodied wine.
3. The proprietors stifled the fermentation of the wine by adding brandy and this was nothing less than a diabolic procedure. The natural development of the wine was stifled without the wine being stabilized, with the result that after an interval it turned cloudy and bitter-sweet. The brandy they used was inferior, whereas only the best brandy should be employed and that not before Martinmas.
4. The proprietors failed to separate the red from the white grapes and this caused the wine to lose its colour and to ferment too easily. They then added elderberries to make up

o

for this and produced a mixture that was artificial and tasteless.[1]

The Factory concluded by saying that the English importers insisted that the wine must be properly stabilized and to be sure of this would not accept wine of less than a certain age. As for their part they could not risk the wine going bad in their cellars, they were obliged to wait for confirmation of the English buyers' orders before they could accept the wine from the growers. All these expensive delays could be avoided if the growers followed precisely the Factory's directions for the preparation of their wines.

The commissaries replied agreeing that the situation was calamitous but laying the whole blame on the Factory. They protested that the Douro wines had enjoyed an excellent reputation as long as they were sold as pure and natural wines without alteration or improvement, but that the Factory had insisted more and more on accepting nothing but rare and full wines and had rejected good natural wines such as the green wines grown in moist and sandy places. Nevertheless they had done their utmost to satisfy the Factory's requirements. They had made the growers separate the ripe grapes and delay picking them until they were thoroughly ripe. Only the sweetest grapes had been used and they had been trodden long hours to make stronger and sweeter wines. All this had been very expensive but still had not satisfied the Factory. The Factory had sought to exceed the bounds of nature and to have wines which burned in the stomach and flashed like gunpowder if they were thrown into the fire, wines dark as ink, having the sweetness of the sugar of Brazil and an aromatic flavour like the spices of India. They had been forced to add brandy to give strength and elderberry to give colour, and as if this were not enough, the Factory added more brandy and more elderberry still, and mixed the green wines sold to them with other green wines of inferior quality. The proof of this was to be found in the quantities of brandy and of elderberries, of sour wines from the mountains and of cheap wines from anywhere which the Factory were known to buy up. These were what they bought from outside, but from the Douro they would only accept wines loaded with elderberry, brandy and sugar, which cost the growers an additional five or six

[1] This correspondence is to be found in S.P. 89/53, but has been often published.

milreis a pipe to make. They rejected the good natural straw-coloured wines from the Douro known as *palhete*, though they themselves bought all sorts of green wines and flat wines from the hinterland of the Douro, such as from the Barro and from Mesão Frio, and also wines from other provinces, from Coimbra, Serra de Estrella and Anadia. The Oporto merchants from whom they bought them cared nothing for the reputation of the trade but only for their profits and for the fact that wines passing as Douro wines fetched a good price. So with one pipe of good Douro wine at forty milreis they mixed eight or nine pipes of cheap wine at ten or twelve milreis the pipe, loaded with sugar, strong spirits and all manner of adulterations. The Factory ought to state their requirements precisely and only buy pure unadulterated wine from the Douro. Only in this way could the reputation of port-wine be saved.

In spite of their mutual recriminations the Factory and the commissaries largely agreed in their complaints. The Upper Douro had great climatic advantages for growing the generous type of wine required, but the supply was limited, and neither side yet fully realized that such wine grew best on the worst-looking soil, where the yield was small but the quality good. Indeed, the best places for growing port-wine were higher up the Douro and still undeveloped. As the demand exceeded the supply both parties bought outside wines to make up but objected to the other party doing so. In this respect the Factory was better placed, for they could sometimes get good wines from central Portugal as well as the wines from the neighbouring Minho, which were cheap and accessible but seldom good. Most of the Douro hinterland on the other hand was hard of access. The Mesão Frio wines were not in themselves bad, but the commissaries probably complained because the Factory got them through the back-door over the pass to Amarante instead of down the Douro, a route which they controlled.

Neither party objected to the use of brandy in itself but only to the use of bad brandy or to its addition too soon. A handbook published in 1720 recommended an addition of brandy during the fermentation of the wine of three gallons to the pipe; this was much less than became the practice later. It is not known when the practice became general on the Douro, but already in 1742 de Castres, then consul-general at Lisbon, apologized for being unable to send any good port-wine to Henry Pelham, because in July it was impossible to find in Oporto any wines which had not been mixed with brandy to such a degree that they were undrinkable. He added that he himself had been obliged to make do with a little indifferent claret until the new vintage. He said he would not forget to send wine as soon as it was available. From this it is clear that he wanted to buy unfortified wine but that this was already difficult.[1]

The practice of adding brandy was also creeping in elsewhere. It was common in Bordeaux, and in Madeira there are references in the 1750s to the addition of a couple of buckets to each pipe, while by 1772 the use of brandy for madeira shipped to America was regarded as essential. Adding small doses of brandy at a later stage was usual. For instance, we find in 1761 John Baker, a Sussex barrister with connections in the wine trade, carefully adding three quarts of brandy to each of his three pipes of new madeira. In Oporto in the early days brandy was probably only added by the shippers and not by the growers. Later, in an attempt to provide the type of wines demanded by the shippers, the growers added brandy, but not always with judgement. It is interesting that the shippers cricitized the growers for adding brandy before fermentation was complete, whereas at the end of the century the defenders of fortified wine took a different view; it was then considered indispensable that the brandy should be used to arrest fermentation in order to preserve some of the sugar content, but at the crucial moment, neither too soon nor too late. Neither the shippers nor the commissaries objected to the use of brandy in itself but only to its abuse, while the growers grudged the additional expense involved.

[1] S.P. 89/42. De Castres to Pelham, 31st July 1742.

CHAPTER X

The Company of the Wines of the Upper Douro

PRESUMABLY the Douro growers did not do badly when the Factory paid high prices to outbid Pancorvo. In the years 1754-55 exports were low but they suffered more from Portuguese competition than from that of other wines. There was a big proportional increase for a year or two in the import of French wines into England, but as the amount involved was only 200 tuns, this did not make much difference. Spanish wines had a peak year of 5,175 tuns in 1753 but declined afterwards, and madeira wines increased from 600 to 900 tuns. If one can judge from the drop in imports into England of 2,000/3,000 tuns in the year after the Lisbon earthquake, Lisbon wines were at the moment the most serious competitor of Oporto wines, but this can only be inferred.

The year 1755, until the earthquake in November, was tranquil for the Lisbon Factory. The Hon. Edward Hay, a new and well-connected consul-general, was appointed. He was a brother of Lord Kinnoul, subsequently minister in Lisbon. The new judge conservator proved to be an active intelligent man who gave satisfaction. The trouble about corn subsided, and when some bullion was seized on its way back to a packet-boat named the *Expedition*, Hay thought the seizures were inspired by officious petty officials, and the minister, de Castres, criticized the captain of the packet for failing to make more discreet arrangements. Carvalho was disposed to be reasonable and both minister and consul reported that the prospects of recovering the money were good. There was again danger of war, but Carvalho seemed to incline towards England. In September the Brazil fleets arrived safely and in the autumn the Lisbon exports of wine were larger than usual. But on 1st November the picture was drastically altered by the earthquake which destroyed most of Lisbon and killed 40,000 people.[1]

In England there was a wave of sympathy for Portugal, and Parliament voted £50,000 for relief measures and sent out stocks of provisions. Other nations followed suit. Hamburg, which had a large Factory in Lisbon, sent a shipload of clothing and three of timber. The Spaniards, after offering money and services, fell into a wrangle about customs duties, but eventually gave 15,000 dollars through their ambassador. The French after a good deal of hesitation sent some supplies. The English on the whole behaved handsomely, as the brunt of the relief organization and of the shipment of supplies fell upon them, but they vexed Carvalho by refusing to pay a so-called voluntary contribution of 4%, which was to be levied on the goods of Portuguese and foreigners alike to defray the cost of building new customs houses. The Factory's attitude was unwise, for they had been the first to complain of the difficulties caused by the destruction of the customs houses, but they were not too much to be blamed, for although they had lost only sixty English lives, the loss of property had been very heavy and no less than 300 British subjects had been rendered destitute and had had to be repatriated. In London the Portugal merchants to the number of sixty-three, supported by thirteen merchants from Norwich, protested indignantly against the levy, and also against the Portuguese customs valuations, which they alleged favoured French goods and overvalued English woollens.[2]

Pombal, as he may now be called though he did not actually receive the title until 1759, rose to the occasion and made heroic efforts to rehabilitate the city. Even the royal family were homeless, and starvation and pestilence threatened to complete the toll of the earthquake. To repair the damage Pombal planned to rebuild Lisbon entirely and to restore Portuguese finances by a whole series of economic plans. These included the establishment of several trading companies.

Not long after the earthquake Pombal received a deputation from Oporto led by a friar named João de Mansilha and was in-

[1] S.P. 89/50, Consul Hay, 2nd April, 16th June, 15th July and 12th August 1755.
[2] S.P. 89/50, de Castres, February 1756, etc. S.P. 89/51, merchants' memorial of 12th July 1758.

formed about the Pancorvo plan and the grievances of the Douro wine-growers and other Portuguese interested in the trade. On the basis of this information plans were made for the foundation of a company to be named 'The General Company of Agriculture of the Wines of the Upper Douro', and the new company with a capital of £120,000 was established by a decree dated 10th September 1756. In the first instance the aim of the company was stated to be the encouragement of the export of port-wine to Brazil in order to compensate the Oporto trade for the loss sustained from the dues imposed by Lisbon on wines coming to the city from Oporto. On this understanding the British consul-general at Lisbon felt that he had no grounds to protest or that it would be wise to do so, as trade with Brazil was a purely Portuguese concern. He believed the English were on a good footing in Portugal and he doubted whether the complaints of a falling-off of the wine trade were justified, as their losses were offset by gains in the Madeira and Azores trade.

Actually the charter of the company affected the whole wine trade and especially English interests. However, ministers in London were growing disinclined to exert themselves to take up the cudgels on behalf of the Factory. They were preoccupied with other matters, and the British Government was unwilling to press the Portuguese very hard, even when Portugal's appeal for help against Spain in 1762, in accordance with the terms of her alliance, afforded an opportunity.[1]

The company's charter provided for the reservation of 10,000 pipes of wine for export to Brazil, but in addition gave the company the monopoly of the export of Oporto wines to all other destinations except the United Kingdom. British shippers could export wine to the United Kingdom as well as the company, but they could only export wines grown in the Upper Douro, passed by the company as Factory wines and approved in Oporto for shipment by one of the company's tasters.

The charter enabled the company to control the wine on the Upper Douro, in transit and in Oporto. No wines could be brought into the delimited district of the Upper Douro or into Oporto without the company's permission, and no Douro wine-grower was to sell any wine other than that from his own vineyards or

---

[1] S.P. 89/50 contains a translation of the charter and consul-general's opinion of 11th February 1756 that English trade was on a good footing.

any greater quantity than that found to be his average production according to an official list to be drawn up by the company. The company was authorized to give credit to farmers up to an amount representing the value of 50% of his annual vintage. A maximum price of 30 milreis a pipe was fixed for the best quality Douro wines, but the company was empowered to take up any wines it chose at 25 milreis for first-quality wine and 20 milreis for second-quality wines. Maximum prices for other wines ranged from 12 milreis and 20 milreis for Upper Douro wines grown outside the district delimited by the company to 4 milreis for wines grown near Oporto. A milreis was 1,000 reis, 5s 4d to 5s 6d. in the years 1750-60.

The company could own warehouses, charter ships and export wines of all qualities to all destinations. It was to prepare all material for casks and to submit all disputes to its own judge conservator, who was given jurisdiction over all carters, boatmen, labourers, coopers and warehouse keepers. In addition the company acquired later, in 1761, the monopoly of the sale of brandy for the fortification of wines.

Foreigners as well as Portuguese could become members of the company by buying shares to the value of 6,000 cruzados (2,400 milreis or a little over £640) and their holdings were guaranteed even in time of war, but the officers of the company had to be Portuguese resident on the Douro or in Oporto.

The preamble to the charter spoke in the name of the principal farmers of the River Douro, the landowners of Oporto and the religious houses and principal families of the Beira, the Minho and Tras os Montes. In practice the large owners in the Upper Douro and certain interests in Oporto were those benefited. The small peasant proprietors of the Upper Douro benefited a little and those of the Minho not at all. On the contrary they lost the sale of their wines for blending, and in the immediate neighbourhood of Oporto the company was authorized to monopolize the sale of all wines and to restrict the number of taverns. This last measure caused riots in Oporto, which were severely repressed. Jacomé Ratton, a French merchant and manufacturer who had been in Lisbon as a young man and had also lived with his parents in Oporto, believed that the riots were not serious but had been magnified by the local Portuguese militia commander in order to increase his importance and to justify his severe measures. Certainly 484 men and 54 women were convicted. Twenty-one of them were condemned to death but several made their escape. Probably the Factory sympathized with the rioters, but they were not accused of complicity and there is no known link except that one of the accused was a servant of an Englishman. The Jesuits were blamed for stirring up trouble. Blameworthy or not they had reason to hate Pombal, who had developed an obsession against them which culminated in their persecution and expulsion from Portugal in 1759/60. Their most important properties were overseas but they also owned religious houses in Portugal. In California and Mexico they planted vineyards at all their missions and they were credited with an interest in vines elsewhere. At one time they owned all the vineyards growing malmsey in Madeira. The name of the Jesuits was associated in England with port-wine, but the author has only found one reference to a Jesuit vineyard in Portugal, at Tourega in the Alemtejo. However the knightly orders of Christ, Santiago and Aviz owned lands on the Upper Douro which probably produced wine, and it was from a commanderie of the Order of Christ that Archbold, one of the first recorded British land-owners on the Douro, acquired for a peppercorn lease the Quinta de Rouriz destined to become famous for vintage port.

When Pombal heard of the riots in Oporto and of the strong protests against the company made by the Factory he was in no mood to brook contradiction. He said that the establishment of the company was essential to redeem a captive trade from slavery. It was presumptuous to question this, and it was the duty of all loyal Portuguese not to question their king and those who did so were ignorant jumped-up wretches. They should take notice of the hatred of the English for the company and draw their own conclusions. Was not the reason for their hatred the fact that the company was instituted for the defence of the Portuguese? The aim of the English was to enrich themselves by draining their unjust gains from Portugal and by taking advantage of Portuguese ignorance and negligence to master Portuguese commerce both in Portugal and Brazil, because the Portuguese like stone statues insensible of feeling were denying the desperate remedies applied to them by their royal physician. Their failure to submit to such a king, who studied to make them happy, proved that the English were right in saying that the Portuguese were half a century behind other nations.

Even in this polemic mood Pombal was as critical of his com-patriots as of the English. In cooler moments he admitted that a system which removed the control of the wine trade from the Factory only to give it to the care of officials not always above suspicion of corruption was imperfect. Pombal owned property on the Upper Douro and vineyards near Lisbon, so he had a personal interest, but according to Jacomé Ratton, who knew him well, he was not corrupt and, if he made a fortune, it was by being a shrewd and careful man of business. British ministers formed much the same opinion and Lord Kinnoul in 1760 said that Pombal was tenacious of his own plans and sometimes mistaken, but that in general his ideas of the commerce with England were just and solid and founded on Anglo-Portuguese interests. So there was no question of doing away with the company. Both sides accused each other fervently of the responsibility for the abuses which had crept into the wine trade, but they were obliged to reach a *modus vivendi*, for the Portuguese still wanted to sell their wines and the British to buy them.[1]

The British were naturally incensed at being reduced to mere middlemen whose only function was to buy the wine the company chose to allow them and to ship it. They threatened to suspend purchases of wine altogether, but were dissuaded from this ex-treme measure. In 1755, 1756 and 1757, the exports from Oporto dropped to 12,000 pipes, but the 1757 fall was largely due to a failure of the vintage, and from 1760 exports again averaged 20,000 pipes. The Portuguese now enjoyed much the same situation in the wine trade as they had in the import of textiles before the Methuen treaty. They enjoyed the protection of severe laws but it did not always suit them to interpret them inflexibly. The company was not in a position to do all the things proposed in its charter, and when it suited the officials concerned there was always scope for an arrangement. The desire to remove the worst abuses of adulteration was general, and Lord Kinnoul even thought that the company had succeeded in improving the quality of the wine. Certainly the proportion of genuine Douro wine increased, and the differences in price for the Douro and outside wines sanc-tioned by the company showed what large profits must have been

---

[1] S.P. 89/50 for Pombal's views of 7th May 1755 and 5th December 1756, and S.P. 89/53 October and December 1760 for Pombal's and Kinnoul's views.

made when cheap wines were used for blending. But some good wines were used for blending too, though they came from outside the Douro, and the Factory complained of being debarred the use of these, though in some seasons and for some purposes they might be better than the Douro wines.

The clamour for and against the company continued in a major or minor key throughout its existence and there has been much argument about its merits and demerits, but on the whole it seems that, during Pombal's lifetime at least, it had a qualified success, as indeed his other companies trading to Brazil had. There was no doubt a wide difference between the company's rules in theory and actual practice, and there were loopholes which did not appear on paper, but there was no doubt that the company was in control and that British shippers were obliged to make the best of the *fait accompli*. The producers, at least for a time, enjoyed the benefit of the increased fixed prices and the shippers, though their privileges had been curtailed, still drew profits from an assured market. The leading shippers, who had been accustomed to buy the best wines for sale to select customers, did not suffer overmuch from the increased prices, but some of the smaller firms who bought for the tavern market were probably squeezed out. The effect on the Factory is shown by a reduction in the number of births and deaths registered by the chaplain, so a few families must have returned home while the majority carried on. In 1775 a visitor named Richard Twiss reckoned that there were about thirty British families in Oporto. The officially approved Factory wine was perhaps a little better than before, and less brandy was added to the wine on the Douro and rather more afterwards. At first most of the wines appear, under the control of the company and subject to the approval of the company's taster, to have been embarked as soon as they reached Oporto. The taster decided whether the wine was fit for export as Factory wine or not, and the Factory complained that his judgement was very arbitrary. Clearly those who contrived to be in the good books of the company had the advantage and the shippers had no opportunity to treat their wines before shipment. But in the next decades an increasing proportion of the wine was kept in Vila Nova de Gaia for a year or more, and this must have restored to the Factory a measure of control over the maturing of their wines, though the amount warehoused continued to be limited by a lack of storage space. But the company's rules made it difficult to bring outside wines to Oporto for blending. One would have expected more wine to have been sent from central Portugal directly to England for this purpose. There are no London port-books for this period to show the extent of the trade with Aveiro and Figueira, or Portuguese export figures until 1796. The Plymouth and Exeter port-books show a fair trade with Figueira in fruit and with Aveiro in salt but comparatively little in wine. Probably some wine from these places found its way into Oporto in spite of the regulations, but the Factory denied this. In 1759 a Factory spokesman said that it had been impossible to stock up from elsewhere after the failure of the Douro vintage in 1757. He said this prevented stocks being built up which could have been used to make up for shortages elsewhere in 1758.

The Douro Company had powers to control the quality of the wine until it was shipped but none to control its treatment after it left Oporto. There is no evidence that the Pombaline legislation had much effect on the quality of the wine sold in England one way or the other. According to Thorold Rogers the price in 1758 was 5/6 a gallon, much the same as before, though owing to increased duties it rose in the 1770s. Probably the temptation to adulterate the wines was somewhat stronger than before owing to the increase in duty, but the better wines, sold at higher prices, continued to be handled by old established firms and to go to places where a traditional market existed, such as in King's Lynn for country gentlemen of the Walpole type. Some of the inferior wines, as the Factory complained, were shipped by the Douro Company to Guernsey. The Factory were not allowed to ship such wines themselves but the company was not above making a profit from them. In the second half of the eighteenth century Guernsey, which had always been a good place for smugglers, built up a thriving trade as an entrepôt for wines. Cheap French wines from the adjacent ports of Brittany were brought in as well as wines from Spain and Portugal, and the numerous apple orchards in the islands and in Normandy and Brittany produced quantities of cider to help out the mixture. It is fair to add that Guernsey also had facilities which Oporto lacked. The great warehouses, or lodges, for which Oporto or rather Vila Nova de Gaia is famous, developed only slowly and were always subject to Douro floods; Guernsey on the other hand had many good dry cellars, where good wine could be matured in an even temperature. Even before the founding of the Douro Company the King's Lynn port-books reveal that ships bringing wine had often called at Guernsey. For instance in 1752 the *Providence* had sailed with a Mediterranean pass for Lisbon and Malaga and came back with lisbon, malaga, and port-wine. The *Neptune*, a ship of 250 tons, had sailed with a pass for Lisbon and brought back forty tuns of port and $12\frac{1}{2}$ of lisbon after calling at Guernsey, while the *Bacchus* with seventeen tuns of port and two tuns of Spanish wines had also called there.[1]

The Portuguese appear to have been satisfied that as a result of the creation of the Douro Company the growers received better prices. A slight improvement of the trade in the second-class wines to Brazil and other destinations perhaps helped to carry the increased costs, but no doubt some middlemen in the Factory were squeezed out and gave point to the Factory's complaints, although the Factory in general suffered comparatively little. However, in support of the Factory's case Consul Whitehead reported in 1764 that the general English trade and shipping in Oporto had notably declined since the creation of the company. His figures showed that in the nine years ending in 1755, 1,294 ships had entered Oporto, while in the succeeding nine years the number had fallen to 757. A commission was set up by Parliament to enquire into the Anglo-Portuguese trade and the customs were asked to submit a survey of the trade for the years 1750-65. They reported in 1767 that exports to Portugal exceeded imports from Portugal by £105,000.[2] Although Schumpeter's figures for the same period are also based on official trade returns they give a very different picture. They show a balance of trade in England's favour of £826,000 in the years 1751-55, of £1,044,000 in the years 1755-60, and of £652,000 in 1761-65. The figures for 1755-60 were influenced by the exceptional exports to Portugal for the reconstruction after the Lisbon earthquake. The figures reported to Parliament left out of account several factors, however, principally the import from Portugal of bullion. The production of Brazil was no longer as great as it had been, a fact which is perhaps reflected in the reduction of total British exports of specie which for

---

[1] King's Lynn Port Book E 190/458 and Mediterranean Passes Adm. 7/87.
[2] Whitehead's report and the customs survey are in S.P. 89/64.

the years 1760-65 were, according to Schumpeter, a third of what they had been in 1729, that is an average for the five years of £1,012,000. Yet according to figures quoted by Fisher the average imports of bullion carried by the packet-boats for the years 1759-1763 were still £680,231. The official report of 1767 seems to have used some traditional figures: for instance the estimate of the exports of fruit from Lisbon and of salt from Setubal was the same as that of Stert in 1729, 50,000 chests of fruit and 40,000 moyos of salt. On the other hand the valuation was substantially increased, though that on wines was lower. Lisbon wines were increased in quantity from 7,000 to 9,000 pipes but reduced in value from £12 to £9 a pipe, while Oporto wines were cut from 25,000 to 22,000 pipes and from £13 10s 0d to £10 a pipe. A surprising feature of the survey was an increased estimate for the Madeira and Azores trade to 12,000 pipes at £20. It will be remembered that Stert had made an estimate of 10,000 pipes for madeira at 28 milreis (£7 14s 0d) and that this seemed high. The 12,000 pipes at the high valuation would have brought the total up to a sum greater than that of the trade of Oporto and some surprise was expressed at the time. It is true that the Azores trade was also included, but the estimate was probably exaggerated, though perhaps nearer the mark than Stert's estimate had been, for the Madeira trade had increased. De Castres some years before believed that this had more than made up for any fall in the Oporto trade, and the Madeira authorities themselves now estimated the total exports, including those to America, to be 11,000 pipes. The imports to England had increased to a peak figure of 1,178 tuns only in 1764, but the increased valuation is easier to agree, for the Lord Steward's books show 3/4 being paid for a quart bottle of madeira at a time when only 1/6 or 1/7 was being paid for port or lisbon.[1]

According to the Oporto statistics the exports of wine did not differ much in the ten years following the foundation of the company from what they had been in the previous decade. They had not gone off but had improved slightly from an average of 17,199 pipes for 1746-55 to 17,706 pipes for 1756-65, while after 1766 they rose appreciably and were helped by some increased exports to destinations other than Britain. There are no figures for Lisbon exports and Portuguese writers use English sources to enable them to calculate the size of the whole Portuguese wine trade. In 1756,

[1] L.S. 9/227, April 1762.

the year of the earthquake, total imports of mainland Portuguese wines into England and Wales fell by about 3,000 tuns, while Oporto exports, though low, were much the same as in 1755 and 1757; the 3,000 tuns probably represented the interrupted Lisbon exports. After the subtraction of the imports from Madeira the totals suggest a drop rather than an increase of the export of Lisbon wines to England. This appears more probable than an increase, because Pombal reversed the process by which Lisbon wines were protected at the expense of Douro wines. When he founded the Douro Company he considered that the Upper Douro was suitable for the production of wine and little else, while a reduction of vineyards in the Lisbon district and in the Alemtejo was desirable to provide more land for growing corn. Portugal was very sensitive on this subject. She had to import half her needs in a good year and more when the harvest failed. At the very beginning of the wine trade with England the ambassador Luis da Cunha had complained that cornfields were being torn up to make place for vineyards and this idea was a popular grievance in Portugal. When allied troops came to Lisbon in 1704 there was an outcry because a miserable-looking sandy patch near the Tagus chosen as a site for a camp was claimed to be sown with corn. No doubt from time to time, when the wine trade boomed, landowners everywhere were tempted to plant vines for easy profits. But in the Minho, which grew so much wine, there was maize enough for subsistence, and in any case most of the vines grew on trellises or on trees and did not compete with the corn. On the Douro, but more especially on the Douro above Regua, where the port-wine district was extended, the best vineyards were on steep and rocky hillsides unsuitable for corn, and the growers slowly came to realize that the best wines did not come from fat valley bottoms. In the Tagus valley and the central parts of Portugal cornfields and vineyards did compete and it was in these districts that Pombal's regulations tried to restrict the vines. Some reduction in the number of vineyards in the Lisbon and Alemtejo areas resulted, and this was compensated by the intensification of the cultivation of vines on the Douro and the eventual extension of the delimited area, where officially port-wine could be grown, higher up the Douro to places which were very suitable for growing quality wine but for little else. Pombal served this policy not only by regulations which obliged the farmers by pains and penalties to replace vineyards by cornfields in suitable places, but also by a reversal of the Lisbon tariff. Lisbon wines had formerly been protected from competition from outside wines, but now wines from Oporto, Madeira and other parts of Portugal, coming by sea, paid dues of 1,000 to 1,600 reis a pipe, whereas local Lisbon wines paid 7,200 reis and Lisbon wines entering the city by land 5,200 reis. The special protection given to Douro wines against the competition of Lisbon wines was perhaps the most important and lasting contribution made by Pombal to the Portuguese wine trade. The trade in Oporto wines with Lisbon, which had for some time been interrupted, was now to some extent renewed and one of the complaints of the Oporto Factory was that this trade was handled by the company and denied to themselves.

Hitherto the only significant outlet for Oporto wines except the United Kingdom had been Brazil. The wine going there was nearly all second- or third-class wine and had perhaps not always been included in the export statistics, though the wines sold to the royal navy and for ships' supplies in general probably were. As nearly all the Oporto exports went to the United Kingdom, the Oporto exports and the British imports could be roughly equated except that the English statistics did not show the Oporto exports to Ireland, Scotland and the Isle of Man, and the Oporto statistics did not include the Lisbon exports or those from Madeira and the Azores. Only after 1781 did Oporto exports begin to exceed the total imports of Portuguese wines into England and Wales. At that period Oporto sent as much as 8,335 pipes in one year to other destinations but only 1,089 pipes were first-class wines. Of these, 889 pipes went to Lisbon and 100 pipes to the British navy. Of the second-class wines St Petersburg and the Baltic ports took 1,356 pipes, Brazil 2,907 pipes and the British navy 2,924 pipes. These figures hardly came up to Pancorvo's expectations or those of the company's charter, but possibly some of the cheap wines going to Brazil in Portuguese ships still avoided being reckoned.

Portuguese figures for the export of Lisbon wines are only available from 1796. By that time there had been an increase in international trade generally and Lisbon exported an average of 10,000 pipes, while Figueira sometimes attained 5,000 pipes. In some years Viana still sent out a few hundred pipes, and there was an occasional shipment from the Algarve. From 1770 to 1790 the Oporto trade prospered quietly, after which it enjoyed a positive boom. Of Portuguese wines only madeira offered Oporto serious competition. Madeira imports to England rose to 2,000 pipes in the years 1788-93 and fetched higher prices than port, while the trade with America was larger than that with England.

Although the wine trade had kept up so well, Consul Whitehead reported in 1767 that the general trade of Oporto had fallen.[1] Some of the decline was due to external causes, for instance the increased competition from Italy and Greece in the fruit trade. Some of the trade was not lost to Portugal but had moved to Lisbon. As a result of Pombal's legislation Portugal was slightly more self-sufficient. More corn was grown in the south of Portugal and some maize was exported from Oporto and the north to Lisbon, while towards the end of the century the improved navigability of the Douro enabled some imports of corn from Castile to replace those from the United Kingdom. A few of the manufactories which Pombal set up survived, for instance the factory for making china and glass at Marinha Grande, which was established under the management of the Stephens family. The contribution of the Company of the Douro to the wine trade was not entirely bad, and was certainly less damaging than the Factory represented, but the maintenance of the trade and the eventual revival of its prosperity was largely due to the fortunate circumstance that a very strong habit of consuming port-wine had been established in England, where the steady increase of population and purchasing power offset the tendency to a decline in the taste for wine. Also, although the total population only increased slowly in the first half of the century, it was the urban population which principally supported the wine trade, and this had already begun to increase proportionately and actually. Between 1695 and 1801 the total increase of population was estimated to be from 5·2 millions to 10·945 millions, but most of this growth took place in the second half of the century. Middle class spending on wines tended to keep pace with the population increase but, until the reduction of duties by Pitt in 1787, was slowed down by the continued increase of duties. Between 1763 and 1782 there were four or five increases, but French wines were penalized even more heavily than before, and though Portuguese wines lost the slight advantage they had enjoyed over Spanish wines they were still the cheapest

[1] C.O. 358, 54, Consul Whitehead's report of 24th January 1767.

P

and able to hold their own against the severe competition offered by spirits and colonial rum.

There was no doubt that the Douro Company seriously interfered with the activities of the Oporto Factory. The resentment between Factory and company was never entirely overcome, but gradually a spirit of compromise gained ground and during the long consulship of John Whitehead between 1756 and 1805 the Factory gained a new dignity and lost a little of its insularity. In the first days of the company only one member of the Factory chose to subscribe to the company and to become a shareholder. This was James Archbold, perhaps a relative of that Robert Archbold of Scottish or Irish extraction who acquired a property near the Upper Douro. James Archbold or Archibald actually accepted a position with the company as an inspector of brandies.[1] He was regarded as a renegade by the Factory and was roundly condemned, but afterwards the Factory showed a more co-operative spirit and some of the members worked together with the Portuguese in the shipping and marketing of wine. One or two firms such as Hunt, Roope & Co and Offley Forrester bought properties on the Upper Douro and took part in the cultivation of vines and in the vintage, but this was exceptional up to the time of Baron de Forrester in the middle of the nineteenth century. Few British subjects stayed long up the Douro, and even when they acquired houses there they were used as temporary offices rather than as residences. On the other hand, as port-wines slowly penetrated to wider markets, the Portuguese took a somewhat greater interest in their development and in the export side of the trade. The Douro Company began to appoint its own agents in England and handled some of the direct trade. English visitors to Oporto went so far as to say that better port-wine could be got from the company than from the Factory, for the Factory cared little for the quality of the wine provided that it could find a buyer. More shocking still, some English visitors to the Factory formed the impression that the English shippers cared so little for good port that they drank inferior wine themselves. In 1774 Colonel Dalrymple wrote that he had been voluptuously entertained at the Factory with rounds of beef and fat turkeys, which made him think he was in sight of St Paul's cathedral rather than in Portugal, but the port-wine given him was so spoilt with spirits put into it

[1] S.P. 89/54. Oporto Factory memorial of 18th May 1761.

that it had become an infernal liquor. He said that he could not understand how men of refinement could persist in drinking such stuff as was regularly sent to the English market. Nevertheless, he thought that the competition of the Douro Company, which was provoking the fury of the Factory by setting up its own agents in England for the sale of its wine, was doing something to drive the worst wine off the market. A few years later Dr John Wright, who had resided in Oporto and claimed to be knowledgeable about wines, said much the same thing and claimed to be able to buy better wine in Oporto from the company than from the Factory. His remarks can be taken with a grain of salt, for it was perhaps after a quarrel with the Factory that he set himself up in England to sell wines as an agent of the company, but the views expressed by him in his essay on wines are very reasonable. Allowance must be made for prejudice and for the fact that the wines passed for export were in any case not drinkable until they had matured, and that the Factory was not allowed to deal in other wines, but their use of such crude wines for their own consumption without excuse or explanation is puzzling.

However, the British shippers were not free agents, for they were obliged to accept the wine that the company's tasters had passed and no other. Presumably the company's officials had some respect for the terms of their charter and had higher standards than were common in some parts of Portugal. These could be very low. An Irishman named Costigan who travelled in the 1770s left an account of conditions at Evora, an old city in the centre of Portugal and far from foreign influence. It was a part of the world where in the fifteenth century the Czech traveller Rozmital had seen vineyards and had commented that the wines were strong and sour, and scarcely drinkable if they were not mixed with water. Costigan said that when he was entertained by the governor only water was drunk except for a thimbleful to drink healths, though afterwards a very sweet madeira was served as a liqueur in half-pint bottles. The only place where he had good wine was at the house of Dr Butler, the only surviving member of the former Irish College at Evora. This gentleman gave him a double flask of excellent wine, of which he had made the vintage himself. He explained that the wine in the inn was not fit to drink and that there was no country in the world which produced better grapes or worse wine entirely on account of the slovenly methods used to prepare it. There was not a barrel or any kind of wooden vessel in the province. The wine was kept in large ill-baked earthen jars and mixed with lime or chalk. It was transported in dried hog-skins, sewed up and patched all over within and without, and was totally unfit for any Christian to drink. A century's experience of the English trade had no doubt improved the standards of the Douro, but it is evident that in the parts of Portugal where foreign influence did not prevail there was much wine about which the Factory would have had trouble to make palatable. Probably some of it was passed by the more venal of the company's wine tasters. On the other hand, to the vexation of the Factory, the tasters were in a position, if they wished, to condemn good and natural wines by not passing them as Factory wines, and to profit by their sale, a privilege denied to the Factory. This would account for the statement not infrequently made that better wines could be got from the company than from the Factory.

Although the Factory had little incentive under the dominion of the company to improve their wines, some progress was being made, and possibly the Dutch and German shippers, who had no privileged position and no sure market, had a greater interest. As has been mentioned, the purchase of a property near Ervedosa by one Robert Archbold is one of the few recorded instances of a British subject residing on the Upper Douro as early as the time of Pombal. It was believed to be the only one, but the research of H. E. S. Fisher has discovered a few more. Archbold was interested in the sporting opportunities which the district afforded, in shooting wolves and bears, and not in cultivating vines. Later the property passed into the hands of Nicolau and Joaquim Kopke, whose family, of German origin, had come to Portugal in the seventeenth century. They planted vines and though the property was not in the delimited port-wine district they obtained permission from the Marquis of Pombal, for whom they acted as agents for some property he held in the neighbourhood, to export their wines. Eventually the property passed into the hands of the Van Zellers, a family of Dutch origin who came to Oporto early in the eighteenth century and founded a firm of well-known merchants and wine-shippers. The property, which became known as the Quintal de Rouriz, was one of the earliest at the turn of the century to give its name to a well-known brand of port and to produce vintage wines. For a time it appears that the Douro Company and the

German and Dutch shippers had a greater interest than the British Factory in the selling of wines of quality, though it is difficult to believe that all the old-established English firms had no pride in their wines. Towards the close of the century, fresh men with fresh capital settled in Oporto much in the same way as in Cadiz and there was a turn for the better.

Materially speaking, the Factory was not badly off in the years when it was dominated by the Douro Company, and in the last decades of the century it achieved a new prosperity. It was then that Consul Whitehead organized the building of the Factory House which still stands as a monument to his labours, the only surviving British Factory abroad of the many which were active through all the trading world from Danzig to Canton.

Consul John Whitehead belonged to a Lancashire family and was an interesting and somewhat eccentric bachelor who lived alone with a Portuguese servant among his many books and papers. He had family connections with the wine trade and was probably allied by marriage with the Warre family, for in 1745 William Warre, a leading wine-shipper, married Elizabeth Whitehead, who was probably the future consul's sister. Personally he appears to have been more interested in his astronomical and scientific studies than in trade. In addition to his learned qualifications he was an architect and himself drew up the plans and superintended the building of the new house for the Factory which was the fruit of the prosperous years of the 1780s. This building, begun in 1787 and completed three years or so later, occupied the site of three old houses which already belonged to the Factory, and a small additional plot bought for the purpose in the lower part of the town near the river and the supposed birthplace of Prince Henry the Navigator. It is said to have cost £20,000 and to have been financed, as will be described in connection with the discussion of the subject in 1826, from moneys raised locally either from levies on English trade paid into what was called the Contribution Fund or from loans advanced by individual British firms who were members of the Factory. The new building was completed and inaugurated in 1790 amid general acclaim except from a few critics like Dr Wright, who found the new building inconvenient and pretentious. It stands today, a plain solid edifice with walls of granite and fine large windows, an impressive entrance hall with massive stone pillars, a broad staircase, a ballroom and two splendid long dining-rooms, in the first of which dinner is served, while in the second the guests take dessert and sip their vintage ports away from the odours of their dinner. Some doubt has been thrown by contemporary travellers on the quality of the port-wine usually served at the time of the building's installation, but by the time of Wellington's defence of Portugal, a member of the Warre family was already able to offer the future duke a vintage worthy to be extolled and there is no doubt that in the century and a half which has since elapsed the Factory has been properly consecrated by a succession of wines which have made history and of which no adverse criticism could be made.

CHAPTER XI

Wine in England in the Last Decades of the Eighteenth Century

KING George III was in his domestic virtues a harbinger of the Victorian age. He was not only a devoted family man but a very moderate drinker. At Worcester he told the mayor that he had never drunk a glass of wine before dinner in his life, but that as a special honour to the mayor, corporation and citizens of Worcester he would not decline a glass of rich, old mountain wine. At home the king's own table was modest. There was still a traditional liking for hock, of which four bottles a day were provided. Claret came next with a consumption of about fifty bottles monthly, but there was no longer any mention of special growths.[1] The court as a whole drank claret first and a fair amount of madeira and hock, and of rhenish, which was classed separately. For a court ball the consumption was eleven dozen and five bottles of claret, two dozen rhenish, four dozen and eight bottles of burgundy, nine dozen and ten bottles of champagne. Among court officials the chaplains figured very prominently with ample allowances of claret and madeira and an occasional bottle of burgundy or champagne. Some of this may have been wine for the Communion, as were probably the wines for the Chapel Royal, the Whitehall chapel and the German chapel; the Whitehall chapel still received a traditional weekly bottle of sack which was otherwise little used. The chaplains also had a fair ration of port-wine amounting to 27 bottles a month, but the yeomen of the guard with seven dozen a month were the chief consumers. Port-wine did not appear at the king's table, though 11 bottles went to the bedchamber

[1] L.S. 13/272.

women, who seem to have done well with 26 bottles of claret, 12 of rhenish, 30 of mountain, and 58 of madeira, while the queen's dressers specialized in burgundy and hock, taking 30 bottles of each. Whether this reflected royal taste upstairs, or tradition, or merely the needs of a department, it is impossible to tell, but the general picture is still of claret reigning supreme in the highest circles, except in so far as it was modified by a lingering taste for hock, and of lower people drinking port. Madeira was well thought of and at 3/4 a quart bottle cost almost as much as claret. The most expensive wine was champagne at 6/1 followed by burgundy at 4/10. With sack at 2/4 and mountain at 1/9 Spanish wines were little dearer than port. These prices were in keeping with those advertised by a London wine merchant in the *Middlesex Journal* a year or two later in 1770. His prices were probably at the lowest for the year because the month was October, just before the new wines came in. He grouped red and white port, mountain, lisbon and sherry all together at 1/6. Tent was 2/4½, rhenish and moselle 1/9, best old hock 3/-, claret 4/6 and brandy 2/4½.

In view of the tastes of the new king it is appropriate that the year of his succession in 1760 coincided approximately with the end of the gin age in England. As has been mentioned earlier, the government had long been perturbed about the excessive consumption of cheap bad spirits, but it was not until 1759 that a bad harvest and an unusual shortage of corn drove them to decree a temporary closure of the distilleries. This made the regulation of the trade for the future easier. Gin did not lose its popularity, but there was a decrease in its consumption. From an annual total of twenty million gallons in the years 1742 and 1743 the figure fell to four million gallons between 1760 and 1780. This development undoubtedly helped to give a new lease of life to the port-wine trade and to preserve it from any decline to which the legislation of Pombal exposed it. It also encouraged the development of port-wines sold in England as fortified wines, capable of serving as substitutes for spirits, rather than as natural table wines. The total official imports of wine into England for the decade beginning in 1760 showed an increase of about 13·9%. Imports of Portuguese wine had a major share with an increase of 23·3%. Port-wines benefited most with an increase in exports of 31·2% to all destinations from Oporto. It is to be presumed that in the early days at least, the Douro Company did something to carry out its declared aim to sell only pure wine and that the wines passed for export were a little less fortified. If so, it is likely that the vintners made up for this afterwards, for there is no record of port-wine in England having become any less strong. On the contrary, twenty years or so later, Sir Edward Barry in his book on wines spoke of port-wine having become stronger. It is doubtful therefore whether even the wine passed by the company was innocent of brandy, and it undoubtedly contained plenty by the time it reached the consumer; on the other hand it is probable that the company retained some of the better natural wines for its own trade; it was free to sell them, whereas the Factory had no such liberty.

In England there was no reason for the vintners to exert themselves unduly to improve the wine, as long as there was an assured market and little competition. A French traveller, P. G. Grosley, who visited London and the south of England in 1765, painted a sad picture. He said that owing to the high duties domestic wines were much drunk in England and the red wine sold was often made of aloes and blackberries mixed with turnip juice. This juice, with wild fruit beer and an admixture of litharge (monoxide of lead) after a slight fermentation, made up most of the port sold in the taverns. Even claret and burgundy were made with similar ingredients. The use of litharge had long been known and could be dangerous. There had been a case in 1696 of litharge being used in the French town of Nancy to sweeten wine, when it caused the death by convulsions of more than fifty persons. The merchants concerned were prosecuted, but only one fine was imposed, of 100 crowns on a woman implicated. Presumably the French learned to use litharge with more discretion, but Grosley said the French excise duties were so high that the genuine French wines were often adulterated or mingled with the poorest dregs from the Langue d'Oc or Provence. Grosley was an informed critic, for he was a native of Troyes on the borders of Champagne and Burgundy, and had a deep respect and love for wine; indeed he felt that the melancholy and phlegm of Englishmen were due to the lack of it, and if only they could be brought to drink good French wines, all their ills would be remedied. He could not stomach the wines in England though he grew to like English beer and cider. He found that the port either had a violent taste of brandy, or if it had matured enough to overcome this, it had lost all flavour and acted only on the stomach by its weight. This impression was confirmed by a German traveller named Archenholz a few years later. He said that Londoners were great drinkers of wine, but they only liked wines which were heavy and powerful, and therefore their favourite was port-wine. They also drank a great number of sillabubs, and all sorts of hot mixtures, for instance gin boiled up with eggs and sugar. Grosley said that even the bordeaux in London was thick and strong and fortified with an infusion of spirits. As for the white wine it was mostly made in England. He had met a Mr Hamilton of Cobham who made genuine white wine from grapes grown in his own vineyard, but it was dark grey in colour, and tasted of vinegar and verjuice with a strong flavour of the soil. During the whole six weeks that he spent in London Grosley claimed to have met good wines only twice; once a surgeon on the Dover coach treated him to a bottle of mâcon which he had brought with him from France; the second time a banker who had an agent in Lisbon gave him a port-wine of a deep colour, but lively and of high spirit, which resembled the best claret he could find in Bordeaux itself.

Grosley was only a short time in England and he was hampered by his ignorance of the language, but he was an intelligent and observant man and his impressions probably give a fair enough picture of the scene as it presented itself to a stranger who moved about freely but had no particular entrée into the highest ranks of society. His opinion of tavern port is corroborated by James Boswell, a man much more familiar with London society. Dr Johnson for long periods abstained from wine for his health's sake, but upon individual occasions could show that he had a stomach of iron. Boswell was a weaker vessel, but he had to try to keep pace with the doctor, for he felt it would have been better to become palsied at the age of eighteen than to forgo the company of such a man. The port they drank together lacked taste and Dr Johnson used to put sugar in his. Boswell found a bottle of such port a thick inflammatory dose and said that it boiled in his veins for several days after drinking it.

Yet port had its apologists and there must have been some good port. John Croft, in his treatize on the wines of Portugal published in 1788, described port as a red wine of a superior mellowness of body and said that it had become such a staple commodity that no Englishman of any decent condition or circumstances could dispense with it after his good dinner, any more than he could with the piece of Cheshire cheese that he took for pretended digestion's sake.

Croft had resided in Oporto as a member of the Factory and described himself as a wine merchant of York. Clearly he had a vested interest but was a man who knew his business. He had been a partner in a very old Oporto firm named Tilden, Thompson & Croft, which had carried on business under that name from 1736 but was derived from a still older firm named Phayre & Bradley founded in 1697. One would expect that in a firm with such long tradition he would have learnt much of the past history of the wine trade in Oporto and it is true that his treatize contains many observations of interest. But much of his history was garbled. For instance he ascribed the foundation of the Oporto Factory to 1727, although it is known to have a continuous existence at least from 1654, the year of the Cromwellian treaty with Portugal, and probably from some years earlier.

Grosley apparently only encountered good port-wine once, and then it was not fortified port but a pure generous wine. Nevertheless, echoes of the old dialogue between port and claret begun by Richard Ames the best part of a century before still found their place in folklore. The epigram devised by John Home as a protest against the enforcement in Scotland of the customs duties on his favourite claret is famous. It appeared in his well-known play *Douglas*, more than a generation after the death of Queen Anne, and reads:

> Firm and erect the Caledonian stood,
> Old was his claret and his mutton good;
> Let him drink port, the Tory statesman cried,
> He drank the poison and his spirit died.

The tradition of good claret indeed lasted in Scotland far longer than it did in England. It was remembered from the old days of Scotland's alliance with France and long after the Union and indeed, until the 1745 rebellion, the law was less strictly applied than in England. Even in the south of England smuggling continued on a large scale until the end of the century; it was common on the shores of the English Channel and comparatively easy in the remoter parts, though of less importance on account of the distance from any considerable market. Tobacco and brandy were the staple articles smuggled rather than wine, but a good deal of wine was perhaps smuggled into Scotland, for although the official imports were small, the northern counties were largely supplied from there. Leith kept its reputation for claret until the nineteenth century and supplied England as far as Yorkshire. The official imports in the earlier part of the century into Scotland were largely sherries but later they turned to port. The French traveller Faujas de St Jean, who visited the Highlands in 1780 not long after Dr Johnson, was offered port at Dalmally in Argyle, and at dinner in Mull the first toast was drunk from a great cup full of port used for a grace-cup, and afterwards decanters of port, sherry and madeira were circulated for dessert. The historian and philosopher David Hume, who died in 1776, was a firm votary of port in spite of the fact that he had been a secretary of embassy in Paris and was perfectly familiar with burgundy and good French wines. He was a great friend of John Home, and the two men used to argue about the merits of their favourite wines. When Hume died he mentioned the fact in his will. He bequeathed ten dozen bottles of his old claret to Home at his choice and also a single bottle of port, to be increased by six dozen more if he finished the single bottle alone at two sittings and provided a certificate to that effect, 'to end the only difference on temporal matters which has ever divided us'.

There were many men of substance who like Home appreciated good wine and managed to supply themselves with it. Some even of the wine which they made for themselves could be good. The Swedish traveller Kalm, who visited England in 1748, found that his landlady at Gravesend made wine out of Smyrna raisins which was so good that those who wished to be thought judges of wine had difficulty in distinguishing it from excellent madeira. An even better story is told of Lord Palmerston's grandfather, Lord Pembroke. He had a great reputation as a connoisseur and was said to make wine of an excellent colour, transparency and taste. Lord Palmerston related that Lord Pembroke always told his guests: 'I cannot answer for my champagne and claret, as I only have the word of my wine-merchant that it is good, but I can answer for my port-wine. I made it myself.'

Lord Pembroke's home-made port was perhaps an exception. The wines described by Kalm sound pretty bad. They were made of cider mixed with beetroot juice, coloured with logwood, and infused with spirits. Much of the imported wine came from

Guernsey, where there were extensive apple orchards and plentiful supplies of second-grade wine from Portugal and Spain and from France, and even from Naples. Guernsey was already noted for the adulteration of wine in 1724 and one of the first complaints of the Oporto Factory against the Douro Company was that the company was using its privilege to ship inferior wine to Guernsey. In 1758/9 one of the few surviving port-books for the inward traffic shows a thriving trade in Portuguese wine brought from Guernsey to Southampton by a shuttle service of one or two small ships making frequent voyages throughout the year. Much of this wine was made-up stuff, but Guernsey also sent good wines, for it had ample dry cellars which could be kept at an even temperature. Such facilities were limited in Oporto as late as 1821, and until the introduction in 1802 of bonded warehouses in London, storage was difficult and expensive too, and entailed the payment of duty as soon as the wine was landed. In 1777 the government tried to suppress the clandestine trade with Guernsey and opened a customs-house there, but found that the only result was to divert the trade to the Breton port of Roscoff. A more successful blow against the contraband trade was struck in the same year, when the Isle of Man, hitherto an appanage of the Earl of Derby and a centre of contraband for the whole north-west coast, was brought under the control of the government. Nevertheless smuggling prospered beyond the end of the century. Returning from the East Indies in 1770 William Hickey saw a smuggler's cutter meet his ship at the entry of the English Channel and take delivery of tea and silks in plain view of a customs vessel which was powerless to intervene in international waters. Payment was made by means of a cheque for £1,800 drawn on the London firm of Walpole & Co. This was big business. The smuggling of wine was not carried out on so large a scale, but many small smugglers continued to operate in spite of the severe regulations governing the use of small boats and small containers. Possibly some of the better wines were brought in by this means through private interests.

There are so many contradictions that the truth about the quality of wines at this period is hard to fathom. Many men who could not tell a good wine from a bad one thought it fashionable to pretend to a knowledge of the subject, and so many political or personal reasons combined to bias talk about wines that a cloud envelopes the truth. It can hardly be said that the eighteenth century lacks records, but the surviving port-books, so useful towards any assessment of the trade in earlier years, are few and far between. Statistics are no fuller and often scantier than at the beginning of the century, and business records are scarce. The commercial community was not given to putting itself down on paper and the age lacks a Pepys. On the subject of wines, somebody approaching him can however be found in the person of the Hon. John Byng, in his last years Viscount Torrington. Byng made several tours on horseback through the Midlands, the south of England and Wales in the years 1770-90 and left a diary recording his experiences. He usually stopped at inns and seldom sought private hospitality. He was a discriminating man of quiet tastes who preferred, as he said, a tolerable dinner, even if it were only of bread and cheese, to a feast with bad wine. As he was very fond of wine he always mentioned what he drank. He found port-wine in almost all the places he visited, and sometimes madeira, but few other wines. Claret was rare though it still had a reputation. Byng told a story of a visit he paid in 1776 to the son of one of his brother's tenants in Bedfordshire. The tenant had been known to him for many years as a real country yeoman, who wore the same suit of coarse-coloured cloth the whole year round and tied his shoes with thongs, but his son was different; he had aspirations to gentility and offered Byng a glass of claret from a bottle with a black seal with the remark :'There, Colonel, perhaps there's as good a glass of claret as you ever drank at St James's.' This was exceptional, for it was unusual to come across claret in small country towns. The Red Lion at Worksop had claret, madeira, port, sherry and lisbon listed on its printed bill of fare, but Byng condemned the inn as pretentious and bad. At Grantham he noticed an old bill for two bottles of claret, but he remarked that money spent on claret in such places was money thrown into the sea. He observed that one might as well ask for champagne at Wapping. He only drank good claret once; this was with a very good dinner of stuffed wheatears and a bottle of excellent port too at the fashionable and sophisticated Castle Hotel at Brighton.

As Byng did not like beer or ale much he took port everywhere, even when it was not good. In the quiet inns which he patronized in preference to the hostelries, noisy with drinking, which were common in the market towns, he found good port fairly often. In spite of the neighbourhood of the Channel, Kent and Sussex were not good counties. The smugglers do not seem to have done their job there. In 1788 he complained that a port-wine which could be swallowed was not to be found in Sussex. Besides the Castle at Brighton, which was exceptional, he only once found good port in the south-east and that was at Godstone. It was perhaps to be expected that the port in remote parts of Wales would seldom be good and not surprising that in Chepstow it was undrinkable; but occasionally he had a pleasant surprise. He found the best inn in Wales at Barmouth, with wonderfully cheap fish, civil usage and good port besides, all of which were doubly pleasant in a situation so lofty and barren that one would not expect to find anything more than a dead sheep to prey on. In Ffestiniog the landlady brought him a bottle of old port which she said had been years in the bottle, and Byng did not doubt that it had been; it was not super-excellent, but he had no difficulty in finishing it. Here and there he was lucky, as at Romsey in Hampshire in 1782, where he found a pigeon pie and a pint of good port-wine, which inspired him to verse. In his first visit to Shrewsbury, his praise of the good port-wine was lavish, but in later visits either his mood or the wine, or both, had changed for the worse. The best part of the world for port seems to have been the east Midlands. At the Three Cranes at Leicester it was very likeable, at Biggleswade very good, at Atherston light and flavourable. At Grantham the port was tolerable and on another visit very good:

> Grantham, the nurt'ring school of Newton's mind,
> That deals out good Oporto to mankind.

At several other places in the district he drank contentedly and finished his quart bottle or even a third pint. At Biggleswade he described the port of the light Lynn kind, which he preferred to the London heavy cut. Among the out-ports, King's Lynn was one of those which had held out against the competition of London in the early part of the century and had preserved a sizable wine trade for the East Anglian squirearchy. Families like the Walpoles were handsome consumers and had broached many a hogshead of port to bring in the right candidate at election time. In the second half of the century the out-ports caught up on London and even surpassed the capital in their aggregate trade. King's Lynn, though no longer the biggest importer of wine after London, still took nearly 500 tuns. No doubt this was where much of the better wine went, and the high-class trade flourished in the rich agricultural districts where noblemen and gentlemen had their finest seats.

Although Byng enjoyed the country inns, he thought that London was a much better place for wine, fish, fruit and most other commodities. He remarked even of the Three Cranes at Leicester, where the wine and the cookery had been very good that after all a good country inn made but a bad London tavern, as a good street of a country town would make but a paltry figure in London. A true taste for eating and drinking was lost in travelling, for it was mostly a case of swallowing tough chops and 'puckering' port, which were only tolerable on account of the good country air and the healthy exercise. Indeed, tours in the country only served to whet the desire for London quiet and London luxuries. A London gentleman could step into a coffee house, order venison or turtle in the instant, and (if known) a delicious bottle of port or claret; upon a clean cloth, without form, he could dine at the moment of his appetite and walk away at the moment without being bothered by anybody.

The words 'if known' are perhaps the key to many of the discrepancies between the impressions of a man like Grosley and of John Byng. Even now the word 'exclusive' is a money-maker and custom can be attracted by affecting to serve only a select clientèle. In former days the segregation of class was more effective and the social category of a man was almost indelibly marked not only by his dress and manners and his house and furniture but also by his table. It was not impossible for enterprising men to rise in the world, but the task of integration in a higher class was made more difficult by the need to acquire many appurtenances. A man was known by his possessions, and although if one was rich it was perhaps not much more difficult to buy a coach then than it would be to buy a Rolls Royce now, there were no great emporia where a man could be fitted out with a substitute for hereditary silver, furniture and pictures. It was hard even to buy wines or to obtain service if one did not know the right people or how to set about it. The best wine merchants tended to deal only with their own select customers, and in town even tavern-keepers did not produce their best to any chance comer. This is not to say that parvenus did not often ape their betters and that some of them did not 'pass', but the social obstacles to their doing so rapidly were considerable. So the nabobs and the great fortunes who came back from the Indies were largely reduced to associating with each other, and permeated the ranks to which their wealth might seem to entitle them quite slowly.

Although the Hon. John Byng had quiet tastes, he was the son of a peer and connected with fashionable circles. His mother-in-law was the extravagant Mrs Forrest described in Hickey's memoirs, and George, his son and heir, frequented fashionable society. Hickey himself, though the son of an Irish merchant, was proof that social barriers could be crossed by men who were well off, gay, convivial and dashing, but Byng was 'known' by reason of his birth. This matter of being 'known' applied even to tavern life, which was then very fashionable. Surprisingly in view of the fact that the opposite was true in later days, a foreign visitor observed that whereas in France a nobleman would entertain at home, in England he might spend ten guineas in a tavern on himself, or would send a turtle to an inn to be eaten by himself and by his friends, and would pay his five guineas club money with the others.

Some light is thrown on the attitude of select wine merchants by a letter addressed to *The Times* on 24th December 1807 by a Mr William Ballantyne. The writer was an old wine merchant who had lived in Oporto, York and London, and knew all the tricks of the trade. It is interesting that by his time claret had been so forgotten that he believed that it was not before 1750 that claret of the first growth and of proper age had been shipped to London; he said that it had been imported by way of Boulogne by two merchants, and they had only latterly been joined by three or four houses who sent it directly from Bordeaux. His relations John and James Ballantyne had had the management of it for fifty years. We know in fact that English wine-lovers had been paying high prices for selected bordeaux at least since the days of John Locke's travels in 1678, and that since 1715 there had been no profit in importing anything but expensive bordeaux wines to England. Nevertheless, the development of vintage wines from particular vineyards was a slow process. The red wines preceded the white wines in this respect, and in 1725 there were said to be only ten or twelve producers in Bordeaux who went in for *grands crus*. In France, where Paris and not so much the court

Q

but the rich entourage of bankers and new men were the greatest consumers and set the fashion, quality bordeaux scarcely penetrated to Paris before 1758, when the Duke of Richelieu introduced Haut Brion, Margaux, Chateau Lafitte and Chateau La Tour. In this respect England had led the way, for the two first names had been well known in the days of Queen Anne and even earlier, but the wines had not been much imported on a commercial basis. Doubtless for some time longer the choicer wines were largely handled by personal recommendations passing between the few select chateau owners and families in Bordeaux who took a pride in these wines, and their traditional customers. It was only lately that the market for such wines had expanded sufficiently to be a matter of common interest to the trade.

The Ballantynes now supplied London, but according to William Ballantyne, until 1770 any good claret for the north of England, for Newcastle, York, Durham or Manchester had to be brought from Edinburgh or Leith. Most wine in former days, he said, had arrived in bad condition and it was not fair to blame the vintners or wine-coopers for their adulteration and defects. It was now possible to buy pure wine in a clean and perfect state, but such wine required careful handling. Wine should not be bottled except for immediate use and all tavern wine was draft wine. The skill of the wine-cooper consisted in producing palatable wine at the lowest prices. It was easy to spoil wine by bad management. His own firm had never mixed their wines, but they had been used to add wine to fill up a hogshead and to strengthen lisbon, which was too thin, by adding Calcavella. White wine tended to ferment in winter and to go foul in summer, and benefited by the addition of a little Teneriffe to stop fermentation. Tastes in white wine were changing. As late as 1780 he had received orders for eighty pipes of white port in a week, but now white port had been superseded by sherry, though in his first three years of business not one butt of sherry had passed through his hands.

Ballantyne dealt in port-wine as well as in claret and sherry. One of his oldest friends, Robert Halcrow of Mark Lane, had come to own two ships, which sailed between Lisbon and Oporto and London. He had become known as one of the greatest shippers of Portuguese goods and was much esteemed by the Portuguese This statement is interesting, as it suggests that Halcrow dealt directly with the Portuguese rather than exclusively with the

Oporto or Lisbon Factory. He also apparently dealt with both Lisbon and Oporto, though in earlier years at least the two trades tended to be separate and not often were both Lisbon and Oporto visited in the same voyage.

Ballantyne admitted that when a pipe of port seemed too old for his customer's taste he added newer wine, and from other observations it is clear that even the best of vintners were obliged to resort to a good deal of tinkering with their wines to make them saleable, and that Ballantyne thought there was nothing wrong in this. Nevertheless he condemned adulteration in good round terms, adding that one of his friends, Paul Amlinck, took the greatest pride in having good wine and would rather have committed robbery than have adulterated it. He knew a hundred of like disposition in London and as many more in the out-ports and in the provincial towns. Yet wherever there were three or four merchants there would always be one to undersell the rest by dealing in bad wine, and there were many such in London. Of late years the excise men had had the right to visit houses and to take them unawares, so less wine was now made by confecting mixtures with sloes and cider, but swindling merchants would still buy wine which had been rejected because it was on the point of going bad. Not all this bad wine was made in England. Much was imported, and he had seen wine imported from Oporto shop-keepers that no wine merchants of repute would have allowed to enter their vaults. Such wines were bought by men who would never presume to supply the tables of gentlemen or of respectable men of business. He was sorry for the poorer sort, who were deceived by houses which advertised wine as 'neat and imported'. He had lived ten years in Oporto before coming to England, where he had travelled on business to most English and Scottish cities. He claimed that he had never met with adulterated wines among the firms which he visited and only complained of the foible of the merchants for ordering the oldest port-wines regardless of cost. In his opinion wines kept long in Oporto turned tawny and vapid (the term tawny was then one of reproach and did not mean, as it does now, a blended wine matured in the wood); two-year-old wines were the best to buy, and if quality were required it was better to buy a young port in England than one which had been in a fever in Oporto for four years. It was safer to rely on the judgement of a good merchant to buy wine on the quay in England than to order it from abroad. Many people thought it smart to pretend to a judgement in wine and imagined they could base an opinion on its name or colour, but a good palate required long practice and this was only to be found among reputable wine merchants. In 1790 and 1791 he had done business with upwards of 170 wine merchants who had taken their port-wine from him, and only ten of them had bought cheap wine, these being importers who sold to publicans and small dealers and had no pretensions to serve gentlemens' tables.

It is refreshing to read Ballantyne's vindication of the better-class trade. From his account taste in wine was by no means dead and there were plenty of people who were prepared to pay a better price for better wine. It is hard to find evidence that they did so. Byng's travels present a picture of a standardized price throughout the kingdom, though sometimes the wine was better, sometimes worse. High prices were certainly paid for the best French wines, but evidence of special brands of port is scarce. In later years Cyrus Redding, who was a stern critic of port and of the amount of inferior port in circulation gave figures for the turn of the century which showed an extraordinary lack of correlation between the price of port and its quality and quantity; nevertheless Thorold Rogers quotes as much as 8/- a gallon being paid for port in 1785 as against an average of 5/6 through most of the century, which still seems to have been a current price for port in the time of Byng. Ballantyne's account of the trade no doubt had some substance.

From Ballantyne's mention of the Oporto shopkeepers it appears that the wicked suburb dealing in inferior wines, which had caused riots at the time of the founding of the Douro Company, had by no means disappeared, but his mention of his friend Halcrow's good relations with the Portuguese implies that English shippers sometimes got good wine direct from the Portuguese without the intervention of the Factory. A principal complaint voiced in the report on the trade in 1767 was that the Factory could not ship any wines except Douro wines passed by the company, and so the company engrossed the trade in these, particularly to Ireland and the north of the United Kingdom.

Ballantyne's practical comments contrast with the high-flown talk of fashionable wine-bibbers like William Hickey's friend William Cane. Cane was living as a remittance man at Tours, having lost his fortune, and wrote to Charles Townshend to ask him to persuade Hickey to repay some money which he owed him. 'If you will assist me in getting me my money from Mr Hickey, you shall receive at your house in London one dozen of La Fite (Chateau de Segur) of 74. If it has not the combined qualities of burgundy and hermitage grafted on right good claret, then I am a Jack. I will decant it here into other bottles as a ten years sediment would totally spoil it, were it to be mixed. If the city of London produces its equal, may I be condemned to heavy port and sour wine "depuis" for my life'.

Ballantyne was sceptical about the merits of old wines in general, but there is no doubt that age was now expected and that knowledge of the art of maturing wines was growing or at least was more widely spread. Byng complained when he was given new madeira, and port was normally kept for some years. By 1809 Warre, a scion of a leading Oporto firm, was recommending port, twelve years old to the Duke of Wellington. Alexander Henderson, who published his classic history of wines in 1824, spoke of Haut Brion being kept six or seven years in the wood before being fit to bottle. He also spoke of sherry being mellowed in the wood for four or five years, and not attaining its full flavour or perfection for fifteen or twenty years. But it is notable that he still thought of the best port-wine as that which had matured with no addition or only a slight addition of brandy. He claimed to have met such wines occasionally and described them as very old wines, which nevertheless had kept their colour. But as the Douro Company was now profiting by its monopoly of brandy and any wine passed by it was presumably fortified, it is hard to know where this good natural wine came from. One can only guess that it was either wine of an exceptionally good year, such as that of 1820, which was naturally generous enough to pass without fortification and to mature naturally, or that it was some exceptionally good table wine, such as the company but not the Factory was empowered to retail.

It is evident that the art of creating a fortified port in perfection developed slowly and did not reach its culmination until after the famous vintage year of 1820, which set up a new standard in vigour and strength, and to equal it inspired new excesses of fortification. Even then the controversy between the defenders of fortified port and the advocates of pure wine continued to rage.

The common view, however, was still that of the inn-keeper, who answered complaints of 'blackstrap' port by saying 'it is black and it makes you drunk. What more can you ask for?'. But there also seems to have been a tradition in the respectable trade that port should be a pure and wholesome wine. This was the epithet which the managers of Ranelagh used for the port served at their fashionable festivities. However, the wine, when not blackstrap, was still wholesome and virtuous rather than refined or elegant. The beefsteak clubs for instance, who only drank port and toddy at their gatherings, had somewhat refined their notions. They dated from early in the century and at first had a reputation for drunkenness and for a membership of gentlemen 'who spent most of their time drinking a muddy kind of beverage, red wines and other sophisticated liquors with a fury and intemperance which consumed many noble estates'. The most famous of beefsteak societies, the Sublime Society of Beefsteak, for over a century consumed much old port but aimed at a higher standard. Its members included royalty and were a model of deportment, using wine as a means to congenial discussion for its own sake. They ordered their port from a neighbouring tavern and doubtless it was the best of its kind. Hogg, the Ettrick Shepherd, attended a meeting in the 1830s and left an eulogistic account. Any member who called for wine other than port was fined 40/-. It was permissible to order punch, but nothing 'above' port. The time when port could universally take an equal place with the best of wines was even then yet to come.

Port-wine evidently varied much in character in the eighteenth century and it is hard to get a true account of it. There is only general agreement on one point, and that is that it was drunk in prodigious quantities. Even on this subject it is hard to divide truth from legend. Three-bottle men are normal in the mythology of the subject, and Lords Dufferin, Panmure and Blayney were commemorated as six-bottle men. John Mytton, whose death at the age of 38 in 1834 was perhaps a culmination of the heroic age of drinking, ordered three pipes of wine for his private use while he was still an undergraduate at Cambridge. His daily consumption between meals was said to have been four to six bottles helped out by a vast consumption of nuts. There were legendary marathon drinkers, such as the Hamburg merchant Van Horn, whose portrait, painted in 1743, hangs upon the staircase of the Wine Trade

Club. He lived in the city of London and presided over a club which met at the Bull in Bishopsgate. He was a faithful member for twenty-two years until his death at the age of ninety and only failed to attend twice, once for his wife's burial and once for the marriage of his daughter. Such men were the athletes of liquor, and there were many like William Hickey who did not aspire to such records but regarded life as one long party, and survived a constant application to the bottle without succumbing at least until a reasonably advanced age. Others, many of them in the highest walks of life, took their liquor as a medicine rather than as a pleasure. William Pitt the Younger depended on port-wine to keep him going and used to drink the better part of a bottle out of a tumbler before going down to the House to deliver a speech. The learned Lord Eldon and his brother on the bench Lord Stowell used to say that in following the law they had drunk more bad port than any two men in England. In later days the Duke of Montrose observed that when he entertained the Cabinet they drank less at a sitting than had been the consumption of a single minister in the days of Pitt.

Doubt has been expressed whether men could really have im-
bibed so much. It has been suggested that the port was weaker and the bottles smaller. This was true to a limited degree. The old pint was about five-sixths of the imperial pint and the bottles perhaps contained more lees. Also the alcoholic content of most port was less than that of vintage port today, though it was a good deal stronger than table wine, and in 1775, according to Sir Edward Barry's history of wines, was growing stronger. However, just as a few men can run a hundred yards in ten seconds, so a few trained drinkers can perform prodigies. Captain Gronow claimed in 1814 that he had known many men who habitually drank two bottles after dinner. This is not impossible, but it must be remembered that drinking sessions could be prolonged until the middle of the next morning and last for twelve hours or even longer, while relief in the Roman manner by vomiting was common. Four or five bottles were not unknown, and the only thing that saved the drinkers was that they drank slowly and out of small glasses. Dr Johnson at the Mitre once told Boswell that they would drink two bottles; and they did so and more. He boasted that he had once drunk three bottles at Cambridge. Johnson was a large and strong-stomached man and his three bottles marked

an exceptional occasion. At the beginning of the century the estimable and serious young men of the Amicable Club split over the question whether one bottle per man per session was enough, and decided that it was. Investigation into the accounts of the Hellfire Club suggests that John Wilkes and his legendary brethren often stopped short of three bottles. It is true that they were votaries of Venus before Bacchus and had to reserve their strength, but their consumption gives some notion of the intake of professed libertines. A record of the proceedings on 13th January 1761 reads 'Account of the element of wine consumed at the private devotion of every brother, when no chapter had been held; brother John of Aylesbury (John Wilkes) one bottle of claret'. Brother John of course could do better than this; on 3rd October 1760 he accounted for two bottles of claret and one of Carcavelos; also on one night, John of Henley, Abbot Francis of Wycombe and Thomas of London drank up two bottles of claret, one of port and two of Carcavelos. Abbot Francis (Sir John Dashwood) made ample provision for contingencies, for upon his death the contents of his cellar were worth £6,000. If the bottles were quart bottles the performances of the brothers were not unimpressive, but one cannot be sure that these epicureans were not assisted by acoloytes, sisters or nuns. Hickey once mentioned that he had finished a bottle of sherry with two gay girls in a tavern, but gentlemen were usually discreet about the ladies present, though they must often have been entertained and are unlikely to have been abstainers. One bottle of port at a draft clearly presented no difficulties and there is no reason to doubt that the bottle which William Hickey drank in the course of his twenty-five mile walk to Erith filled him, as he said it did, with new vigour.

The diaries of John Byng seem to prove that a quart bottle was well within a normal man's drinking capacity and that three bottles in the course of the day, and a little more besides, were not too taxing for a man in good health who was taking plenty of exercise. John Byng loved his wine, but he was not a hard drinker for the sake of drinking alone. In his earlier days at least he limited himself to a pint as often as not, and only took more when the wine was really good. The vexed question, whether the bottles were quarts or pints, can often be checked up against the bills which he carefully kept. The standard price for a pint was 1/3, so we can determine that at the Three Cranes at Leicester, where both dinner and port were good and Byng and his friend were tempted to exceed but did not do so, they drank a quart only at dinner and another pint in the course of the day. Byng alone seems to have drunk a quart upon occasion, though not always at one sitting. In his later tours he sometimes drank more. He had many domestic worries and financial troubles to account for the dark moods which replaced too often the *joie de vivre* of his earlier days, but too much port may sometimes have contributed to them. In 1793 he himself said that he had drunk three pints a day besides half a pint of brandy, because the port was good, and for the same reason he had boozed away at Higham Ferrers, Kettering and Lutterworth. His statement is largely though not entirely confirmed by his bills. Even Byng perhaps allowed a touch of bravado in his tales of his drinking; one must allow for the odd glass left, or offered to a friend or to his landlord. Byng was a believer in being civil to landlords; it enabled him to hear the gossip and often inclined the landlord to charge less. Describing his first evening at Biggleswade, he said 'then to supper upon a cold fowl, peas with a pint of port-wine and half a pint of brandy. Gods, how I drink, jolly Bacchus, god of wine'. According to his bill he had the brandy, but the pint of port was a quart. He had three dinners and suppers at Biggleswade and had a quart of wine for dinner and a pint for each supper plus the brandy for dinner on the first day. However, the port was the lighter Lynn variety and he may have offered a few glasses to the Reverend Mr Newman, the *bon vivant* vicar, whose conversation he mentioned enjoying; on the other hand he may well have called on the vicar and if he did so he would not have escaped without a whet. At Higham Ferrers he had a quart rather than the three pints he claimed, but at Stone he had a full 3/9 worth. At Lutterworth he arrived in the morning with a headache. He took 3d worth of brandy in a gallon of tea to cure this and a quart of port for dinner and a pint for supper. Byng was not a regular three-bottle man, but this seems fair evidence that he could have been and that with hard training some of the feats of drinking which have become legendary may upon occasion have been approached.

Byng's earlier tours took place at a time when for the first time for over a century the duties on wines were reduced. The duties fell between 1788 and 1795 to 4/6 a gallon on French wines and to 3/- on Portuguese wines. With a peak of 35,525 tuns imported in 1792, the imports were more than double those of 1786, but the proportion of Portuguese wines continued to be about three-quarters of the total. Spanish wines benefited and French wines a little, while the slender trickle of Rhenish wines, which for some reason from 1788 paid rather more duty than French wines, was further reduced. Old hock at 36/- a dozen in 1794 was no more expensive than madeira, but there was no demand. According to André Simon, the year 1783 was the marvellous year for hock in the century. 'The wine was good and plentiful and there was nothing like it before or after'. In that year German wines were not unfavourably treated, but only 196 tuns were imported. The rates of duty had a considerable effect, but old habits were hard to change, and the market seems to have responded very little to the changes of quality of wine in any particular year.

CHAPTER XII

The False Dawn of Lower Duties

THROUGHOUT the eighteenth century the duties on wines had multiplied. There was a pause after the war of the Spanish succession broken only by an increase of duty of £8 a tun on French wines and of £4 on other wines in 1745, but there were similar increases in 1763 and 1780, and a slightly larger one of £8 8s od a tun on French wines and of £4 4s od on other wines in 1778. There were also additional duties of 5% on the existing duties in 1779 and 1782. So in 1782 French wines paid fifteen separate duties and other wines thirteen. According to a parliamentary report on the customs tariff, published in 1897, the total duties payable in 1784 were £96 4s 1d on French wines, £45 19s 1d on Portuguese wines, £46 19s 1d on Spanish wines and £50 6s 3d on German wines plus some fractions of a penny. Other authorities give slightly different figures and the net payments after allowance for various deductions were somewhat less.

In 1786, as a result of a report submitted to Parliament, an effort was made by Pitt's government to simplify the tariff and the customs procedure. The duties dating from before 1745 were left untouched, but the later duties were repealed and were replaced by an excise duty of £35 14s od on French wines and of £17 17s od on all other wines. In 1787 another act was passed to sweep away all the old duties and to implement a commercial treaty recently concluded with France by reducing the duties on French wines. Wines were now subjected to only one excise and one customs duty. The excise duty amounted to £17 17s od on French wines and to £11 18s od on all other wines, the customs duty to £29 8s od on French wines, £19 12s od on Spanish and

Portuguese wines, and to £33 12s od on all other wines. So Portuguese wines lost their small preference over Spanish wines, but retained their advantage over French, Italian and German wines. Wines imported in ships of their own nationality continued to pay more, £4 4s od in the case of French ships and £2 16s od in the case of Portuguese ships. The reduction for wines landed at the outports was kept, but wines brought to London after being imported elsewhere had as before to make up the difference in duty. Formerly the cost of transport had seldom made this particular evasion of the customs worth while, but latterly the improvement in the roads and the easing of the restrictions on the importation of French wine in bottles and of other wines in small containers had increased the smuggling of wine into London, after it had paid the lower duties at Channel ports, enough to alarm the authorities and to cause them to introduce new and stringent regulations to prevent this abuse. Wines at the outports, except at Chester and the remaining Cinque Ports, which were excepted by special charters, still paid prisage, but otherwise the duties were reduced to one excise and one customs duty. This was a great simplification, though some arguments about what should properly be paid continued. Records of actual customs duties paid at Bristol in 1789 show French wines paying £25 4s od and Portuguese wines £16 16s od.[1]

In the first year of the reduced duties the total imports rose by half. Portuguese wines benefited most, and the relief given to French wines was not enough to cause any general change in the pattern of trade. Although luxuries were spreading with the increase of prosperity, the middle classes did not take to French wines again and the taste for them was confined to aristocrats and wealthy men. These were numerous enough to cause the importation of French wines to rise in 1787 from 475 to 2,127 tuns (or from 419 to 1,857 tuns after deduction of re-exports), but the average fell again afterwards to 1,000 tuns. This was twice as much as before but not enough to be a threat to the domination of Portuguese wines. From 1789 madeira, which had been out of fashion for twenty years, was imported in quantities of over 1,000 tuns and took the lead as a quality wine.

In Bordeaux the character of the wine trade had substantially changed. After the loss of the English market the Netherlands

[1] Bristol Port Book E 190/1239/1.

had been the mainstay of Bordeaux exports. Towards the middle of the century the Dutch had taken as much as 69% of them, but afterwards the trade declined and fell to 10%. The loss was not as great as it appeared, for much of it was due to the fact that the wines for Scandinavia, which had formerly been shipped by way of the Netherlands, now went directly, but it was still considerable. The exports to Scandinavia therefore showed a big increase, but on the whole the exports of Bordeaux wines to foreign countries had declined and had become less important than the home and colonial trade. In 1723 exports abroad had been 69% of the total; towards the end of the century they were only 14%. At the beginning of the century the French colonies were still small and the home market for Bordeaux wines was surprisingly limited. They were of course drunk by the citizens of Bordeaux itself, but the peasants and country people drank little wine, both by custom and because they could not afford to do so. The old aristocratic conception of wine still prevailed. Wine was drunk by the upper classes as a matter of course and was dispensed by them to their guests and dependants in generous quantities. Wine drinkers recruited in this way were numerous enough and included most of the bourgeoisie in the towns and many tradespeople and hangers-on, but did not spread much outside the towns and the peripheries of noble houses. This was especially the case in the south. The nearer that one approached to the climatic frontier of the vine, the more wine was appreciated. So wine drinking had in earlier days been more common in northern France and perhaps even in England than in the south where vines could most easily be grown. Bordeaux was in this respect nearer the north than the south, but the peasants only drank pin-pin, the weakest strainings of the second or third pressings, and the best Bordeaux wines were more drunk abroad than in other provinces of France. A good deal of Bordeaux went to Brittany, but carriage by land was so expensive owing to the poor roads and the heavy duties payable by goods passing from one French province to another that the market elsewhere was limited. Paris had been practically inaccessible to Bordeaux wines, and it was only recently that they had begun to become fashionable there. The court had known burgundy and champagne, but Bordeaux hardly at all. The change is said to have been initiated by the Duke of Richelieu, who in 1758 gave a series of lavish banquets to celebrate his capture of

Port Mahon from the English, at which he served the best wines from Bordeaux.

By the closing decades of the century the French colonies had become an important market and wine was being drunk much more generally by all classes throughout the country. Naturally it was the cheaper wines which were in most demand. Consequently the average price of Bordeaux wines sold had dropped to about two-thirds of what it had been. Nevertheless the production of quality wines continued and on account of their value played a much greater part in the trade than their quantity indicated.

The United Kingdom had been the principal market for the most expensive Bordeaux wines since the seventeenth century and it continued to be so. Although in 1789 the English trade only accounted for 4·7% of the diminished Bordeaux export trade, in 1787 its value was as much as 26%. The château wines which were now fashionable at Versailles as well as in London only amounted to 8,000 tuns annually, but they were the most valuable part of the vintage. They were the monopoly of a comparatively small group of the leading families and citizens of Bordeaux. In the Middle Ages the Bordeaux district had played a major part, but in the earlier half of the eighteenth century the High Country wines had threatened their pre-eminence. From 15% of the total exports in 1715 they had increased to 66% in 1766. Now they had shrunk again to 9%. They were used for blending with Bordeaux wines but they were no longer to the same extent exported under their own names. This blending was general and was practised even with the best wines, indeed more so, for to prepare wines for the English market strength and a deep colour were required. Brandy was added and to give colour the strong dark Beni Carlos wines from the borders of Catalonia and Valencia were commonly used, or sometimes hermitage from the Rhône valley. These were shipped by way of Marseilles or Cadiz, but the hermitage could also come by the Langue d'Oc canal. A fair quantity of second-class wine found its way to England by roundabout routes. Much went to Guernsey, whither it was shipped directly or by way of Brittany, and was used together with wines from Poitou or the Charente to make cheap port. According to Charles Higounet, the historian of Bordeaux, more wine was shipped from Bordeaux to Ireland than to England, and in 1786 the figures were 1,285 tuns and 225 tuns respectively. The total official imports to England in that year were 475 tuns, rising in the following year after the reduction of duties to 2,127 tuns, after which the average for several years was a little over 1,000 tuns. Much of the increased quantity was imported from Dunkirk or Rouen rather than from Bordeaux directly.

Portuguese wines now lost the small advantage they had enjoyed over Spanish wines and paid the same customs and excise duties. The difference was not large, but its abolition helped the revival of the Spanish trade. From Oporto the sailings of British ships increased from ninety-four in 1783 to an average of over 150 in the years following the reduction of duties. Sailings were still most frequent in the months following the vintage but were now spread more evenly throughout the year. As the average time for maturing port-wine grew in length, provision of ample storage became essential. A shortage of storage remained a problem in Oporto, but by the end of the century considerable stocks could be accumulated there, though most of the wine was shipped to be stored in England or Guernsey.

Under the 1787 Act, wine could not be imported into England in ships of less than sixty tons burthen, but the average tonnage of merchant ships and particularly of ships engaged in the wine trade remained small. Comparatively few were over 200 tons and many were under 100 tons. After the burst of development in the sixteenth century merchant ships had altered slowly and the changes made in them had mostly been of a minor character such as rearrangements of the sailplan and improvements of the methods for the storage of cargo. Where more seasoned and mature timber was used, ships could be more accurately and strongly built, but the supply of oak and pine from the diminishing forests of Europe was rapidly decreasing. England was able to compensate for this shortage by using more American timber and American-built ships, but the wood was not so good and the ships were shorter-lived. By the end of the century the introduction of exact chronometers facilitated the definition of longitude, but the improved instruments were by no means general in the merchant service until the nineteenth century. It might be thought that ships engaged in the wine trade, navigating European waters not far from the coast, could find their way easily enough. But even men-of-war found the entry to the English Channel by means of soundings and sometimes failed to do so, as the disaster to Sir Cloudesely Shovell early in the century bore witness.

Until the seventeenth century warships and merchant ships had been largely interchangeable. During the seventeenth and eighteenth century they became more and more specialized. Already by the beginning of the eighteenth century most men-of-war rated over 500 tons, while very few merchant ships were over 300 tons and the average size even decreased. One reason for this was that the need or the advantage of a merchant ship being defensible and capable of being converted into an auxiliary cruiser slowly decreased. For service in home waters, in the Baltic and as far as the Strait of Gibraltar, economy in running became more important than strength or speed, while in time of war merchants looked to the navy for protection rather than to themselves. As a main source of expense was the cost of the crew, and larger ships used a smaller number of men per ton, one would have expected an increase in size rather than the reverse. But other factors were important. Ships of 300 tons were used for distant ocean voyages and for the timber trade with the Baltic because the cargoes were so bulky, but the majority of merchant ships were small. A proportion even of the ships going far afield were only of 100 tons, and the average size of ships trading from London to Portugal and Spain in the second half of the century was 117 and 108 tons respectively. The average for ships from the outports was smaller still, 92 tons for Spain and 95 tons for Portugal. This was the case in spite of the fact that a high proportion of the ships engaged in the peninsular trade made triangular voyages which took them to the West Indies or America. As late as 1840, a visitor to Oporto saw a few fine ships from Liverpool in the Douro but was struck by the small old-fashioned look of the majority of English ships loading wine. Many of them were under 100 tons. Foreign ships and even many Portuguese ships looked better. In 1830, when most of the ships calling at Oporto were British, only two were over 200 tons. Most of the ships were regular callers; three voyages a year were common and four not unknown, though this had been rare in the eighteenth century.

Although larger ships were more economical to run they involved a larger initial outlay, and to justify the capital invested required a regular trade and the certainty of a good return freight. Some ships making regular runs to Lisbon, Oporto or Cadiz could

comply with these conditions, but many were tramps taking cargo
where they could find it. For this purpose small ships were convenient. They could be delayed or laid up with less cost, and they
could move in or out of small ports or awkward entries with less
difficulty. Many of the out-ports suffered from such disadvantages,
and the entry to the Douro was dangerous. Small ships could pick
up a sufficient return freight more easily and could be diverted
from one port to another. The gains were smaller, but so were the
risks, and ship-owners with little capital were chary of putting
many eggs in one basket. Therefore, although as the years passed
more big ships were built and the total tonnage of shipping and
of trade grew larger, the average size of merchant ships diminished
a little in the first half of the eighteenth century and only increased
slowly afterwards.

The principal exception to this was the East India trade, which
always employed large ships. Yet it was not until 1769 that the
East India Company ordered three ships of 800 tons. These were
scarcely bigger than the Venetian galleys of the fifteenth century,
and smaller than Henry VIII's *Grace de Dieu*. Little ships predominated and still sailed the ocean. The *Peggy of Topsham*,
which with a crew of six made the triangular trip out to Newfoundland and back to England by the way of the Peninsula in 1770,
was only forty tons. Besides the ships in the Baltic trade there
were comparatively few other sizeable ships, mostly sailing to the
Levant, the Far East or America.

The regular East Indiamen in the mid-eighteenth century were
always rated at 499 tons but were actually larger. They carried
100 men and twenty-six guns, for they had to be defensible. This
applied also to ships bound for the Levant. Few other ships were
so well found, but a surprising number continued to carry guns
of some kind though not so often the gunners to man them. Ships
bound for Mediterranean ports beyond Malaga, or carrying fish,
or having two decks and sixteen guns, were exempt from the 1%
Mediterranean tax on outward and inward cargo. This was a slight
inducement, but the carriage of guns was mainly a matter of
custom and did mean that in case of need ships after taking on a
few more men could be converted into privateers. As late as the
last decades of the eighteenth century about a third of the ships
applying for Mediterranean passes were listed as carrying guns
of a sort, though with small crews, so they could seldom have

R

been capable of making much use of them. In time of peace guns were no longer required in home waters, or so much in the Strait of Gibraltar after treaties had been made with the North African powers. Nevertheless the Algerian pirates and the Sallee rovers were in business until the nineteenth century. In 1770, four Danish ships were taken by the Algerians, and a Portuguese ship carrying wine from Teneriffe was captured by the Sallee rovers. But they no longer appeared in the English Channel, and for the most part the maritime powers had ships of war enough at sea to ensure that the treaties they had concluded were respected.

Occasionally a ship with four guns or more was found bringing wine from Lisbon or Oporto, but this was rare with those in the regular trade. Most merchant ships, and especially those in the wine trade, aimed at taking as much cargo as possible and using only a small crew. For this purpose they were built on the lines of the Dutch fly-boats. At first in the seventeenth century these were all built in the Netherlands and those sailing under the English flag had all been acquired by capture during the Dutch wars or by purchase. Afterwards they began to be built in English yards. They had greater length than their predecessors and were not very beamy, but they won cargo space by having round bows and narrowing very little fore or aft. They had lighter and more varied sails, which made them easier to work, and were adequate for their business but neither speedy nor very well found. The principal change they brought about was the progressive diminution in the size of their crews. Between the early years of the seventeenth century and the end of the eighteenth century the average of tons per man rose steadily. A ship of 120 tons trading to Cadiz in the 1630s required a crew of eighteen of nineteen men and fifteen or sixteen men later in the century. By 1700 the number had fallen further and by 1760 a crew of nine was nearer the average.

The replacement of heavy sails by more and lighter ones, which were better rigged, made a ship more easily manageable, and as there were fewer men the accommodation for them could perhaps be a little better. There was a gradual improvement in many small things, and a long ocean voyage was somewhat safer and more regular, but we only have to read William Hickey's account of his voyage to India at the turn of the century to realize that there were still in 1800 many hardships and dangers. The conditions of 1800 were easier than those of 1600 but not so very much so in the small ships carrying wine and other merchandise in the European trade. In the mid-seventeenth century Edward Barlow had vividly described the hard lot of an old seaman with many years of service 'always in need, and enduring all manner of misery and hardship, going with many a hungry belly and wet back, and being always called "old dog", and "old rogue", and "son of a whore", and suchlike terms, which is a common use among seamen and that would be a great grief for an aged man'. It was true that years of war outnumbered years of peace for long periods and that in war-time the wages of such merchant sailors as managed to elude the press-gang were much higher. But throughout the eighteenth century in time of peace wages rose little, averaging in the 1770s 25/- a month with a shilling or two more in the African and Far Eastern trades. In peacetime in the seventeenth century seamen had earned almost as much.

The papers have survived of a ship named the *Fanny*, who made a voyage of five months to Portugal in 1746.[1] She carried a crew of ten and rated about 150 tons. It was a year of war against Spain and the English able seamen were paid 40/- a month. Two men taken on board in a temporary capacity at the last moment only received 10/- monthly. The four Portuguese seamen and the Portuguese cook were paid £4 10s 0d a month and £3 13s 6d respectively. Foreigners could command a higher wage because they were not liable to be pressed for the navy, but by law the majority of the crew had to be British. When the Portuguese were paid off in Oporto they were only given £1 3s 9d a month, but they had each been given an advance of £2 12s 9d and it is to be supposed that there were other deductions. The mate received £4 a month and the boatswain £3, so £4 10s 0d was good pay. The captain, Samuel Clarke, who was a son of the owner and after his father's death became the owner of his father's ships, was only paid £6. When he came into his inheritance he owned two or three ships, but he does not appear to have gone to sea again. About one in ten sea captains owned their ships, but many more owned one or more shares in their ships or were responsible for their administration as well as their command. Conditions on ships engaged in the wine trade were perhaps better than in some other trades. Such ships encountered plenty of rough weather on the voyage to the peninsula and even in the Mediterranean, but the times

[1] C. 103/146. Papers of Samuel Clarke.

spent at sea were comparatively short and the climates visited relatively benign. The beverage wine was probably no better than it had been in Barlow's day, but it was usually available, as were oranges and lemons, which were such an innovation on oceanic voyages in Captain Cook's ships and did so much to preserve the health of his men.

The *Fanny* brought home 202 pipes and one hogshead of wine from Oporto, which at a rate of £3 10s 0d a tun earned £374 7s 6d in freight. The wine was all purchased from Messrs Lambert, Croft & Co, one of the older Oporto firms, and was delivered in London to thirteen consignees. The *Fanny* also called at Figueira de Foz, where she took on an almost equal amount of cargo for a freight of £226 7s 0d. This cargo could have included wine, but as there was no mention of wine was probably southern fruits. The circumstance is interesting, as instances of ships taking cargoes at more than one Portuguese port are not commonly recorded. Consul Whitehead complained in 1767 that after the foundation of the Douro Company the Factory was prevented from sending wines to Lisbon or from loading wines for England on ships which had already partially loaded in Lisbon.[1] The fact that he complained suggests that the practice had not previously been entirely prohibited, but the Portuguese customs had always been inclined to subject any foreign ship to a full examination and payment of dues, regardless of whether she had already been cleared into a Portuguese port, and for this reason British ships seldom included Lisbon and Oporto in the same homeward voyage. Weather conditions and the difficulty of crossing the Douro bar to enter the river also tended to make a diversion into Oporto on the way to or from Lisbon unduly long. The voyages of another ship of Samuel Clarke tend to confirm this. This ship, the *Caroline* of 150 tons, after one voyage to South Carolina engaged in regular voyages between London and Oporto in the years 1754 to 1766. She made fifteen voyages to Oporto for wine, but only one to Lisbon and one to Malaga. There are no particulars of her cargoes, but she took wine up to a maximum of 289 pipes and occasionally fruit. She had a crew of eleven, which sometimes included as many as five Portuguese.

An occasional reference can be found to a ship taking corn to Lisbon and then proceeding in ballast to Oporto to pick up wine.

[1] C.O. 358/54, Consul Whitehead, 24th January 1767.

There was no difficulty about a ship calling at two Spanish ports or first at a Spanish port and then at a Portuguese one. For instance the *Neptune* of King's Lynn of 250 tons brought both Portuguese and Spanish wines to King's Lynn in 1754. However, she had called at Guernsey as well as at Oporto so might have picked up some of the wines there. Before going to Portugal she had been to Danzig, so was probably a timber ship, which would account for her comparatively large tonnage and for her bringing only a small load of wines, not being of the regular trade. These amounted to 40 tuns of port-wine and 16½ tuns of Spanish wine.[1]

Oporto and Malaga were the two principal ports of the wine trade. Lisbon and Cadiz were larger but depended more on general international trade than on wine. The *Caroline* made only two voyages to Oporto in the same year once or twice, but it was common for ships engaged in the regular trade with Oporto or Lisbon to make two voyages in a year. The same was true of Cadiz but not of places beyond the strait. This applied even to Malaga, for although Malaga was a bare hundred miles from Cadiz, wind and current often made the return voyage through the strait difficult, particularly in the autumn and winter months succeeding the vintage. This should not have prevented a ship calling at Malaga in the early summer and again in the autumn, but instances of two voyages in the same year are not common.

In the early days the risk of wine deteriorating soon was very great and it was wise to ship it as soon as possible. After port-wine began to be stabilized by fortification, shippers did not care to accept it until it had been kept some time and they could feel sure that the fortification had been properly done. Nevertheless, owing to a shortage of storage space, most of the wine was shipped as soon as it had come down the river to Oporto. In 1775 Richard Twiss reported seeing spacious wine vaults belonging to the Factory, but the figure he gave of their capacity was only 6,000-7,000 pipes, which would have accommodated less than half an annual vintage. Most contemporary accounts spoke of the wine being shipped quickly. This might not be done before the spring, because the wine often did not reach Oporto until February. At Lisbon the wine did not have to come from so far and the problem was easier. In Cadiz the Spanish regulations were obstructive and the short voyage down the Guadalete river from Jerez caused delays,

[1] King's Lynn Port Book, E 190/458.

because it was Spanish policy to discourage the warehousing of wines and they were often not despatched from Jerez before there were ships in port ready to load them. But there was more general trade in Cadiz, which made the shipping problem easier. Ships calling at Oporto were more dependent on a return freight in wine, but not entirely so, for they often returned with southern fruits and no wine at all. At first nearly all the wines were shipped in the early months of the year or in the late autumn but in the later decades of the eighteenth century shipments were spread through the months more equally. This happened in Oporto first because the wine began to require to be matured as soon as fortification became general, but was dependent on bigger firms with sufficient capital entering the business. In Cadiz the same tendency made itself felt at the end of the century, when older wines were shipped and business also began to be organized on a large scale.

Ships engaged in the triangular trade between England, America and the Peninsula had in any case no time for more than one voyage in the year. A high proportion of these sailed from west-country ports. King's Lynn had something more like a regular trade with Spain and Portugal. The ships took out corn and returned with 100 pipes or so of wine and other southern products. More often than not they made only one voyage a year to the Peninsula, though not infrequently they made a second voyage with corn to a French port or with other cargo to the Netherlands or even to Sweden. Towards the end of the century two voyages in the year to Lisbon, Oporto or Cadiz became more usual, particularly from western ports which lay well to windward in the prevailing south-westerly winds. No port-books are available in the later years of the century for Exeter, but a Bristol port-book for entries from foreign ports has survived for 1789. It shows thirteen shipments arriving there from Oporto, four from Cadiz, four from Lisbon, and seven from Malaga. None of the ships enumerated brought wine from more than one port, but the *Princess Royal* of 170 tons made two voyages to Oporto, returning with 102 tuns of wine in January, and with oranges and lemons and 100 tuns of wine in May. This was an unusually quick turn-round. She had difficulty in disposing of her second cargo, for in November she was still in port and unloading the last of her wines. Another ship, the *Elizabeth*, the third of her name to make the voyage to Oporto in the year, also made two voyages. No ships made two voyages in the year to Lisbon or Cadiz, but another ship called the *Princess Royal* brought thirty-four tuns of wine from Cadiz in February, sailed again to Lisbon from King's Lynn in October after making an intermediate voyage from Bristol to Waterford, where she loaded Irish linen and 1,637 quarters of oats for King's Lynn.[1]

From 1788 imports of madeira, which after a spurt in the 1760s had suffered a decline, picked up and in 1789 attained 1,174 tuns. There were few direct shipments from Madeira, but almost every ship reaching Bristol from the West Indies brought at least a few gallons or a hogshead or two. An occasional ship brought more. *The Friends*, for instance, arrived from Jamaica on 10th June with sugar, coffee, logwood and sixty-five tuns of madeira. It is not clear whether this had been originally intended or whether a glut of wine in Jamaica had prevented the sale of the wine there. Such choice wine was a valuable commodity, but on this occasion it took some months to sell, for it was the end of September before the last of it was unloaded. There were forty or fifty purchasers; one or two sales were of five or six tuns but most were of smaller quantities. Several purchasers however came back for more, one or two three times.

In 1789 the Duke of Grafton still enjoyed the ancient privilege of prisage granted to his ancestor by King Charles II and in the Bristol port-book there are entries for the redemption by the duke's agent of two tuns of wine on each cargo over twenty tuns and of one tun on each cargo between ten and twenty tuns, upon payment of prisage at the rate of £12 11s 2d a tun. At the time of the original grant the duke had been able to claim the wine without charge; from the time of James II he had to pay prisage, but the privilege was still valuable as the wine was worth a good deal and the prisage was less than the normal duty. Prisage was not finally abolished until 1811, but the Treasury bought the duke out a little earlier than this in 1806 in return for an annuity of £6,370 payable to himself and after his death to his lawful successors. This nobleman, as also the Duke of Ormonde, who held the right of prisage for Ireland must have had great quantities of wine at their disposal. Belonging to the limited class which was still interested in choice wines, they perhaps did something to keep up the standards of the better-class trade by purveying to their

[1] Bristol Port Book, E 190/1239/1.

friends better wines than could commonly be got in the open market.

Some wine reached west-country ports including Bristol by way of Ireland, and although ships tended to trade back to their home ports they did not always do so. Ships for instance going to London, or even to King's Lynn or Sunderland, sometimes dropped part of their cargo on the way at ports such as Exeter. The coastal traffic carried wine between adjacent ports, and sometimes, though less often, between major ports such as Exeter and London, or London and King's Lynn. Transport by land was rarer on account of the expense. A little went from Bristol to London, for instance a quarter of a tun of Spanish wine by the carrier in the midsummer quarter of 1788 and a few bottles of Portuguese wine packed in a hamper. It is to be supposed that the latter was something special.

In the year 1789 the wines imported into England and Wales reached an official total of 24,281 tuns, a figure which had been surpassed only twice before in the century. The reduction of duties in a time of general prosperity had been the main factor in bringing this about, but a serious effort had also been made to help trade by simplifying the customs law. A long list occupying many pages of the volumes of parliamentary proceedings had been submitted of the employees of the numerous departments of customs and excise. In 1786, a Mr Frewin offered Pitt a proposal for the reform of the obsolete customs acts. It took some years to consider his suggestions and war broke out before more was done to implement them. It was only at the end of the Napoleonic wars that he was commissioned together with a Mr Jickling, the author of an exhaustive digest of the customs in 1,375 pages, to embody his proposals. He was handsomely rewarded for his work with a commissionership of customs and a cash payment. The customs and the excise services, whose overlapping and bitter rivalries had long been a bar to efficiency, were finally amalgamated and the new accretions of duties, which in the course of the war had produced a fresh and complicated network of regulations, were swept away. This is to anticipate by several years, but something was already done in 1786 and 1787, when the customs and excise were co-ordinated. In spite of this, the customs and excise continued to quarrel about precedence. Officers of either department were entitled to board ships to make the first search; the question of precedence was solved by granting priority to the first department to arrive; the customs probably won more often as they had better facilities in the way of launches.

Until the next outbreak of war the problems of importers were easier, but the reductions of duties were not enough to make smuggling unprofitable. The rate of duty on French wines was not much lower than it had been in the middle of the century, and the duty on double brandy and even on colonial rum was very high. French wines were delicate and difficult to handle; fair quantities infiltrated, but they were not a subject for large-scale smuggling like brandy, tea and tobacco. To bring them in, the smugglers were often organized in gangs strong enough to repel the forces of the law, but they were usually ready if pursued to abandon some of their goods, a policy which ensured their own escape and enabled the authorities to display zeal and make adequate seizure with less danger to life and limb.

After 1779, French wine could be imported in bottles again either directly or by way of the Channel Islands. This enlarged one loophole for evasion, but in other respects the regulations were tightened up. By the 1787 Act, the duty-free allowance of merchant seamen was restricted to ten gallons a head, or three dozen bottles. The facilities allowed the navy were also defined, and in 1793 a scale was laid down which was later extended to cover the marines. By modern standards the allowances were generous. All commissioned officers were allowed to keep on board or to purchase duty-free for consumption on board half a tun a year; captains of ships were allowed a tun, captains of first-raters three tuns, and admirals more upon an ascending scale according to rank.

Although the reduction of duties helped Portuguese wines and made little change in the general pattern of the trade, a breath of competition was beginning to steal into the Oporto trade and the Douro Company was not altogether inactive. It had abandoned the fervour for pure and unadulterated wine recommended in its charter, and was very ready to take the profits arising from its monopoly of the sale of brandy. Whereas in 1793 the average quantity of brandy added to the pipe of port was believed to average 15 to 20 litres, in the war years that followed the proportion rose to 34 litres a pipe and later even higher. Because the production of wine was greater and the proportion of brandy also increased, the annual quantity of brandy sold by the company, according to statistics quoted by Guerra Tenreiro, rose from 2,647 pipes in 1798 to 3,895 pipes in 1801 and to more than 4,000 pipes subsequently. The wine from Oporto entering England was therefore more fortified than ever, but on the other hand the art of fortification was beginning to be better understood and the average period for maturing wines was creeping up to three years and often more. Mature wines were paler and the fashion for very dark wines was for a time replaced by a demand for paler wines, so that the merchants ceased to use elderberries and even added grapes with white skins to the vintage. Elderberries were now again decried and the company revived the strict regulations preventing their cultivation.

The company also introduced some genuinely progressive measures, such as harbour improvements at Oporto, and the final removal in 1792 of the rocks which barred navigation at Cachão de Valeira (or Baleira) on the Upper Douro just below its junction with its tributary, the River Sabor, not far from Moncorvo. This improvement had been contemplated for many years and was eventually begun in 1778 and financed by a tax of 40 reis on each pipe of wine taken down the river. Portuguese sources gave the credit for the promotion of the work to a local priest, Father Antonio Manole Gamelo, a native of the neighbouring village of San Jõao de Pesqueira, and to two engineers, Bento de Moura Aragão and an Italian named José Maria Iola. English writers thought an Englishman had done the job but did not give his name. No doubt in the course of years several engineers were asked for advice, but in any case the rocks were at last removed by the use of 4,000 charges of dynamite. An official party with a representative of the Douro Company on board was able to navigate the rapids in 1788 and in 1792 they were opened to commercial traffic. Boats could now go up the river as far as the neighbourhood of Moncorvo and even to Barca de Alva on the Spanish frontier. This facilitated the trade in corn with Castile and the development of the Moncorvo district, but only indirectly helped the port-wine trade. Few wines were grown so high up the river, but the general increase in navigation was beneficial. On the other hand the extension of the delimited port-wine area to the Upper Corgo in 1788 encouraged the cultivation of vines higher up the river, where in fact the climate and the nature of the soil was most suitable. The lengthening of the frontiers of the delimited area also made it easier for unauthorized wines to be brought in from outside. It was now at last understood that for the production of port-wine the slatey parched mountain-sides above Regua were better than the gentler reddish clay slopes of the lower valley with their damper climate. The extension of the district undoubtedly promoted an increase in the production of wines handled by the company. The average grew from 31,770 pipes a year in the years 1783-87 to 48,136 pipes in 1792.

Though the company now competed with the Factory in shipping wine and the Lisbon wine trade had also revived, there was enough for all and the Oporto Factory did not suffer. There was some increase in the export of port-wines to countries other than England, and for a time there were good hopes of finding new openings in the American market. After the Declaration of Independence the United States were anxious to negotiate reciprocal commercial treaties with European countries and placed France and Portugal high on their list. Wine still played a much smaller part in American life than spirits, but madeira was popular in spite of the fact that the duty on it was high, ranging from 40 cents a gallon on wine directly imported from Madeira to 49 cents on wine imported by way of England and 56% *ad valorem* on the special wine called London Particular. The duties on other wines were 30 cents a gallon on French wines, 33 cents on San Lucar sherry, 25 cents on lisbon and port-wine, and 20 cents on Fayal (Azores) and canary. The correspondence of the firm of John Norton & Co of Virginia between 1750 and 1790 throws some light on the attitude of Virginian gentlemen towards wines at this period. The Nortons were general merchants, who extended their business to include wine mainly because they were interested in supplying their own cellar. They liked to do a deal in burgundy or champagne occasionally, but their staple wine was madeira. They had a standing order for an annual pipe for their own consumption from a Madeira firm named Lamar. They had connections with both Lisbon and Oporto, but made no mention of shipping wine from either place. There was evidently still some demand for French wines in Virginia, for during a visit to St Eustatia (near St Kitts) in the West Indies, one of the Nortons heard of a bargain in the form of 1,000 hogsheads of Bordeaux claret of good sound quality. This consignment was prize wine and was offered at the very low price of 57/6 a hogshead. Norton thought he might have cleared 100% profit, but unfortunately the naval authorities required payment in cash and would not accept a bill of exchange, so as he did not have so much money with him he lost the opportunity.

The general American preference for madeira was shared by George Washington, but his colleagues Jefferson and Adams preferred French wines and there was a great enthusiasm among Americans for all things French as a result of the support they had received from France during the revolution. When Jefferson was engaged in a diplomatic mission in France he took a personal interest in wines and was always on the look-out for good ones. It is interesting that even in France he concluded that wine merchants were seldom reliable and that he could only be sure of getting the best wine if he went directly to the growers. In his official capacity Jefferson was hopeful that a commercial treaty could be concluded between France and the United States, though there had not hitherto been much trade between the two countries, and the American importation of French wines was not more than 2,000 tuns. But this was as much or more than the United Kingdom had been taking, and he thought that if upon the outbreak of war with France England declared, as she was expected to do, an embargo on French goods, there would be a good opportunity for America to step into the breach. He remarked that France had wines and America had useful things to give for them in exchange. He thought that even without a formal treaty trade between the two countries ought to flourish, indeed that all the government required to do was to refrain from hindering. He had the support of many leading people in the States who were anxious to promote French wines. The State of Virginia actually went so far as to pass a law in its legislative assembly annulling the import duties on French brandy and proposing to give French wines the same privilege, if the Constitution permitted.

Unfortunately the Constitution did not permit, and also little came of Jefferson's high hopes of a treaty or of a general reduction of duties. He continued however to buy Bordeaux, Frontignan and burgundy for his own use. He was also interested in madeira and thought that the strength of Portuguese wines would always recommend them to American taste and that the United States would soon be able to absorb the whole of Portuguese production. He anticipated a decline in the English market and that in consequence American purchases would be all the more welcome to the Portuguese. Nevertheless, though the discussions began well, the negotiations for a commercial treaty with Portugal fared no better than they did with France. The Portuguese minister, the Chevalier de Pinto, was unable to give any encouragement to Jefferson's hopes that Portugal might agree to concede the right of free trade with Brazil to the United States, though he was generally sympathetic, and the talks never progressed further than amiable exchanges of views, so that after a time the negotiations petered out leaving the predilections of Americans for Portuguese wines to take care of themselves, and the pattern of American-Portuguese trade much as it had been before. But the trade in madeira continued to flourish; much of it was the much-travelled wine so popular in England and after its voyaging was imported from there. Among the well-to-do both in Virginia and New England there was also a certain cult for port-wine following that in England.

In the last decades of the century the growth of America and the expansion of British shipping over the seven seas became noticeable. The use of port-books, which had been such a valuable guide to the development of shipping, was discontinued, but a general idea of the trend can be gathered from the lists of ships applying for passes to the Mediterranean and also from the returns of seamen's sixpences. The names and tonnage of most ships going to Spain or Portugal or transoceanic destinations are given in the returns of Mediterranean passes, but many ships only called at a Mediterranean port on the return voyage and did not therefore apply for a pass when they left England. The seamen's sixpences, described in connection with the Cadiz trade, were paid upon return to the United Kingdom and the returns give the last port of call and in this way are more informative, but the returns at the Public Record Office do not include the ships which called first at an out-port and paid their sixpences there.[1] These constituted the majority, for in the mid-summer quarter of 1789, £1,857 was collected in the out-ports compared with £490 in London. On account of its large coastal trade in coal, Newcastle-on-Tyne collected most, but Falmouth was a large contributor, for although

[1] Adm. 7/106, Mediterranean passes, 1789. Adm. 68/206, Seamen's sixpences.

it was in itself a small port it was a first port of call for ships entering the Channel. By 1789 the returns showed a fair number of ships rated at over 400 tons, but the peninsular trade was still mostly carried by ships of less than 200 tons. The connections of the wine trade and particularly of the Spanish trade with the west country and with Ireland were still strong, while Oporto still traded with King's Lynn. Ireland had a thriving export trade to the Peninsula in butter, bacon and corn, and although Ireland was a poor country she had a larger population relative to that of the rest of the United Kingdom than she had later, when the population of England and Scotland had enormously increased, and emigration and the potato famines had depopulated Ireland. She handled more trade at this period than Scotland, and although her peasants starved she maintained a number of gentry who were good customers for wine. Scotland maintained her traditional taste for wine, even French wine, as far as her scanty means allowed, and handled through Leith much of the claret drunk in the north of England. But the customs returns were so meagre that one supposes that smuggling must have played a great part. A fair number of Scottish ships traded with Spanish and Portuguese ports not only from Leith but from minor ports such as Fraserburgh, Portsoy and Montrose.

In 1789, a good year for wines, Guerner rated the Oporto exports to England at 39,698 pipes. The official Portuguese statistics, also available, including second-class wine and exports to all destinations, gave a total of 49,902 pipes. In 1792, the last year of peace, English imports of Portuguese wines were 53,876 pipes, plus 2,504 pipes from Madeira and 10,790 pipes from Spain. The English sources for these two years do not differ much, but for 1792 the Oporto exports to the United Kingdom as shown by Guerner and the official source show 2,000 and 5,000 pipes more. The omission of second-class wine or of the Guernsey trade could perhaps account for all or part of the discrepancies. Certainly with regard to a period not very much later, in 1812, the Oporto customs showed 135 pipes and twenty hogsheads going to the island of Guernsey, whereas the London customs showed 2,545 pipes and 162 hogsheads of port-wine entering from Guernsey in the same year. Some of this perhaps came out of stocks, and much more wine was kept for a time before shipment, as was shown by the fact that exports of wine from Oporto were distributed much more evenly through the year. As far as London was concerned, there were more ships coming from Lisbon than from Oporto. In 1789 the return of seamen's sixpences, which showed perhaps half the total number but gave the right proportion, recorded sixty-seven ships from Lisbon and forty-seven from Oporto. The Portuguese figures for the exports of wine from Lisbon and other Portuguese ports only begin in 1796 but show a total of from 15,000 to 20,000 pipes in good years, mostly from Lisbon but with Figueira attaining 5,000 pipes in certain years. Most of this went to the United Kingdom, and except for the island wines most of the Portuguese wines reaching the United States passed by way of England. The Navigation Act no longer prevented the direct carriage of wine in English ships from Portugal to America, and there was some direct trade in Portuguese ships from Oporto, but not very much, as the Douro Company's monopoly prevented the Factory from shipping their wines except to the United Kingdom.

CHAPTER XIII

The Years 1793-1815

War broke out between England and France in February 1793 and in the course of the year drastic measures were taken by France to prevent the introduction of British manufactures. These measures were modified during the years of the Directory, as the French felt they could not afford to trample too hard on the rights of neutrals. The British at first showed less inclination to respect neutral rights and were expected to follow a rigid policy and to prohibit the entry of all French goods. They did not do this, but declared a blockade and asserted their right to seize all cargoes bound for French ports, regardless of whether they were carried in neutral ships. At first the carriage even of foodstuffs to France was prohibited, but after a while this measure was revoked, and the export of food and corn as well as of British manufactures to enemy territory was positively encouraged. The need to pacify the United States also led to a softening of British policy towards neutrals. Except during the years 1797-98, when Cadiz was blockaded by the British fleet, the trade in wine with Spain was well maintained in the early years of the war; that with Portugal declined, but not very much except in the years 1796-98. Some wine continued to come in from France. In 1794 this did not amount to more than 757 tuns (or 451 subtracting re-exports), but afterwards French wines were imported on much the same limited scale as before the war, in spite of the fact that two penalizing increases in the excise duty on French wines, amounting to £60 a tun, came into force in 1795. Some of the wine imported was prize wine taken from enemy ships. The remainder came in neutral ships, which were allowed to leave French ports if they declared that they were bound to a neutral destination. They had no difficulty in calling at a British port en route.

Although the total imports were appreciably swollen by captures of prize goods at times, most of the wine imported came in the normal way. In spite of the totalitarian aspect of the revolutionary and Napoleonic wars which eventually engulfed all Europe, and in spite of the policy so ardently embraced by both belligerents, the trade in many products between them remained astonishingly large and in the latter half of the long war increased rather than diminished. For the wine trade there were a few lean years, but on the whole imports of wine kept up through the whole twenty-two years and in the majority of years exceeded 30,000 tuns, which was as much as had been imported in the preceding years of peace.

Of the three principal wine-producing countries only France was lucky enough to escape becoming a battle-field. Portugal and Spain suffered several campaigns, but their exports of wine were comparatively little interrupted and their production hardly at all. In some other wars, for instance the Thirty Years War in Germany, devastation had been very general and the vineyards had suffered very much. Vineyards were less vulnerable than corn-fields, because they were often situated on steep hillsides and because they were in any case nubbly places to march across or to encamp on, but this did not mean that they were always spared, and wines in cellars or warehouses were particularly vulnerable to looting. But it happened that the principal battles were not fought in the more important wine-growing areas either in Spain or Portugal. An exception was Cadiz, which was blockaded by the fleet in 1797/8 and besieged by the French from 1810-12. On the first occasion the imports of Spanish wines to England were low, but the fleet itself is said to have taken on board 20,000 pipes, which must have compensated for the loss of exports. On the second occasion the French occupied Jerez and Malaga, but there was little fighting in the neighbourhood of the vineyards, and the largest engagement was fought away from Jerez and San Lucar at Chiclana north of Cadiz. Exports fell in 1811 but in 1808-10 the trade in Spanish wines in general with England touched unusually high figures.

Throughout the war the Atlantic islands were largely accessible only to British or neutral ships. Madeira was occupied by a British

s

garrison and regularly sent a few hundred tuns of wine annually to England in the early years of the war. From 1801 the figure exceeded 1,000 tuns and in 1809 it attained a maximum of 2,902 tuns. Madeira could claim to be the most universally appreciated wine throughout the war, for small quantities reached every country where English trade extended, even to the young city of Sydney, Australia. The Canary Islands also sent wines to England in small quantities from about 1800 and after 1808, when they declared against King Joseph and in favour of the Spanish insurgents, the trade was resumed on a large scale and almost equalled that with Madeira. Portugal itself was fought over widely and was for a short time entirely occupied by the French. Many vineyards in the Estremadura were affected, and the lines of Torres Vedras were the centre of the district producing Bucellas wines. The trade in Lisbon wines was much interrupted between 1808 and 1812, but Wellington's soldiers learnt to like the Bucellas and Lisbon wines and revived to some extent the English taste for them.

The Oporto trade also suffered vicissitudes but on the whole was luckier. There was little fighting in the actual wine district of the Douro, and although Oporto was twice occupied by the enemy, first in 1808, then after a few months of uneasy peace for a short time in 1809, the wines ready for shipment were in both cases embarked and saved from the enemy. There was a sharp fall in exports in 1811, but the bad years for exports were on the whole more occasioned by bad weather than by the disturbances of war.

There were nevertheless several alarms before Portugal was actually invaded by Marshal Junot's army at the end of 1807. Towards the beginning of the war in 1796 John Offley, the representative of a well-known London and Oporto firm, led a deputation of leading wine-shippers to call on William Pitt and to express to him their anxiety for the safety of their Oporto property in the event of a French occupation. Although some years later there were still complaints of the want of storage accommodation in Oporto, the increasing time needed to mature the wines favoured the accumulation of stocks and the lodges of the Factory must already have been fairly capacious. Offley spoke of stocks of wine amounting to 40,000 pipes valued at £800,000. This was a large quantity, but still represented rather less than the total export in a good year. Pitt thought that the merchants' concern was premature, as indeed it proved to be. No doubt after each fresh alarm they tried to run down their stocks, but in 1803 Offley was still talking of stocks worth £60,000 being in jeopardy, perhaps referring in this case to those of his own firm. A few years after the end of the war, in 1829, a much larger figure of 42,000 tuns was attributed to the stocks.

The crunch in Portugal finally came in August 1807, when the French delivered an ultimatum demanding that all Portuguese ports should be closed to British shipping, British property in Portugal sequestrated and British subjects told to leave the country. However, the Portuguese succeeded in hedging for some months without actually agreeing to the French demands and the Oporto Factory was able to profit by this respite to evacuate their families and to send the church plate and their valuables and as many wines as possible home. They collected as many of their debts as possible and in October sixty heavily-laden ships left Oporto and twenty-four sailed from Lisbon. Finally the French lost patience with the Portuguese and at the end of November Marshal Junot crossed the frontier and marched rapidly towards Lisbon. The British Minister was on the point of leaving, but a British squadron stood by, and at the last moment he succeeded in persuading the Regent and the Portuguese Royal Family to embark with him together with his court and the ministers and to sail for Rio de Janeiro. As they passed the bar of the Tagus the French army was already marching into Lisbon. The Portuguese Royal Family was to remain until 1821 in Brazil, and soon after their arrival there a new treaty was concluded with England which superseded the Methuen treaty, though Portuguese wines enjoyed their preference over French wines for some years longer, until 1831, and the privilege of having judge conservators in Oporto and Lisbon was not abolished until the treaty of 1843. The British Factories as corporations in the eyes of Portuguese law were abolished, and after its dissolution by the French occupation the Lisbon Factory scarcely figured though the Oporto Factory as a private institution revived after the war. The trade with Brazil was made free for all nations and, as English trade with Brazil could now be conducted openly and directly and no longer had to pass through Portugal, Anglo-Portuguese trade diminished.

The French occupation interrupted communications between England and Portugal and the price of port-wine in London rose steeply, but before long Marshal Junot began to give licences for ships with wines to sail from Oporto and Lisbon, so that already in April 1808 six ships with wine on board reached London. The French realized that there was little point in cutting off one's nose to spite one's face and that the export of wine could pay for imports needed by Portugal. Junot went so far as to give permits for American ships to bring colonial goods, often of British origin, though for doing so he was censured by Napoleon. In June 1808 the Portuguese rose in the north against the French, and when Wellington's expeditionary force sailed for Portugal he was able in August to land at Oporto, which was occupied by an insurgent junta led by the Bishop of Oporto. Proceeding down the coast of Portugal Wellington landed near the mouth of the river Mondego and advancing towards Lisbon won a battle at Vimiero. He was not in supreme command or allowed to follow up his victory, but the French signed the Convention of Cintra, under the terms of which they agreed to evacuate Portugal. In this way the country was freed until a new French invasion began early in 1809.

The departure of the French from Portugal was hastened by the news of a rising in Spain. Revolutionary juntas had been formed at Seville and in other cities. In August Spanish insurgents won a signal victory at Baylen in the north of Spain. There was a revulsion of feeling in England against the easy terms which Sir Hew Dalrymple, the commander-in-chief appointed over Wellington's head, had granted to the French. Sir John Moore was sent out to take charge in Portugal and advanced with an army into Spain, but arrived too late to join forces with General Baird, who was landing an army at Corunna, or to prevent the Spaniards being severely defeated at Durango in November. Napoleon came in person to Madrid in December, and Moore was obliged to undertake his famous retreat to Corunna where he fell on the field of battle as his army was re-embarking.

Spain fell largely into French hands again and Napoleon's brother Joseph was set up as King of Spain in Madrid. Only Andalusia and some of the coast remained in the power of the insurgents, and Portugal was again threatened. However Wellington, who had returned to England after the Convention of Cintra, was made commander-in-chief in Portugal and landed in time to save Lisbon from an advancing French army, though another army coming from the north reached Oporto and occupied the city.

One of the most notable of the men left in charge of British firms in Oporto after the Factory was evacuated was an American citizen named Joseph Camo. He had become a partner in a firm named Webb, Gray, Campbell & Camo, who were the direct successors of the seventeenth-century firm of Bearsley and the predecessors of the twentieth-century firm of Taylor, Fladgate & Yeatman. Camo did his utmost to ship the 1808 vintage, but was held up by bad winter floods on the Douro. When the enemy advancing from Galicia reached Oporto, the wines were already on board but the ships on which they were embarked had not yet crossed the bar. There they remained throughout the French occupation, fortunately without being molested. Luckily the occupation only lasted a few weeks, for Wellington with reinforcements landed at Lisbon on 18th April, and before another month had passed marched over two hundred miles to Oporto, recovered the city and drove the French back to the Spanish frontiers. Oporto was not again occupied by the enemy during the war, though there were several alarms, particularly in September 1810 when the battle of Bussaco was fought in the neighbourhood of Coimbra, halfway from Oporto to Lisbon. Consequently, though from time to time members of British firms visited Oporto to see to their interests, it was not until 1815 that the British community returned in a body and that the Factory was reconstituted and given possession of the Factory House. But as the Portuguese government were always careful to point out, the Factory newly set up was no longer a legal and privileged body representing the entire British community, but only a private club owning the Factory House and consisting of the consul and such wine firms as could show proof that they had been members of the Factory before the war.

During the interregnum, production of wine went on much as before. It flagged during the years of the French invasions in the years 1809-11, but the amount registered by the company recovered rapidly from 1812 onwards. Exports did not recover so quickly, but it is difficult to say whether this was due to the absence of English direction, since soon after the war a general downward tendency began, due to circumstances extraneous to Portugal. During the last years of the war the Portuguese and neutral managers in charge of the shipping firms seem to have managed well enough, and the prestige of port-wine positively benefited by the presence of Oporto men serving with Wellington's army. As knowledgeable men on Portugal their services were welcome, and apart from Oporto visitors or men temporarily attached, there were several regular officers belonging to Oporto families. One of them was General Warre, a relative of a well-known port-shipper. George Sandeman, the founder of the famous firm, had started business with Oporto in the 1790s and during the war was often a guest at Wellington's mess. He is said to have drawn Wellington's attention to the extraordinary merits of some wine of the 1797 vintage still in stock and to have arranged for a couple of pipes to be sent to the Duke of York. It is a curious circumstance that in the accepted list of Douro vintages that of 1797 is described as unusually bad, but as the well-known authority on wines Warner Allen pointed out, an individual wine can be an exception in a bad year and even be outstandingly good. These 1797 wines, which Sandeman extolled and purveyed, were long remembered, and in any case the many talks at headquarters, supported by potations of the best of the wines themselves, drunk by tired campaigners to whom luxuries were precious, must have done much to help the rise in the social scale which port-wine was soon to experience.

In spite of the war the export of Portuguese wines had held up well until 1807 with an export of 10,000 pipes from Lisbon in most years and often of 5,000 pipes or more from Figueira. The Figueira exports then diminished notably until the end of the war and the Lisbon exports flagged. The year 1811 was the first really poor year in Oporto, when 21,000 pipes, or about half the total of the previous year, was exported. Recovery in the following years was slow in spite of the fact that 1811, although a critical year, was actually a turning-point in the war, and by 1813 the French were rapidly being driven out of the Peninsula. There was a big demand for imported goods in Spain, which stepped up the exports of wine in 1812 to over 8,000 tuns again, but the Spanish market was soon sated and the merchants who had hurried to send large consignments and for a time had made quick sales and good profits soon found that they were being left with goods on their hands. One reason for this was that during the French occupation of Spain the Spanish colonies had begun to trade with England directly rather than through Cadiz. The opening of direct trade between England and Brazil had similar effects in Portugal. At the same time there was a slump in England.

Therefore at the very moment when the allies were beginning to win the war and the wine trade with countries previously occupied by the enemy might have been expected to benefit, it fell off in Portugal and after one good year in 1812 in Spain too. Also peninsular wines now began to face appreciable competition from Madeira, the Canaries, Sicily and the Cape of Good Hope, whose wines in 1814 represented about a fifth of the total English imports.

From the beginning of the war until the declaration of war by Spain in 1796, Spanish wines were imported at a higher level and from 1799 this was resumed. More damage seems to have been done to trade by the destruction of the Cadiz custom-house by fire in 1793, and by the yellow fever which was particularly bad in the summers and autumns of 1800 and 1804 but became an annual visitant, than by the accidents of war. Except during the interlude of the peace of Amiens, Spanish wines were carried in neutral vessels until 1808. Licences were usually liberally given by the Spanish authorities. The French were often in a situation to prevent this, but even when they were in complete control they tended to adopt the same attitude. Clandestine trade was always a fine art in Spain, and during the war the Spanish authorities developed a specially blind eye, and Gibraltar and afterwards Malta became great depots for British trade. Some useful ideas of what actually happened and of the methods by which trade was carried on can be derived from the papers of Antony Gibbs, an Exeter merchant who had begun to do business in Spain before the war.[1] His principal business was in textiles, but he did a two-way trade which included fruits and wines. His career illustrates the impulse which the coming of new men and fresh capital could give to the wine trade, as it did both in Cadiz and Oporto, and also the part which social rank and good connections could play perhaps more in the wine trade than elsewhere. These were not of course an absolute guarantee of success, for Gibbs suffered many reverses and for long did not do more than break even, but they were certainly helpful to him. He also tried to behave like a gentleman by refusing to smuggle, at least first hand, and by insisting on high quality in the goods he sold. It is arguable whether too much emphasis on these virtues always brings success

---

[1] These extracts can be found in published work. The complete MS can be seen at the Guildhall Library, City of London.

in business, but in the long term they did so in this case, for they won his firm an unusually good reputation, which stood it in good stead when better times finally set in and floated it on the Victorian tide to a lasting prosperity.

Antony Gibbs appreciated the advantage of obtaining a thorough knowledge of the trade at every stage from production to consumption, and though he himself was often short of capital he fully realized the essential need for it. In his early years he travelled constantly between Spain, Portugal and England to study the market and the sources of supply for a two-way traffic. He made it his business to arrange not only the purchase and consignment of goods but also the provision of ships to carry them. At the beginning of the wars he was the representative in Spain of various textile exporters and also a partner with Juan Pomar of Malaga, an exporter of southern fruits and wines. He had had the advantage of three years' residence in Madrid and had made himself well-known in Lisbon, Seville and Cadiz. He had been one of the few English business men resident in Spain, for when the French were obliged to leave Spain in 1794 after the outbreak of war between Spain and France they were said to number 27,500, while there were only 140 English. There were certainly many more French than British, but the numbers quoted do not give a true picture, particularly of Cadiz, where there were many Irish and other Roman Catholics of British origin who could pass as Spaniards when it suited them.

In 1794 Gibbs was able to arrange for the despatch of seven shiploads of fruits and wines from Malaga for delivery to customers whom he had personally canvassed all over England. His business was going well until in July 1795 Spain made peace with France and followed this up in October 1796 by declaring war on England. All British subjects, except the Irish, were ordered out of Spain and their property was declared to be embargoed, but neither Gibbs nor his friends suffered. Trade was hindered but not stopped, and the chief danger was from French privateers infesting the strait until Admiral Collingwood's fleet appeared there in 1797. Trade on a reduced scale still continued through Gibraltar and Lisbon or with Guernsey by means of neutral ships. There was peace again with Spain in September 1801 and this continued until 1804 officially, though relations were strained and war soon broke out again with France. Antony Gibbs was sufficiently hopeful to open an office in Cadiz and to renew his partnership with Juan Pomar of Malaga. He resided for some time in Cadiz and was not unsuccessful, though he found that the Irish resented his competition and he had few friends, as there were not many English residents. But he was on good terms with the consul James Duff and his relative by marriage, William Gordon. Both these men had been established in Cadiz for some time and were to play a leading part in the revival of the wine trade of Cadiz. They brought capital and fresh enterprise to a trade which in the hands of a few small exporters and under the thrall of Spanish officialdom had been languishing for some time. There was an earthquake in Malaga in 1803 and the yellow fever, which had been especially bad in Cadiz in 1800, returned in 1804 and became chronic every summer. The quarantine regulations were more hindrance to trade than the sickness itself and kept Gibbs from visiting Cadiz in the autumn of 1804, though he got as far as Seville and stayed some time there. He remained there until the February after the outbreak of war, when he was finally ordered to leave. But he was still able to keep in touch through Lisbon, and although his private property in Cadiz was embargoed, he succeeded in transferring all his trade goods into the name of a Spaniard named Vallarino and they were untouched.

Gibbs returned to England in September 1805 and began to work on a plan devised by himself and Vallarino to ship his unsold goods in Vallarino's name in a Spanish ship to South America. Most exceptionally, through the influence of his brother Vicary Gibbs, who had recently been elected M.P. for Totnes and was Solicitor-General in William Pitt's last government, he procured, though with some difficulty a licence to ship the goods, valid for eighteen months on condition that the ship returned to an English and not to a Spanish port. He returned to Lisbon together with his son Henry and arranged to meet Vallarino on the frontier in order to deliver the licence. When this arrangement fell through he actually entered Spain and met Vallarino at San Lucar near Cadiz. He found that Vallarino had succeeded in selling stock to the value of £1,000 but was having difficulty in finding a ship to go to South America. The delay made the embarkation of the goods impossible before the English licence expired and Henry Gibbs had to go back to London to try to obtain an extension. He was successful and both father and son visited Seville again and Cadiz in October 1806 and returned safely to Lisbon in spite of the war. While in Spain Antony Gibbs transferred the balance of his goods from Vallarino to other Spanish friends, and Vallarino diligently continued his search for a Spanish licence and a ship. Eventually he succeeded and loaded the goods on the Spanish ship *Hermosa Mexicana*, which successfully reached Peru and sold the goods in Lima. The completion of the plan was frustrated by Vallarino's brother, who had sailed with the ship and brought her back to Vigo instead of to an English port. This jeopardized the validity of the English licence but after some hesitation Vicary Gibbs agreed to use his influence and this was sufficient to prevent it being cancelled.

Again through influence, Gibbs procured a passage on a man-of-war for his son Henry to proceed to Gibraltar early in 1808. Lisbon was now occupied by the French and was closed as a channel for correspondence, which now had to go to Spain through Gibraltar. The Spaniards had declared the sale of all British goods in Spain illegal, but Gibbs was still able to receive and to arrange to accept an order for textiles to be sent to an Irish friend named Lonergan, resident in Cadiz. In Cadiz Gibbs employed another Irishman or naturalized Spaniard named Mardon, who was working as a clerk in a Spanish firm, to look after his interests. As a Spaniard Mardon could not obtain permission to travel to Gibraltar, nor as an Irishman could he leave Gibraltar to return to Spain, but he obtained employment as a courier to take despatches to the Spanish Consul General in Tangier and by this means was able to meet Henry Gibbs there in March 1808. Soon afterwards, in June, the Seville Junta began the insurrection against the French but refused at first to allow the fleet to land a British force to defend Cadiz. After the battle of Vimiero the Junta reconsidered their decision and sent their secretary Esteller to Gibraltar to negotiate. Henry Gibbs knew Esteller personally and obtained leave to accompany Esteller and the governor of Gibraltar's son, Captain Dalrymple, back to Cadiz and to Seville. The fleet was still anchored off Cadiz and Henry Gibbs witnessed the landing of an expeditionary force, for which the Spaniards had now given permission. He also saw the Spanish bombardment of the French warships blockaded in Cadiz harbour and their surrender.

Henry Gibbs successfully did his business in Seville and afterwards set up an office in Cadiz and recovered some of his father's stock. About £400 worth was paid in wines, which were shipped from Malaga by Juan Pomar. It was not until the spring of 1809 that Antony Gibbs ventured on any new business; then as the danger of the French returning to Cadiz seemed to have receded, he chartered a ship named the *Sylph*, and afterwards two more ships, and loaded them for Cadiz. The *Sylph* was delayed and did not return to England before the end of August. She had been successful in selling her English goods in Spain but missed the market for the wine she had loaded. Upon reaching London she found herself the last of thirty-one ships with Spanish wine waiting to unload, and incurred heavy charges for demurrage. From the time of the victory of Trafalgar in October 1805 the British had commanded the sea and there had been no means of removing the stocks of wine accumulating in Spanish ports except on ships receiving English naval protection. The Spaniards were always glad to sell their wine and the French were not always in a position to prevent this, and even when they were, they were often ready to connive at the grant of export licences and upon occasion even openly to approve them. For these reasons the exports of Spanish wines in the years after Trafalgar were unusually large. In 1808 the import into England rose to a peak of 11,987 tuns and were almost as high in the two succeeding years, in spite of the fact that the French army was encircling Cadiz and had occupied Jerez and Malaga and that for one year 1809 an additional duty of 1/1 a gallon was imposed on Spanish red wines, which presumably came more from French occupied territory than did the white ones.

The import of English manufactured goods into French-occupied Spain was stopped from the English side, but until 1811 neither the English nor the French objected to the trade in Spanish wines or in the colonial goods which were sent to Spain to pay for them. Consul James Duff returned to Cadiz in 1808 and remained there throughout the blockade by the French army. Although the French occupied for some time the landward side of the Isle of Leon, on which Cadiz was built, and the fort of Matagorda a mile away across the entry into Cadiz harbour, they made no serious assault. A British garrison remained to support the Spaniards and Cadiz remained open to British ships. There was little trade with Cadiz itself, but under British naval protection ships were able to bring back from America millions of dollars in specie. Even before the insurrection William Gordon and John Murphy, British residents in Cadiz, had in 1806 arranged a deal with the Spanish government, by which they agreed to supply dollars in exchange for British licences for ten shiploads of British manufactured goods to be sold in the Antilles for colonial goods and precious metals. In the years 1808-10 the bullion reaching Cadiz went far to defray the expenses of Wellington's army in Portugal and of the Spanish insurgent government. An incidental result was an increase in the sale of Spanish wines to England at the expense of Portuguese wines. In 1810 the French were in possession of Malaga and of all the wines ready for shipment there, but they saw no advantage in keeping it there to go bad, and much of the wine was shipped in neutral vessels or to Gibraltar, and was able eventually to reach England. Export licences were not difficult to obtain and some British subjects were given British licences to reside in enemy-occupied territory to attend to this business.

Thus although Wellington's armies were driven back into Portugal more than once and Cadiz was in grave danger, British trade with the Peninsula continued and was even able to recoup some part of the losses occasioned in the north when Napoleon gained control of the whole of the coast of Europe as far as the Baltic. So the wine trade flourished with Spain during the French occupation, but declined when Spain was finally delivered. There was a good year in 1812, when British goods poured into Spain to supply the depleted market and the imports of wine into England were again over 8,000 tuns, but the British Government tightened their regulations to meet economic difficulties, and discouraged imports, including wine, while on the Spanish side trade suffered by the failure of Cadiz to recover her monopoly of the Spanish colonial trade.

While the tide of French occupation and power was highest, the export of Peninsular wines to England had benefited because neither belligerent had any interest in stopping it. The enemy were glad to receive colonial goods in exchange for wines and the English benefited not only by the consumption of the wines but by taking over a large share of the trade of the enemy in Europe and America with neutrals and by re-exporting considerable quantities of wines and brandies which exceeded normal British needs. All the declarations made by Napoleon against the iniquity of the English trade and the Draconian decrees, and the similar diatribes

on the English side against French trade, were aimed at manufactures rather than against natural products and against exports
rather than imports. Both sides also had from time to time to
temper the wind for the sake of neutrals. As neutrals rapidly grew
fewer this consideration diminished, and in the last years of the
war Great Britain actually went to war with the principal remaining
neutral, the United States. But even the rigour of the campaign
against enemy manufactures had to be modified sometimes
by both belligerents in order to meet their own needs. When
Napoleon lost command of the sea he was obliged to make large
concessions to obtain goods which could only reach him by crossing
it. Towards the end of the war the belligerents came near to a tacit
agreement to allow a limited amount of open trade on a reciprocal
basis.

Furthermore, though it was logical to suppress enemy trade it
was hard to give up the profits derived from trade in general.
Great Britain needed funds to carry on the war and Napoleon's
need was even greater. An easy way to help the exchequer was to
countenance any trade which did not specially help the enemy and
to sell exemptions from one's own laws. This was what was known
as 'fiscalism', and whenever arguments could be found for relaxing
restrictions they were eagerly seized. There was always strong
pressure from interested parties for the safeguarding of exports,
and the enemy on reciprocal grounds could often be brought to
tolerate the corresponding imports if they were urgently needed.
Goods were incontrovertibly contraband if they directly helped
the enemy's war effort, and England had usually been inclined
to extend the definition of contraband rather than to limit it. But
now her interests as a great trading and manufacturing nation led
her to adopt the same attitude as formerly had been that of the
Dutch, when in the war of the Spanish succession they had refused
to ban trading with the enemy. In the earlier years of the war
leather and cloth were allowed to reach Holland, so that a Speaker
in the House of Commons was moved to admit that the uniforms
of Napoleon's armies were largely made of Yorkshire cloth. Both
sides had qualms about foodstuffs. England began the war by
declaring that corn and flour carried in neutral ships was contraband, but was not averse to carrying corn for enemy consumption
in English ships, and if she limited exports of corn, it was in order
to conserve her own supplies, and not in order to starve the enemy.

England was usually in greater need of corn than France, and Montalivet, Napoleon's home secretary, did suggest in July 1810, a time when England was short of corn, that the export of corn to England from the North Sea or the Baltic should be stopped, as this would cause a famine. At about the same time Napoleon prohibited for a time the export of corn, but it appears that he too only did this in order to conserve his own supplies. Napoleon was well aware that England needed corn, but until France herself faced a shortage had given export licences lavishly because he considered that corn was a profitable export and that England had alternative sources of supply and was not dependent on French-controlled corn. He told his ambassador in St Petersburg: 'The English, having need of corn, will naturally let vessels enter and leave, because the corn is a prime necessity for them.' But as he explained in 1811, he did not propose to try to starve England out, because she could always obtain adequate supplies from America, which was outside his control, and from Poland and Prussia, which were within his sphere of influence but not under his absolute control. So his prohibition in 1812 of the export of corn was due to a failure of the French harvest and to his need to build up supplies for the Russian campaign and not to any ambition to deprive England, though after another bad harvest in 1811 she was in as great need again as she had been in 1808 and 1809. There was a shortage and the price of corn in England rose very high, but Napoleon's view was shown to be right, for England came through successfully without any need for corn imports from France. These imports, in 1810 had been considerable, but they only represented a comparatively small part of England's total imports.

If the two belligerents found it prudent to be tolerant on the subject of bread, they found it still wiser to be liberal about wine and brandy. Brandy was a valuable export for France and its production enabled large quantities of cheap wine, which could not be exported under war conditions, to be converted into this precious and durable commodity. Normally the English distillers opposed the import of foreign spirits, but in time of war the government was inclined to discourage the production of the distilleries in the interest of the conservation of corn supplies. Another consideration was the fact that the smugglers continued to bring in brandy in considerable quantities and it was undesirable to encourage them further by reducing official imports and thus placing a premium on smuggling and losing the heavy duties payable. In addition, during the war the re-export of brandy was a valuable trade. In 1808 for instance, when 4,893 tuns were imported. 2,526 tuns were re-exported. Two thousand and twenty-four tuns went to Sweden, much of it no doubt continuing to other countries with which direct trade was closed by Napoleon's blockade. In 1805 and 1809 the imports of brandy were higher still, attaining 10,567 and 11,704 tuns respectively, but the value of the brandy exported in the years 1808-12 exceeded that imported by £54,000. This is only a token figure, as the values both of the imports and exports were official values and not current values, but they indicate the extent of the re-export trade.

In the early years of the war, until 1805, figures submitted to Parliament show a decrease in the home consumption of wines and a re-export trade amounting to two or three thousand tuns a year. But two or three thousand tuns of duty-free wine used by the Royal Navy must be added to the consumption figures, and if this is taken into account the pattern of consumption was not very much altered, except that in some years more Portuguese wines were drunk, in others more Spanish wines. Surprisingly there was an increase in the importation of French wines but this was offset by increased re-exports. In 1792, 836 tuns of French wines were imported and 300 tuns were re-exported. In 1805, 640 tuns were consumed and 1,466 tuns re-exported. After this the increase in the import of French wines was remarkable, amounting to 7,838 tuns in 1808 and attaining a maximum of 13,105 tuns in 1809. In 1808 no less than 5,869 tuns of the total were prize wines. In 1809 the importation of brandies and wines both from France and Spain was so large that the docks and quays were absolutely encumbered and many ships had to wait to unload. Six thousand, three hundred and eighty tuns of these French wines were re-exported in 1808 and 9,481 tuns in 1809. Considerable quantities of Portuguese and Spanish wines were also re-exported. Over 1,000 tuns of the French wines and 250 tuns of the Spanish wines were prize wines. In the circumstances the government had no reason to be alarmed and indeed had good grounds for satisfaction, but they took fright and imposed an additional duty of 6/- a gallon on French wines in 1809.

The list of applications to the Board of Trade for licences for neutral vessels gives some idea of what happened in 1809.[1] The applications numbered several thousand and there is no knowing how many were actually used, but they indicate the way in which basic prohibitions were undermined by considerations of policy or by personal influence. The applications were made by firms or individuals to import goods from enemy territories in English or in neutral ships. A case of an obvious exception to the rules suiting both belligerents was the permit given to the British ship *Duchess of York* to provide a packet service for the regular carriage of passengers and cargo under the name *Henrietta* to Dunkirk and to Holland. Sometimes a blanket permit was given, for instance the permit to the firm of Garland, Baker & Man to import twenty cargoes of grain from Germany. On the other hand applications to take grain to Spain or to import it from France were refused, as was a permit to take cheese to Portugal. The grant or refusal of a permit seems to have depended on the circumstances and often to have been arbitrary. A permit to bring four cargoes of brandy from Valencia was allowed, but another application to bring three cargoes from the Charente was refused, although a permit for wine to come in the same vessels was granted. Four cargoes of wine from Bordeaux were allowed but eighty pipes of port-wine from the same port were disallowed. On the other hand an application supported by Lieutenant-General Sir John Doyle to bring a cargo of port-wine from La Rochelle to Jersey was granted.

In the earlier years of the war neutrals carried much of the trade, but as the war progressed neutrals became fewer and Great Britain was successful in carrying much of the French and former neutral trade of Northern Europe. The belligerents were indeed feeling their way to a kind of reciprocity. The French handled the internal trade of Europe, while Great Britain carried the maritime trade. Both sides rejected the manufactures of the other but were willing to admit exchanges of cargoes and to grant licences liberally for the importation of colonial or natural products. The trade with the Peninsula was mostly carried in British ships, but the Americans carried a great deal of the Atlantic traffic. It had been necessary to modify the Navigation Laws in their favour and the principle by which goods could only be carried directly to England from the country of origin in English ships or in the ships of the producing country was eroded by an increasing number of exceptions.

[1] Board of Trade 6/195. Licences to neutral vessels.

The direct trade with France was subject to constant changes of policy. In 1810 Napoleon gave licences for imports liberally on condition that the outgoing ships took wine and brandy or other French goods to the full value of the cargoes they proposed to import. Napoleon was also anxious to encourage the export of French silks, but here he ran into strong opposition on the English side. Otherwise the dispute between the belligerents was about which party should take the first step rather than any dis-agreement about licensing the import or export of reciprocal cargoes. In October 1810, when Napoleon was tending to be liberal, the British took a stiffer line and began to refuse licences, and to insist that licences to import wine or brandy would only be given in return for the export of English manufactures of similar value. But they were faced by such determined protests from the trade that they allowed the balance of the licences already issued to be used and in 1811 resumed the grant of new ones. Meanwhile the regulations were infringed by various abuses. On the French side shippers, in order to obtain French licences, went so far as to load their vessels with worthless wines and shoddy silks which could be thrown into the Channel without great loss. In this way they could present themselves at British ports in ballast or with very few enemy goods and easily obtain British export licences. Alterna-tively, in order to obtain French licences they took on board works of art at an exaggerated valuation, which satisfied the need to show an export quota. Napoleon countered these evasions by encourag-ing smuggling to England of wines, brandies and silks. He made arrangements for them to be welcomed at Dunkirk, whence they took on clandestine cargoes, which were transferred to other ships off the English coast or sunk at an agreed spot offshore, where they could be picked up.

At the end of 1811, when licences began to be issued again, a more precise reciprocal system was adopted. English licences to import a tun of wine were given in return for the export of a muid of sugar (12 cwts), 10 cwts of coffee, a ton of copper or English manufactures to the value of £100. Napoleon reciprocated by licensing the import of colonial goods against the export of wine. The year 1811 had been a time of stiffer policies and diminished trade, but in 1812 there was a revival, which was very noticeable in the wine trade. Portuguese wines, which had fallen very low in 1811 to 9,260 tuns, revived to 15,007; Spanish wines increased

T

from 4,541 to 8,068, French wines from 3,441 to 5,100 and Madeira from 1,518 to 2,035. No statistics are available for 1813 on account of a fire at the London custom-house which destroyed all the records, but in 1814 fewer wines were imported from France and Spain and about the same amount from Portugal. On the other hand rather more wines were imported from miscellaneous sources and a substantial preference was given to Cape wines by a reduction of duty from 9/- a gallon to a little over 3/-. This produced a boom in Cape wines, but it only lasted a year or two after which about 2,000 tuns a year were imported on much the same scale as madeira and canary. The 1811 additional excise duty of 9/- a gallon on French wines was taken off in 1814 as soon as news of Napoleon's abdication was received, but the other high duties remained, and when the re-export trade diminished with the signature of peace the import of French wines reverted to the pre-war level of about 1,000 tuns.

The last years of the war had seen a vigorous contest between the exporters of manufactured goods, who wished to recover their trade in Europe and opposed the blockade, and the traders with the Peninsula, the Baltic, the Mediterranean and the Far East, who did not suffer from the blockade and had no objection to it. In 1812 the opponents of the blockade were winning and the orders in council, particularly those directed against the United States, were repealed on condition that, and in the expectation that, France would revoke the Berlin Decrees. The outbreak of war with the United States in June 1812 revived the orders in council until 1814, but the strength of American commercial interests was such that American ships went on carrying goods in defiance of the American wartime regulations. In 1813 English trade with Europe was growing again in spite of the French ban on English manufactures and the restrictions on the import of French brandy into England. In the months January to August 1813 ninety ships entered English ports from France and sixty-eight ships took colonial goods to France. Forty-three ships brought wines from France, but as soon as peace was signed the wine trade slackened. After French wines Portuguese wines were the greatest losers, except for madeira wines which retained their trade. Nevertheless port-wines, or wines purporting to be port-wines, were still the most consumed. All wines were more expensive than they had been before the war and Spanish wines had caught up a good deal on Portuguese wines, but otherwise the pattern of the wine trade remained surprisingly little altered.

The royal household still had its allowances, though the king himself was out of action, and with a few changes and reductions reflected the fashion. The royal dukes lost their allowances in 1806 and at about the same time the chaplains and the bedchamber women lost their traditional generous allotments. There was no ban on French wines during the war and a few bottles of hock still figured, but port-wine had become the staple supported by other Portuguese wines, Carcavelos, lisbon and madeira. Sherry however was beginning to be used, and by 1797 a little Cape wine was being supplied, perhaps a patriotic gesture.[1]

[1] L.S. 9/247.

CHAPTER XIV

The Years of Vintage Port

ALTHOUGH a few British subjects returned to Oporto again in 1808, most of them left again and did not return until the end of the war, although in 1812 the consul-general from Lisbon visited Oporto and called a meeting. During the interregnum the Factory House was run by a Portuguese named de Queiroz, who let out some of the rooms for shops and for an eating-house used by English sea-captains. This sub-letting continued for a time even after the return of some of the British merchants. Bento de Queiroz was the name of a well-known Douro farmer and also of the court scrivener; he may well have taken over the administration of the Factory House as the representative of the ultimate landlord, the Portuguese Crown. In any case, Wellington's officers were able to be received at the Factory when they entered Oporto, and in due course the representatives of the former Factory resumed possession without opposition, though for some time the handling of their business remained in the hands of Portuguese agents. But the London representatives of the Oporto firms were active in defence of their business and in 1813 complained to Parliament that the Royal Douro Company was exercising a monopoly in restraint of trade and in defiance of the new Anglo-Portuguese treaty signed in 1810. The company denied the charge and pointed out that in 1811 they had only exported 7,337 pipes of wine out of the total of 18,536 pipes, so the British had handled more than themselves. It was true that some of the balance had been sent under Portuguese names, but they maintained that most of these were acting on behalf of British principals. So the British had more than a fair share, for while the company had forty-four representatives in

London, all respectable firms, the Factory had only mustered thirty-five signatures for their memorial and these included the names of a German, of two Portuguese, and of several firms which had been out of business for a number of years. The Factory memorial was not therefore properly representative. This assertion was not altogether unfounded, for although the defenders of the Factory, led by William Warre, a wine-shipper and latterly deputy British consul in Oporto, stoutly blamed the company for every ill which beset the wine trade, the committee of the Privy Council looking into the matter found to their surprise that the company had many defenders in England. Naturally the company's own agents in England stood up for it, but other merchants also supported the company's contention that it had access to better sources for its wines and agreed that they could buy better wines from the company at a better price than from the Factory. It was therefore only after some hesitation that the British government replied officially to the Portuguese government that the company's privileges infringed the guarantees of free trade given by the 1810 treaty. The Portuguese refused to agree to this and prolonged the life of the company by a new decree, but although the company continued for some years longer to fight a strong rearguard action in defence of its privileges, its influence and functions slowly diminished. Meanwhile the majority of the war-time duties remained in force in England until 1825; the duties on all wines except French wines, which paid a third more, and on Cape wines, which paid half-rate, were then reduced to 4/9¾ a gallon. In 1831 the duties on all wines, including French wines, were fixed at 5/6 a gallon. Cape wines still paid half.

In Oporto the Factory soon began to re-create itself in its own image. But it functioned on a reduced scale, for in 1824 it only had fourteen members. The British community as a whole however was much enlarged, particularly after 1820. Some of the newcomers were in the wine trade, and many of them exported a little wine from time to time, but they were not admitted to membership of the Factory as a matter of course.

Not long before the French invasion, the vesting of the property of the British Factory in the name of the British consul and of the Factory had been confirmed by a renewal of the lease of the site in perpetuity by the Portuguese Crown. The existence of the Lisbon and Oporto Factories as corporations in the eyes of the Portuguese law had been ended by the Anglo-Portuguese treaty of 1810, but the English merchants returning to both cities still regarded themselves as members of a Factory and tried to claim their privileges. In Lisbon the Factory had no claim to the ownership of any building, but in Oporto such survivors of the old Factory as returned to live in Oporto undertook the responsibility for the maintenance of the Factory House and regained possession without any difficulty.

The old firms tried to exclude the new arrivals, who dealt mostly in woollen and cotton goods, though some of them dealt in wines, from the use of the Factory House. They recognized that the Factory no longer had the same status as before and was now only a private house or club, but they claimed that they were entitled to undisputed possession as private persons and successors of the pre-war owners. To emphasize this contention they no longer styled themselves the British Factory but adopted the name of British Club. However, after a year they decided that this name too was inappropriate and baptized themselves again the British Association, a name which they have kept until this day.

So when the Rev. W. B. Kinsey visited Oporto in 1828, he found that the Factory was possessed by what he called the aristocratic faction, consisting of the consul and about fourteen firms who were either the representatives of pre-war Factory firms or in one or two cases new members co-opted by election among themselves. So the Oporto community was divided into 'ins' and 'outs', and there was great jealousy between them. Kinsey could scarcely cast any aspersions on the 'ins', whose generous hospitality and wines he had enjoyed, but confessed that he could not help feeling a certain sympathy for the 'outs'. He added that Portuguese society was equally torn asunder by dissensions.

Since the war Portugal had become separated from Brazil, and after the death of King John VI divided into two factions, the absolutists who wanted Dom Miguel for their king, and the constitutionalists who preferred Dom Miguel's brother, the Emperor of Brazil, Dom Pedro, or else Dom Pedro's daughter Maria Gloria. As long as Dom Pedro remained in Brazil Dom Miguel was Regent, and in 1823 a revolution in Oporto and several other parts of Portugal declared in favour of Dom Miguel and of an absolute regime. This insurrection was quashed and in 1826, with the backing of the great powers including Britain, a new charter of parliamentary government was taken to Lisbon by a British ambassador and imposed upon the reluctant Dom Miguel. But he soon began to rule absolutely again and the struggle between the two factions continued with unabated rancour. In 1829 a regency was established in the Azores on behalf of Maria Gloria, and in 1831 Dom Pedro resigned his empire of Brazil and sailed to Europe to back his daughter's cause. In July 1832 he landed near Oporto.

The revolutionary atmosphere of Portugal infected the British communities, who showed a similar disposition to split into factions and to fight each other with more enthusiasm than rhyme or reason. There were troubles in Lisbon, Madeira and Oporto. In Lisbon the appointment of a new vice-consul was a bone of contention. To facilitate their recognition by the Portuguese authorities these junior officials had latterly been given royal commissions and had been recommended to adopt some distinctive uniform to board ships or perform their public functions. But they were still paid from local funds and elected by the Factories: their only government character was the possession of a commission, which could not be given without the recommendation of the minister or consul to the crown. Consuls and consul-generals had been appointed in much the same way, and it was not until 1825 that a regular service of officers paid by the government was instituted, although in certain posts such as Algiers and Leghorn the consuls had always had a diplomatic character and had drawn government salaries. In Lisbon also the consul-general had sometimes been chargé d'affaires, or had been promoted to be minister, and had come to be regarded as a government official rather than as a Factory representative. In Oporto the consuls had hitherto been Factory men, but now the same evolution was taking place. After the end of the Napoleonic wars the deputy consul, John Hatt Noble, was a Factory merchant, but he had to leave Portugal as a result of becoming implicated in local politics on behalf of the constitutional party, and the consul, John Crispin, was a paid government servant. But he retained the office previously used by his predecessor William Warre in the Factory House without payment of rent, and it was only when he finally resigned his membership of the Association that the office of consul as such became clearly distinct from that of chairman of the Factory. Particularly in this period of transition, consuls were often caught between two fires. They had to face the complaints of an ebullient community, on whose good opinion they were largely dependent, and at the same time to carry out orders from home which were sometimes distasteful or impracticable. More-over their parishioners often found means to voice their complaints directly to the secretary of state, who by no means always took the side of his own officer, though he did so firmly in the Lisbon dispute about the appointment of vice-consuls. The consul-general had complained that the Factory recommended their favourite paupers to be made vice-consul regardless of their ability to per-form their duties, and was told without equivocation that the final decision rested with the representatives of the crown.[1] Both in Lisbon and Oporto similar disputes arose about the appointment of chaplains; the right of the crown was asserted with regard to these appointments also, but by the act of 6 George IV, Cap 87, which put an end to official consulage, the crown undertook to supplement the salaries of chaplains and to double the amount raised in any year by voluntary contributions paid to a fund organized by the consuls and the local merchants. The same con-dition applied to funds required for the upkeep of the chapels themselves. In Oporto there was a period during which the local merchants paid contributions towards the chaplain's salary but refused to pay for general expenses or anything towards the hospital. It was after some years of dispute that this question was put on a good footing by the offer of adequate subscriptions locally.

In Madeira the British merchants were prospering and, al-though from about 1830 the wine trade began to flag, continued to do so until the onset of disease put a stop for some years to production. The consul, Henry Veitch, indited a despatch twenty pages long to enlarge on the inadequacy of his salary to keep up, in consequence of this unusual affluence, with the local standard of living. At the same time the merchants or a vociferous section of them were trying to oblige him to summon general meetings without giving him any notice of the agenda to be discussed and to insist that the decisions taken at such meetings would be binding. He wrote a careful report and was more fortunate than his Lisbon colleague, another harassed consul and the father of eleven children, who received such a thunderous reply from Canning

[1] F.O. 63/271, Lisbon despatches of Consul-General Matthews.

regarding a complaint about the form of receipt for his salary asked by the Lisbon chaplain, and a well-meant offer to mediate in the troubles of the Oporto Factory, that he would no doubt have preferred a second Lisbon earthquake.[1]

In Oporto the consul, John Crispin, had infinite trouble over the dispute of the 'ins' and 'outs'. The 'outs' were more numerous and at this time transacted more trade than the 'ins', who remained however more influential, being able to use their traditional connections and the hospitality of the Factory House to support them. Crispin was a conscientious man, and in the fullness of time produced excellent reports. But information on the background of these old disputes was hard to come by, and his dilatoriness wore out the patience of the secretary of state.

The quarrel came to a head in the year 1824. The 'ins' wished not only to exclude the 'outs' from the Factory House but also from the management of the 'Contribution Fund', into which moneys collected locally for the Factory and for community expenses were paid. The 'outs' maintained that the expenses of the Factory had always been defrayed from the moneys raised for the 'Contribution Fund' by the whole British community and that it was illegal to deny them the right of access to the Factory House. Complaints that Consul Crispin did not invite the 'outs' to the meetings of the Contribution Fund at the Factory House reached Canning, the secretary of state, who after consulting his legal advisers instructed Crispin through the minister at Lisbon that all resident British subjects, including Roman Catholics, were entitled to be summoned to meetings. Crispin then summoned all British subjects who were heads of British firms to a meeting. Even this caused difficulty, for a number of Portuguese had been in charge of British firms during the war years and had come to expect British protection while in charge of British interests. There were also British subjects in charge of foreign firms, particularly one Edward Murphy, who was manager for a Hamburg firm named Diedrich Feuerheed. Crispin refused to include him or any foreigners and on this point received the approval of the secretary of state.[2]

The 'ins' did not venture to dispute the ruling about the admission of all qualified British subjects to the meeting, but they failed

---

[1] F.O. 63/271. Consul Veitch's despatches.
[2] F.O. 63/290, Consul Crispin, 23rd June 1823, 28th June 1824.

to attend the meeting themselves or to agree to the decision taken at it to recommend the Reverend Whiteley for the vacant post of chaplain. In the following year a new complexion was given to the situation by the repeal of the act of 8 George I, Cap 17, which authorized the collection of consulage for the Contribution Fund, and its replacement by a new act, which provided for consuls to be paid by the government and for local community expenses to be met from a voluntary contribution fund to be organized by the consul and to be regulated by the votes of the majority at a general meeting of resident British subjects to be called by the consul.

Strictly speaking the Contribution Fund, which had existed from about 1690, that is from a date before the act of George I, was derived from consulage, which consisted of specified fees collected on each ton of goods imported on English ships. Consulage, authorized by an act of 1736, was collected in Cadiz in a similar way. But the fund came to comprise money collected on the outward freight carried in British ships, which in Oporto at least amounted to much larger sums than the consulage proper. The Acts of Parliament authorized the consulage to be used for expenses generally, but in order to evade the objections of Spaniards and Portuguese it seems to have been applied to purely British purposes such as the relief of distressed British subjects and the payment of the chaplains' salaries, while the levy on exports was said to be voluntary and was used for local expenses such as the relief of resident British subjects, and the upkeep of the hospital and chapel. In Cadiz the two funds do seem to have been kept separate, and payments for sick seamen, etc., to have been made to local Catholic hospitals, at least upon occasion. The distinction does not seem to have been observed so clearly in Oporto, though Consul Crispin stated that even in Consul Whitehead's time the meetings of the Contribution Fund had not been held at the Factory but at the consul's residence, and the expenses of the maintenance of the Factory had been administered separately. However, even the 'ins' only maintained that they had paid all the expenses of the Factory since 1807, and admitted that before that date some of the cost of the new Factory House had been met from the Contribution Fund, and the rest by themselves by means of loans advanced on the security of the Contribution Fund. It appears that there had been a Factory House of some sort since 1727 at

least, though until the building of the new Factory House by
Consul Whitehead it had been comparatively small.[1]

The 'outs' argued that the whole community had contributed
to the cost of the Factory House and of the purchase of the
additional plots of land required for the site and that the whole
community therefore had equal rights in the Factory. They did
not however suggest that non-British subscribers had any rights,
nor make any distinction between the consulage authorized by a
British Act of Parliament and obligatory on British subjects and
the payments amounting to 400 reis on a pipe of wine, 100 reis
on a pipe of oil, etc., collected on outward freight. Such payments
could not be obligatory in a foreign land but nevertheless had to
be paid, because in case of refusal the consul could refuse to clear
the ship. After 1825, when consulage ceased, all payments to the
Contribution Fund became voluntary and as mentioned above,
the government paid the consul's salary and offered to pay half
the chaplain's salary and general expenses too, if local people paid
the other half. There were long quarrels about this, and the 'outs'
were also able to back their claim to a share in the Factory by
showing that the renewal of the lease of the property from the
Portuguese Crown in 1806 had been specifically made in the name
of the consul and his successors and of the British nation in perpetuity, and that it could not have been made in any other form,
because in Portuguese law leases in perpetuity could not be made
to private individuals or entities. Under Portuguese law it was
necessary from time to time to obtain confirmation of such a lease
from Lisbon and to pay a fee. When in 1832 this confirmation
was due, Crispin in order to avoid personal responsibility asked
the treasurer of the Factory to forward the application. He did
so but obtained no reply, but the secretary of state in the meanwhile, after further consultations with his legal advisers, inclined
to the view that the confirmation could only be given to the consul
and that the Factory did belong to the British community. Crispin
was therefore told that he must not allow the Factory to obtain
by what the secretary of state called 'surreptitious means' a con-
veyance of the lease to themselves. Crispin then applied to Lisbon
himself and a favourable reply was actually on the way when it
was held up by the outbreak of civil war and the landing in July

[1] Some account of the history of the Factory is given in F.O. 63/427,
May and October 1830.

1832 of an army led by Dom Pedro, who occupied Oporto and for the next year was besieged there by the Miguelists.[1] A pause then ensued in the battle between the 'ins' and 'outs'. Through all the preceding years the secretary of state, sometimes by cajolery, sometimes by threats, had been trying to obtain a conclusive report on the subject from Consul Crispin. The consul, who was the butt of all parties, only procrastinated and indeed was genuinely unable to reach any conclusion, because all the pre-war Factory records had been taken home in 1807 by Consul Warre and had since disappeared. In 1832 Crispin did send a report, still inconclusive, but for practical purposes he had been succeeded as consul by Colonel Thomas Sorrell, who was accredited to Dom Pedro. He was a man of higher status than poor Crispin, and in a much stronger position, for during the siege of Oporto both 'ins' and 'outs' were dependent on his good offices. He gave them to the satisfaction of all and used his influence to the utmost to bring together the warring factions. He also finally, on 8th January 1834, produced a conclusive report saying that the legal claim of the 'ins' to the sole possession of the Factory was doubtful, but that it was impracticable for the British government to accept the responsibility. He suggested that the best solution was a reconciliation of the two parties and he actually achieved this. The Factory issued invitations to the ball to celebrate the victory of Dom Pedro to all resident British subjects and all accepted with the exception of Lawrence Ormerod, who for many years had been a leader of the 'outs'. So the old feud was assuaged and soon afterwards many of the principal 'outs' applied for membership of the Factory and were admitted. But the Factory remained in the possession of the wine firms and a century later those who dealt in other commodities were still 'outs'. The claim of the possessors of the Factory was perhaps disputable, but they had undoubtedly earned their rights by many years of bearing the costs.[2]

Although the British Association claimed to be the heir of the old Factory and preserved for a time the names of a few eighteenth-century firms, in fact a new set of men took over in the generation which succeeded the Napoleonic wars. Consequently, towards the end of the century Charles Sellers, the author of *Oporto, Old and*

[1] F.O. 63/391, Consul Crispin's despatches.
[2] F.O. 63/427, Consul Sorrell, 8th January and 18th August 1834.

New and the classic historian of the Oporto Factory, with which he had been long and intimately connected, found it hard to glean any information about the earlier history. He said that all the families had changed and that it was easier to collect information in England than Oporto. We have seen that even in the 1820s Consul Crispin both by his own disposition and by force of circumstances found it impossible to find the facts about the past and to draw up an objective report. Some facts were conveniently forgotten, but it was the nature of the old wine-shippers to stick to their business and not to be given to literary composition. During the eighteenth century the tradition had been maintained by the continuous existence of several families and firms; after the war the tradition lost none of its force, but it operated through collateral relationships and through the marriages of newcomers with the relicts of old families rather than through direct descents. Many records disappeared during the various vicissitudes which Oporto experienced, and there are actually more papers to be found in England than in Oporto, and about the earlier period than the later. Now that the nineteenth-century firms have in many cases been succeeded in their turn by new combinations a few old documents may yet turn up, but in the meanwhile few records are left to illustrate the change from the eighteenth to the nineteenth century. The impressions of William Henry Giles Kingston, however, form one of the rare links. Kingston was a grandson of John Kingston, whose name appears in 1772 in that of the firm of Lambert, Kingston & Co, successors of the original seventeenth-century firm of Peter Dowker. In his *Lusitanian Sketches*, published in 1845, he gave an account which has been much quoted of Portugal and the wine trade. He was a keen critic of the Douro Company and quoted statistics to show that its influence had been harmful. During this period between the Napoleonic wars and the Portuguese civil war of 1832-34 the Factory campaigned against the Douro Company as well as against the 'outs'. . . . On the other hand Kingston spoke warmly of the Portuguese and took exceptional pains to do justice to them. The defence of Portugal against Napoleon by Britain had left a certain legacy of good feeling, and the relations of the Factory with the good Portuguese families was better than usual. For a time the Portuguese entertained more, and the Factory families of good social standing, which as Kingston admitted did not mean all of them, went quite often to Portuguese houses. This good feeling was in some ways strengthened by the common experiences during the siege of Oporto, though this struggle also created many bitter divisions and resulted in the withdrawal from society of many Miguelist families. But the families which had sided with Dom Pedro remained, and the English, though they had been obliged to keep up an appearance of neutrality during the war, had mostly had Pedroist sympathies and therefore were on good terms with the new government. During these years the British Association made an effort to maintain cordial social relations and some of the leading merchants married Portuguese ladies and even in the course of the century were the recipients of Portuguese titles of nobility. Kingston spoke warmly of the good qualities of the Portuguese of all classes and said that the English at this period also took part with pleasure at a lower social level in the many traditional Portuguese celebrations centred on the anniversaries of local saints and the festivals of the Church.

Nevertheless, in the years immediately after 1815 the British shippers had to face the continuation of the high English customs duties and a post-war recession. In his trade report for 1823 Consul Crispin spoke of 23,578 pipes of Factory wine and of 5,526 pipes of second-class wine.[1] Nearly all the latter went to the Argentine en route for Brazil; the Factory wine nearly all went to England. Shipments of both Factory and second-class wines directly to the British colonies were small and only 115 pipes went to the United States, none of it in British ships. Of the exports of Factory wines the British shippers only handled 11,317 pipes; this relatively small share was not due to the intervention of the Douro Company, who only handled 1,750 pipes, but to Portuguese and non-British shippers, who handled as much as 10,510 pipes. Both the volume of trade and the British share in it diminished in the post-war years, but the fortified wines were now often matured for eight years and were attaining high standards of excellence and fetching high prices. The vintage of 1820 was particularly strong and generous and led to demands in succeeding years for more wines like it and to even more liberal additions of brandy in the attempt to achieve this. The reductions of the English duties in 1825 and 1831 both helped the trade, though the increase in each case after the first year of reduced duties was less than had

[1] F.O. 63/271, Consul Crispin.

been hoped. From 1831 all wines paid the same duty of 5/6 a gallon, which meant a sizeable reduction in the duty on French wines and an increase of a few pence on other wines. Most surprisingly French wines did not benefit; on the contrary the British public turned away from the cheaper French wines to buy more expensive port-wines and sherries. The total import of wines increased slightly, mainly to the benefit of Spanish wines. Throughout the period the middlemen had tended to profit at the expense of both producers and consumers. According to Guerra Tenreiro the Douro grower received in 1756 about 12% of the price paid by the English consumer but this had shrunk to 3·2% in 1815 and 1820, in spite of the fact that in the latter year the price of port to the consumer had fallen from £250 a pipe to £220. This price was still about 150% more than that paid by the first importer after payment of customs duties. The cost of the freight from Oporto apparently never changed, though the proportion of its cost to the total had halved. There are many discrepancies between the statistics taken from various sources; changes in measurements were partly responsible; the Oporto pipe was 138 gallons, and the English pipe 126 old English gallons, but from 1824 the old English gallon was replaced by the imperial gallon, which was a fifth larger. But it seems fairly clear that in the years since the foundation of the Douro Company the Douro growers had gradually lost what they had gained and the middlemen, both in Portugal and England, had secured a larger share of the turnover and probably of the profits.

The campaigns of Wellington's armies in the Peninsula and particularly their stationing in Portugal had undoubtedly helped to preserve the popularity of port-wines, which were now increasingly confronted by competition. They also helped a revival of the trade in Lisbon wines; in the years immediately following the war their export averaged 11,493 pipes and in the years 1826-31 15,985 pipes. The Lisbon wine trade had never been so much in the hands of the British as that of Oporto and was only one of many Lisbon trades. Records of it are scanty, but at long last some light is thrown upon the subject by the papers of Aquila Brown kept between 1819 and 1831.[1] Brown was an American merchant from Philadelphia: he was a banker as well as a merchant of various commodities and at this period an elderly gentleman

[1] C 103/53 and 54, papers of Aquila Brown.

of independent means and of good social standing, who very much
liked to be on good terms with the best people. He was Anglicized,
or at least Europeanized, and his wife and daughter had left him
in 1819 to live in London. Though somewhat estranged the
couple continued to correspond. Brown's carefully kept books give
a good picture of his activities as a banker, general merchant and
wine merchant. He seems more often to have been losing a gentlemanly £1,000 a year than making profits, but he did business on
a large scale and took pains to find good wines for his distinguished
friends and clients. It seems that a high-class wine business
afforded almost as good an introduction to society as the purchase
of landed property. Brown was a good example of a not uncommon
type of man, who turned his trade into a profession, a hobby and
almost an art. Such men were a link between the business and
upper classes and in matters of wine had genuinely high standards.
One way to keep on good terms with the nobility was to become
one of their tenants at an attractive rent. The Lisbon firm of
Purry, Mellis & Vismes, for instance, had been lessors of Pombal's
town house. The Mellishes at least must have prospered, for they
founded a county family in England. Brown followed this custom.
In London Mrs Brown was a tenant of the Duke of Bedford,
whose family had always been good buyers of wine; the duke also
had connections in Lisbon. In Portugal Brown leased a country
property from the Duke of Cadaval, who was the hereditary owner
of many vineyards. Brown supplied wine to the Duke of Bedford
and to successive British ministers and ambassadors. These included Sir William a Court, later Lord Heytesbury, who went
from Lisbon to St Petersburg as ambassador, where Brown continued to send him wines.

Brown often dealt in port-wines, sometimes having wine sent
to Lisbon, sometimes directly from Oporto to England. There
was apparently no longer any difficulty about shipping wine for
export by way of Lisbon. Several prominent Oporto names figured
in his business. They included John Ormerod and John Graham,
both 'outs' and prominent subscribers to the Contribution Fund.
Other correspondents were already 'ins', George Sandeman, like
Graham the founder of a very famous wine firm, and Quarles
Harris, who had only begun to export wine in 1817 but was a successor of the old firm of Dawson and Harris. Brown also had
correspondence about the shipment of a pipe of port with one of

the Van Zeller family, who later became owners of the Quinta de Rouriz. Rouriz was already known for vintage wines and at the time of his death in 1832 Brown had thirty-three dozen bottles of Rouriz in his cellar. Port-wine predominated in it for he also had eighty-eight dozen bottles of superior port, one hogshead of old port, and one hogshead of ordinary port. Other Portuguese wines consisted of a quantity of madeira and sixty-six dozen bottles of Bucellas. The madeira included twenty-one dozen unspecified madeira, five-and-a-half dozen Sercial and five dozen Old Jenifer. This name commemorated that of the ship which brought the wine, for it was the custom to name vintage madeiras accordingly. Brown often dealt in Bucellas, described as superior and old, and it was Bucellas with sealed corks that he sent to the ambassador at St Petersburg. The other Lisbon wines mentioned by him were principally Carcavelos; Colares was only mentioned once and no red Lisbon wines were spoken of. Brown shipped Lisbon wines to Philadelphia as well as to London. Those for Philadelphia were rather cheap; he quoted £24 a pipe for Lisbon, £28 for Carcavelos and £34 for Bucellas, all f.o.b. The prices for London seem to have been higher, but they were per dozen bottles c.i.f. and may have included the duties. They were 52/- a dozen for Bucellas, 55/- for Malvasia, and 60/- for superior old port. The most expensive wine in this London shipment was East India madeira at 75/-.

Brown also dealt from time to time in claret and sherry. He ordered the sherry from Jean Haurie & Sons. Jean Haurie, nephew of the founder of the firm, had been a contractor to Napoleon's armies and consequently disgraced and driven to bankruptcy, but he was still trying to carry on. In Bordeaux Brown corresponded with Messrs Nathanael and Johnson, and in 1815 he ordered 900 bottles of brandy and wine to be sent to Oporto for transhipment to London. Later his Bordeaux orders were shipped direct to England. Johnson was presumably of British descent and was mentioned by Ballantyne as one of the first to revive the direct trade between Bordeaux and London at the end of the eighteenth century. According to Ballantyne, in the middle of the century claret for England had always been sent to the north of France for transhipment. The Johnson family remained leading wine-shippers for some time, and by the middle of the nineteenth century were owners of one of the Bordeaux chateaux, while the son of the house was a French deputy. In the year 1810 or

U

thereabouts, according to Warner Allen, Johnson was one of the first to experiment with the maturing of vintage wines in the bottle and to discover its merits. After the close of the Middle Ages British subjects had not played any great part as Bordeaux shippers or producers, but from the end of the eighteenth century one or two British names again figured in the claret trade.

Brown's dealings in wine may have been in his last years something of a gentlemanly hobby, but his books were meticulously kept, and illustrated a type of high-class trade which depended on limited sales of expensive wines to the upper classes and was not without influence. On the one hand Brown was on good terms with such distinguished people as Lord Amelius Beauclerc and the Duke of Cadaval. On the other he was in touch with correspondents in Philadelphia, New York, Bordeaux, Cadiz, Jerez, Lisbon, Oporto and London. He was in a position to place orders and to arrange credits by means of bills of exchange in all these cities. It was not then enough to look up an address in a directory and to give a bank reference. Connections had to be built up gradually. For the tavern-trade wine could be bought and sold in the open market, but the private trade depended on personal connections and private recommendations. The best French wines had always been sold by these means, but such connections only became requisite in the port-wine trade when vintage wines began to be sold at high prices and to play an important part. In this way, although the total turnover of the Portuguese wine trade tended to decline, the increased value of the high-class trade compensated for this.

Brown died in 1832 before the disturbing effects on the trade of the spread of the civil war to the mainland of Portugal began to show themselves. Actually the effect on Portuguese exports was less than might have been expected, though they were naturally noticeable in the exports from Oporto in 1832. Dom Pedro landed near the city in July, and for almost a year Oporto was closely encircled by the Miguelist forces, though British ships were always stationed in the Douro and communications by sea were never entirely cut off. But although the Pedroists held the city and occupied the Convent of the Serra on the top of the precipitous hill facing the north-east side of Oporto across the Douro, the Miguelists occupied all Vila Nova de Gaia and the quarter of the wine lodges on the south bank of the Douro. The Miguelists declared a blockade of the Douro, but supplies could be landed in Oporto from boats, and the protection of British lives and property was ensured by a man-of-war lying in the river and a British squadron anchored outside the bar. Consul Thomas Sorrell, who had been accredited to Dom Pedro, tried to bring about an agreement between Pedroists and Miguelists to enable British-owned wines to be shipped from Vila Nova de Gaia. He failed in this, but the government of Dom Miguel agreed to allow the British to send their wine by bullock cart to be shipped from Aveiro or Figueira provided that they paid the export duties. Most of the shippers decided that this was too dangerous and only Messrs Newman, Hunt, Roope & Co sent 301 pipes from Aveiro by this means because their lodge stood in the line of fire and in such danger that this seemed the lesser evil. They soon got into serious trouble with the Pedroists for doing this. Shortly before they evacuated Gaia in August 1833 the Miguelists set fire to the lodges of the Royal Douro Company. Some of the British-owned wine had already been sold, and some had been stored for safety in other lodges, so that the British losses were not too heavy, but several thousand pipes of boiling port were poured into the river. The fire threatened to spread to the British lodges but a naval party was able to land and to prevent this happening. The Miguelists then threatened to set fire to a number of other Portuguese-owned lodges situated near and between the British lodges, but were deterred by strong British protests. Soon afterwards news came of the success of the Pedroist squadron which had left Oporto for the Algarve with troops on board, and of the declaration of Lisbon in favour of the constitutionalist forces of Dom Pedro. The Miguelists then gradually raised the siege and the blockade. As soon as they were out of Gaia twenty ships waiting outside the bar entered the river and loaded the wine which had been waiting. So in spite of the fact that Oporto had been besieged for most of 1833, the wine-shippers were able to embark over 19,000 pipes for the United Kingdom, according to the individual returns listed by the consul for each exporter.[1]

In 1834, after the victory of Dom Pedro and the end of the civil war, the privileges of the Douro Company were suspended. They were renewed in 1843 and were not finally abolished until 1859,

[1] The despatches of Consul Sorrell covering the siege are in F.O. 63/392, 407-9 and 425.

but neither the suspension of the company nor its rehabilitation, nor the many discussions by all concerned of the troubles of the wine trade, had any marked effect upon its development. The exports of port-wine to the United Kingdom according to the Portuguese statistics fell to an average of 23,000 pipes in the 1830s and to 21,000 pipes in the next two decades, while the exports of lisbon dropped to practically nothing. On the other hand the exports of port-wine to other destinations, which had been cut off during the civil war, slowly expanded and between 1851 and 1859 was nearly 17,000 pipes, a figure approaching that of the English trade. The purchasing power of England reflected the increasing population, but changes in the way of living produced a further decrease in the relative importance of wine. Cyrus Redding calculated that the consumption per head in the United Kingdom fell from a little over a gallon per head in the 1790s to about half a gallon in the 1840s. He attributed this to the increased consumption of spirits, but a more important factor was perhaps the part played not only by beer, coffee and tea but also by the many new luxuries and comforts upon which money could alternatively be spent. In addition a religious revival, principally among Nonconformists but also in the Church of England, not only discouraged drinking but promoted in many sectors of the population total abstinence. This was a comparatively new idea. Drunkenness had often been decried, but hitherto some form of alcoholic stimulant had been considered to be normal and almost a necessity. Now that life had more to offer, abstinence was more practicable and the loss to the wine trade would have been greater still but for the great increase in the population and spending power. It must also be said that a high proportion of the wines consumed were fortified and went further than table wines of low alcohol content. Nevertheless wine was a rarer thing in normal life than it had been, and except for port and lemon, which found favour with working men and was considered proper for their ladies, wine was not much drunk except by people of considerable social pretensions and on occasions of special festivity.

However, the comparative success of the sherry trade showed what could still be done and that the Oporto trade, which did not lack capital and the backing of substantial interests, might have done better. Canary wines fell off again after 1815, but the sherry trade steadily improved and the importation of Spanish wines into the United Kingdom in the 1840s caught up with Portuguese wines and in the 1850s passed them. The beginning of the revival of the popularity of sherry is often attributed to the Prince Regent saying that he preferred sherry to madeira. No doubt the taste of the Prince Regent helped, but the decline of madeira dated from about 1831, whereas the revival of sherry began a good deal earlier. William Ballantyne, in his letter to *The Times* in 1807, spoke of 11,000 butts of sherry being imported at that time and said that he had begun to order sherry from Mr Duff, the consul at Cadiz, twenty years before, when a fashion for sherry succeeded that for white port. The Duke of Clarence was drinking sherry regularly from 1797, and in 1820 the pages of the royal household began to be allowed a bottle of sherry a day instead of port as heretofore, so sherry by no means depended entirely on the patronage of the Prince Regent.

For a visit to the sherry district in the year 1831 we have the account of an Australian, interested in the cultivation of wines, named James Busby. At that time the import of sherry to England was about half that of port-wine but was beginning to catch up. The natural wine of the country preferred by Spaniards was too light to suit the English taste for a fiery draught, but for the export market substantial additions of brandy and stronger wines were made, particularly for the more ordinary qualities. Even the short voyage by water down the Guadalete river from Jerez to Cadiz or Port St Mary had often been enough to hamper exporters, but it was nothing like as far as the journey down the Douro to Oporto, and as many of the shippers were also growers, there was not the same rivalry between the two sections of the industry. Busby was entertained by James Gordon, a Scottish Spaniard long established in Spain. He owned vineyards and cultivated them, and also had large warehouses capable of holding as much as 4,000 butts. The better wines according to Busby were never shipped until they had been kept at least two years. Busby also met Pedro Domecq, another head of a founder firm. He was also a man of French origin but naturalized in Spain. The revival of the industry was led by men of foreign origin with capital, experience and knowledge of foreign markets. In Oporto there had usually been some men with these qualifications, and after the war new men had come in, but although relations with the Portuguese became somewhat closer than they had been they were not integrated in the same way as they were in Spain. The English shippers were liked and respected by the Portuguese, and for most of the nineteenth century and indeed until 1890, when ill-feeling arose on account of the British attitude towards the Portuguese colonies, they were not so aloof. But they never took more than a small share in the actual growing of the wines. In Spain the situation was different. The government was no more settled than that of Portugal, and there were quite as many revolutions, but the agriculture of the Spanish peasants was better, while foreigners both took a greater part in production and were in closer touch with local life. It is noteworthy that whereas in our generation after the Spanish civil war, travellers entering Portugal could not but be struck by the spick and span appearance of the countryside compared with Spain, in the early nineteenth century the reverse was the case. Cadiz was scourged annually by cholera, but the city and its neighbourhood looked white and clean, whereas Lisbon remained magnificent, but as filthy as ever.[1]

Busby also visited Malaga, where the trade in old malaga or mountain had almost disappeared and more grapes were being turned into raisins than into wine. Nevertheless there were still a number of Irish engaged in the wine trade. They were finding a good market for light dry wines in America, where they had positive allies in the temperance societies, who had declared spirits as Public Enemy No. 1 and by contrast regarded wines almost as friends. Canary wines, which had enjoyed a revival during the wars, were still quoted towards the middle of the century at prices comparable to those paid for port and sherry, but after the equalization of duties in 1831, their imports dropped to 200 tuns or less and in the 1850s the vineyards were largely destroyed by the *oidium* disease.

Cadiz still kept up its old connection with the west country. Bristol in the nineteenth century was declining as a port but maintained a traditional connection with the sherry trade and was the headquarters of Messrs Harvey, one of the largest importers. Many of the early Oporto firms also had roots in the west country, for instance Newman, Hunt, Roope & Co, though in the nineteenth century London took the major share of the trade. There was a good deal of interchange between Oporto and Cadiz, and some of

[1] The Cadiz Consular Despatches for this period are in F.O. 72/64 and 80.

the leading firms developed connections with both towns. Such were the Sandemans, the Harveys and later Gonzalez, Byass, who became a leading firm in Jerez but afterwards established themselves in Oporto.

In Oporto the Factory maintained its guiding influence in the wine trade. In Cadiz, although the revived sherry trade was after the Napoleonic wars largely led by men of British origin, not all of them were members of the Factory and the Factory itself came to an end in 1825. There were as many changes of government and dissensions between liberals and absolutists as in Portugal, but the industry still progressed. In Oporto the close oligarchy of the Factory flourished on the profits from the growing market for expensive wines, but the extent of the market continued to be limited and would have decreased more but for the lucky accident that it was a time of reduction of duties and an increasing population. The Factory enjoyed some support from the British government, which in 1830 ordered the old report of 1767 on the Douro Company to be reprinted and also the exchange of letters in 1813 between the British ambassador and the Portuguese secretary of state. The fight against the privileges of the Douro Company was pursued, and as often as the liberal cause prevailed in Portugal, with some success. In the 1840s the Factory had to meet criticisms from within its own ranks when James Forrester reopened with vigour the old controversy between the votaries of so-called pure wine and the defenders of the fortified variety. In an anonymous pamphlet entitled *A Word or Two on Port-wine*, Forrester echoed the complaints of almost a century earlier, saying that port had fallen in the estimation of persons capable of judgement and had become a nauseous fiery compound of sweets, colours and alcohol. Consequently it was appearing less often at the tables of private gentlemen and was in danger of falling gradually into disuse. This violent statement produced a violent reaction. Another pamphlet was published with a similar title *A Word of Truth on Port-wine* and there were many polemics. Among contemporary writers T. G. Shaw, himself a Leith merchant and the brother of a man who had fought for Dom Pedro in Portugal, spoke up for Forrester. He compared the fortified wine unfavourably with the fine, highly flavoured, light old port which the English merchants had formerly kept for their own use. Others defended fortified wine, and accounts of port-wine in contemporary English literature do not confirm that it was toppling towards its fall. The novelist Thomas Love Peacock was a genuine wine-lover and in *Crotchet Castle*, published in 1831, described the dinner parties of the wealthy Aberdonian Jew Mr Crotchet in loving detail. There was already much talk of vintage claret, though in vague terms. By 1860, the date of the later novel *Gryll Grange*, ideas were clearer on the subject. At Crotchet Castle madeira came in for more praise than port, but port formed a substantial background, and like a Greek chorus the old-fashioned Scot Mr McBorrowdale was constantly chiming in, 'I hold to the opinion I've always expressed, this is as good a glass of port as ever I have tasted'.

The novels of Surtees, published a few years later than those of Peacock and dealing with life in the shires and the hunting field, give a vivid though more critical picture of the taste in wine of the times. In *Ask Mamma* Lord Scamperdale, an ardent hunting man of simple, hearty but parsimonious disposition, preferred at home to drink glasses of gin with his crony and huntsman, though he did not disdain port or champagne if others paid for them. When he dined with the pretentious Mr Jawleyford at Jawleyford Court his host wished to give every appearance of grandeur and did not stop at port, sherry and lisbon, but served Chateau Margaux and champagne too. But Surtees suggested that they were not the real thing and that Jawleyford did not know where to get good wines or grudged paying for them. His wines were bought as cheaply as possible from a local man named Wintle. Surtees itemized what he paid for them. Wintle's port was 36/- a dozen and Jawleyford also took a little of the best at 48/-. The pale sherry was 36/-, the brown sherry 48/-, the Bucellas 38/-, and the lisbon 32/-. The marvellous creaming sherry was 48/- and the Margaux 66/-. In the end Jawleyford had to pay quite a lot. He might have done better if he had gone to an accredited wine-merchant. The sting was that Jawleyford did not know of one or how to go about finding one. Good wines could only be bought from high-class merchants and they were apt to confine their dealings to a distinguished and discerning clientèle. Crotchet was more of a man of the world than Jawleyford and served better wines, but from the account of both there is no suggestion that port was in danger of losing pride of place at gentlemen's tables.

Later Forrester denied that he had been attacking the Factory wine. He claimed that he was only attacking its abuses. There is no doubt that he was devoted heart and soul to the wine trade. He published many works on the subject and composed with infinite labour the first complete detailed map of the River Douro in reward for which he was made a baron by the King of Portugal. When he met his death in 1861 it was by drowning in the famous Cachão rapids of his beloved Douro and he died universally loved and respected. Yet his aim in attacking the adulteration of wines was inspired not only by an altruistic desire for improvement but by a legitimate ambition to enlarge his own trade. The company's tasters passed or condemned wines arbitrarily, sometimes taking some wines and rejecting others which were not only of the same growth and vintage but came from the same vat, but British firms were not allowed to export the rejected wines to England, still less those which although of excellent quality came from outside the port-wine district. Naturally they sometimes tried to evade these restrictions by smuggling the wine or shipping it by way of Hamburg. Forrester realized that he could handle such wines, and that if he could export them freely, they might easily prove more profitable than the port-wines with their expensive additions of brandy and lengthy periods of waiting for maturity. He himself was one of the few English shippers who grew wine as well as exported it, and his firm, Messrs Offley, Forrester, were second or third in the list of Factory exporters with an annual average export of 1,100 pipes. Naturally Forrester had his knife into rival firms and aroused a keen opposition, but several of the Factory firms refrained from signing the manifesto condemning him and among the Douro growers he had a strong following. Forrester himself claimed that the Factory manifesto had been framed and that not all the firms who signed were really against him. There were some firms who did not sign and in addition there were a certain number of British shippers outside the Factory and a fair number of Portuguese and foreign shippers. The Douro Company itself at this period was not a large exporter; it handled only 420 pipes in 1844 and 235 pipes in 1845.

The case for Forrester was presented most strongly at a dinner given by him at Messrs Offley's quinta on the Douro near Regua on 8th October 1845. This dinner was attended by the Viscount of Santa Marta, who was a former commander-in-chief of the Portuguese army, and by a number of Portuguese notables and owners of vineyards. The only prominent English guest was

Colonel Owen, who was a peninsular war veteran and a friend of the British consul in Oporto. Only pure Douro wines, prepared in the old way, were served at the dinner and general regrets were expressed that the days of Pombal when adulteration was impossible were long past and that the wine trade had fallen on evil days. Amid scenes of enthusiasm speakers asked that Forrester's advice should be taken to sell only wine and not brandy mixed with wine. Most of the producers of the Douro and of the Douro local municipal councils backed Forrester. They liked his suggestion that wines should be sold and paid for at the time of the vintage without the need for a long wait and for heavy expenditure on additions of brandy and colouring matter. The Portuguese in general attacked the Factory with the same fanaticism and exaggeration as the Factory used to defend itself. Nevertheless, much of the advice given by Forrester had often been urged by the Factory itself. Most people agreed that the grapes should not be picked until they were thoroughly ripe and that care and discrimination should be used, and that the grapes should be thoroughly trodden before they were run into the vats or any brandy added. They would also have agreed that only good wines should be chosen which could look after themselves, for wines initially bad could not be confected to take the place of good wines. But his contention that the fermentation should never be checked by the addition of brandy was strenuously confuted. He himself does not seem to have meant that Factory wines should never be treated, but only that their vintage should be carefully handled and any addition of brandy be made with discretion.

The English firms were not the only ones to disagree with Forrester. Messrs Kopke, for instance, denied that the falsification of wines was the chief cause of the low prices lately paid and blamed only the general stagnation of trade. Forrester quoted on the other hand a letter from a vineyard owner who said that he had never used to add brandy to his wines but had lately begun to do so to meet the insistent requests of the Factory. Yet William Kingston, who was a very knowledgeable and reasonable man, laid down that some addition of brandy to check fermentation was essential and that the art lay in choosing the right time and the right amount, for if the fermentation was allowed to continue the wine would become bitter and turn to vinegar. This directly contradicted Forrester's statement that the addition of brandy was unnecessary and even harmful. The fact remains that good wines had long been made without resort to brandy but that to be suitable for export and to improve their quality rather than to lose it with maturity they had to be rather special wines in the first instance. On the other hand good wines could also be made with brandy, but the process took some time for the wines to mature, and port-wines in particular needed careful maintenance if they were to be palatable. Brandy was also used with success in other wines, in Bucellas which sometimes went by the name of Lisbon port, in the heavier sherries, and even in claret. But it, or a liquor in which brandy had a part, was often added after the fermentation had fully worked itself out. Forrester himself insisted on the need for a long and thorough treading of the grapes but in his cooler moments did not exclude the uses of brandy for some wines. On the other hand few disagreed with his contention that the use of brandy must be restrained and every care devoted to the vintage, while the abuse of brandy, colouring matter and chemical additions ought to be stopped.

In spite of all the polemics and the zeal of Forrester the Oporto trade continued to flag. The wine trade as a whole from 1850 onwards also suffered from a disease of American origin called *Oidium Tuckeri*, which attacked the vines everywhere and for some years almost destroyed the production of madeira and gravely impaired that of bordeaux. Forrester published a book on the subject. However in 1859 the English wine trade, and port-wines in particular, were given a fillip by the first of Gladstone's acts, which reduced the duties on all wines to 3/- a gallon. But the act which followed in the succeeding year struck a blow at port and heavy wines by reducing the duties on wines with an alcohol content of less than sixteen degrees on the Sykes scale to 1/- a gallon. Another act in the next year modified the effect by extending the low duties to wines with a content of less than twenty-six degrees on the Sykes scale, but the higher duties still missed most French wines while applying to the majority of ports and sherries. So the preference which port-wines had so long enjoyed was finally reversed and light French wines could compete freely. The scales were positively weighted against heavy wines, for the light wines paid less duty than they had since the early years after the Restoration, while the duties on port-wines were still quite high. From 1862, when there was a further small reduction in duties, heavy wines paid £28 17s od a tun and light wines £11 10s od. In 1745 all Portuguese wines had paid £25 3s 11d net and Spanish wines a few shillings more, plus 20% which must be reckoned for the change from the old wine gallon to the imperial gallon.

The importation of sherries regularly surpassed that of port-wines from 1859 onwards and continued to go ahead; it did not benefit by the first reduction of duties on light wines but rose by some 5,000 pipes after the passage of the 1862 Act. Port-wines suffered by the 1861 Act and derived only slight benefit from the 1862 Act, but they lost no more ground and it was a long time before the lighter French wines began to benefit appreciably from the lower duties they now paid. The taste of the British public was conservative and slow to change. The expensive heavy port-wines still commanded a solid well-to-do market and their rivals were the heavier sherries and a few strong wines from the south of France rather than the French table wines. In 1861, soon after the reduction of duties, *The Times* published an article under the title 'Unimaginative' which described English contemporary taste in wines. It said that Englishmen stocked their cellars exclusively with the exports of Oporto and Cadiz, and it was but a few years since claret had been a rare and expensive luxury, only brought to the table after the company had been well soaked with port, though such a thin and delicate wine could seldom do much good or give much satisfaction after the stomach had been loaded and the palate seared with wine as strong as brandy. But even this appearance of claret had been uncommon, the regular wines had been port and sherry only, so constantly and religiously produced in couples that the very decanters containing them were manu-factured and sold by the pair. This almost implied that claret came in with the cheese and port with the fish! This heresy is not supported by Peacock's account of a dinner at Crotchet Castle, though claret did arrive with the dessert as well as port. Earlier in the meal the chief mention was of sherry, hock and madeira. But it is true that at the hunt dinners and public occasions de-scribed by Surtees, port and sherry, varied by bumpers of cham-pagne, appear to have reigned all the time. John Jorrocks, master of fox-hounds, ex-grocer, bon viveur and Surtees' hero, was apt to turn to brandy or what he called sherry negus at any time, but refused nothing ever offered to him, port, sherry, champagne or claret.

However, Gladstone's lower duties finally took effect. The consumption of French wines first exceeded in quantity that of port-wines in 1866, and ten years later almost trebled and passed that of the sherries, which were at the peak of their popularity and on the point of losing favour again. But the onslaught of *phylloxera*, another scourge originating in America, now attacked the French vineyards and then spread to vineyards all over the world, even in Australia. The havoc caused by the disease provoked a shortage of good wines and again set the clock back, giving a new impetus to the evils of adulteration and imitation which the Gladstonian acts had combated. Good wines continued to be an expensive and hallowed mystery enjoyed only by the elect; Victorian prosperity enlarged the numbers of the elect very considerably and the average consumption of wine per head, which was estimated to have fallen from an average of 1·08 gallons in 1700 to ·23 gallons in 1851, slowly began to recover, but many of the middle classes seldom drank wine at home.

With the opening up of the New World and of many other countries where the climate favoured vineyards, new wines might have been expected to appear with other colonial products in the European market. Some of the new countries began to supply their own needs, but their wines were slow to appear in Europe. The American contribution was for long confined by the two terrible diseases, the *oidium* and the *phylloxera*, though it is fair to add that American rootstocks proved to be the best means to combat the *phylloxera* and to render possible the renewal of the devastated vineyards. The only exception in the first half of the century was the Cape wines, mainly white wines resembling hock; after they were given preferential duties in 1814 they boomed for a time but the fashion for them did not last. Algeria became a wine-exporting country towards the end of the century, but otherwise only Australia entered the lists. Vines were introduced into Australia in the 1830s but in their turn were ravaged by the *phylloxera* and Australian wines did not figure in England before the twentieth century. In spite of the equalization of duties and the preference given to light wines the trade changed its pattern very slowly.

Though it had lagged for so long during its period of monopoly and did not improve its share of the market in the earlier part of the nineteenth century, the port-trade nevertheless was the most enterprising during this half-century. In the wine lore of the time it had climbed to the summit, so that the mid-Victorian novelist George Meredith found himself moved to describe it as 'our noblest legacy, combining the strength of youth with the wisdom of age'. Such a reputation ensured that the rewards of a comparatively limited trade were very profitable. In addition, and particularly after the passage of the Gladstone acts, port-wines penetrated downward again in the social scale and kept their place in the taverns as the equals in favour of beers and spirits. It cannot be said that wines other than port and sherry played any great part in the life of the English people: the wines of quality remained a prestige symbol reserved for festivities rather than for daily use. At this level they made great progress. Warner Allen spoke of the years 1811-78 as the golden age of vintage wines. He ascribed some knowledge of them to classical times and the author is of the opinion that they had not been entirely forgotten in the intervening centuries, though they had become the rare exception. Warner Allen described the art of maturing wine in the bottle as unknown before the Napoleonic wars. Undoubtedly it was unusual until then, though wines had occasionally been kept in bottles and incidentally matured in them at an earlier date. The provisions legalizing the importation of French wines in bottles in the year 1779 also suggest that wine was beginning then to be kept in bottles for this purpose. Nevertheless it was port which led the way, for port was the first wine which was habitually matured over a period of years. Claret followed and the perfecting of vintage wines in the bottle was a great triumph which Warner Allen suitably celebrated. He admitted that port and claret were the principal beneficiaries, for Germany as a white wine country was less indebted to the bottle and wine growers in Jerez held that their solera system matured wines admirably without the bottle's intervention. Nor did the bottle play so great a part in burgundies, and while champagne could claim to be the earliest wine to have benefited by its use, its life in the bottle was comparatively short and modern champagne serves a long apprenticeship in the cask. But port and claret reached unprecedented perfection in the bottle, and both in bottle and cask better wines were made in the nineteenth century and in far larger quantities than had been possible before.

So with the end of the preference given to port and with the advent of the modern scene we can take farewell of the wine trade.

Wine was not the earliest of bulky commodities to be traded or transported far afield. The existence of Stonehenge and the Pyramids prove that for religious motives men even with very limited resources could make prodigious efforts to carry about objects far heavier and more bulky than an amphora or a cask. They were moved by religion, and religious motives influenced the first uses of wine, as also its association in lands where it did not grow with prestige, associations which endure until this day. On the other hand earthier considerations also played a part; the introduction of wine to Gaul was much advanced in the first instance by the lustful thirst of the barbarian for firewater. This gross desire in the marginal countries of the north shaded off into the more respectable thirst for an exotic product which could add colour and interest to life and diet through a long dark cold winter. The cult of wine-drinking and even the cultivation of vineyards had been followed with the most enthusiasm not in the Mediterarnean countries where the vine grows most freely, but in the regions of the north near the climatic frontier of the vine's cultivation. In the south the invasion of Islam narrowed the areas where wine was drunk and left a lasting legacy of suspicion of its enjoyment. Italy and to some extent Greece were the only southern countries where wine was uninterruptedly consumed as an article of diet. For that reason it was less regarded and, in Italy especially, surprisingly little developed as a luxury and an export. The Rhineland too had a history reaching back to Roman times of uninterrupted cultivation of the vine, but it was also a climatically marginal country.

England for practical purposes was beyond the frontiers of the vine but near enough to them for wine to exercise its full magic as a commodity of prestige as well as of use. It became very early the prey of the tax-gatherer and the economist. Customs duties or prohibitions ultimately could have their way with it, but it was more resistant to plain matters of cost than any other commodity. It took half a century for the English to forget about French wines after 1690 and, even in the accelerated tempo of the nineteenth century, some years for them to be reminded of them again. Once the habit of port-wine had become ingrained it persisted and yielded to economic and political factors urging change most reluctantly. Yet wine was a delicate product. Vintages often failed; wines went sour, and convoys were unable to sail. Then the vintners showed remarkable skill in confecting wine where the natural product had failed. In the hey-day of the Middle Ages wine-drinking had almost become a national habit in England, at least in the cities and principal centres, and although in the later Middle Ages and in Tudor times wine was less drunk, the taste for it was still more pronounced than it became in the eighteenth century and particularly from 1740 onwards. Nevertheless there always remained a sizeable minority ready to sacrifice their purses and even their stomachs to drink wine or something bearing its name. The trade in wine retained an importance sufficient to interest legislators and even to influence national policies. The trade in wine remained indissolubly wedded to the cloth trade and to such considerations as the feud with France and the alliance with Portugal. These influences were what prevailed in the end, but the Englishman's liking, whether it was for a glass of claret, or of port or of sherry, also acquired and retained for some time a force of its own which reacted on English policies. Wine was in the last resort a luxury trade. It was something which man could do without but not easily. It is this permeation of the wine trade of all quarters of history and of all quarters of the globe which renders its story of such uncommon interest.

Statistics of the Wine Trade

ALTHOUGH estimates of the volume of the wine trade must for the most part be derived from the same sources they differ widely, not only in early times but even in the opening decades of the nineteenth century. As far as the eighteenth century is concerned Sir G. Clark has described some of the pitfalls in his *Guide to English Commercial Statistics*, 1938. The few figures quoted below can only suggest what was believed to be the state of the trade at various periods. The earliest detailed ones are those taken from the Bordeaux customs and begin in 1303. According to figures published by M. K. James and by Charles Higounet, the historian of Bordeaux, the total wine exports of Bordeaux averaged:

At their peak in the years 1303-37	83,165 tuns
During the middle century crises 1337-56	14,282 tuns
During the government of the Black Prince 1356/69	30,000 tuns
During the crises of 1366-69	11,400 tuns
During the difficulties of 1440-53	11,000 tuns

No complete English import figures are available, but it is computed that during the English occupation of Aquitaine in the later Middle Ages, about half the Bordeaux exports went to England and at their peak amounted to 30,000 or even 40,000 tuns. During the Hundred Years War there were great fluctuations and a steady decline and at the time of the final loss of Aquitaine English imports from Bordeaux are believed to have fallen as low as 3,000 tuns. Afterwards they recovered, perhaps to 5,000-6,000 tuns in 1475 and to 8,000-10,000 tuns in 1476-79.

Throughout this period other French wines from La Rochelle and the Loire, and also from Auxerre, played a part though they never rivalled in quantity those of Bordeaux. Rhine wines were always imported but never in quantity. From the early fourteenth century wines from Italy and the Levant were popular; they never rivalled the Bordeaux wines in quantity but they fetched a better price and were subject to higher customs duties, so their regulation attracted a good deal of attention.

By the reign of Henry VIII better customs records were kept, and from them Professor Schanz was able to compile detailed records of the trade of London and fifteen out-ports. They show the distinction between wines imported in English and foreign ships, and between non-sweet wines, sweet wines and the mal-voisies or malmseys, which now came largely from Spain and excelled the other sweet wines. Foreign ships handled much of the trade in London and western ports except Bristol, and a large share of the malmseys, which were principally imported by London and Southampton. The following are the average imports in tuns for the whole of the reign, showing A, imports in English ships, B in foreign ships.

Non-sweet wines		Sweet wines		Malmseys		Total
A	B	A	B	A	B	
6,959	1,604	14	103	687	435	9,800

There were great fluctuations, ranging from a total of 4,194 tuns in 1509, the first year of the reign, to 17,518 tuns in 1521/2 and 15,494 in 1542/3. Another big total of 17,082 tuns is shown for 1519/20, but there seems to be some mistake here, for this total is reached by the inclusion in the London imports of 10,069 butts (5,035 tuns) of malmsey, which is three times as much as that imported in any other year, while the total for malmsey in the summary for imports to London and the fifteen out-ports is shown as 2,206 tuns only.

André Simon estimated that the total import of wines may at times have reached 30,000 tuns in the reign of Henry VIII, so the figures of Schanz are perhaps on the modest side. Simon estimated the total imports in later Tudor times as 25,000 tuns in 1558/9, rising sometimes to double this figure in the 1560s and dropping towards the end of the century to 35,000-40,000 tuns. Precise estimates in early Stuart times are lacking, but the total imports seem to have been maintained or increased in the more prosperous years of James I and to have fallen markedly as the Civil War approached, though they recovered somewhat in the time of the Protectorate. During this period Spanish wines were popular and kept pace with, or even exceeded, French wines.

The Restoration brought about an increase in the wine trade and in the varieties of wines, but precise customs returns of the total imports were not compiled before 1675. In that year the total imports to London were given in tuns as:

French	Portuguese	Spanish	Italian	German	Total
7,495	20	4,012	30	539	12,096

In 1677, the penultimate year before the prohibition of French wines the totals were:

French	Portuguese	Spanish	Italian	German	Total
9,789	177	5,272	104	808	16,150

During the seven year prohibition of French wines from 1679 to 1685 the totals were:

French	Portuguese	Spanish	Italian	German	Total
$\frac{1}{2}$	5,833	5,781	112	2,748	$14,474\frac{1}{2}$

The averages do not show the violent fluctuations from year to year. Spanish wines rose to 8,420 and 11,286 tuns in 1680 and 1684 but were not much above the normal in other years. German wines also had two big years, 5,959 tuns in 1680 and 7,072 tuns in 1681. The most remarkable increase was shown in Portuguese wines, which attained 13,861, 16,772, and 12,186 tuns in the years 1682, 1683 and 1685, though in the remaining four years they remained between 1,000 and 2,000 tuns. It is accepted that many French wines were entered under other headings but the amount cannot be determined.

During the reign of James II French wines returned though Portuguese wines and other wines, except Spanish wines which were tending to go out of fashion, maintained some improvement. The totals were for the years 1686-89:

French	Portuguese	Spanish	Italian	German	Total
13,401	434	3,914	159	796	38,704

During the war against France from 1690 to 1696 no French wines were officially imported except 770 tuns before the embargo took effect. Excluding these the totals were:

French	Portuguese	Spanish	Italian	German	Total
—	5,491	6,253	61	839	12,954

The following figures for the six years of peace from 1697 to 1702 include the imports into the out-ports, given in brackets.

French	Portuguese	Spanish	Italian	German	Total
1,193	5,789	7,586	1,319	560	16,447
(447)	(787)	(1,069)	(64)	(81)	(2,446)

The totals for the war of the Spanish succession 1703-12 were:

French	Portuguese	Spanish	Italian	German	Total
826	7,960	2,376	1,305	521	12,848
(424)	(1,727)	(586)	(54)	(38)	(2,829)

The above figures for the trade from 1675 to 1712 were given to Parliament in 1713 by Charles Davenant, the inspector-general of customs, to assist the consideration of the whole question of trade with France, and with Spain and Portugal. They are of some importance in so far as they influenced the attitude of Parliament in the debates in 1713 which resulted in the rejection of the most favoured nation articles in the commercial treaty with France and the maintenance of the Methuen treaty with Portugal.

Davenant's returns were based on the entries of wines through the customs in each port, and whatever the truth of the original entries they represent, apart from mistakes, duplications, and omissions, the total of wines entered which paid customs duty. Portuguese and Spanish wines were usually entered together, while German and French wines were kept separately. Separate sheets were sometimes mislaid and inevitably some mistakes must have been made in compiling the returns, but on the whole they add up.

Subsequent statistics published have been based not directly on the original port-books but upon résumés made by the inspectorate of customs. For the eighteenth century the most generally accepted statistics of the wine trade were those published in 1824 by Alexander Henderson in his *History of Wines*. This series was also used by Cyrus Redding in *Modern Wines* and continued by him until 1850. Latterly the figures compiled by E. B. Schumpeter have been regarded as more reliable. They were published in 1960 in *English Overseas Trade Statistics 1697-1808* and were taken from the *Ledgers of Imports and Exports of England and Wales, 1697-1780*, and the *Reports on the State of the Navigation, Commerce, and Revenues of Great Britain from 1772*. The early figures for the period to 1712 do not differ largely from the Davenant returns but diverge afterwards from those of Henderson and Redding. This is less the case for the Portuguese imports, which often correspond, and can be checked as regards the general trend against the figures for exports of wine from Oporto published by Guerner and reproduced with much other statistical information by Guerra Tenreiro, whose figures for exports of wine from Oporto are also given in John Marshall's *Digest of all Accounts* published for Parliament in 1834.

The discrepancies between the figures derived from various authorities are sometimes due to plain mistakes, but more often arise from the use of different copies of the same original documents, which sometimes omitted peripheral imports such as madeira or canary, or carried on to the next year figures which had been entered late. The differences are appreciable in some years and are more marked in the case of Spanish than of Portuguese wines. Proportionately French wines, which were often entered separately, showed even larger differences, but in their case the total imports were small. Over a period of years the discrepancies tend to average out. For instance the imports of all wines for the years 1757-66 amounted to 163,659 tuns according to Schumpeter and to 163,114 tuns according to Henderson, if one includes the Italian wines which he omitted.

From 1697 onwards a complete set of figures for imports is available in the 1897 parliamentary report. These, however, have the disadvantage that they are in imperial gallons, while contemporary figures and those of other authorities are given in tuns of 252 old gallons (five imperial gallons equal six old gallons). For the period 1757-66 the total figure according to the parliamentary report, converted into old tuns, is 162,558. After 1787 the situation changed, but until then the Schumpeter figures are more convenient and the following statistics are taken from this source.

Table I, overleaf, shows the imports of wine in tuns for the first years after the end of the war of the Spanish succession according to Schumpeter.

It is to be noted that the imports of Spanish wines continued at the higher average until the outbreak of war in 1741 and were resumed at the lower average at the end of the war in 1748. Portuguese wines fell below 10,000 tuns in four out of six years before 1756 but recovered afterwards to 10,000 tuns and above. Italian wines fell below 100 tuns from 1757 and were not again

Table I

	French	Portuguese	Madeira	Spanish	Canary	Italian	German	Total
1713	2,548	5,861	112	4,116	1,663	1,228	379	15,907
1714	1,196	8,652	308	5,605	1,648	1,120	104	18,633
1715	1,261	10,334	387	6,768	1,997	467	503	21,717
1716	1,568	8,923	179	4,718	1,951	990	476	18,805

The following are the averages for ten-year periods beginning:

	French	Portuguese	Madeira	Spanish	Canary	Italian	German	Total
1717	1,297	12,066	195	7,458	809	225	446	22,496
1727	845	12,311	380	8,467	380	237	412	22,932
1737	374	12,330	542	3,305	101	158	222	17,032
1747	490	10,321	607	3,867	55	117	212	15,669
1757	541	11,221	754	3,555	46	56	191	16,564
1767	491	11,849	952	3,554	93	69	157	17,165
1777	436	11,300	548	2,434	47	7	142	14,914

imported in any quantity until Nelson's fleet in Sicily made Marsala popular.

From 1787 the figures of the 1897 parliamentary report are used. They reflect the great changes which were coming about owing to the reduction of customs duties even before the out-break of the revolutionary and Napoleonic wars introduced new factors. At this period wines began to be re-exported on a con-siderable scale, so that the figures of internal consumption differ greatly from those of the total trade. The parliamentary report gives the totals for internal consumption from 1787, but it is not always clear under which heading wines allowed free of duty to the navy are included; also wines re-exported were sometimes taken out of bond and had not paid duty; on other occasions they had paid duty but upon re-export the whole or part of the duty was refunded. Another complication is that the imports into Scot-land were usually included from about 1791 but not usually the larger imports from Ireland. Imports into Scotland varied from 804 tuns in 1785 to between 1,261 and 1,548 tuns in the years 1811-21. The averages for the next two decades are taken from the 1897 parliamentary report and give some figures for U.K. consumption only as well as the total imports (Table II). For com-parison the Schumpeter figures representing imports for internal consumption are also given. The latter from 1791 include imports into Scotland but not Ireland. Azores and Cape wines are included in miscellaneous. The figures are in old tuns.

Table III shows the ten-year averages (for 9 years in 1807-16, be-cause the 1813 records were destroyed by fire) taken from the 1897 parliamentary report and are in new tuns of 252 imperial gallons.

From 1853 the imports are classified according to the country of shipment and the imports for U.K. consumption are given in less detail (Table IV).

The supremacy of Great Britain at sea during the Napoleonic wars stimulated the trade in island wines. Marsala from Sicily, madeira, canary, Azores wines and wines from the Cape supplied in the post-war years over 6,000 tuns, or about a fifth of the trade.

THE RE-EXPORT TRADE

Although the total trade was maintained throughout the war years and afterwards, internal consumption flagged, in spite of the

Table II

	French	Portuguese	Madeira	Spanish	Canary	Rhenish	Italian, etc.	Total
1787–96	3,009	23,636	1,039	6,474	110	142	34	34,444
For U.K. consumption	2,541							31,759
Schumpeter's figures	946	19,794	981	5,159	111	114	24	27,129

According to Redding the average total Irish imports for eight of the ten years was 5,266 tuns.

	French	Portuguese	Madeira	Spanish	Canary	Rhenish	Italian, etc.	Total
1797–1806	2,455	24,561	1,039	7,378	175	103	84	35,795
For U.K. consumption	578							23,964
Schumpeter's figures	1,797	20,308	1,060	6,292	175	86	85	29,803

Average Irish imports for the decade were 5,672 tuns.

Table III

	Cape	French	Portuguese	Madeira	Azores	Spanish	Canary	Rhenish	Misc.	Total
1807–16	350	4,478	16,729	1,801	56	7,522	1,326	64	872	33,198
For U.K. consumption, 10-years average		663								21,528
1817–26	2,406	1,545	12,548	1,973	245	6,240	1,083	176	665	26,881
For U.K. consumption	2,242	928	10,602	1,300	24	4,452	593	140	315	20,596
1827–36	2,313	1,584	12,689	1,248	49	11,401	995	268	1,548	32,095
For U.K. consumption	2,243	1,193	11,286	783	12	8,479	355	241	1,099	25,691
1837–46	1,560	2,214	11,274	953	17	13,112	1,031	277	2,207	32,645
For U.K. consumption	1,686	1,565	10,294	408	1	9,713	110	225	1,702	25,704
1847–52	1,108	2,405	11,480	692	9	13,485	505	261	2,230	32,175
For U.K. consumption	1,009	1,220	10,109	291	1	9,831	73	211	1,726	24,471

Y

increase of population and purchasing power, until the encouragement of light wines by Gladstone's legislation. T. G. Shaw calculated that the number of bottles of wine consumed per head in
the United Kingdom fell from 2·9 in the 1790s to 1·3 in the 1840s
and did not pass two bottles again until the 1860s. The real decline
in individual consumption was greater, or rather the tendency was
to drink less wine, for the reduction of duties before the war and

Table IV

1853-62

Cape	1,723		
Australia	28		
France	4,907		
Portugal	12,056		
Madeira	286		
Azores	24	*For U.K. consumption*	
Spain	16,779	France	3,740
Holland and Germany	1,662	Portugal	9,242
Italy	1,235	Spain	12,087
Miscellaneous	1,078	Other countries	5,618
Total	39,778	Total	30,687

again in 1831, and the increase of wealth and population, had been
counter-factors. It was the rise in the re-export trade which maintained the level of the total trade and even increased it. According
to the 1897 parliamentary figure the excess of imports over U.K.
consumption amounted on the average to a little over 3,000 tuns
in the decade ending in 1797, and averaged over 11,000 tuns
during the war until 1816 and about 7,000 tuns after the war and
until 1862. According to Crouzet a tun of wine could be bought
in Bordeaux during the war for £8 and sold in a Baltic port for
£45, so that the incentive to re-export French wines was very
great. In 1809, which was a peak year, Crouzet estimated the re-
exports of French wines at 9,481 tuns and of Spanish and other
wines at 5,020 tuns. The *House of Commons Journals* and the customs returns for 1809 give a somewhat lower figure, 7,999 tuns
of French wines including 1,087 tuns of prize wines, and 1,161
tuns of Spanish wines including 252 tuns of prize wines. On the
other hand the figures obtained from the 1897 parliamentary
report by subtracting the totals for U.K. consumption from the
total imports are larger, amounting to 22,731 tuns in 1809 and to
17,053 tuns in 1810. The totals vary according to whether the
wines issued free of duty to the navy, exported out of bond or

brought in as prize wines are included. Sometimes in a given year more Portuguese wines are shown as going out than coming in. John Marshall's *Digest of all the Accounts*, published for Parliament in 1834, shows minus figures for Portuguese wines in 1829 and 1830 of 1,123 and 1,058 tuns. The 1897 report gives 1,123 and 1,057 tuns. Old wines could of course be re-exported long after their original importation and the fortified wines were often blended and thus increased in volume. Marshall's figures for 1827-30 show the composition of the re-exports.

They averaged: *Spanish*, 2,888; *Cape*, 536; *Madeira*, 363; *Fanary*, 598; *French*, 374; *German*, 32; *Portuguese*, 213; *Italian*, 213: *Total*, 5,385. With these figures those of the 1897 report agree.

Marshall also shows the destination of the re-exports for the years 1827-30. During the war the re-exports had been mainly of French wines to Baltic countries, and indirectly to Germany. In the 1820s they were largely Spanish wines. In the years 1827-30 an average of 945 tuns went to Europe, 831 tuns to the West Indies and 238 tuns to the U.S.A. Figures for the East Indies are only given for 1823-7, when the average was 922 tuns. In the same years fortified wines sent to the Indies to mature on the voyage and reimported thence amounted to 478 tuns. Possibly a little genuine oriental wine from Shiraz was included. These imports do not seem to be included in the total imports from elsewhere. The figures for exports to specific countries leave a balance of 5,000 tuns or so unaccounted for, which possibly represents the wine allowed to the navy or to merchant ships for ships' stores.

Bibliography

MANUSCRIPT SOURCES

At Public Records Office
State Papers. S.P. series.
   Portugal. S.P. 89 series.
   Spain. S.P. 94 series.
Colonial Office. C.O. 388 series.
Lord Steward's Books. L.S. series.
Port Books, E 190 series. London, King's Lynn, Exeter, Dartmouth, etc.
Chancery. C 103 series.
High Court of Admiralty. H.C.A. series.
Ships' Logbooks. Adm. 51 series.
Mediterranean Passes. Admiralty. Adm. 7 series.
Seamen's Sixpences. Admiralty. Adm. 68 series.
Board of Trade. Licences to neutral vessels. B.T. 6 series.
Foreign Office. F.O. 332. Cadiz Factory Records, 1748-1824.
   From 1790. F.O. 63 series, Portugal.
             F.O. 72 series, Spain.

At British Museum
Additional Manuscripts (Add. MSS.):
4163.   A. Pope to Wanley.
11569/70. Thomas Burnet correspondence, Lisbon 1727, etc.
20799.   Sebastião de Carvalho (Marquis of Pombal) correspondence as Portuguese minister in London, *c*. 1740.
20817/8. Da Cunha's memoirs as Portuguese minister in London. 1690-1715. In Portuguese.
23634 & 23627. Lord Tyrawley's correspondence in 1727-28 and 1752-57.
23726.   Diary of Thomas Cox. Lisbon, *c*. 1700.
32639.   Seventeenth-century reference by A. Rose to a mediaeval vineyard at Lincoln.
34727.   Poley/Davenant correspondence.
35101.   Lisbon Legation. 1668-80.
38153.   Southwell Papers. Ireland, etc., 1687-1706.
Sloane Collection:
   2,294. Account of Portugal. In French *c*. 1690. Much of this

has been published by E. Prestage in *Arquivo Histórico de Portugal*. Lisbon, 1935.

Egerton Collection:
921. Some letters of Thomas Burnet.

At Coimbra University

MS 2974. Correspondence of Da Cunha Brochado, Portuguese minister in London, 1713-16.

At Maidstone (Kent) Record Office

Chevening MSS: U1590. Correspondence of John and Paul Methuen, and of Alexander and James Stanhope, etc.

At Althorpe, Lord Spencer's archives

John Methuen correspondence with Lord Halifax.

At Corsham House

Lord Methuen's archives. Little remains of John Methuen's correspondence but a good deal of Sir Paul Methuen's and some accounts for wine.

Archives of the Haberdashers Company

Accounts of expenditure on wine.

At Kansas University, U.S.A.

John Methuen's correspondence with Sir William Simpson.

Published Manuscripts

Calendars of State Papers.

Calendars of Treasury Books.

Historical Manuscripts Commission: Reports (Bath, Buccleuch). Dartmouth Papers, etc.

CONTEMPORARY WORKS

Adams-Jefferson Correspondence. 2 vols. Williamsburg, 1959. Ed. E. J. Cappon. Notes by Bohm.

J. Addison, *Collected Works*, Ed. R. Hurd. 6 vols. Articles in *Guardian, Spectator*, etc.

J. Archenholz, *Picture of England*. 1789.

C. Arnoux, *Dissertation sur la situation de bourgogne*. London, 1727.

Andrea Bacci, *De naturali historia vironum*. Vol. vii. Rome, 1596.

J. Baker, *Diary*. Ed. C. P. Yorke. 1937.

S. Baldwin, *A Survey of the English Customs*. 1770.

J. Balsall, accounts of, purser of the *Trinity of Bristol*. Camden Miscellany. Vol. xxiii. 1969. 4th series. Ed. T. F. Reddaway and A. A. Ruddock.

J. Baltharpe, *The Straits Voyage.* Ed. J. Bromley. Oxford, 1959.

Edward Barlow, *Journals*, Ed. Basil Lubbock. 2 vols. 1934.

A. M. de Boislisle, *Correspondence des intendants.* 3 vols. 1883.

Bolingbroke, *see* Henry St John.

J. Boswall, *London Journal.* Ed. J. Pottle. 1950.

Bolton Letters. Ed. A. Simon, 1928, and Vol. 2 privately produced by Graham Blandy. Madeira, 1960.

W. Bromley, *Travels through Portugal.* 1702.

British Merchant. Collected edition. 3 vols. Ed. C. King. 1721.

G. Burnet, *Letters & Travels.* 1685/6. Pub. 1724.

Burney Collection of Newspapers at British Museum.

Hon. J. Byng, *Torrington Diaries.* Ed. J. B. Andrews. 4 vols. 1934.

J. Busby, *Journal of a Recent Visit to the Vineyards of Spain and France.* 1834.

Cadiz, Voyage to. Camden series, ns. 32. 1883.

Carnota, Conde de (J. A. Smith). *Memoirs of the Marquis of Pombal.* 1871.

Suzanne Centlivre, *Works.* 3 vols. 1740.

G. Chalmers, *Treaties.* Vol. 2. 1790.

Colleccâo de leis extravagantes. (pragmatica). Vol. 11. Coimbra, 1819. Ed. F. C. de Franca.

W. Congreve, *Letters and Documents.* Ed. J. C. Hodges. 1964.

A. W. Costigan, *Sketches of Society and Manners in Portugal.* 2 vols. 1787. A mixture of fact and fiction.

Tench Coxe, *A view of the U.S.A.* Philadelphia, 1794.

J. Croft. *A Treatise on the Wines of Portugal.* York, 1788. Croft is not always historically accurate but he represents the views held at the time by men with experience of the Oporto Factory.

R. Cumberland, *Memoirs.* 1806. They relate to the middle of the century.

L. da Cunha, *Obras.* Vol. 1, 1920. The obras stopped at Vol 1, but da Cunha's memoirs for the period 1690-1715 are in Add. MSS. 20817/8.

A. W. Dalrymple, *Travels through Spain and Portugal.* 1776.

Charles Davenant, Inspector-General of customs. *An account of the trade between Gt. Britain, France, Spain, Portugal, etc.* 2 parts. 1715.
Collected Works. 5 vols. 1771.

Lady Fanshawe, *Memoirs.* Pub. 1907. Refer to *c.* 1670.

J. Farington, *Diary*. 8 vols. Early nineteenth century. Ed. J. Greig. 1922.

G. Farquhar, *Collected Works*. Ed. G. Stonehill. 2 vols. 1830.

J. J. Forrester, Baron, *A word or Two on Port-wine*. 1844.

        J. S. Oliveira Prize Essay on Portugal. 1853.

S. Fortrey, *England's Interest and Improvement*. 1663.

Antonio Oliveira de Freire, *Descripcão del reino de Portugal*. 1739.

Thomas Gage, *Diary*. 1648. Ed. A. P. Newton. 1928.

J. Gee, *Trade & Navigation in Britain*. 1732.

R. H. Gronow, *Reminiscences and Recollections*. (*c.* 1814.) Ed. J. Grego. 1900.

P. J. Grosley, *A Tour to London*. 2 vols. 1772.

Christovaõ Guerner, *Discurso analytico sobre o establecimento da companhia general de agricultura das vinhas do Alto Douro*. 1815. Guerner's statistics have been widely quoted.

Hakluyt Society, *Travels of Baron Rozmital*. 1465-7. Series ii. Vol. 108. Vols. v and vi of *Voyages* for sixteenth century voyages to the Levant, Spain, Canaries, etc.

        Papers of Thomas Bowrey. Series ii. Vol. 47.

T. Heywood (attributed), *Philocothonista*. Pamphlet pub. in 1635.

W. Hickey, *Memoirs*. 4 vols. 1925.

J. Houghton, *Improvement of Husbandry and Trade*. Collected letters composed *c.* 1690 and pub. in 1727.

House of Commons Journals.

House of Lords Journals.

W. Howell, *Familiar Letters*. 1638. 2 vols. Ed. J. Jacobs. Interesting for a description of wines in the early seventeenth century.

David Hume, *Letters to Strachan*. Ed. C. Hill. 1888.

Henry St John, Viscount Bolingbroke, *Letters and Correspondence*. Ed. G. Parke. 4 vols. 1798.

P. Kalm, *A visit to England*. 2 vols. Trans. J. Lucas. 1892.

Sir Benjamin Keene, *Correspondence*. Ed. Sir R. Lodge. 1933.

Martin Lister, *Journey to France*. 1698. In Pinkerton's Voyages. Vol. iv. 1809.

John Locke, *Travels in France*. Ed. J. Lough. 1933.

Norton & Sons, Merchants of London and Virginia. Ed. F. N. Mason. 1968.

Original Documents Concerning the Impolicy of a Further Continuance of the Royal Company of Oporto. 1813.

Sarah Byng Osborne, *Letters*. 1738. Pub. Stanford University, California. 1930.
Samuel Pepys. *Diary*.
Letitia Pilkington. *Memoirs*. 1712-20. Ed. J. Isaacs. 1928.
Purefoy Letters. 1735-53. Ed. C. Eland. 1931.
Jacomé Ratton, *Recordacoës*. 1747-1810. London, 1813.
Lewes Roberts, *Map of Commerce*. 1677.
William Salmon, *The Compleat Physician*. 1693. This is a medical dictionary but gives contemporary descriptions of wines.
St Evremond, Marguetel de St Denis, Comte de. *Oeuvres*. Ed. P. de Maizeaux. Amsterdam. 5 vols. 1739.
H. Saxby, *English Customs*. 1757. A very useful work of reference for customs' duties between 1660 and 1750.
Statutes of the realm.
Richard Steele, *Articles in the Guardian*. Ed. A. Dowson. 1885.
Jonathan Swift, *Correspondence*. 6 vols. Ed. F. E. Ball. 1913.
John Taylor, the water poet, *Works*. Ed. Charles Hindley. 1872.
J. Townsend, *Journey through Spain*. 1792.
R. Twiss, *Travels in Spain and Portugal*. 1775.
G. Uztariz, *The Theory and Practice of Commerce and Maritime Affairs*. Trans. from the Spanish by J. Kippax. 1751.
Viajes de estranjeros en Espana. Vol. iii. Ed. J. Garcia Mercedal. Contains accounts of most of the travellers to Spain, including many published elsewhere in English or French.
Edward Ward, *The London Spy*. Ed. A. L. Hayward. 1927.
Antony Wood, *Life and Times*. 5 vols. 1891. Ed. A. Clarke.
Wine Trade of Portugal. Proceedings of a meeting held at Offley, Webber & Forrester's quinta on the Douro in Oct. 1844.
J. Wright, *Essay on Wines*. 1795.

LATER WORKS

H. Warner Allen, *Sherry*. 1933. *Port and Sherry*. 1952. *In Contemplation of Wine*. 1951. *A History of Wine*. 1961. *The Wines of Portugal*. 1963. One of the best modern writers on wines, erudite but readable.
W. Arnold, *Sublime Society of Beefsteaks*. 1871.
J. Ashton with J. Mew, *Drinks of the World*. 1882.
J. Ashton, *Social Life in the Reign of Queen Anne*. 1882.
H. Atton and H. H. Holland, *The King's Customs*. 2 vols. 1810.
J. V. de Azevedo, *Épocas de Portugal Económico*. 1957.

Sir E. Barry, *History of Ancient Wines*. 1775.

G. Blandy, *Madeira*. 1960.

E. L. Bogart, *Economic History of the U.S.* London, 1907.

E. W. Bovill, *The Golden Trade of the Moors*. 1956.

C. R. Boxer. *The Golden Age of Brazil*. University of California. 1962. *The Portuguese Seaborne Empire*. 1425-1825. 1969.

H. L. Bradfer-Lawrence, *The Merchants of Lynn*. (Clement Ingleby, Supplement to Bloomfields, Norfolk.) 1927.

F. Braudel, *La Mediterranée et le monde Mediterranéen a l'époque de Philippe II*. 2 vols. 1966.

T. E. Bridgett, *History of the Holy Eucharist*. 2 vols. 1881.

R. Burwall, *Madcap Progress; The Life of John Mytton*. 1927.

D. Burwash. *English Merchant Shipping*. 1460-1540. 1947.

Cambridge Economic History. Vol iv. 1967.

Cambridge Modern History. Vol iii. 1904.

The New Cambridge Modern History. Vol vi. 1970.

E. Carus-Wilson, *Mediaeval Merchant Venturers*. 1957.

E. Carus-Wilson and O. Coleman, *England's Export Trade*, 1245-1547. 1963.

Chapman, *see* Shillington and Chapman.

Sir Marcus Cheke, *Dictator of Portugal*. (Pombal.) 1938.

G. Cobb, *Oporto, Older and Newer*. 1966. This work brings up to the twentieth century the story of the Oporto Factory by C. Sellers.

Sir W. Clowes, *History of the Royal Navy*. 6 vols. 1898.

G. Connel Smith, *Forerunners of Drake*. 1954.

Jan Craeybeckx, *Les vins de France aux anciens pays bas*. 1957.

R. Croft-Cooke, Madeira. 1961

C. Crouzet, *L'économie britannique et le blocus continental*, 1808-13.

C. G. Cruickshank, *The English Occupation of Tournai*, 1513-19. 1971.

Ralph Davis, *The Rise of the English Shipping Industry in the Seventeenth and Eighteenth centuries*. 1962.

Roger Dion, *Histoire de la vigne et du vin en France*. 1959.

S. Decatur, *Private Affairs of G. Washington*. Boston. 1943.

R. Druitt, *Report on Cheap Wines*. 1865.

J. Duncan, *History of Guernsey*. 1941.

M. Epstein. *The Early History of the Levant Co.* 1908.

Ferguson, *see* Pan Ferguson.

H. E. S. Fisher, *The Portugal Trade*, 1700-70. 1971.

H. W. Flinn, *British Population Growth*, 1700-1850. 1970.

A. D. Francis, *The Methuens and Portugal*. 1966.

R. V. French, *19 Centuries of Drink in England*. 1884.

A. Gayer, *Growth and Fluctuation of the British Economy*, 1740-1850. 2 vols. 1953.

D. Gardiner, *Historic Haven: The story of Sandwich*. 1954.

W. D. George, *London Life in the Eighteenth Century*. 1930.

A. Gibbs, *History of Antony and Dorothy Gibbs*. 1922.

V. Magalhães Godinho, *Os descubrimientos e a ecónomia mundial.* 1963.

H. Gonzalez-Gordon. *Jerez Xerez-Scheris*. 1935. The best Spanish work on sherry.

J. A. Goris, *Les colonies marchandes meridionales*. 1925.

N. S. B. Gras, *Early English Customs*. 1918.

Guerra Tenreiro, *see* Tenreiro.

C. S. Gutkind and K. Wolfskehl, *Das buch von wein*. 1927.

G. Harrison, *Bristol Cream*. 1958.

E. F. Hekscher, *The Continental System*. 1922.

A. Henderson, *A History of Wines*. 1824.

M. Herrero-Garcia, *La vida española del siglo xviii. Las bebidas*. 1933.

C. Higounet, *Histoire de Bordeaux*. 6 vols. 1962-68. This is a general history of Bordeaux but is the best authority for the history of the Bordeaux wine trade.

E. Hyams, *Dionysus: A Social History of the Wine Vine*. 1965.

W. B. James, *Wine Duties*. 1855.

Julian Jeffes, *Sherry*. 1961. The recommended English work on the subject.

N. Kerr, *Wines Scriptural and Ecclesiastical*. 1882.

W. H. G. Kingston, *Lusitanian Sketches*. 1845.

W. B. Kinsey, *Portugal Illustrated*. 1828.

H. H. Lamb, *Britain's Changing Climate*. 1966.

F. Lane, *Navires et constructeurs à Venise pendant la renaissance*. 1965.

Lawrence, *see* Bradfer-Lawrence.

R. Lennard, *Englishmen at Rest and Play*. 1930.

E. Lipson, *Economic History of England*. 1956. Vols. ii & iii.

H. V. Livermore, *History of Spain*. 1958.

Rose Macauley. *They Went to Portugal*. 1946.

J. B. de Macedo, *A situacão económica no tempo de Pombal.* 1951.

F. M. McNeill, *The Scots Cellar.* 1956.

Magalhães Godinho, see Godinho.

T. Malvezin, *Histoire du commerce de Bordeaux.* 4 vols. 1892.

F. Martin, *History of Lloyds.* 1876.

F. Mauro, *L'expansion européenne.* 1964.

R. F. Michel, *Les Portugais en France.* 1882.

E. Freire de Oliveira, *Elementos para história de Lisboa.* 1898.

R. Ollard, *Escape of Charles II.* 1960.

M. Pan-Ferguson. *La vendimia y sus problemas en el siglo xviii.* 1952.

H. M. Panzer, *Book of the Wine Label.* 1947.

C. McKew Parr, *Jan van Linschoten.* 1964.

T. L. Peacock, *Crotchet Castle.* 1831. *Gryll Grange.* 1860.

J. H. Plumb, *Sir R. Walpole.* 1956. *Men and Places* (Walpole's wine.) 1963.

E. Power and M. Postan, *Studies in English Trade in the Fifteenth Century.* 1933.

C. Rambert, *Histoire de commerce de Marseille.* Vol iv. 1934.

Peter Ramsay, *Tudor Economic Problems.* 1963.

Cyrus Redding, *Modern Wines.* 1851.

Lionel Rothkrug, *Opposition to Louis XIV.* 1965.

A. Ruddock, *Italian Merchants and Shipping in Southampton, 1270-1600.* Southampton Record Society, ns. i. 1951.

C. Ruggles-Brice, *Sealed Bottles.* 1939.

G. Sandeman & Co., *Port and Sherry.* 1955. An account of some of the history of the firm.

G. Schanz, *Englische Handelspolitik gegen ende des mittelalters.* 2 vols. 1881.

E. B. Schumpeter, *English Overseas Trade Statistics.* 1960.

G. Scott-Thomson, *Life in a Noble Household, 1641-1700.* 1937.

C. Sellers, *Oporto, Old and New.* 1899.

A. Sergio, *Antologia dos economistas Portugueses.* 1942.

T. H. Shaw, *Wine, the Vine and the Cellar.* 1863.

G. Sherburn, *Early Career of Alexander Pope.* 1968.

Shillington and Chapman, *Commercial Relations of England and Portugal.* 1907. The classic work on the subject of its time.

A. Silbert, *Le Portugal Mediterranéen.* 1966.

André Simon, *History of the Wine Trade.* 3 vols. 1906-09. This is a classic work on the subject and very rich in statistics and quotations, not always co-ordinated. *Port.* 1934. *Champagne.* 1934. *Bottlescrew-Days.* 1926. This carries the history of the wine trade into the eighteenth century.

A. Stanislavski, *Landscapes of Bacchus. The Vine in Portugal.* Univ. of Texas, 1970.

M. Strachan, *The Life and Adventures of Tom Coryate*, 1962.

R. S. Surtees, *Ask Mamma and Handley Cross.* Many editions.

A. Guerra Tenreiro, *Douro. Esboços para sua história económica.* Oporto. Vols i and ii. 1942. *Conclusões.* 1944. *Ainda o tratado de Methuen.* 1943.

Thomson, *see* Scott-Thomson.

G. Trevelyan, *English Social History.* 1944.

E. Trochmé et Marcel Delcasse, *Le commerce Rochelais de la fin du xvme siècle au debut du xviime siècle.* 1952.

Warner Allen, *see* Allen.

Carus-Wilson, *see* Wilson.

Wine Trade Loan Exhibition Catalogue. 1933.

L. B. Wright, *The First Gentlemen of Virginia.* 1940.

M. G. A. Vale, *English Gascony.* 1970.

J. V. Vives. *An Economic History of Spain.* Princeton, 1969.

C. E. Vulliamy, *Life of Mrs Delany.* 1935.

W. Younger, *Gods, Men and Wine.* 1965.

ARTICLES IN PERIODICALS

P. Boissonade, 'Le mouvement commerciale entre la France et les Iles Britanniques au xvième siècle.' *Revue Historique.* Vols 134, 135. Paris, 1920.

C. R. Boxer, 'Vicissitudes of the Anglo-Portuguese Alliance.' *Faculdade de Letras.* Lisbon, 1958.
'Brazilian gold and British traders in the first half of the 18th century.' *Hispanic American Historical Review.* Vol 49, iii. 1969.
'Lord Tyrawley in Lisbon.' *History Today.* Nov. 1970.

H. Braure. 'Quelques aspects des relations commerciales entre France et l'Angleterre au xviieme siècle.' *Annales du Midi*, Vol 65. Toulouse, 1953.

H. Enjalbert. 'Comment naissent les grands crus, Porto, Bordeaux, Cognac?' *Annales (E.S.C. Èconomies, Sociétès, Civilizations).* 1953.
'L'alto Douro.' *Cahiers d'outremer.* Bordeaux, 1949.

H. E. S. Fisher. 'The South-West and the Atlantic Trade'. *The South-West and the Sea*. Exeter, 1968.

R. Gravil. 'Trading to Spain and Portugal.' *Business History*. Vol 12.

A. C. Hess. 'The Moriscos'. *American Historical Review*. Vol 64-i. 1968.

C. Huetz de Lemps. 'Le commerce maritime des vins d'Angleterre, 1698-1716.' *Revue Historique de Bordeaux*. Jan./June, 1965.

M. J. James. 'Les droits commerciales des negociants en vins gascons en Angleterre durant le fin du moyen age.' *Annales du Midi*. Toulouse. Jan. 1953, and English version in *Economic Hist. Review*. iv. 2nd series. 1951/2: 'The Fluctuations of the Anglo-Gascon wine trade in the 14th century'.

E. Power. 'The English wool trade in the reign of Edward IV.' *Cambridge Historical Journal*. ii. 1926/8.

J. Richards. 'Diary.' *Retrospective Review*. 1853.

C. Samaran. 'Franco-English relations at the end of the Hundred Years War'. *Annales du Midi*. Vol 65. Toulouse, 1953.

G. Thornton. 'The Stephens Brothers and Marinha Grande'. *The Anglo-Portuguese News*. Lisbon, 22 March 1969.

STATISTICS

Middle Ages and Bordeaux:
    Charles Higounet. *Histoire de Bordeaux*. 6 vols. Principally for the early period, but some statistics throughout.
    M. K. James. Article in the Economic History Review. iv, 2nd series. 1951/2. 'The Fluctuations of the Anglo-Gascon wine trade during the fourteenth century.'
Tudor Period and Early Stuarts:
    G. Schanz. *Englische Handels Politik gegen ende des Mittelalters*. Leipzig. 2 vols. 1881.
    André Simon. *History of the Wine Trade*. 3 vols. Principally for the earlier period but some figures throughout.
From 1675:
    Journals of the House of Commons. The parliamentary figures 1675-1714 are also used by Henderson, Shillington and Chapman, etc.
Eighteenth Century:
    A. Henderson. *History of Wines*. 1824.
    Shillington and Chapman. *Commercial Relations of England and Portugal*. 1907.

E. B. Schumpeter. *English Overseas Trade Statistics*, 1697-1808.

For Oporto wine exports from 1678, and for the Portuguese wine trade in general in the last decades of the century, A. Guerra Tenreiro. *Douro. Esboços para a sua história económica.* 4 vols. Oporto. 1941/4.

Also available in a continuous series from 1695 are the import figures given in Parliamentary Report C 8706 LXXXV.1 published in 1898 with the title *Customs Tariff of the U.K.* The drawback to the use of these figures for the eighteenth century is the fact that they are all in imperial gallons, a measure which was not adopted until 1824 officially.

Napoleonic Wars:

Journals of House of Commons. Vol 61.

Customs 10/1, etc., at P.R.O.

P. Crouzet. *L'économie Britannique et le blocus continental.* 2 vols. 1958.

Nineteenth century:

Parliamentary report C 8706.

J. Marshall. *A digest of all accounts.* Submitted to Parliament in 1834. This gives complete figures for 1826-30 and some for the preceding years, including details of re-exports. It also gives Guerners figures published by Guerra Tenreiro for Oporto wine exports from 1678.

Some statistics are also to be found in T. G. Shaw, *On Wine*, 1863, and in W. B. James, *Wine Duties*, 1855.

Index

z